Visual Basic for Behavioral Psychologists

Visual Basic for Behavioral Psychologists

by

Mark R. Dixon
University of Southern Illinois

and

Otto H. MacLin
University of Northern Iowa

Foreword by

Steven C. Hayes
University of Nevada, Reno

Context Press

Reno, NV

Visual Basic for Behavioral Psychologists
Paperback pp. 280

Library of Congress Cataloging-in-Publication Data

Dixon, Mark R., 1970-
Visual basic for behavioral psychologists / by Mark R. Dixon and Otto H. MacLin ; foreword by Steven C. Hayes.
p. cm.
Includes index.
ISBN 1-878978-44-6
1. Psychology--Research--Methodology--Software. I. Maclin, Otto H., 1958- II. Title.
BF76.5.D59 2003
150.19'43'02855133--dc21

2003008255

933 Gear Street, Reno, NV 89503-2729

Printed in the United States of America

Table of Contents

Foreword

The hallmark of behavioral psychology is its commitment to empirical work. Behavior analysis is still sometimes called "the experimental analysis of behavior" – a term that emphasizes experimentation as a defining feature of the behavioral tradition. In the modern era, empirical work has been enormously enhanced by the ability to program experiments and observational systems on computers. Even twenty years ago, experimentation in behavioral psychology involved "programming" done with wires and switches arduously arranged into simple logical circuits and behavioral observation and data recording was done largely by hand. Personal computers changed all of that.

Of the many modern programming languages available, none is more popular than Visual Basic. Flexible and powerful, Visual Basic allows for control of virtually every parameter related to the conduct of experimental research. Particularly as basic behavioral psychology moves more into human experimentation, flexible control over the presentation of stimulus materials, and careful measurement of the dimensions of responding are essential to successful research programs. Visual Basic gives the researcher the tools needed to accomplish those ends. Programming has become a key ally to the intellectual development of the field.

In the present volume, Mark Dixon and Otto MacLin take readers from the earliest stages of Visual Basic programming to the use of this language to program complex human studies. The ability to program your own experiments is a godsend to students and researchers. Nothing delays research progress quite so much as the delay between an idea and its implementation. I have seen over and over again that students and researchers who are able to make their own research projects happen, finish more quickly and do so in a high quality way. I am sometimes told by graduate students (usually as they are learning how hard it is, and how expensive it is, to find someone else to program their ideas) that they do not have time to learn how to program. In fact, taking the long view, they do not have time to waste *not* knowing how to program. The hours put into learning pay off very quickly, usually within a matter of weeks. It does not make sense to delay the process, especially when learning tools are available that shorten the learning curve so dramatically.

The present volume is such a tool. It has the considerable advantage of being written by two young professionals who just a few years ago helped many of their fellow graduate students learn to program, and since have helped many of their own students learn how to take advantage of this powerful technology. The authors are driven by the sense of satisfaction that comes from empowering others. The examples and sample programs are precisely relevant to the preparations behavioral psychologists and student will want to be able to program. This book will empower behavioral psychology. It will empower you.

Steven C. Hayes

Preface

Looking Ahead

We can not stress enough the importance of learning how to program your own experiments. The time you spend learning Visual Basic.NET will be nothing compared to the time you will spend attempting to explain to a computer programmer what you want your experiment to look like and what it needs to do. These folks don't come cheap, they don't work on your schedule, and they don't really care about your deadlines. Take the time now to learn how to program, and it will pay for itself soon enough. Learning how to program is a liberating endeavor, much like knowing how to speak the foreign language of a distant country that you will be visiting. There is so much you can do with the repertoire, and so little you can do without it.

There are so many ways to use the power of Visual Basic.NET in your professional research career. They include conducing basic operant research in the laboratory, collecting observational data in an applied setting, computerizing traditional paper survey instruments, and computing data transformations. Every project you conduct as a behavioral psychologist could probably be enhanced in some way with a form of computerization. Teaching students and other professionals how to do the same will benefit our entire science, in addition to your own career.

By teaching you Visual Basic, we are giving you the tools to create many things. Many people might think we are crazy for doing so. Instead we should have opened a software company and designed custom programs for top dollars. Others have done so. Our reinforcers are simply different.

This book is dedicated to Linda J. Hayes and the members of her Human Operant Laboratory at the University of Nevada who undertook this programming adventure with us or inspired us to continue. They include Ruth Anne Rehfeldt, Michael Clayton, Ramona Houmanfar, and Deirdre Fitzgerald-Beebe. We would also like to thank the many graduate students at Southern Illinois University who test-programmed the chapters of this book to make sure that they actually worked. They include Daniel Fienup, Kimberly Zlomke, Jamie Dake, Zach Shoemaker, and Janice Marley. Lastly we would like to thank Steven C. Hayes and Emily Neilan of Context Press who made this book much more sophisticated than we ever thought it could be.

Mark R. Dixon and Otto H. MacLin
Makanda, IL
March 2003

Chapter 1: Introduction

Overview

Technology and Research

As we venture into the 21st century, computerized technology is accelerating at exponential rates. Computerized equipment that was state of the art five years ago is now obsolete. Such rapid changes in technology may have a considerable impact on the research agenda of the behavioral psychologist. Equipment and software purchased with start-up or grant funds are often outdated before the end of the project. Furthermore, additional monies are regularly needed to hire computer programmers to reprogram software to handle changes in experimental parameters or new hardware. This often leaves the behavioral psychologist at the mercy of technical staff that have varying degrees of knowledge about the purpose of the experiment.

Furthermore, behavioral psychologists interested in the study of human operant behavior are under increasing demands to automate their experimental procedures. Tabletop procedures where stimuli are presented to the subject by a human experimenter are often criticized for potentially containing methodological flaws. While these flaws can be reduced through careful training of experimenters, they can never be completely eliminated. Using a computer to present stimuli eliminates many uncontrolled variations in stimuli positioning, orientation, and inter-trial intervals. Computerization also eliminates experimenter demand characteristics and any across-experimenter variability.

This text is designed to provide the behavioral psychologist with the necessary skills to adapt their human operant research agenda to the changing face of science in the 21st century. We will show you how to atomize your experimental apparatus, stimulus presentations, and data collection procedures. We will also provide you with specific programming routines (code) that you can customize and incorporate into your own experiments. But most importantly, we will provide you with the skills to program your own research, whatever that research may be.

In this book we have attempted to illustrate the creation of some popular types of experiments a researcher of human operant behavior may wish to conduct. The list is far from exhaustive. Yet we believe we will present the skills necessary for you to program any other type of experiment you can conceptualize albeit similar or totally different from the ones found in this text. We will walk you through the experiment programming experience step-by-step. In doing so, we believe that two goals will be accomplished upon successful completion of each chapter. First, you will learn more specific techniques about Visual Basic.NET and observe their application in an actual computer program. Second, you will craft an actual working program that may be useful in the classroom, the laboratory, or the applied setting.

If nothing else, each chapter's program can serve as a backbone for your own experimental creations.

If you have ever purchased or browsed through commercially available textbooks on programming in Visual Basic.NET, you may have discovered that most of the information found in them is irrelevant to psychological research. They are written for computer programmers more generally. In this book we have attempted to greatly accelerate the learning curve for crafting your own computer programs for your own research agenda by only including those programming routines that are necessary for research purposes. The programming repertoire we present in this book has evolved over many years of hunting, searching, and foraging for the correct answers to many programming questions in vast sources of texts, list-serves, chartrooms, emails, and personal connections. Our programming abilities are a repertoire that has been considerably shaped by the contingencies of reinforcement for programming (or the punishers for failure to correctly program) that will be delivered to you the reader in somewhat of a "rule-governed" fashion.

To reduce and hopefully eliminate the deduction that programming will become easy after reading this book, or that a program can be created in a liner fashion from start to finish, we have programmed each experiment found in this text in a rather roundabout manner. That is, we will have you take steps backwards and often times run you into a dead end before finishing the program that is created in each of the chapters. We feel this approach more accurately approximates the real programming experience. Our non-liner method may frustrate you as you work through the chapters, but we believe it will prepare you in the long run for your own programming adventures that lay ahead.

Utility of Programming in Visual Basic.NET

Visual Basic.NET is an "object orientated" programming language that is relatively easy to use. What is meant by "object orientated" is that the programming language is based on the placement of objects on the screen that perform some type of action when they are clicked on or triggered by keystrokes or timers. By being an "object orientated" language, Visual Basic.NET takes the labor out of many once time consuming tasks. In previous versions of the "BASIC" programming language, programmers needed to write pages and pages of "code" in order to get an object to increase or decrease in size. In comparison, Visual Basic.NET allows this type of operation in less than two sentences or even with the simple click of the mouse. If you are familiar with programs such as Microsoft Word, PowerPoint or Excel, you already possess some of the necessary skills to program in Visual Basic.NET. For example, Visual Basic.NET uses the same procedures to cut, paste, and copy images or text within the program as well as utilizes the mouse pointer to drag, drop and resize objects on the computer screen.

Another useful feature of Visual Basic.NET is that it is seamlessly connected to other common desktop software programs developed by Microsoft. We are not attempting to develop a loyalty to a particular brand of software for all your computing application needs, but this feature is quite valuable to expanding Visual Basic's capabilities. For example, you might wish to design a variety of experimental conditions using different stimuli and reinforcers. Using the streamlining capabilities of Visual Basic, you as the researcher could enter these values beforehand in an Excel spreadsheet, and have Visual Basic.NET "read" them into your program during the running of the experiment. All your condition changes now are just made in Excel, not the actual computer program. Plus, your data output file can be written directly into Word or Excel formats for easy data analysis.

The ease of creating a computerized experiment in Visual Basic.NET will also allow the behavioral psychologist to reduce the time necessary to run a given experiment. The researcher will not need to train graduate students or research assistants in the meticulous methodological procedures of a given study. Once the experiment is programmed, they will only need to show the assistant which button to click on the mouse to start the procedure. Additionally, by using a computerized procedure it may allow for the simultaneous running of multiple subjects given the appropriate research facilities. By placing the experiment on a server or the web, the behavioral psychologist could increase his/her sample sizes or experimental conditions significantly without adding any additional time for data collection.

System Requirements and Installation Procedures

Hardware and Software

Before we get started working with Visual Basic, you will need to make sure that your computer contains the appropriate hardware and software to run the program. Our experiences with Visual Basic.NET and above will require you to have:

IBM-compatible computer equipped with CD-ROM drive, monitor and mouse
Pentium-based microprocessor (Pentium 3 or above)
Audio card and speakers (for multimedia purposes)
Microsoft Windows 2000 Professional or XP Professional or above operating system
256 Megabites of RAM (or more)

While these are the recommended minimum requirements for running Visual Basic.NET, newer equipment and software along with faster processors will improve performance.

Editions of Visual Basic.NET

While Visual Basic.NET comes in different varieties or editions (Academic Edition, Professional Edition, and Enterprise Edition) we recommend that you purchase either the Professional or Enterprise Edition. Many of the multimedia features discussed in this text may not function properly with only the Academic Edition. We have developed and tested all our programs found in this text using the Professional Edition of Visual Basic.NET.

Installation

To begin the installation process, place the Visual Basic.NET CD into your CD-ROM drive. The installation process will begin automatically. If, for some reason it does not, click on the start button in the bottom left corner of your screen. Next, click on *Run*, click on *Browse*, change directories to your CD-ROM drive, and then double-click on *setup.exe*. Now click on *OK*. Visual Basic.NET should begin installing. If installation is still not accomplished, please see the owner's manual that accompanies your software.

One option that will appear during installation is the type of install you want to undertake. A "minimum install" will only place the essential files for most components of Visual Basic.NET to operate correctly. While this will save hard drive disc space, it is not recommended for programming the types of programs we will present in this text. The "standard install" is also not recommended. Most of the programs found in the following chapters will work correctly with this option, but not all of them. Therefore, we strongly recommend that you conduct a "full install" of Visual Basic.NET / Visual Studio to minimize any programming incompatibilities between information found in this text and your attempts to reproduce the programs on your own computer.

Programming Interface

The Project

Open the Visual Basic.NET program by first clicking on the *Start* button in the bottom left corner of your computer screen, then on *Programs*, and finally on *Microsoft Visual Basic*. Depending on your installed version, your third option may say something like "Visual Studio.NET" or "Visual Basic.NET." Once the program opens you will see a small window entitled "Start" prompting you to make a selection between *New Projects* or to open an existing project. Select *New*, and then *Windows Application*, and then click *OK*. This option is probably already highlighted as the default option when the program loaded. In the future you can use the *Existing* tab to quickly access projects that you previously worked on.

It should be noted at this time that throughout the course of this book some buttons or names will appear using *italics*. This has been done by the publisher to assist with reading ease and clarity, but these items are not written in *italics* in Visual Basic.NET. When VB.NET code is written, it is set apart in a different font. When these lines of code are too long to fit on a single line, the subsequent lines are indented to indicate that the previous line of code is continuing.

Project Explorer

Programming in Visual Basic.NET takes place in, what is called, a "Solution." This "solution" can be conceptualized as the environment that houses your program. As a default, Visual Basic.NET has named this solution for you as "WindowsApplication1." As you examine your computer screen, along with Figure 1.1, you will see a novel looking tool bar down the left side of the screen along with four smaller windows containing a variety of information within the larger main window of Visual Basic.

Take note of the smaller window in the upper right hand side of the screen. This window is called the "Solution Explorer." The "Solution Explorer" is your outline of the various components that currently exist in your program. Currently your program, entitled "WindowsApplication1" contains a file folder consisting of a form called "Form1.vb". Right now if you were to run your program, a blank window with

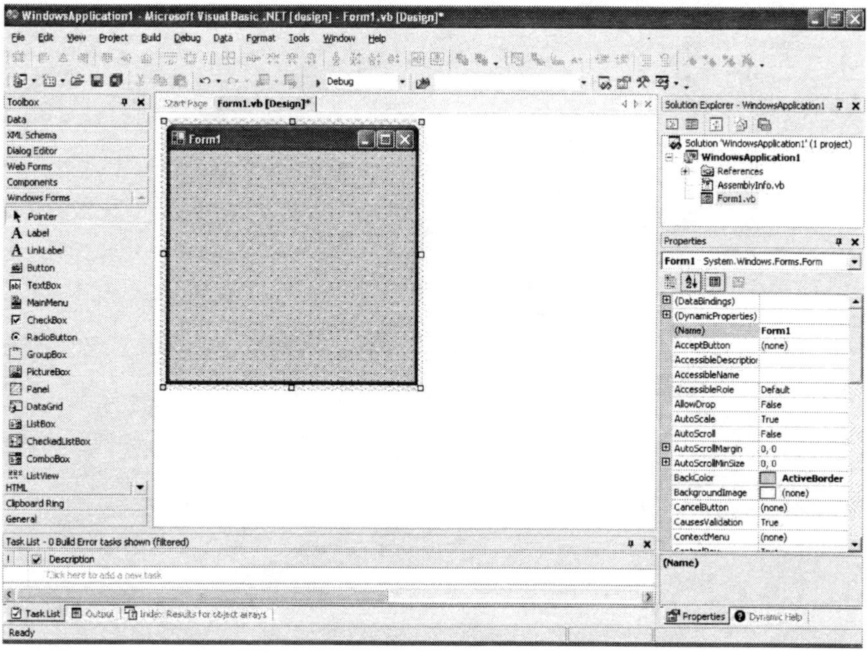

Figure 1.1 displays an overview of the Visual Basic.NET programming environment.

a name of "Form1" would appear on the computer screen. Try this by clicking on the *Debug* option in your main toolbar at the top of the screen followed by the *Start* sub-option. To terminate the program, again click on "Debug" but now select the sub-option *Stop Debugging.*

As you add more materials into your computer program besides a blank window called Form1.vb, the detail of the Solution Explorer will grow. Clicking on the Solution Explorer files and directories is quite useful when your program becomes larger and you need to locate specific portions of the program quickly. If for some reason you accidentally close the Solution Explorer window, and it will happen, simply click on *View* and then *Solution Explorer* from the main toolbar. The other two file options besides Form1.vb under "WindowsApplication1" are technical computer coding procedures needed to make VB.NET run on your comuter. They are what makes it possible for you to program with Visual Objects and easy to understand English language Style commands instead of "computer friendly" 0s, and 1s. Understanding these sections of VB.NET (the "References" and "AssemblyInfo" folders) is unnecessary to create the programs you will probably make for research purposes.

Forms

To the left of the "Solution Explorer" window is a larger window called "Form1" containing a window "Form1" inside of it. This layout mimics what you also see in the "Solution Explorer", yet in graphical form. Again, we currently have a solution called "WindowsApplication1" and a form called "Form1" within it. You already saw Form1 in action. So far, it doesn't do much. Yet this little form can quickly become quite powerful.

Properties Window

Directly below the "Solution Explorer" window is a slightly larger window entitled the "Properties Window." In our current project, the name in the Properties Window reads "Properties-Form1." This window displays a variety of modifiable properties of the form. Some of these properties are more important for psychological research than others, with the most commonly used options described here. Other form properties will be detailed in later chapters as their use becomes more context relevant.

For now, take a look at your first form property, the name. You can change the name of your form to something more descriptive than "Form1." To do this simply double-click on the "(name)" option. It should be the first available option. The text "Form1" will become highlighted. Change this text to your new form name. For illustration purposes, lets call the form "frmGreetings." This name might be relevant if our form served to greet users or subjects when they begin to interact with our program. The name of your Properties Window should now have changed to "frmGreetings". Figure 1.2 displays this change.

A few sections below the "(name)" option is the "Backcolor" option. Click on this option, select *custom* and change the color to a shade of yellow. Note the changes in frmGreetings in Figure 1.3.

Below *BackColor* is the *FormBorderStyle* property. This property of the form determines if a user will be able to resize the form during run time (i.e. minimize or maximize the window). It is likely to be the case that you will not want your subject to alter the size of the screen's form during run time of the experiment. Doing so may disrupt subject attention to the stimuli conditions programmed into the experiment. Alter the BorderStyle property in different ways, and run the program each time, trying to change the size of the form. Note the differences with each property option. You may have had a problem trying to run your program at this time. A new error window probably popped up saying there were build errors. Click on the *NO* Button when asked if you want to continue. To fix this error, click on *WindowsApplication1* in the *Solution Explorer* (to highlight this selection), then click

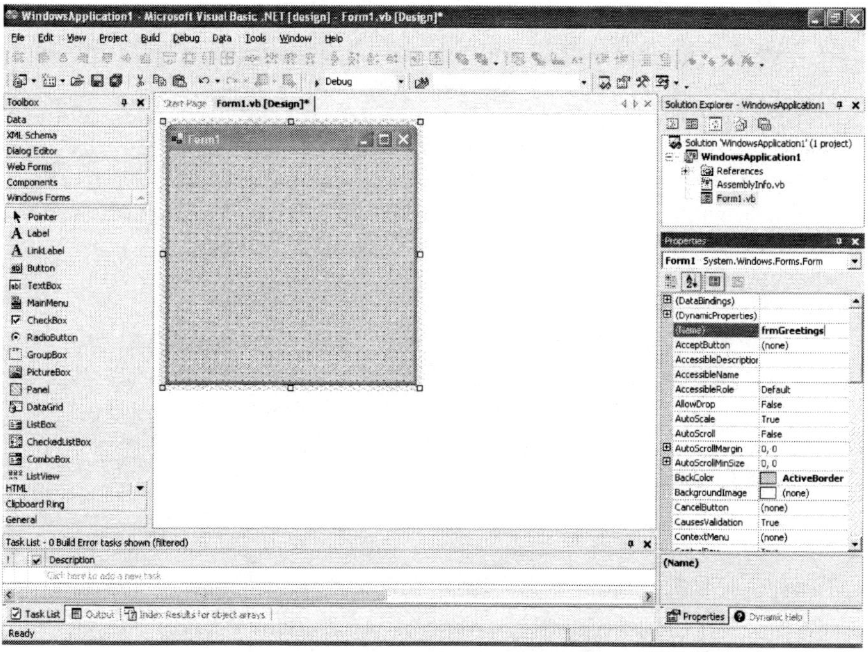

Figure 1.2 shows the alterations made in the Properties Window following the renaming of Form1.

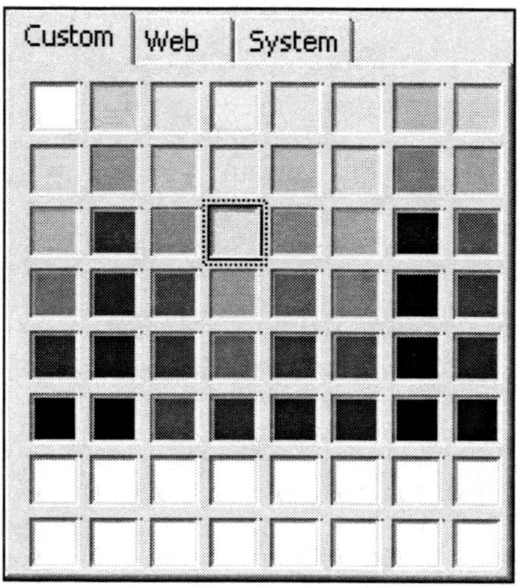

Figure 1.3 displays the BackColor property color customization window.

Project on the main menu, then on the *Properties* option. Now change the *Startup option* from *Form1* to *frmGreetings*, and click *OK.* Try running the program, it should now work.

Scrolling down the Properties Window you will find an option entitled *WindowState.* The default option for WindowState is *Normal.* This means that during run time your form will appear with the same size dimensions that existed by default when you began your program. Yet, if you want the form to become larger, say the entire size of the computer screen, all you need to do is change this property to *Maximized.* Run the program. Your yellow frmGreetings form should encompass the entire computer screen. Note though, that it will no longer be possible to stop the program using the *Run* and *Stop* sequence as before – frmGreetings covered it up. Stop the program using the X in the top right hand corner of frmGreetings. If you selected a BorderStyle of *None* and wish to stop the program you will need to actually use a CTRL-ALT-DELETE command sequence. Varying levels of program termination and form size can work to your advantage when attempting to reduce subject distraction during your experiment.

Form Layout

The Start Position property provides you with a way of altering your form's look during run time on your computer screen. You can shift your form's position by changing this property. Try moving your form here, and then try running the program. Note how your form is positioned in different sections of the monitor screen based on the selection you made. The Start Position property only works to aid you when your form is in the WindowState *Normal* mode. Most programs you will create will contain forms that are Maximized.

Toolbox

The most dynamic window that resides on your Visual Basic.NET desktop is the Toolbox. This window contains all the necessary devices for you to create your own experiments. These "tools" which are contained within the toolbox can be incorporated into your program by using your mouse button to select, drag, and drop them onto your existing form. Since we are creating Windows-based programs (as opposed to web-based or other types) the Windows Forms tools are displayed by default. If not, click on this option.

The first tool is the default mouse pointer. You can click here if you accidentally selected a tool you don't want and need to obtain a different one, or if you clicked on a tool by mistake and simply want to return to other activities within your form and program. The next tool is a Label, and is depicted with a large capital letter *A.* Placing this tool on your form will result in a rectangular box with the text "Label1" located within it. Note that the default property highlighted in the Properties Window is "Text" - "Label1." Double-click on the section and type in a different caption, like *Hello* and press Return. Notice how your Label on your form now has changed its text from *Label1* to *Hello*.

Figure 1.4

Figure 1.4 and 1.5 display the effects of altering your form's position with the Start Position Property.

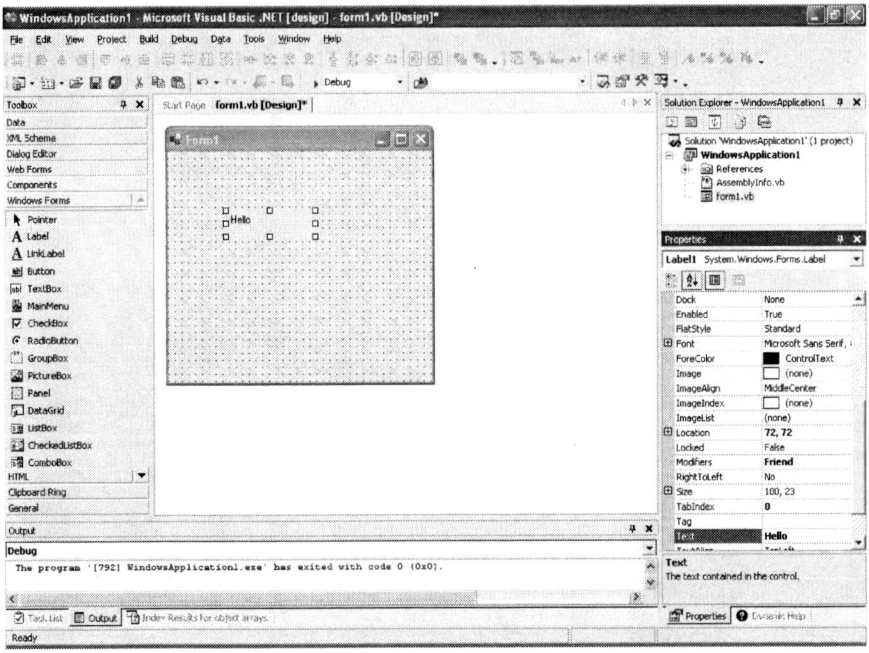

Figure 1.6 displays the form, PictureBox, and Label.

Another tool is the PictureBox. Adding a PictureBox to your form will give you the ability to place graphics into your computer program. Add a PictureBox to your form and note the default property highlighted in the Properties Window is "Image (none)." Double-click on the "(none)" section and notice that you are presented with an explorer window to select a picture from your computer's files. Browse for a picture, select it, and click *OK*. Your picture should now reside in your PictureBox. The PictureBox contains a property called *SizeMode* located a few options below the Image property. Altering this property to *StretchImage* will allow your graphic to be resized to fix exactly within the display box. This is a very valuable property which will save you considerable time if you are left having to resize all your graphical images to fix exactly within your Picture objects. This tool also contains the ability for participants to respond, or click, directly on it during an experiment. This is of considerable value if you are presenting stimuli directly within a PictureBox and wish for the participant to make a response to that stimulus rather than an adjacent Button or CheckBox.

Another tool is the TextBox and is depicted with a small case "a b |" display. Placing this tool on your form will result in a rectangular box with the text "Textbox1" located within it. This TextBox looks very similar to your Label box, yet the important difference is that a TextBox allows a user to enter information during run time by typing in the box, while a Label will not. A Label is used to display information, while a TextBox is often used to acquire information from the

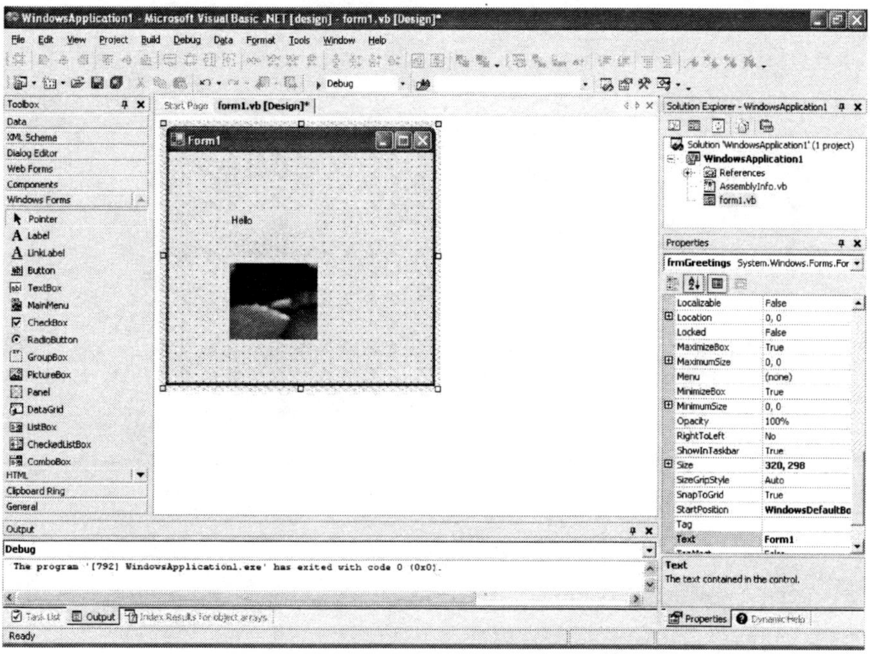

Figure 1.7 displays a PictureBox on the form.

participant. There are exceptions to this case, but in general this rule does hold true. Notice that the default property highlighted in the Properties Window is "Text – TextBox1." Double-click on the *TextBox1* section and type in a different line of text, like *Welcome to my form* and press Return. Notice how your TextBox on your form has now changed its text from *Text1* to *Welcome to my form*. Now locate the Font property for your TextBox and double-click on it. Notice that you are now presented with more property options like Name, Size, Unit, Bold, etc., that allow you to make a variety of changes to the characteristics of your font for the text in your TextBox. Play around with some changes, and note the changes on your form. Run your program and notice how you can edit the text of your TextBox and how you cannot edit the text of your Label.

A GroupBox is a rectangular object on the form that can hold other tools within it. It is essentially a type of "mini form" within your existing form. Add a GroupBox to your form and note that the text displayed above it is *GroupBox1* and that the default property highlighted in the Properties Window is "text" – "GroupBox1." Double-click on the "text" property and change the text to *How are you?* and press Return. Notice how your text has changed. Within your new Frame you can place specific tools to enhance the design style of your form's layout. There are other and more pragmatic properties to the GroupBox tool that will be covered in later chapters.

Figure 1.8 displays the form, PictureBox, Label, and TextBox.

Another important tool is the Button. A Button is a tool that a user or participant clicks the mouse pointer on during an experiment. It can be thought of as a computerized version of a lever in a traditional operant chamber. The Button can be used as the primary response operanda in many experiments. Two or more Buttons can also function as response options in choice situations. Add two Buttons to your form, within your GroupBox. You can stretch or shrink them by manipulating the sides of the Button. Make them about the same size, and locate the "text" property of Button1. Change that property to *Great.* Note the change on the form. Now select Button2 and change the "text" property to *Bad.* Note the change on your form.

The CheckBox and RadioButton tools allow you to create a means for participants to select from an array of options presented to them. You might use these tools to create a means of assessing participant age, sex, race, and other demographics. They might also be used in survey research to measure self-reports to different psychological questions.

The ComboBox and ListBox tools provide you with yet another way in which a participant can select from a list of options presented to them. These tools work best on forms containing many objects and materials because they only require minimum space and can store a large number of response options.

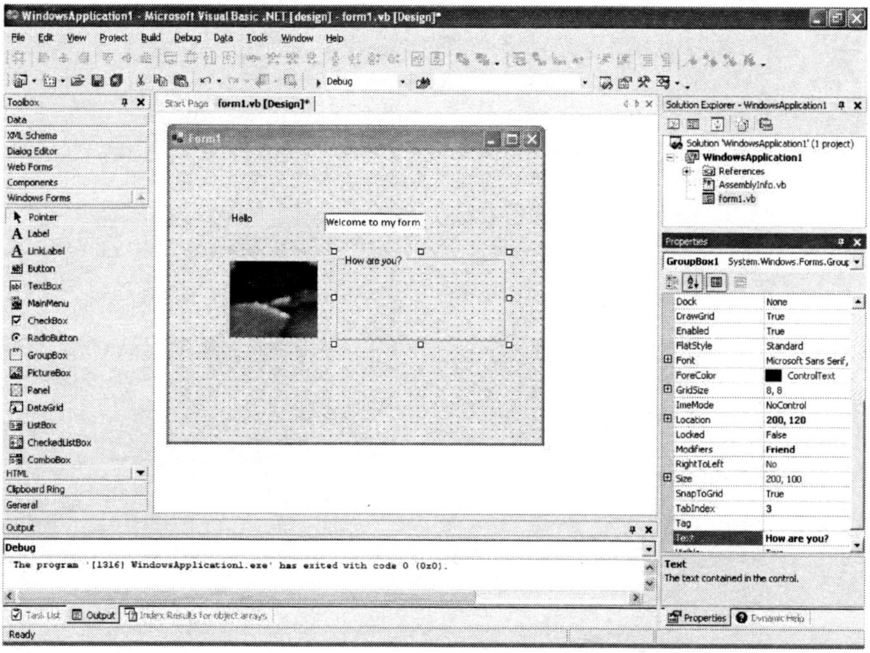

Figure 1.9 displays the form, PictureBox, Label, TextBox, and GroupBox.

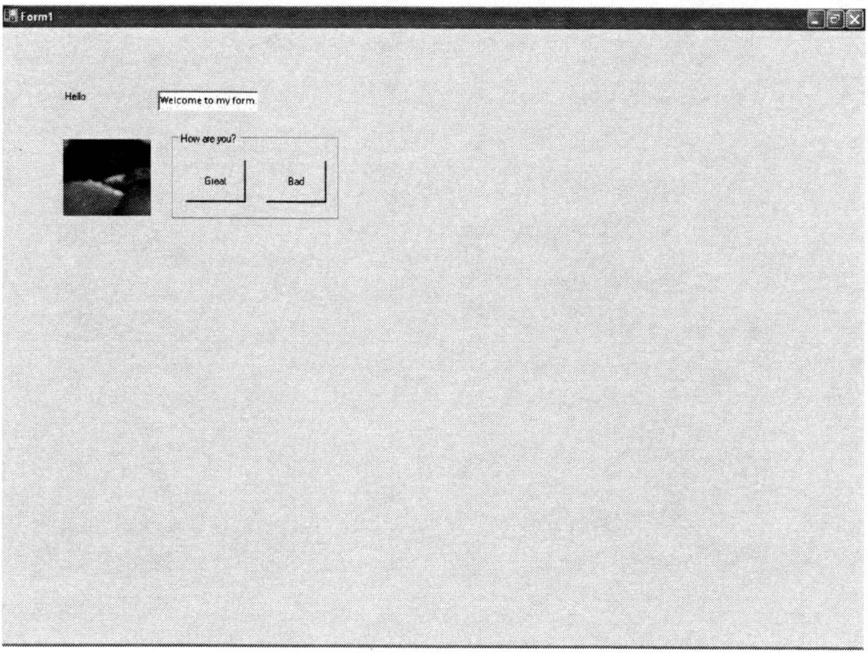

Figure1.10 displays the form with the newly added two Buttons.

The *Timer* tool has considerable utility for programmers of behavioral research. It is sometimes called the *Timer Object.* The Timer is depicted by a little stopwatch in the toolbox. Add a Timer tool to your form. Notice how it immediately was removed from your form and placed in the empty space below it. this is done because the Timer Object is never visible during runtime. Look in the Properties Window and notice that this little tool has only a few properties compared to other tools like the TextBox, Label, GroupBox, etc. Altering the *Interval* property of the Timer from "0" milliseconds to some value can control the duration stimuli are displayed on the form, specify the length of an experimental phase, or delay the onset of a reinforcer.

There are other tools within the toolbox that we have not mentioned here, but will be highlighted in subsequent chapters as their utility becomes more apparent. However, most programming can be completed with the simple tools we have outlined above.

Output Window

The Output Window found on the bottom of your screen is a new feature in VB.NET. Its purpose is to provide you with a listing of problems that occur during the test running of your program. Hopefully this window will remain relatively

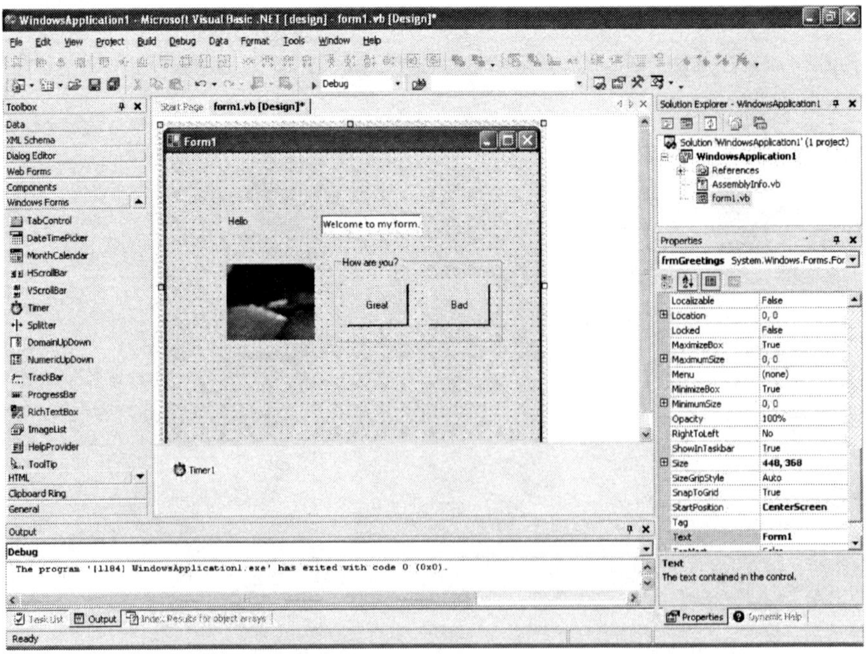

Figure 1.11 displays the form with the added Timer.

empty as you learn to program, but if not, it does highlight where your errors are, and provides you with "hints" about how to fix the error(s).

Beyond the Visual Interface

Menu Bar

The Menu Bar in Visual Basic.NET is quite similar to the Menu Bar found on your other popular Microsoft Office products. Some of the response options are in fact identical. You have the *Cut*, *Copy*, *Paste* features, the *Open* and *Save* features, and the *Undo* and *Redo* features. Other response options are more idiosyncratic to Visual Basic. Here you can *Add a project, add a windows form,* or *add a new component.* Like the other Microsoft products, these options are simple shortcuts to perform actions that are also found in the dropdown menus located at the top of the screen under headings such as *File*, *Edit*, *Properties*, etc. We will highlight the most commonly used response options of this Menu Bar as we construct the programs found in the following chapters. Explore them a little now to become familiar with their location. Often sought after options are the "Properties Window" and "Toolbox". There have been many times that we have accidentally closed one of these windows, and need to pop them back open quickly. It can become rather frustrating when you can't remember how to do so.

Code

By now you probably double-clicked on your form somehow and accidentally opened a window containing a white background and the title text of "Public Class frmGreetings." If not, do so now. Simply place your mouse pointer anywhere on your form and double-click. This underworld of your form is actually called the *Edit Level*, *Code Level*, or *Programming Level* where you write syntax to make your form do the things you want it to do during the running of the experiment. It is here where you make stimuli in PictureBoxes appear and disappear, Timers turn on or off, sounds play, screens change colors, etc. Believe it or not, you will be able to do so by the end of the next chapter. With the right direction, the programming all of these fascinating events is relatively quite easy to do.

An Unfortunate Flaw

There will be times when you attempt to run your program, and your form just does not show up. Your mouse can still move on the screen, but the form seems to be missing. this is a flaw in the VB.NET program that will hopefully be solved in future editions. To minimize the probability of this happening, make your WindowState property *Maximized.* If all else fails, stop the program, and just try running it again. This flaw is annoying, yet it will not affect the running of the final program once it is totally built.

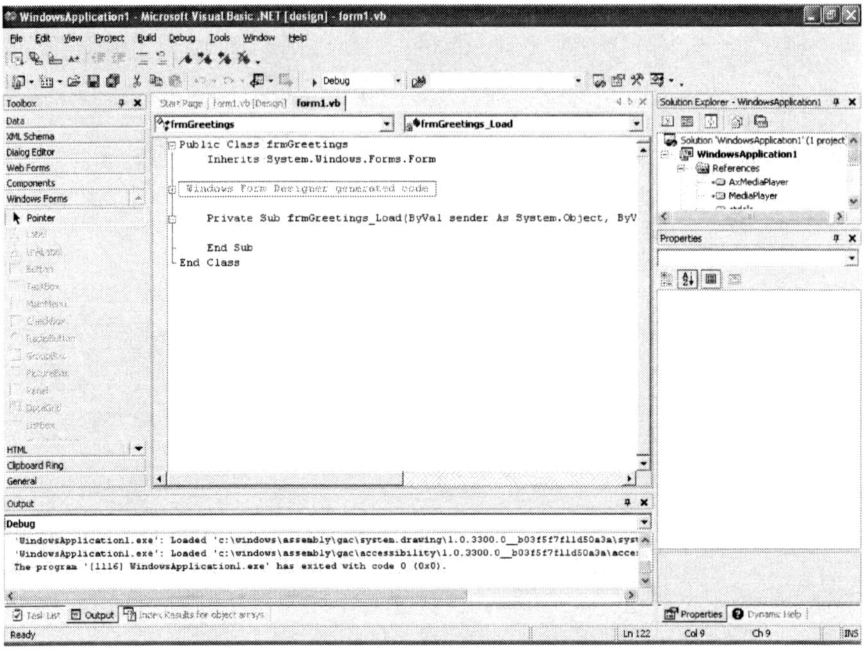

Figure 1.12 displays the "Code" or "Edit" level of the form.

Chapter 2: Simple Routines in Visual Basic

Windows States, Screen Colors, and Key Previews

Window States

Open a new "Windows Application" project and change the name of the Project and solution to *Forms*. It is a good practice to start off by saving your form and project immediately before you begin working on it. This helps avoid any loss of information from computer crashes or unexpected power outages. To save all your related forms and information found in your Forms Solution, click on *File* in the main menu, then click on *Save All*.

Select the form by clicking on it, change the name of the form to *frmForm*, and change the text to *This is a form*. Now run the program using the menu. Make sure to change the Start up object as noted on page 14. You can use the controls box in the upper right corner to minimize and maximize the form during run time. Close the form.

Allowing the subject to be able to change the size of the form is sometimes undesirable when running experiments. Also, it may be more useful for subjects to see the experiment encompass the entire computer screen to reduce distractions. It is easy to configure these options prior to running the program. To do so, change the *WindowState* property to *Maximize*. Now run the program using the menu. Close the program using the control box in the upper left corner.

Screen Colors

You can change the background color of the form by altering the BackColor property in the property toolbox. Simply click on *BackColor* and choose your preferred color. There are a wide variety of colors you can choose from. These colors can add contextual cues to specific programming procedures, or just a flash of color to a rather boring preparation. You may wish for the screen color to change when the subject clicks a specific object, or after a given amount of time has elapsed. Both of these options are easily constructed, as you will see below.

Key Preview

The key preview information is useful for creating programs that would require a subject to press a specific key in order for a specific event to happen. For example, you might have a subject press the *X* key to turn off a loud aversive noise, but only after he/she has pressed the *G* key twice. Or, you might have the space bar advance images in a signal detection task. The key preview function allows you to figure out which keycode is associated with each key, and with that information you can compose code for the computer do something if the keycode = 34 (or whatever the number of your desired key might be).

Double-click the form to go to the edit level. There are two drop down boxes at the top of the editor. The left drop down lists the objects residing on the form. Currently there are no objects other than the form, and two items called *(Overrides)* and *(Base Class Events)*. Select *(Base Class Events)*. The *(Overrides)* option found here will be discussed later.

The right drop down box will now list all of the events or *(Base Class Events)* associated with the form (or whatever other object is highlighted in the left drop down box). With the *(Base Class Events)* listed in the left box, select *KeyUp* in the right box. A new subroutine will appear called Form_KeyUp (ByVal sender as Object, ByVal e as System.Windows.Forms.KeyEventArgs) handles Mybase.KeyUp. Directly below this line and above the line *End Sub* type:

```
me.Text = e.KeyCode
```

Now return to the properties toolbox and change the form property of *KeyPreview* to *True*. Run the program using the menu and try typing in numbers or letters. Remember to change the Startup Object. Notice that the text displays different numbers each time you press a key. This is because each key has a unique number associated with it. Each time you press a key and then let it up, the associated number is displayed in frmForm's text. Close frmForm using the upper right control box.

Under your last line of code type:

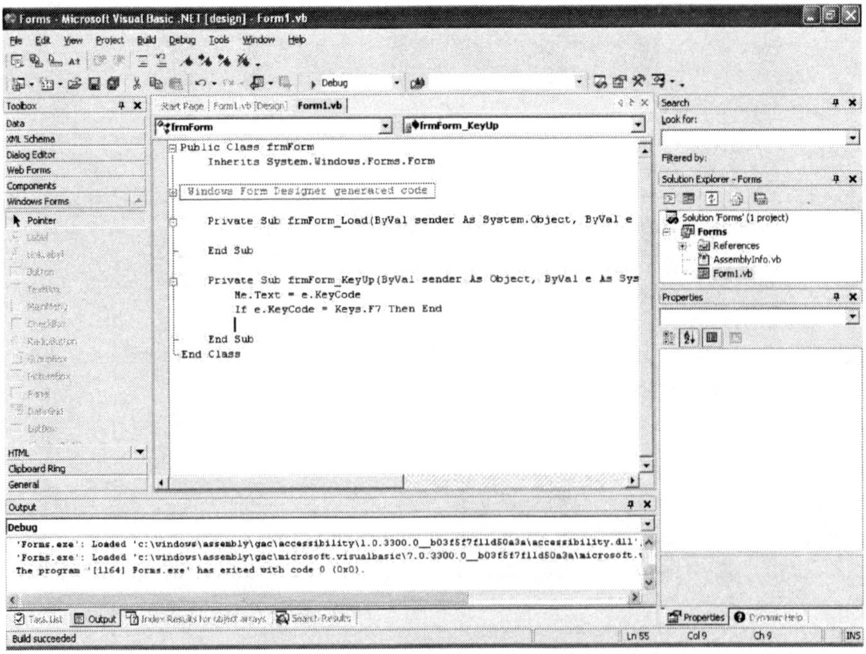

Figure 2.1 displays an example of the keypreview function.

```
If e.KeyCode = Keys.F7 then End
```

Now run the program and press the F7 key. Your program should automatically end.

Altering Form Properties

Form Resizing and Buttons

Double-click on the form to go to edit level. Using the left event drop down box, select *(Base Class Events)* and using the right drop down box, select *SizeChanged*. A new subroutine called *frmForm_SizeChanged...* will appear. Below this line type:

```
me.Text = me.Height & "," & me.Width
```

Run the program using the menu. Use the control box to restore the form. Move the mouse cursor to the edge of the form. The cursor will turn into a double headed arrow, then press down on the left mouse key and resize the form. Notice how the form properties *Height* and *Width* are displayed in the text and change each time you resize the form. This information may be useful if you are designing a program with multiple forms where each will occupy only a portion of the computer screen.

Return to your project and click on the Button object in the toolbox. Place the Button on your form and change the name of the Button in the properties box to *cmdButton*. Resize the Button by clicking on it, and then move your mouse cursor to the edge of the Button. When the mouse cursor changes to a double arrow, hold down the left mouse button and resize the Button by moving the mouse in any desired direction. You can also resize the Button by changing the *Size* properties in the properties box.

You can also move the entire Button by pressing down on the left mouse key when it is over the Button. Then simply drag cmdButton to any desired location on the form. Another way to move cmdButton to the left or right is by changing the *Location* property in the property box. If cmdButton disappears don't worry, you have probably entered a value that is larger or smaller than the visible area of frmForm. Now try moving cmdButton by changing the *Location* property in the properties box. While this appears rather trivial right now, keep in mind that you can change object properties while the program is running. This can be very useful in a variety of experiments. We will illustrate such usage in later chapters.

Now, change the text property of cmdButton to *Color Switch*. Double-click on cmdButton and insert the code directly below the subroutine cmdButton_Click...:

```
me.Backcolor = Color.Bisque
```

Run the program, and click on the Button. You will see that your screen changes from whatever color you chose earlier to a light tan color. You could add other Buttons for other colors too.

Utilizing a Button with code to terminate the program is also very useful. For example, if you are attempting to assess a subject's persistence on a given task like a slot machine and you allow them to quit when they "feel" they can't win any more. Some human subjects' committees may even require a program termination option to be in your experiment. Such an option allows the subject to terminate the program at anytime they feel uncomfortable.

Change the text property of cmdButton to *Close*. Double-click on cmdButton and insert the code directly below the subroutine cmdButton_Click:

```
End
```

While you have previously been starting your program using the icon on the menu, you can also run it by pressing the *F5* key. Give this a try and click on the *Close* button. The program should end.

You might be wondering right now what this "code" you are typing in actually means. Especially that "me" word. Well "me" is shorthand for the active form in the program. When you have more than one form in your program "me" becomes quite important.

Events

An event is something that happens, most often due to the user clicking on the mouse or pressing a key on the keyboard. When the user clicks on the cmdButton, as described above, this is called an event. The same is true with the KeyUp procedure that you created earlier. Visual Basic.NET programs are most often run via a series of events that occur right after each other. Your experiments will undoubtedly be event driven by the subject. Let's begin an example of an event that links multiple forms together.

Linking Multiple Forms

Open the Forms Solution if it is not already open, and add a new form using the menu. Click on *Project*, then *Add WindowsForm*, then double-click on the *WindowsForm* Icon. Rename the form *frmForm2* and change the text of frmForm2 to *Form 2*. Change the WindowState to Maximized. Now add a Button and rename it *cmdPreviousForm*, and change the text of cmdPreviousForm to *Previous*. Next, double-click on cmdPreviousForm to enter edit mode and under cmdPreviousForm_Click type:

```
me.Visible = False
```

Now press the enter key. On the next line type:

```
Dim x as New frmForm()
x.Show()
```

Return to frmForm by double-clicking on its name in the Solution Window. Add a Button and rename it *cmdNext* and change the text property of cmdNext to *Next.* Move cmdNext to any new location on the form. Double-click on cmdNext to enter edit mode, type the following code below cmdNext_Click:

```
me.Visible = False
```

Press the enter key and then type:

```
Dim x as New frmForm2()
x.Show()
```

Press the F5 key to run the program: Click on the *Next* Button: Click on the *Previous* Button. Notice how the Buttons take you from one form to another.

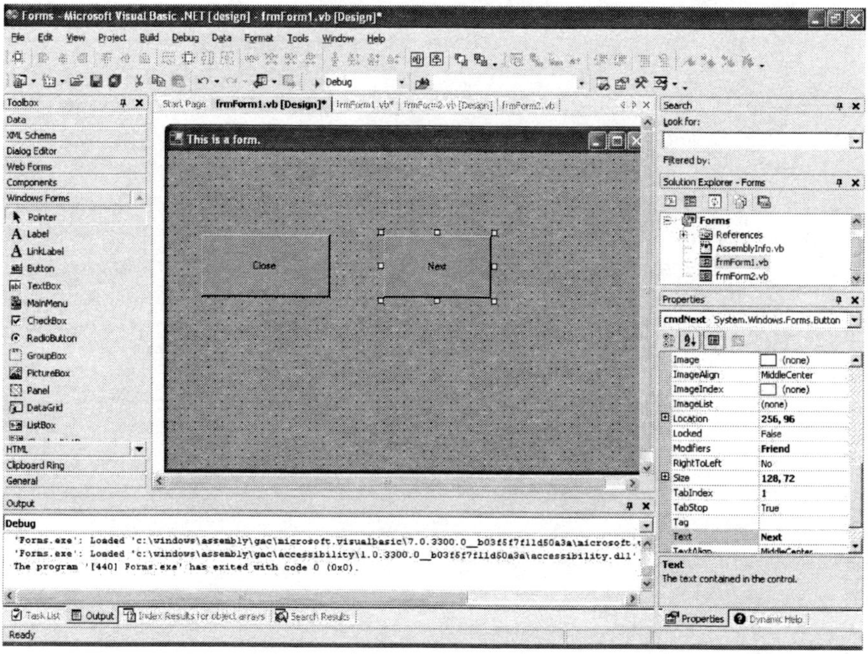

Figure 2.2 displays an example of the incorporation of Buttons with multiple forms.

Notice how the screen flickers when you change from one form to another. This is because you are hiding one form before showing the next. If you reverse the order of the code under cmdNext so that the show property of *X* is *True* before you change the visible property of frmForm to *False* then the flicker will not occur. Change the order of the code under frmForm2 as well, and run the program using the F5 key.

While the *me. Visible=False* code explains itself the *DimX...* code probably does not. What happens here is that we need to take the frmForm2 Object (i.e. Windows Form) and make it equal an arbitrary entity (i.e., *X*). Then we simply tell *X* to show itself. Variables such as *X* will be explained in more detail as we progress.

Labels

Open the VB.NET Solution *Forms* if it is not already open and go to frmForm by clicking on its name in the Solution Explorer. Add a Label to the form by clicking on the Label icon in the toolbox. Change the name property of the Label to *lblInstructions* and change the text property of lblInstructions to *Click on the NEXT button to go to the next form*. Notice that the Label is too small to display all of the text. Resize the Label so that the entire text is displayed, move the Label to the upper left corner of frmForm and run the program.

Changing the Font properties in lblInstructions can be done rather easily. Click on lblInstructions to select the object, and then locate the font property in the property box. Double-click on the font property so that more font options appear. This is very much like font options that are used in Word and Excel. This is because VB.NET uses existing Windows libraries to make VB.NET a more powerful program, as well as one that you should be somewhat familiar with if you use other Microsoft products. Using the font dialog box, change the font size and any other properties you might desire. Finally, close the font options by double-clicking on font property again and resize lblInstructions if necessary. Run the program.

In addition to changing font properties, you can also change the TextAlign property of lblInstructions. The default alignment of the text for lblInstructions is set to the left. Yet, if you wish to center the text, select lblInstructions by clicking on it, locate the TextAlign property in the toolbox, and change the alignment property to center. Run the program.

Another possibility you may wish to consider when using Labels for providing instructions to your subject is changing some of the Label properties while the program is running. This might be done to ensure orientation to a specific Label at a specific time. To do this, add another Button to frmForm, change the name to *cmdLeft*, and change the text of cmdLeft to *Left*. Double-click on cmdLeft to enter edit mode and type the following code under cmdLeft_click:

```
lblInstructions.TextAlign = ContentAlignment.MiddleLeft
```

Now, add another Button and position it to the right of cmdLeft. Change the name of this new Button to cmdRight, and change the text property to *Right*. Double-click on cmdRight to enter edit mode and type the following code under cmdRight_click:

```
lblInstructions.TextAlign = ContentAlignment.BottomRight
```

Run the program. Try clicking on the Left and Right Buttons.

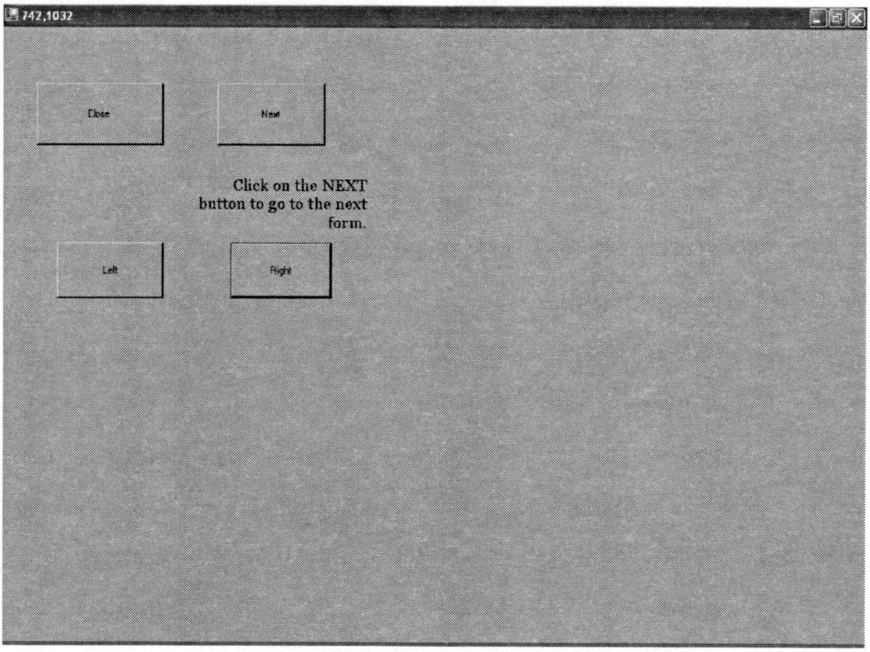

Figure 2.3 displays an example of using Labels for the display of instructions

Array

Button Array

So far we have worked with single objects (forms and Buttons). Now we will create what is called a control array. A control array is a group of more than one object (such as a Button or Label) that controls a similar function in your program. For example, if you have three Buttons that a subject could click on to indicate a preference among three options, much less code would be needed if we created a control array than if we put three separate buttons on the screen and typed similar code underneath each of those buttons.

Open the VB.NET Solution Forms if it is not already open, and select lblInstructions from frmForm. Now select *Edit* and then *Copy* from the main menu. Go to frmForm2 and select *Edit* and then *Paste* from the main menu. Now we have duplicated the same Label on two different forms with duplicate names. We can have duplicate objects with the same names because they are on separate forms. This is because they are really named *frmForm.lblInstructions* and *frmForm2.lblInstructions* (Note the period separating the form name and the label name is called "dot notation"). Yet, something different happens if we want two objects on the same form with the same name.

Create a new Button on frmForm and name the Button cmdLocation1. Change the text to *Top*. Now, select cmdLocation1, then select *Edit* and then *Copy*, and finally, *Edit* again and then *Paste* all from the main menu. Now we will have two Buttons that we want to call cmdLocation. So change the name of this second Button to cmdLocation2, and the text to *middle*. Select either of the cmdLocation buttons and repeat your earlier steps. The third button should be identical to the other two except it has the name of cmdLocation3, and a text of *bottom*.

To turn the three separate Buttons into a control array (in other words to link the click event of one to each other), you simply need to change a little existing code. Double-click on cmdLocation1 and go to the edit level. Note the line of code directly above your cursor:

```
Private Sub cmdLocation1_Click (...)
```

Notice at the end of this line of code it states:

```
Handles cmdLocation1.click
```

Just add the following code after cmdLocation1.click:

```
, cmdLocation2.click, cmdLocation3.click
```

Double-click on either of the other two cmdLocation Buttons and note that each cmdLocation button now handles all three Buttons.

Advantages of the Control Array

One benefit of this newly constructed control array is that you can reduce the amount of program code you use. Remember on frmForm the Buttons to change the alignment of lblInstructions? Under each Button you had to have a new line of code. With the array we can alter object properties with one line of code for all three cmdLocation Buttons.

To change the text displayed in our Label object when any one of our new cmdLocation Buttons is clicked, add the following code under any one of the three Buttons:

```
Dim buttonClicked as Button
buttonClicked = CType (sender, Button)
lblInstructions.Text()= "You pressed" & buttonClicked.Text
```

Now when you press any cmdLocation Button, the text of that Button will be translated into the text property of the Label. Run the program and click on the different Buttons.

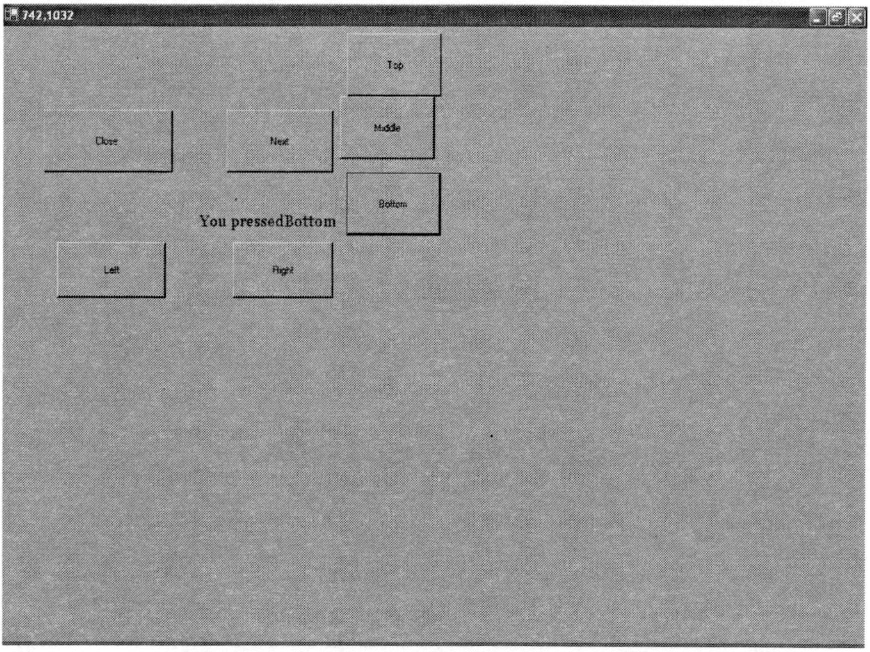

Figure 2.4 displays an example of using Command Arrays

Simple Audio

Beep

Sometimes it is good to have simple sounds incorporated into your program to get the users attention. There are several ways to do this. The easiest way to add a sound is to utilize the "Beep" function. This Beep is code that will tell VB.NET to play the actual default sound your computer plays during the running of any windows application.

Let's add a new form to our existing project. Click on the *Add New Item* icon and notice that there are many types of Items we can add. However for now just click on *WindowsForm*. For now let's name the form frmForm3. While this is not that clever of a naming convention, it is consistent with the naming convention we have started. Change the text of frmForm3 to *Form 3*, and the Windows state to *Maximized.* Now we need to access frmForm3 from the main page, or from frmForm. Go to the frmForm and add a Button called *cmdForm3* and change the text to *Form3.* Double click cmdForm3 and enter the following three lines of code below Private Sub cmdForm3_Click():

```
Dim x as New frmForm3()
x.show()
me.Visible = False
```

Go back to frmForm3 and add a Button called cmdBeep, change the text to *Beep*. Double-click cmdBeep and add the following code below Private Sub cmdBeep_Click():

```
Beep
```

That's it. Just "Beep." Run the program, click on the *Form3* Button, and then click on the *Beep* Button.

Simple Graphics

Image Graphics

There are several ways to add graphics to your program. For now we will use the object called a PictureBox. Go to Form3 if you are not already there. Add a PictureBox to the form and call it imgForm3 for lack of a better name at this point. An outline of a box will appear on your form. Stretch it to whatever size you desire. Under properties find BorderStyle. Change the BorderStyle from *None* to *Fixed Single*. You will see your PictureBox take on new dimensions. Now find the Image property, double-click on the small box to the right of the image description, and browse your directory for any picture that you might like to put in the PictureBox. Many standard images can be found in your Windows directory. Chances are the PictureBox will not be the identical size as the picture you want to place in it. Therefore, BEFORE you add your picture to the PictureBox, change the *SizeMode* property to *StretchImage*. If you do this after you add your picture, it will not work. So again, change the *SizeMode* property of the PictureBox before you add your picture. Now the picture will fit, but it may be distorted because the aspect ratio (proportions) has changed. Select imgForm3 by clicking on it once. Try to resize the PictureBox by clicking and dragging on the blue resizing boxes in and out until you have the proportions that best accommodate your picture.

Adding a Graphic During Run Time(while the program is running)

A very useful feature of the PictureBox is that it will allow you to add or change the image within it during the running of the program. This is extremely beneficial if you are presenting a variety of stimuli to the subject across a series of trials and do not want the subject to see all of them at the onset of the experiment. Just think of the headache it would be if you needed to create a new PictureBox for every stimulus you had for your program.

First you need to figure out ahead of time what the path and file name are for the desired pictures. Lets say the picture is called *Picture1.bmp* and is located in the *c:\My Documents* directory. To work through this example, actually find an image on your computer, copy it to the *My Documents* directory, and rename it *Picture1.jpg*.

Add a new Button to Form3 called *cmdImage* and change the text to *New Image*. Locate cmdImage just below the PictureBox you previously added to your form. Double-click on the cmdImage and add the following code below Private Sub cmdImage_Click():

```
Dim path As String = "c:\My Documents\Picture1.jpg"
imgForm3.Image = Image.FromFile("c:\My
   Documents\Picture1.jpg")
```

Now run the program, go to Form3, and click on the New Image Button. Note that there is a space between the word *My* and the word *Documents*. If you do not add this space your program will not find the image. Also, keep in mind that if your image uses a capital letter or a space between a multiword picture name, you must have these same capitalization and spaces or VB.NET will not be able to find the image file. Lastly, you must add the file extension to your picture's name. In the above example, we used a .jpg. You can also use GIF files and BMP files, which would result in .gif or .bmp file extensions respectively.

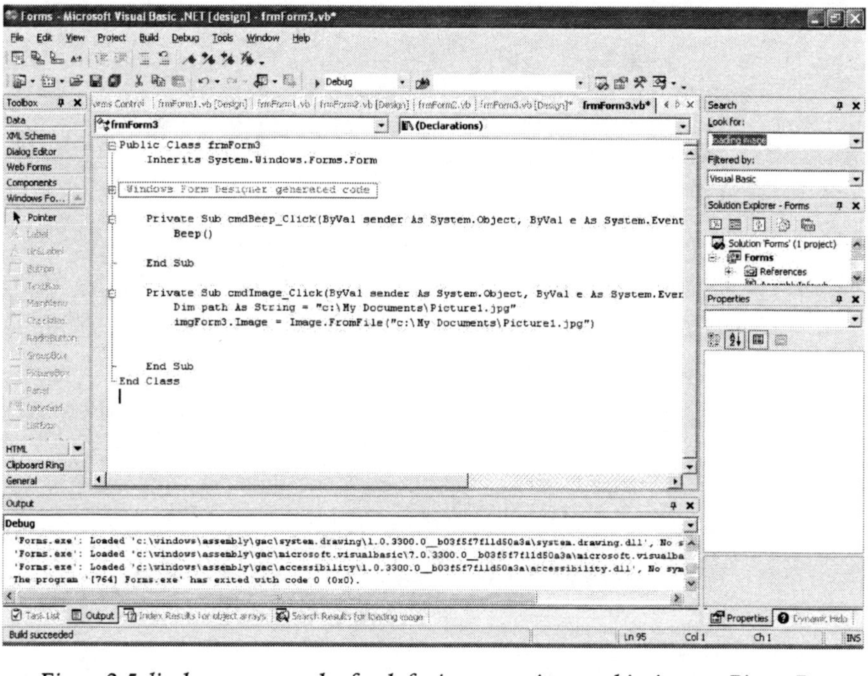

Figure 2.5 displays an example of code for incorporating graphics into an PictureBox

Adding Multiple Graphics During Run Time

For this exercise we will need to use a variable to keep track of the pictures. Double-click on Form3 and enter the edit mode. The left dropdown menu should say *frmForm3*. Click on this once, and select the *(Base Class Events)*. Type the following text *above* the Public Class frmForm3 code::

```
Option Explicit On
```

Then just below *Inherits System.Windows.Forms.Form* type:

```
Dim vPicCount
```

The *v* will remind you later that this is a variable, or an entity that contains values. We will talk more about variables later, for now though simply understand that a variable keeps track of values that we can assign during programming, or the subject can generate and alter during run time. Under the same dropdown box, now select the *(Base Class Events)* option again. You will see that the default event that is associated with the form is *(Declarations)* (this appears in the right dropdown menu). Change this option to *Load*. The subroutine will look like this:

```
Private Sub frmForm3_Load()
End Sub
```

This means when the form loads, VB.NET will do what ever is in the subroutine. Currently nothing is here. So when the form loads, it waits for the user to click on a Button to start some action. Yet, we want the form to do something, in this case load a picture, before the user even clicks on a Button. Therefore, we will have the form generate a value associated with our newly created variable and use that value to determine what type of picture will appear in the PictureBox. We will want the initial value of variable, vPicCount to equal 0. So type the following in this blank subroutine, directly under the text Private Sub frmForm3_Load().

```
vPicCount = 0
```

Now, when frmForm3 opens, the variable will be initialized to a value of 0. We also need to develop the following subroutine so we can cycle through three pictures (Picture1.jpg, Picture2.jpg, Picture3.jpg). Therefore, double-click on your cmdImage Button, and take a look at the following line of code you previously typed.

```
Dim path As String "c:\My Documents\Picture1.jpg"
imgForm3.Image = Image.FromFile ("c:\My
   Documents\Picture1.jpg")
```

This code calls one specific picture into the PictureBox at run time. Yet, now we want a variety of pictures to be displayed. Again, we will use pictures that are located in *c:\My Documents* directory. If you do not have at least three pictures in that directory, add them now, and change their names to Picture1, Picture2, and Picture3. Remember to note the file extensions.

What we want the computer to do is to show Picture1, then Picture2, then Picture3. To do this we need to learn to concatenate a string. This is actually very easy in VB.NET. Therefore, let's assume vPicCount has a value of 1 (vPicCount = 1), and if we do, the following sections of code are equivalent:

```
("c:\My Documents\Picture" & vPicCount & ".jpg")

("c:\My Documents\Picture1.jpg")
```

What this new, and somewhat different looking section of code says is, load a picture which has the first part of its name *Picture*, the second part of its name being equal to vPicCount (our new variable we created), and the last part of the name being the file extension (in this case a .jpg). Or in other words, load *Picture1.jpg*. If we increase the value of vPicCount by one (vPicCount = vPicCount + 1) then the following two sections of code are equivalent because now vPicCount = 2.

```
("c:\My Documents\Picture" & vPicCount & ".jpg")

("c:\My Documents\Picture2.jpg")
```

Because we want the picture to change each time we change the value of vPicCount, delete your previous code under the Button and type the following three lines of code directly under Private Sub cmdImage_Click():

```
vPicCount = vPicCount + 1
Dim path As String = ("c:\My Documents\Picture" &
   vPicCount & ".jpg")
imgForm3.Image = Image.FromFile ("c:\My
   Documents\Picture" & vPicCount & ".jpg")
```

Run the program, go to Form3, and click on New Image Button. Notice that when you passed the third picture (Picture3.jpg) and error message occurred because the was no Picture4 and you drove the computer crazy looking for it because it assumed there was a Picture4.

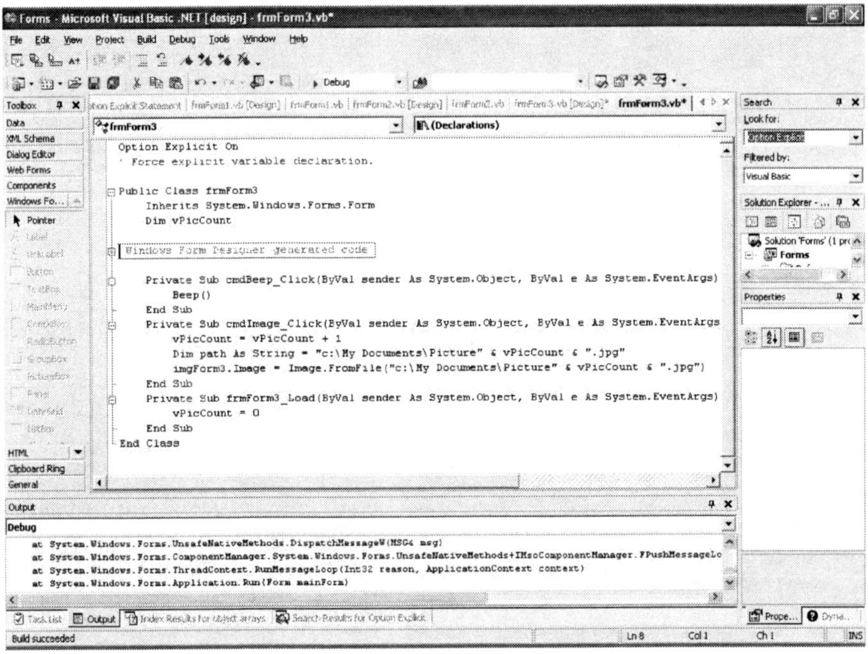

Figure 2.6 displays an example of code for incorporating sequential graphical images into a PictureBox.

There are two ways you can fix this run time error. The first is to tell the computer only increment vPicCount if it has a value below three (If vPicCount < 3 the vPicCount = vPicCount + 1). So add this line of code below vPicCount = vPicCount + 1.

```
If vPicCount < 3 then vPicCount = vPicCount +1
```

We don't want to run both lines of code that advance vPicCount so we want to *remark out* the old line. You do this by putting a 'in front of the old line. Notice how the old line turns a different color (probably green). The ' remarks out the line of code telling the computer to ignore it. *Remark out* is also very helpful if you want to put notes in your code so you remember what you were writing earlier. Just put the quotes at the front of anything you want to type in, and the computer will ignore it. Your subroutine should now look like this:

```
Private Sub cmdImage_Click()
'vPicCount = vPicCount + 1
If vPicCount < 3 then vPicCount = vPicCount + 1
```

```
Dim path As String = ("c:\My Documents\Picture" &
   vPicCount & ".jpg")
imgForm3.Image = Image.FromFile ("c:\My
   Documents\Picture" & vPicCount & ".jpg")
End Sub
```

Run the program, go to form3, and click on the New Image Button. You should have solved the error problem now. Your pictures should change three times, and stay on your third one, no matter how many more times you click on *New Image*.

The Error Trapper

The other way to prevent the error message is to include an error trapper. While topics such as error trapping and debugging are usually held back until later chapters in programming books, it is important to get into the habit of using them in your programs. Many types of error trapping will be discussed later, we won't go into that much detail yet, and just show you the code. Note that you have to take the remark off of the old line that was originally causing the error and place a ' in front of the line of code starting with the *If* statement. For fun we will make the computer also Beep to let you know you have made an error, but the Beep is not required to make the error handler work. Therefore, rework your code under Private Sub cmdImage_Click() so that it looks like this:

```
Private Sub cmdImage_Click()
On Error GoTo Handler
vPicCount = vPicCount + 1
'if vPicCount < 3 then vPicCount = vPicCount + 1
Dim path As String = ("c:\My Documents\Picture" &
   vPicCount & ".jpg")
imgForm3.Image = Image.FromFile ("c:\My
   Documents\Picture" & vPicCount & ".jpg")
Exit Sub
Handler:
Beep
Exit Sub
End Sub
```

Run your program. After you click on your *New Image* Button three times, all consecutive clicks will result in a Beep. This allows you to become aware that an error or incorrect value has been now associated with your variable.

Randomizing Picture Presentations

Sometimes you may want the order of pictures to be random. For example, if you are presenting a series of pictures to children and require them to respond on one Button if the picture is of a stranger and on another Button if it is of a friend/

family member. Here you probably do not want the list of pictures to be in a set repeated order. Randomization of pictures is quite easy to do in Visual Basic.NET.

VB.NET has a random function (RND) that works off of the computer's internal clock. Unless you what to display the same random pattern each successive time you run the program (and you may) you have to *randomize* Visual Basic.NET each time you start the program. To do this you use the RANDOMIZE function which is different from RND. Note that while the Randomize function can be added just about anywhere in the program, it is best to include it at the very beginning with the first form that is opened. So go to frmForm and double-click the form to go to the form editor. Select *frmForm* then *Load* from the drop down boxes at the top of the editor. Type the following code below Private Sub Form_Load().

```
Randomize
```

Now the program will use a new random pattern each time you run it. Go to frmForm3.

While serving a slightly different function from Randomize, the RND function also generates random values. Here though RND pulls a random number between 0 and 1 each time it is used. This seems rather useless, but it can actually add great possibilities to your program. To explore this simple process, add a new Button to frmForm3 and call it *cmdRandom* and change the text accordingly to *Random Number*. Double-click cmdRandom and add the following code to the subroutine:

```
me.text = Rnd
```

Run the program, go to frmForm3, and click on cmdRandom. Notice in the blue text bar above frmForm3 a small number with several significant digits appears. This is your random number. Now to incorporate this into our picture presentation, we need to get this number into a number between 1 and 3 so we can randomly display our pictures. Remember that RND makes numbers between 0 and 1. If we multiply 3 x 0 we get 0. If we multiply 3 x 1 we get 3. Now if we multiply 3 times a number between 0 and 1, we will get values between 0 and 3. To explore this change you code for cmdRandom to:

```
me.text = 3 * Rnd
```

Run the program. Notice that the numbers are like 0.33453, 2.6443, 1.73545 etc. While entertaining, we need integers like 1, 2, and 3 to correspond to our pictures. To make this occur, and change the code to generate whole number integers, simply type:

```
me.text = Int(3 * Rnd())
```

This tells the computer to round down the values to the nearest integer. Run the program and see for yourself.

We are now getting random values of 0, 1, and 2. To get values between 1 and 3 we simply need to shift the distribution by 1. To do this, change the code you have been working to look like this:

```
me.text = Int(3 * Rnd()) + 1
```

Run the program and see. Remember that we want to display a random picture in our PictureBox, and because we know the numbers will be between 1 and 3, we probably don't need our error trapper (but well keep it intact anyway). Instead of incrementing vPicCount each time we press the New Image Button as we did before, we can just assign it a random number. Remark out the old code vPicCount = vPicCount + 1 using the apostrophe. Make sure it turns green in color. Insert a new line of code to read:

```
vPicCount = Int(3 * Rnd()) + 1
```

Run the program and click on the New Image Button. You'll notice that sometimes when you click the Button, the image doesn't change. This is because the numbers are random and there is a one out of three possibility that the same number will come up consecutively. We have now created a small routine that will generate random stimuli presentations via clicking on a Button.

Timer

The Timer Object

In the previous section we worked with displaying graphics in a PictureBox when the subject pressed the New Image Button. Here one of three images appeared in a random order. There may be times when you want the images to appear "on their own" without having the subject be required to press a Button. This can be done using a Timer object. Note that VB.NET also has a timer function that returns the current computer time. This is easily confused at first with the Timer object. We will use the computer time timer function later.

A Timer object can be found in the toolbox. Go to frmForm3 and add a Timer. Notice that there are very few properties associated with this very important object. Of these we are only going to use Name, Enabled, and Interval. Use the Name now by calling it *tmrPicture.* Enabled equals True means that the Timer is working. Enabled equals False means that it is turned off. The Interval property is used to tell the timer how often to display a new picture, or whatever task we assign it to do. The interval is measured in milliseconds so 1000 equals 1 second. Notice that there is no Visible property. The Timer is always invisible during run time.

Because we want the Timer to start when we tell it to, change the enabled property to false. Let's say we want to display a picture every 5 seconds. Change the interval property to 5000. Just as we had the code for the New Image Button execute the subroutine each time the Button was clicked, we want the Timer to execute the same command every 5000ms. Double-click on tmrPicture to open a new subroutine. Copy the code in the cmdImage subroutine and paste it into the tmrPicture subroutine you just created. Make sure you only copied the code and not the `Private Sub cmdImage_Click()` or the `End Sub` otherwise you will get an error. Now we need a way to start the Timer. Add a Button to frmFrom3, call it cmdStart and change the text accordingly. Double-click on the Button and add the following code in the subroutine:

```
tmrPicture.Enabled = True
```

Run the program. After you click on your new *Start* Button, your images will randomly appear in the PictureBox once every 5 seconds. Keep in mind you could get the same picture more than once in a row.

Random Timer Intervals

Suppose you want the pictures to be displayed at random intervals between 0 and 5000ms. This is easy to do because we just learned about how VB randomizes. To do this we simply need to add a line of code that changes the interval property each time the Timer displays the image.

Notice that we want the full range of values. If we just wanted discrete values of 0, 1000, 2000, etc. we need to include the INT for integer values, but we want the full range of values. This code has to be located below the new Timer interval to show the current interval value. Add this line of code under your Timer object.

```
tmrPicture.Interval = 5000 * Rnd
```

Your new tmrPicture subroutine should look like:

```
On Error GoTo ErrHandler
'vPicCount = vPicCount + 1
vPicCount = Int(3 * Rnd()) + 1
'If vPicCount < 3 then vPicCount = vPicCount + 1
tmrPicture.Interval = 5000 * Rnd
Dim path As String = ("c:\MyDocuments\Picture" &
   vPicCount & ".jpg")
imgForm3.Image = Image.FromFile
   ("c:\MyDocuments\Picture" & vPicCount & ".jpg")
Exit Sub
ErrHandler:
Beep
Exit Sub
```

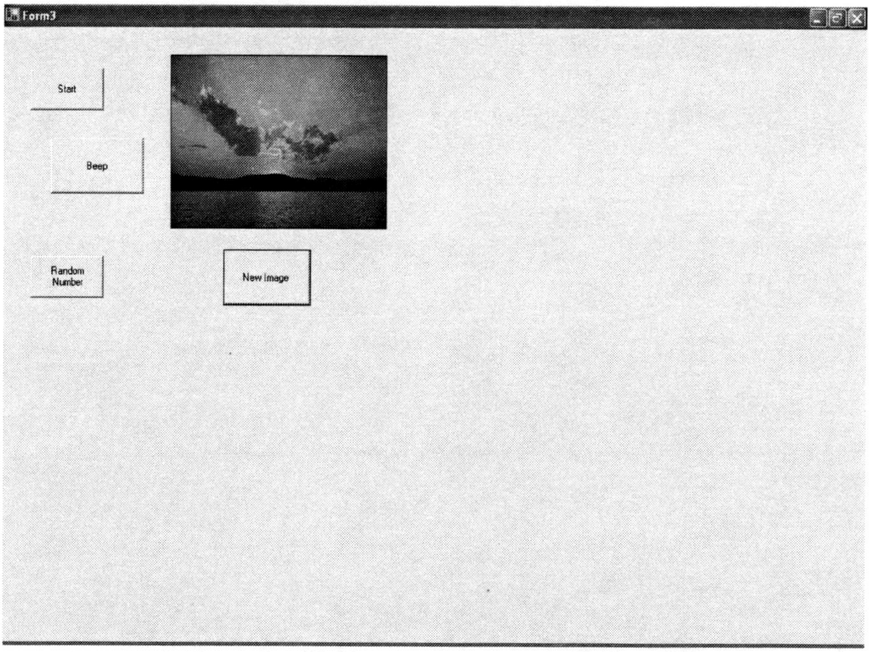

Figure 2.7 displays the lyaout of FrmForm3 during runtime.

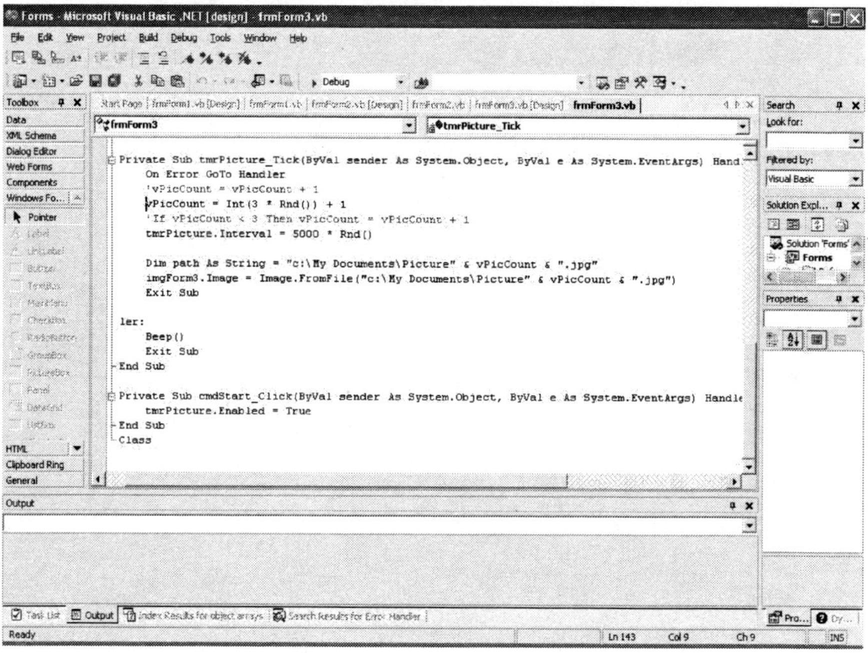

Figure 2.8 displays code incorporating a Timer to initiate random stimulus presentations.

In summary we have just created your first computer program. On one level this program does nothing more than a few interesting tricks. Yet on another level, this program contains much of the code you will use for most of the programs you will ever make in Visual Basic.NET. Study these little tricks closely, they will save you time, again and again.

Chapter 3: Schedules of Reinforcement

Overview

For the most part you have learned many of the necessary tools to prepare you to write some basic behavioral programs. There are some advanced topics you still might wish to learn that will be included in this chapter and others that will be discussed in detail later in the book. Let us begin by programming some simple schedules of reinforcement that you might wish to integrate into your research agenda. These are very simple examples, and might be useful for classroom demonstration. The programs themselves may not be ideal as stand alone programs, but they illustrate many concepts of Visual Basic.NET that are critical for creating your own experiments.

In this chapter we will program the following schedules: 1) Fixed Ratio; 2) Variable Ratio; 3) Fixed Interval; and 4) Variable Interval. We assume that you are already somewhat familiar with the contingencies applicable for each schedule. If you are not familiar with these concepts you may want to refer to a textbook such as Learning (Catania, 1998) before beginning to write the following programs.

Fixed Ratio

Initial Preparation

For this program we want to display a reinforcer after the participant clicks on a Button a specified number of times. In this case the reinforcer will be a smiley face icon and points added to a cumulative total. *Note: We will use code that identifies our picture as "Face" but your picture can be anything you want.* Open a new Windows Application and name it FixedRatio. Now rename the form frmFR and save it as FR.vb. Add a Button called *butFR* and change the text to "...", a TextBox called txtFR, and an PictureBox called imgFR and place them on frmFR. Once you have placed the objects where you want them, you will need to change some of the properties of the objects. Use the properties window and change the following:

TxtFR's TextAlign Property to *Center*
ImgFR's Image Property to whatever picture, gif, jpg file you want.

Notice that imgFR resized to fit the icon. You may want the icon to be larger or smaller, so you will need to change imgFR or resize the image. To do this change imgFR's SizeMode property to *Stretch Image.*

Now we are ready to begin writing the code. There are several considerations we need to think about first. We have not specified how many clicks will be needed before the participant is reinforced. At this point we will have to change this value during programming, however later we will learn how to do this during runtime. Making such changes during runtime will allow experimenters or research assistants

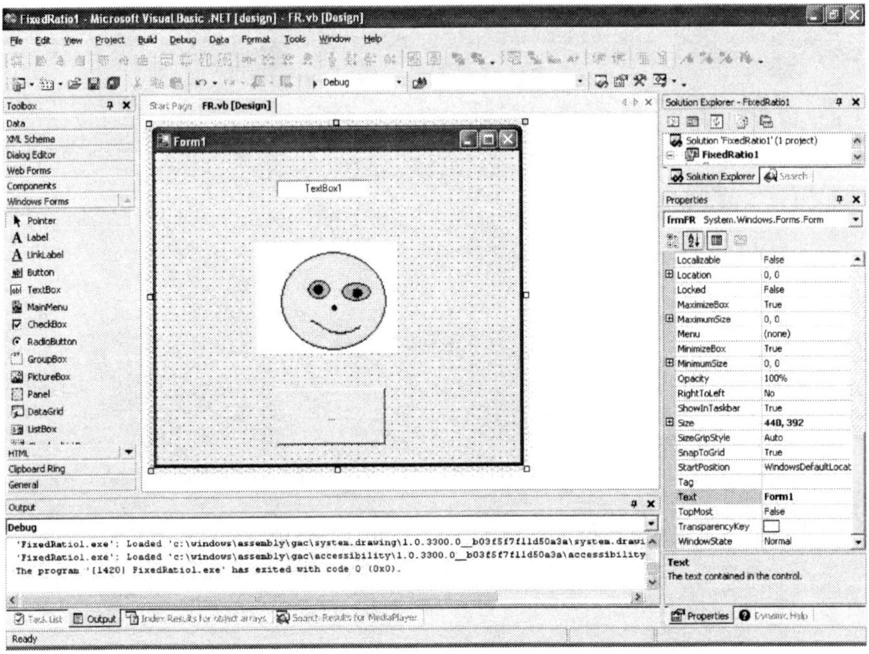

Figure 3.1 shows a possible screen configuration for the FR schedule.

to customize the program to the specific experimental condition without having to learn code or modify the actual program.

We must also think about things that were not specified such as how big do we want the PictureBox, Button, and TextBox objects? What color do we want the objects and the form? What do we want the text on the form and Button to read? When do we stop the program? Do we want to allow the participant to be able to terminate the program? How long is imgFR displayed when it appears? Should it remain on for a specific amount of time or when the participant next clicks on butFR? How many points do we award for the reinforcement? There are probably a dozen other things that you haven't thought about just yet. The point is that as the programmer, you have to make many decisions that are often taken somewhat for granted at the initial phase of designing an experiment. For now, you can decide how you want to address these questions.

Change your objects to the sizes and colors you want. Keep in mind your preferences at all stages of programming. We believe it is best to write these ideas down before beginning to write the program. While you may not have all the specifications up front, the more you can do initially, the better. See how the simple FR schedule quickly becomes quite complex?

Appearance During Run Time

Now consider what do we want the participant to see when the program begins? Probably butFR and txtFR, while imgFR should be invisible. In this case, you will need to change imgFR Visible Property to *False* in the property window. What do we want displayed in txtFR? Should txtFR be blank, have a value of *0*, or a value of *1*? Let's change txtFR's text property to *0* and run the program. So when the program begins the participant should see butFR and txtFR with the value of *0*. When you click on butFR nothing happens. That is to be expected, because there is no code written under the Button just yet. Now, end the program. The first thing you may have noticed is that your window state property of your form is not maximized. To have your schedule program encompass the entire screen, change the WindowState property to maximized.

Using Variables to Create a Point Counter

Next double-click on butFR so we can write some code. Move the cursor above the `Public Class frmFr` code and type the code:

```
Option Explicit On
```

We will need to keep track of the number of clicks so we will need a variable to store this value. Under the line Inherits System.Windows.Forms.Form, type:

```
Dim vCount
```

This will declare the variable. The *v* is just a naming construct we use to let us know that Count is a variable. Visual Basic.NET does not require it. The name vCount is not a magical name that counts things either. We could have called our variable vPotato, or simply Moose. The name is up to you. We prefer to use a theme of prefexes that designate what the types of variables are along with names that are somewhat programatically relevant. The choice is yours though. Now, when the participant clicks on butFR we will need to advance vCount by one. Therefore, under Sub butFR_Click() type:

```
vCount = vCount + 1
```

This literally means make vCount equal vCount plus one. Now we need to tell the computer to display imgFR and advance txtFR's. Let's decide on 5-points after 10 clicks have been made on butFR. Utilizing these values, on the next line type:

```
If vCount > 9 Then
imgFR.visible = True
txtFR.Text = txtFR.Text + 5
```

An "End If" line of code should have been automatically added after the last line you typed. If not, add it manaully. Now run the program and start clicking. If all goes well on the 10th click, imgFR is displayed and txtFR is increased by 5 points. Nothing happens as planned on the 20th click and it is difficult to keep counting to see what click number you are on. So we still have some work to do. Our image remains on the screen, our counter is now adding by five, and things appear to be getting out of control. End the program.

To begin fixing these flaws, often called "bugs" in the world of programming, under the line vCount = vCount + 1 type:

```
me.Text = vCount
```

This will keep track of the number of clicks we make on our Button in the top or text part of our form. When the program is finished we can just remark out this line of code with the ' key or even delete it because we don't want the participants to see it during run time. Now we have to figure out how to reinforce every 10th click. We just need to reset the value of vCount each time we reinforce by typing the following code just below the code to display the image (imgFR.Visible = True):

```
vCount = 0
```

Now run the program. You will see that vCount is resetting after the 10th click and txtFR is advancing by 5 each 10th click, by viewing the values displayed in the Form's text.

Turning On and Off an Image

While our point counter is working just fine, imgFR stays on all of the time once it appears. There are several things we can do at this juncture. First, we could set up a Timer so imgFR disappears after a given interval. Second, we could make imgFR disappear after butFR is clicked. Or third, we could have the participant click on imgFR to make it disappear. Let's decide on the third option. Now, when imgFR appears, butFR should disappear. And when imgFR is clicked on it disappears and butFR appears. Double-click on butFR to enter edit mode. Under the code to make imgFR.Visible = True, type:

```
butFR.Visible = False
```

Next select imgFR from the leftt drop down box and click from the right drop down box at the top of the editor to open the *Click* subroutine. Under Sub imgFR_Click() type:

```
imgFR.Visible = False
butFR.Visible = True
```

Run the program. It should now work just fine.

Terminating the Program

The final line of code that we might need is one that automatically terminates the program. Let's just decide for now that we want the program to end after 10 reinforcements. There are several ways we can do this. We know that after 10 reinforcements the value of txtFR will be 50. So when txtFR = 50 we can end the program. But what if we change the number of points awarded? Then we would have to remember to change the cutoff point. Another way is to divide the total points by the pay off and if that value equals 10 then we can end the program. For now let's decide on terminating when txtFR = 50. Double-click on butFR to enter edit mode. Just below the *End If* statement type:

```
If txtFR.Text > 49 Then End
```

Now, since 50 is greater than 49, the program will end once the subject obtains 50 points. Run the program. You can experiment with the program by changing the reinforcement schedule and see if it still works. For example, you might try adding an *Exit* command Button and the *End* statement so the participant can terminate the program. Try changing other object properties and program parameters.

Don't forget to remark out the `me.Text = vCount` line of code when you run the program for a real participant. This was only used during programming to allow us to check that the variables we created were working properly.

Disabling a TextBox from User Input

One possible kink in your well-designed program is the fact that your participant may "cheat" and change the value of your TextBox, hence changing when the program ends, their points, and giving you a bunch of grief. You can fix this problem by clicking once on the TextBox, and changing the property *Enabled* in the property toolbox from *True* to *False*. Your problem should now be solved.

Variable Ratio

Initial Preparation

Let's suppose you want to make a program with a Variable Ratio schedule of reinforcement. For the variable ratio we want reinforcement to occur after an average number of clicks. To do this we need to specify a range of values and then find a random number between those values before the reinforcer is produced. This program is very much like the Fixed Ratio program. We can recycle some of the code for our new project. Open a new project and name it *VariableRatio*. Move your cursor to the Solution Explorer where the forms are listed and right click the mouse on the highlighted text of the Variable Ratio Project to view a popup menu. Select *Add*.

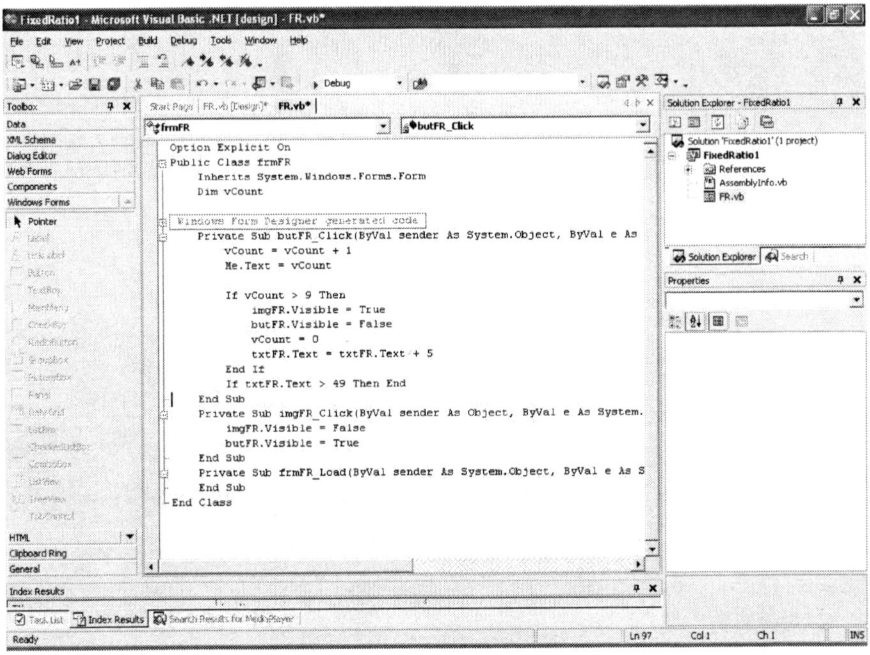

Figure 3.2 displays the code for developing a fixed ratio schedule of reinforcement.

Then click on *Add Existing Item*. Next, from the browser locate and select FR.vb, then click on the open button. You should see frmFR added to your list of forms. We have no use for the default form1 so locate your mouse over form1 in the Solution Explorer and right click. Select *delete* from the popup menu. Now only frmFR should remain in the Solution Explorer. You might think about changing the PictureBox image for your new schedule.

Editing an Existing Form

We also want to make some changes to FR.vb so it can become a variable ratio, but we don't want these changes to be shown when we run the fixed ratio program. So we need to change the name of the form. Locate your cursor over frmFR in the Solution Explorer and right click. Select the rename option, and change the name to *VR.vb*. This will create a new form to be used in the VR project, and keep your frmFR form in tact. Any changes we make will not affect the other program. Finally change the name property of VR.vb to frmVR and run the program.

Changing Object Names

We now need to rename txtFR to txtVR; butFR to butVR; and imgFR to imgVR. Enter the edit mode and change the code to reflect these changes. Rather than change all of the code from FR to VR by hand, you can use the search and replace function. While in edit mode press ctl-h to open the *Replace* dialog box. In the *Find What* text

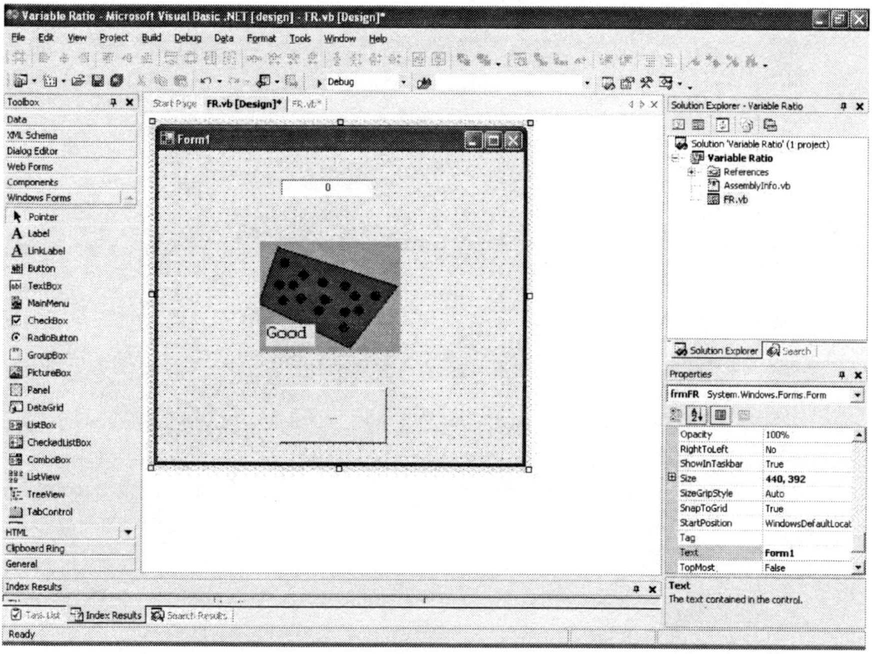

Figure 3.3 shows a possible screen configuration for the variable ratio schedule.

box type FR and in the *Replace With* TextBox type VR. Click in the *Replace All* button. Close the dialog box.

Notice that we accidentally changed frmVR to VRmVR. Now if you try to view the design window for VR.vb you will receive an error stating "Failed to parse method InitializeComponent." Click back to VR.vb (the code window), click on *Edit*, and finally on *Undo*. This dead end will hopefully make you aware that you need to be very careful when changing the name of objects and properties. In this case it is best to change these items by hand. Make the corrections both in the code and in the Properties Window, and then run the program. It should work just like the FixedRatio program, which is good at this point.

Using Random Numbers

We still need to make the schedule a variable ratio. Because we are going to use a random number we have to tell the computer to randomize the number strings each time the program is run. This is done by double-clicking on the form to enter edit mode and opening a new frmVR_Load subroutine. Under Sub frmVR_Load type:

```
Randomize
```

Each time the form is loaded the number string is randomized. Next we need to write a subroutine independent of any one object to find a random number according to our specifications. To do this, at the bottom of all text (above "End Class") in the editor type:

```
sub rand_number
```

and press return. Something called a subroutine will automatically be created for you.

Subroutines

A subroutine is a section of code that performs an action like generating random numbers, writing to file, displaying images, etc. This same code could be located under a Button or other similar objects, but if we want the action to occur at various times during the program, a subroutine allows us to call that action without retyping the code under every different Button or object. After you hit the return key you should see the following text in the editor (you don't need to type it, VB.NET has done this for you already):

```
Sub rand_number()
End Sub
```

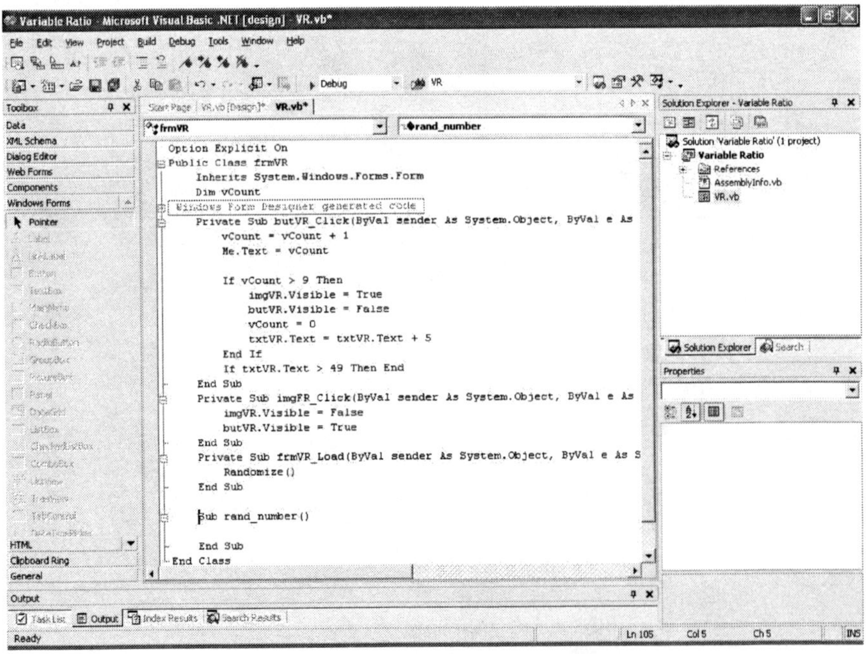

Figure 3.4 displays the Edit window after changing the FR code to the VR code.

The underscore in the subroutine name is just a construct that tells us rand_number is a stand-alone subroutine. The creation of this name and underscore within the subroutine is for our convenience to keep track of our work and make it more readable later on. However, a specific name or the underscore symbol is not required by VB. A subroutine can be called anything you like. Some programmers never even use subroutines. While we didn't either in our early programming days, we learned the hard way that subroutines are a very wise method to organize code.

Generating Numbers

Now we need to define the range of integer values. Let's say 10 plus/minus 3 so we will have a range of 6, or in other words a VR10 with a range of 7 to 13. We need a new variable to hold the random number, so near the top of the editor under your last Dim vCount line of text type:

```
Dim vRand
```

Now under Sub rand_number() type:

```
vRand = Int(Rnd * 7) + 7
```

This code tells the computer that you want to generate an integer (Int) value. It also states that you want the random value between 0 and 1 that the Rnd function will generate to be multiplied by 7. This will give you a value of 0, 1, 2, 3, 4, 5, or 6 because the Int function always rounds down to the next integer value. We then add 7 to the integer value to shift the distribution into the desired range between 7 and 13 inclusive. Now we can generate a value between 7 and 13 every time we call on this subroutine. Let's generate a value for vRand when we load the form. To do this type the name of the subroutine inside the frmVR_Load () subroutine, on the next line following *Randomize*:

```
rand_number
```

Now when the program starts we will have a new random number. We also need a new random number after each reinforcer is delivered so next type the name of the random subroutine just below the line of code in your Button that sets vCount = 0:

```
rand_number
```

Because we want the reinforcement to occur each time vCount=vRand we have to change the following code

```
If vCount > 9 Then
```

to

```
If vCount >= vRand Then
```

We may also want to see what vRand equals during the program development. We still want to see the number of clicks so we have to change the following code:

```
'me.Text = vCount
```

to

```
me.Text = vCount & ", " & vRand
```

This code will display the two values separated by a comma and a space. Run the program. It should run fine. The first number displayed in the Form Text is the number of clicks you are making on the Button. The second number is the random number that the computer generated first upon loading the form, and afterwards each time the reinforcer image is clicked. Now go ahead and experiment by changing object properties and program parameters.

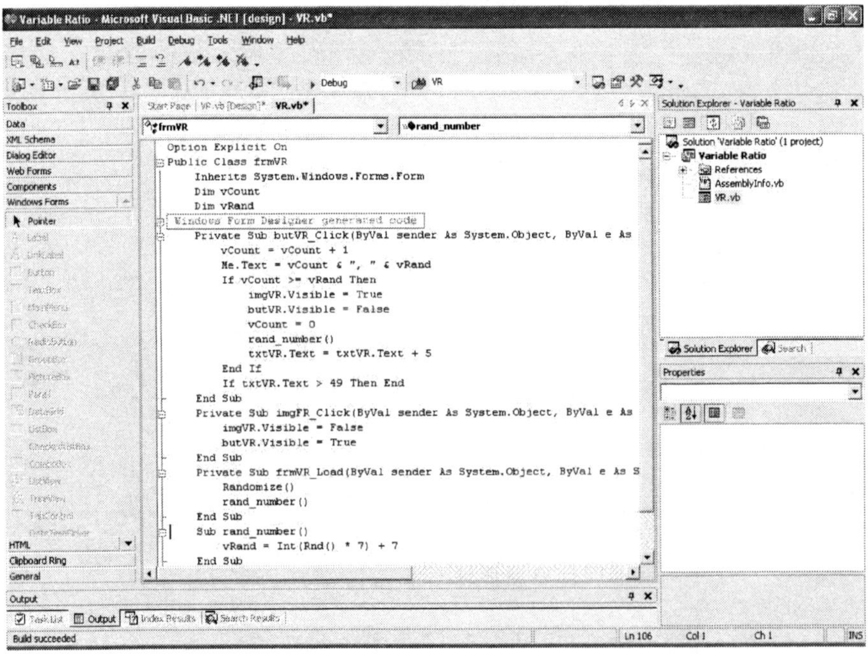

Figure 3.5 shows the final code to create a variable ratio schedule of reinforcement.

Fixed Interval

Initial Preparation

For the fixed interval schedule we need to display a reinforcer on the first click after a fixed period of time has elapsed. So each time the participant clicks on a

Button, the program needs to check to see if that predetermined amount of time has passed before it displays the reinforcer. This program is very similar to the FixedRatio program so let's recycle frmFR again. To do this, open a new project and change the name to *Fixed Interval.* Add FR.vb and remove form1 as detailed in the Variable Ratio section. Change the name of the form to *frmFI.* Click on the Fixed Interval project in the Solution Explorer to highlight it. Now right-click and select *Properties*. Change the Startup Object to *frmFI.* Save both the new form and your new project by holding down the Ctrl+Shift keys and pressing the "S" key.

As before, rename the objects txtFR to txtFI, imgFR to imgFI and butFR to butFI in the properties window. Now change the respective lines of code in the editor too. Run the program. It should still work on the fixed ratio schedule; therefore we have some changes in the code to make. One of the first modifications might be to change the image in the PictureBox.

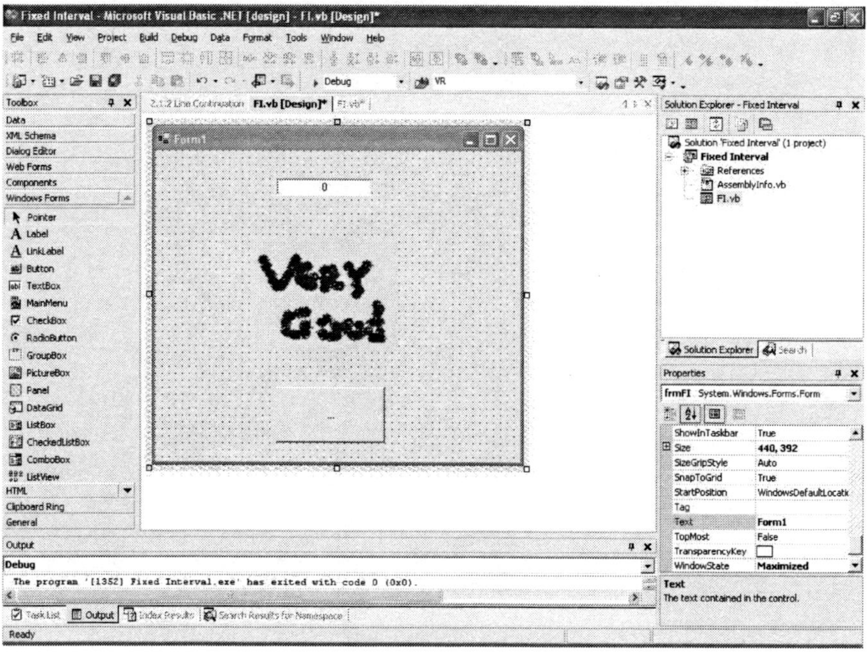

Figure 3.6 shows a possible screen configuration for the fixed interval schedule.

The Timer and If-Then Statements

Each time we click on butFI we want the computer to check and see if the predetermined amount of time has passed. VB.NET has a function called *Timer* (not to be confused with the Timer object). Timer returns a value based on the amount of time elapsed according to the computer clock. The actual value is not important because we are only interested in the difference of time between two sampling periods. Thus if we store the timer value at time1 and subtract that value from the timer value at time2 (time two will be larger) then we can ask if that value is greater than the allocated time interval. We will see how that is done using VB.NET code.

First we need a new variable called vTime so add a line of code below Dim vCount to read:

```
Dim vTime
```

Move the cursor down to the frmFI_Load subroutine and insert the following code to set the initial time.

```
vTime = Microsoft.VisualBasic.Timer
```

Although we will not be counting the number of clicks we will keep the vCount and associated code for use later on. We have to decide on the value of our fixed interval. Let's say 15 seconds. Now change the existing conditional code located under your butFI Button

```
If vCount > 9 Then
```

to

```
If Microsoft.VisualBasic.Timer - vTime > 15 Then
```

We also need to reset the timer value when the participant clicks on imgFI. Insert the following code into the imgFI_Click() subroutine:

```
vTime = Microsoft.VisualBasic.Timer
```

We additionaly want to display the amount of time passed in the form test so change the existing code

```
'me.Text = vCount
```

to

```
me.Text = Microsoft.VisualBasic.Timer - vTime
```

Run the program and it should work.

Rounding Time and Numbers to Whole Integers

Notice the time values written to the form text. They are written up to the 14th decimal point. You can change these to whole numbers by editing the text code to read

```
me.Text = Int(Microsoft.VisualBasic.Timer-vTime)
```

Experiment on your own with changing object properties and program parameters.

A Shorthand Shortcut

You may have started to become irritated with the repeated typing of long lines of code such as `Microsoft.VisualBasic.Timer`. Luckily for you, VB thought you might too. So, to create a shorthand for this line of code, typ the following text below the Option Explicit On:

```
Imports VB = Microsoft.VisualBasic
```

Now replace your long line of code with the shorthand: `VB`. This comes in quite handy as the programs become larger.

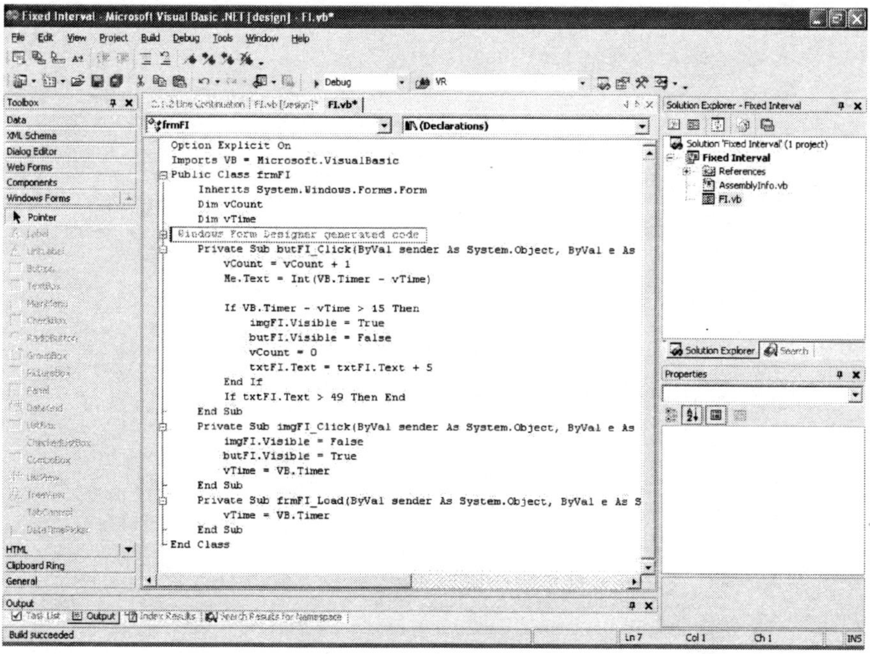

Figure 3.7 displays the code for creating a fixed interval schedule of reinforcement.

Variable Interval

Initial Preparation

The variable interval is similar to the fixed interval with the exception that the reinforcer is delivered on the first click after an average of a specified amount of time passes. The Variable Ratio program has the variable subroutine so let's recycle that program, but we will still use some of the code from the Fixed Interval program. So open a new project and name it Variable Interval. Add VR.vb, rename it VI in the

Solution Explorer Window and change its name in the Properties Window to frmVI. Change the names and respective code of the objects to imgVI, txtVI, frmVI, and butVI. Change the startup object to frmVI. You might also want to change the picture in your image box. Run the program. The program should work like it did for the variable ratio.

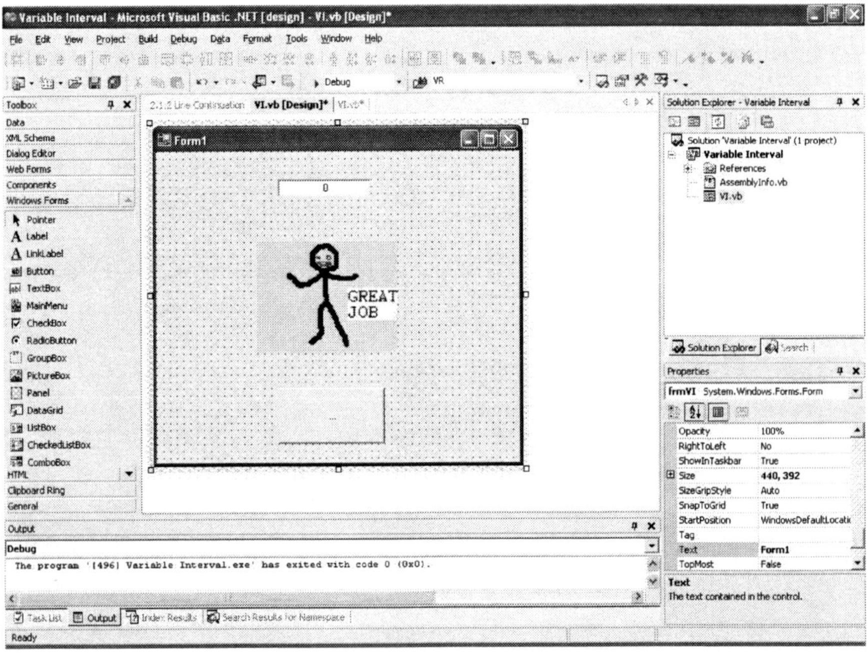

Figure 3.8 shows a possible screen configuration for the variable interval schedule.

Now we need to change some code. Under Option Explicit On, add the following code:

```
Imports VB = Microsoft.VisualBasic
```

Now under Dim vRand type:

```
Dim vTime
```

Here again, we are creating the new variable vTime. Now add the following code below the rand_number code in the Private Sub frmVI_Load() routine:

```
vTime = VB.Timer
```

You should also add this same code at the end of the imgVI subroutine (yet before *End Sub.*) This will result in the computer resetting the time interval when the program starts and also when the participant starts a new trial by clicking on imgVI.

Shifting Variable Range Distributions

We now have to determine the VI range. Let's say 15 seconds plus/minus 5 seconds. We need to change the existing code

```
vRand = Int(Rnd() * 7) + 7
```

Since the range is now 10, we need to change the 7 to a 11 and because the lowest number will be 5, we need to shift the distribution by that amount. Change the new code to read:

```
vRand = Int(Rnd() * 11) + 5
```

Next we have to change our conditional if statement to determine if the correct passage of time has occurred. We need to change the statement:

```
If vCount >= vRand Then
```

Rather than counting clicks, we need to find the difference between time1 and time2 by subtracting vTime from the timer function. The new line of code should read:

```
If VB.Timer - vTime > vRand Then
```

And of course we will want to see what values the program is using while we are programming, so we can change

```
me.Text = vCount & "," & vRand
```
to
```
me.Text = VB.Timer - vTime & " ," & vRand
```

Run the program. Experiment with changing object properties and program parameters.

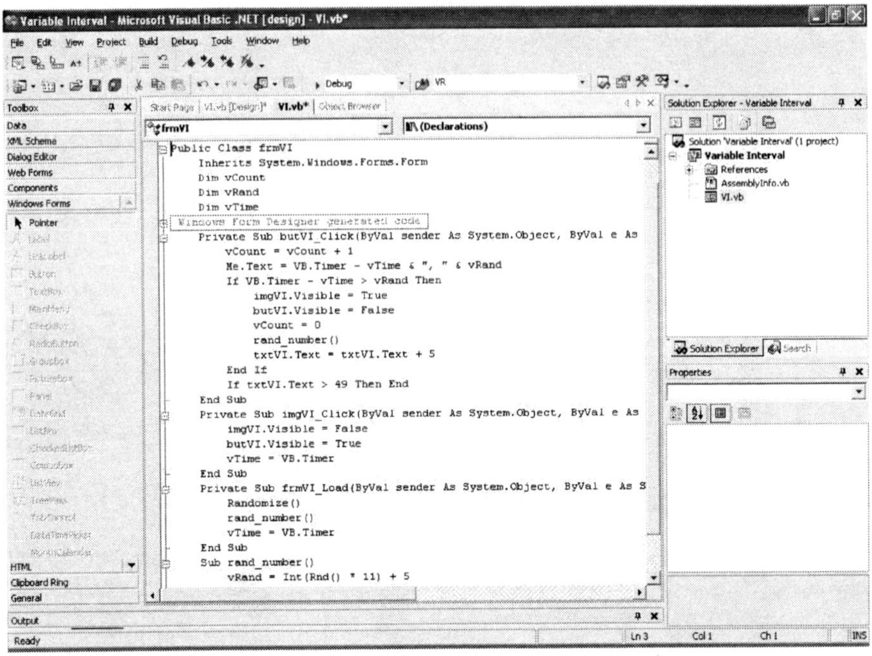

Figure 3.9 shows the code necessary to create the Variable Interval schedule.

Reference

Catania, A. C. (1998). *Learning*. Prentice Hall: New York.

Chapter 4: Control Panels: Programming for Multiple Conditions in an Experiment

Combining Four Schedules of Reinforcement

Overview

In the last chapter we completed the programming of four basic schedules of reinforcement using four separate programs. In this chapter we will begin discussing advanced topics such as the integration and synthesis of simple programs into a more complex, stand alone program that is managed via a control panel. A control panel consists of a form that loads when the program starts, that contains a number of parameters the experimenter can control and alter during run time. As you might have suspected in our last chapter, to make simple changes like making an FR10 into an FR5, you need to go back into the code and rewrite the program. This might be fun for a small percentage of researchers, but there is a much easier way to do this. In general, the control panel captures values that are inputted by the experimenter and transfers the values over to other forms, in this case the simple schedule of reinforcement form, and alters the values during that running of the program. This way, each time the program is run, new values can be entered without changing the code. Such flexibility is priceless when running multiple conditions or parameters of the same basic program.

Getting Started

Open a new project and name it *ControlPanel*. Rename the form *frmControlPanel* and change the text to *Control Panel*. Also change the Start up object from *Form1* to *frmControlPanel*.This form will be used to allow the experimenter to change object properties and program parameters. Right-click the mouse while the *ControlPanel* project is highlighted in the Solution Explorer or by using the Project dropdown menu located at the top of the screen to open a popup menu. Select *Add* from the popup menu, then select *Add Existing Item*, and add the four schedule forms we created in the previous chapter. *Note: You can also use Shift+Alt+A to add existing forms.* Make sure you just add the FI.vb, FR.vb, VI.vb, and VR.vb forms and not their associated projects.

Multiple Document Interface Form (MDI)

To create one large program with multiple forms we can use what is called a Multiple Document Interface form (MDI) to link them together. The MDI form allows an experimenter to create an application (i.e. program) that contains multiple forms within a single "encompassing" or larger container-type form. This container form allows for various other forms to be displayed within it during run time. Without using a MDI form, you could only have one form displayed and running at a time in VB. The MDI form is the encompassing form of the other forms and is called a "parent" form, while the others are called "child" forms.

Add the MDI form using the *Project* dropdown menu located at the top of the screen. Select the first option "Add Windows form". Rename the form *mdiSchedule*, change text to *Schedule* and change the WindowState to *Maximized.* Because we are using this form as a MDI form, we need to change the *IsmdiContainer* property to *True.* This tells Visual Basic.NET the MDI is the "parent" form and the others are dependent (or "children") to the parent form. Again, this will cause the children forms to be contained within mdiSchedule. Make sure you save your forms in a different directory so they will not overwrite your previous schedule programs. Depending on your VB.NET settingsthe forms may already be automatically be stored in the folder created for the ControlPanel project. Change the Startup object to mdiSchedule. This will allow the MDI form to bring "child" forms into it. To draw a child form, say frmControlPanel, into mdiSchedule double-click on mdiSchedule to enter the edit mode and type the following under mdiSchedule_Load:

```
Dim x as New frmControlPanel()
x.mdiParent = me
x.Show()
```

Run the program. When the program runs you should see frmControlPanel contained inside of mdiSchedule. Try moving frmControlPanel around by dragging it from the blue text bar. Notice how the form stays inside the MDI. Maximize both forms and notice how frmControlPanel opens inside mdiSchedule. We can use this MDI/Child form relationship to our advantage when programming.

Menus

Creating Menus

Now that we have our project ready, we need to add the four schedule forms, and find a way to display the desired schedule form during run time. One way to do this is to add them to a *View* menu. This is easy to do because VB.NET has an editor to create menus. Just like the menus at the top of your screen in Visual Basic.NET, as well as any other Microsoft program that normally consist of items such as *File*, *Edit*, etc., you can make custom menus for your own project. To use the menu editor in Visual Basic.NET, open mdiSchedule by double-clicking the form in the Solution Explorer. Select the Main Menu Object from the toolbox and place it on your form.

Let's make a menu that contains options named *File* and *Exit* so we can exit the program. At the top of our form where the text *Type Here* is highlighted, type the

Figure 4.1 shows the MDI parent and child form relationship during runtime.

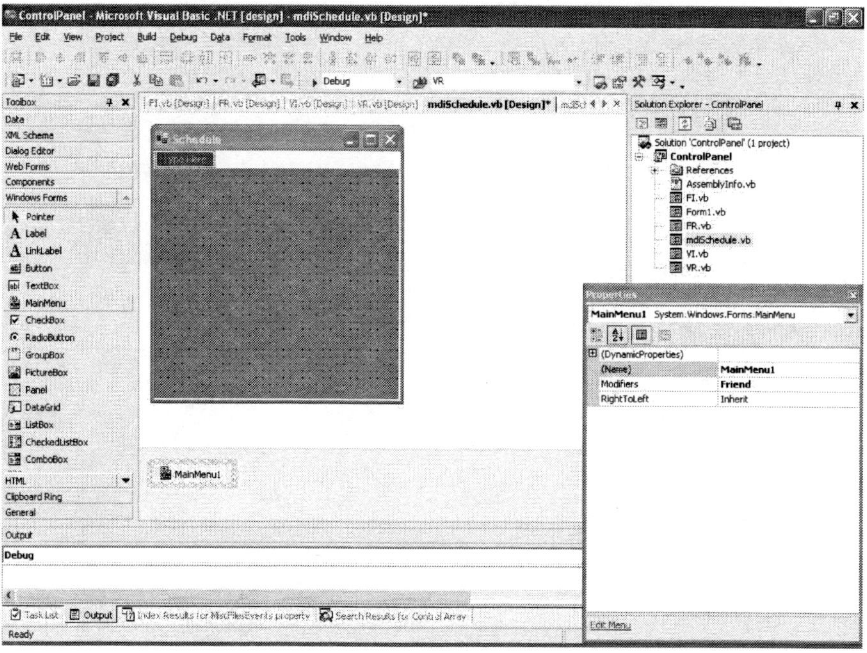

Figure 4.2 shows the menu editor for creating your own drop-down menus.

text *&File*. Notice that once you hit the *Enter* key, there is a new name property entitled *MenuItem1* in the properties window. Change this to *mnuFile* where *mnu* indicates that the subroutine is a menu.

Next add the text *&Exit* directly to the right of the *&File* text. Change the name of this menu item to *mnuExit*. Finally change the *Menu* property of *mdiSchedule* from *none* to *MainMenu1*. Run the program.

Notice that *File* and *Exit* both appear in the main menu. We wanted *Exit* to appear under *File*. To do this close the program and go to the mdiSchedule form. Click on *File* in the menu and cut and paste *&Exit* from the top row to reside under *File*. Now click on the *File* menu and then on the *Exit* menu to open the editor at the mnuExit subroutine. Type the following in the subroutine:

```
End
```

Now run the program, and try to exit the program using the *File*, *Exit* menu of mdiSchedule.

Linking Forms Via Menus

Suppose we want another menu that allows us to view the schedule forms or the control panel during run time. To create a menu option entitled *View*, open the mdiSchedule form and place the text *&View* on the first level (where the *Exit* text used to be). Now create a new sub level called *Forms* by entering the relevant information in the *Type Here* option that appears below the *View* menu. This is identical to what we just did with the *Exit* option. We want the list of the four forms to be located under *Forms* so shift the highlighted *Type Here* box to the right of *Forms*. Continue by entering text for each of the four forms VI, FI, VR, FR, also change their respective name properties to mnuVI, mnuFI, mnuVR, and mnuFR. Now close the Menu Editor dialog box and return to the mdiSchedule form to examine the new menu. Don't run the program just yet.

Notice when you click on *View*, *Forms* appears with a small arrow pointing to the right. This indicates that there are more options available. Remember, this is to be done with the program NOT running. Move the cursor to the right of the arrow and the names of the four forms will appear. Double-click on VI to enter the edit level. Now change the two drop down menu items in the code editor so that you have selected *mnuVI* in the left, and *Click* in the right. Now type the following code under the mnuVI_Click subroutine:

```
Dim x as New frmVI()
x.mdiParent = me
x.Show()
```

To complete the other three subroutines repeat this process and enter the necessary code to make the forms appear when that menu option is selected during runtime. Run the program. Try the menu.

Finally, we need to add a menu option for frmControlPanel under the *View* menu. So, return to mdiSchedule, open the Menu Editor, and make the necessary changes. Place *ControlPanel* under the four forms in your *View* option. You may have also noticed that when you run the program the MDI form does not automatically maximize the "child" forms. If you want the "child" form maximized enter a line like the following at the bottom of the four menu subroutines:

```
x.WindowState = FormWindowState.Maximized
```

You may also want to add the following line of code at the bottom of mdiSchedule_Load() subroutine to make frmControlPanel maximized when the program begins.

```
x.WindowState = FormWindowState.Maximized
```

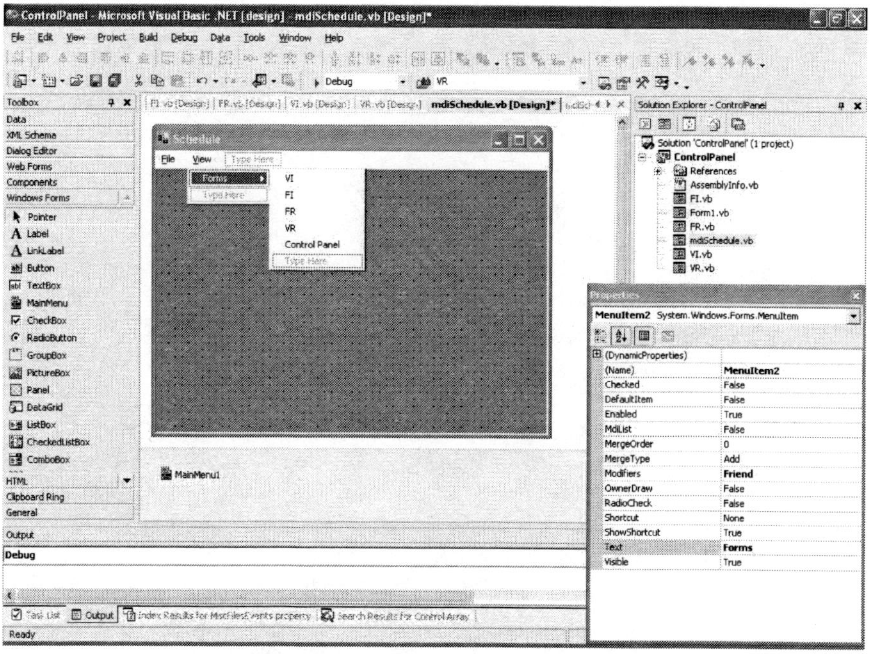

Figure 4.3 shows an example of the MDI parent form.

Dialog Boxes

When we began programming the four schedules of reinforcement we had to make several decisions about the program properties and parameters. Because we are using multiple forms, we can design a control panel to allow the experimenter to manipulate these values during runtime. Suppose we want to let the user change the background color for each of the forms. To do this we need to open frmControlPanel and add an object called a ColorDialog that will allow us to use a type of Dialog box common to Windows and familiar to Windows users. If the ColorDialog icon does not appear in your toolbox, right click on the toolbox and select *Customize Toolbox* from the popup menu. With the *.NET Framework Components* option selected, select *ColorDialog* from the list by checking the box to the left and clicking on the *OK* button.

Once you have the ColorDialog icon in your toolbox, double-click to add it to the ControlPanel form, and rename it to colBackColor. Like the Timer object, the ColorDialog icon will not appear during runtime. Now add a GroupBox to frmControlPanel by double-clicking on the GroupBox icon in the ToolBox. Change the name of the GroupBox to gbBackColor and the text property to *BackColor.* Similar to the MDI forms, GroupBoxes are containers. When something is added to the GroupBox, it only appears when the GroupBox is visible. Once an object is placed in a GroupBox, it cannot be moved off of the GroupBox. You must cut and paste the object to move it from GroupBox to form or form to GroupBox. This will become clear later.

Because we want to change the BackColor properties of the forms independently, we will need to add four Labels to the GroupBox. Add a Label to the GroupBox by selecting the Label icon from the toolbox and drawing the Label inside the GroupBox. If you double-click on the Label icon, the Label object will be placed on the form and not the GroupBox. So don't do this. Change the name of the Label to *lblBackColor* to mirror the name of the GroupBox that contains it. We want to make an object array so select the Label by RIGHT-clicking it once with the cursor and select *Copy*. Right-click again and then select *Paste.*

The Label should belong to the GroupBox and be located in the upper left corner of the GroupBox. Move the new Label below the original one. We still need two more Labels. Repeat this process two more times. You can use keyboard commands to do this as well. *Ctl-C* = copy, *Ctl-V* = paste. Try it.

Change the text of the Labels to the form names that correspond with your four schedules. The order is not important at this point. Also change the names of these Labels so that they are lblBackColor0 through lblBackColor3 (going from top to bottom then left to right). Now we need an object to show what color the form will be. ThePanel object is useful for this purpose. Select the *Panel* icon and draw a Panel in fraBackColor. Name the Panel *pnlBackColor0.* The Panel may overlap the Label, so you may decide to resize the Label. Now we need a Button to activate the ColorDialog object. Select the Button icon, draw a small Button in fraBackColor, name it *butBackColor0,* and change the text property to "...".

We still need to make three more sets of Panels and three more sets of Buttons. Select one of those two types of objects (either Button or Panel), press the Ctl-key and then select the other. Both should now be highlighted. Copy and paste them into the GroupBox. Locate the new object pairs directly beside the Label and change their names so they correspond to lblBackColor#. Move the objects around to place them where you like, then resize fraBackColor to fit around the objects it contains. Repeat this process two more times until you have four Buttons, four Panels, and four Labels above them as shown in Figure 4.4.

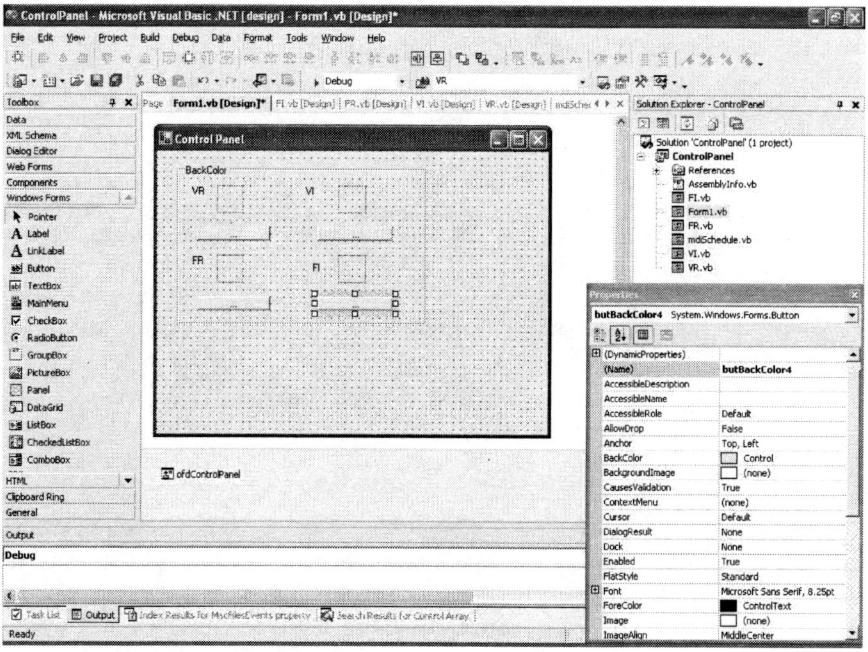

Figure 4.4 displays the control panel with BackColor color options.

Double-click on the first of the four Buttons, and enter the edit mode. Change the subroutine from *butBackColor0_click* to *butBackColor_click*. Now add the other three Buttons names to the end of the *Handles* section of the subroutine. It should now read: “Private Sub... Handles butBackColor0.click, butBackColor1.click, butBackColor2.click, butBackColor3.click”. Finally add the following code under the butBackolor_click (by val... butBackColor3.click) subroutine:

```
colBackColor.ShowDialog()
Dim x as Button
x=CType (sender, Button)
If x.Name = "butBackColor0" Then pnlBackColor0.BackColor
   = colBackColor.Color
If x.Name = "butBackColor1" Then pnlBackColor1.BackColor
   = colBackColor.Color
If x.Name = "butBackColor2" Then pnlBackColor2.BackColor
   = colBackColor.Color
```

```
If x.Name = "butBackColor3" Then pnlBackColor3.BackColor
   = colBackColor.Color
```

Now we need to make some changes in the schedule forms. When the forms load we want them to take on the BackColor of the Panels. To do this add the following code in the frmFI_load subroutine of frmFI:

```
Dim x as New frmControlPanel
me.BackColor = x.pnlBackColor0.BackColor
```

(Note: Your suffix number could be 0, 1, 2, or 3 depending on how you labeled the various Panels.) Notice that we had to tell frmFI the full name of the pnlBackColor by first declaring an instance of frmControlPanel on our frmFI, and then reference that instance with *x*. Now make the corresponding changes to the other three schedule forms, replacing the *FI* with *VI*, *VR*, and *FR*. Use the same code as above, but replace the 0 with 1, 2, and 3 so that they correspond to the Button butBackColor associated with the other three schedules of reinforcement. Run the program and try clicking on one of your four Buttons. The standard windows color dialogue box will appear. Select your color. Change some of the BackColors and then select *View* and then *Forms* from the main menu.

You may have noticed a little problem during run time of the Control Panel program at this time. The ColorDialog boxes open just fine, their colors are placed inside of pnlBackColor0-3 just fine, but when you attempt to run the actual schedule of reinforcement, none of those color changes actually appear as a new background color on your schedule form. Any guesses as to why? Take a look at the code you just placed under your form_load subroutines for your four schedules. In this case, frmFI:

```
Dim x as New frmControlPanel
me.BackColor = x.pnlBackColor0.BackColor
```

This first line of code is creating an instance of frmControlPanel on frmFI when frmFI loads. Yet, it is creating a *New* instance of that form. That means it pulls the original properties of the form that we created prior to runtime and stores all that information within frmFI and waits for it to be called on. Guess what? Our original properties of frmFI contained pnlBackColor panels that were all gray in BackColor. Now those gray BackColor values are being shifted over to our frmFI instead of the new preferred colors that we just modified on frmControlPanel during runtime. One "instance" of frmControlPanel is sitting inside of the mdiSchedule Parent form, and another new instance is sitting waiting to be called on in frmFI. It appears that we have a problem.

If we attempt to fix this problem by calling on the instance of frmControlPanel that is sitting inside of mdiSchedule, we are in a sense trying to get a Child form to pass information to a Parent form and over to another Child form. Here we would need to store the values of the pnlBackColors of frmControlPanel as instances in the mdiSchedule form and also make an instance of the mdiSchedule form occur on the various schedule forms. See how working with multiple forms can quickly become quite complex? While this solution would probably work, think about another alternative. Step back from the error in front of you and examine your program more broadly. Is there an easier way to accomplish the task of controlling parameters of these four schedule forms?

Take a look at mdiSchedule. All this form is doing is housing the frmControlPanel, and it is this frmControlPanel that really is doing all the work in generating program parameters for our four schedule forms. mdiSchedule only serves the function of generating the menu which allows us to select from our various program options. If you were to place the menu options on frmControlPanel, mdiSchedule would not even be needed. Then, you would only need to shift the values of pnlBackColor across one form, not two. Plus it would reduce the code needed, hence streamlining the program. Most importantly we could then capitalize on the menu options that are creating new instances of the schedule forms when they are clicked on. If we generate some code that places the new properties of the pnlBackColor panels onto these instances prior to them being displayed, we could get around the error or "bug" we are stumbling with using this code under the form_load subroutines.

To begin this program restructure, first cut and paste the *MainMenu1* from mdiSchedule and paste it on to *frmControlPanel.* Next change the Startup object from *mdiSchedule* to *frmControlPanel.* Also delete *mdiSchedule* from the entire project. It is no longer needed. Because we just deleted our Parent form, we need to now create a new Parent. Change the ismdiContainer property of frmControlPanel from *False* to *True.* This will change the background color of the form slightly, a cue that this is our new Parent. Delete your existing code under the "Control Panel" option in the menu editor since it is now the Startup object and you will automatically access this form upon loading the program. Add the following code to the "Control Panel" option in the menu:

```
me.gbBackColor.Visible = True
```

Also add the following code under the "Exit" option on the menu.

```
End
```

This was the same code as on your mdiSchedule form, but when you deleted the form, the code was deleted with it. Although you copied your *MainMenu1* over to *frmControlPanel,* the corresponding code contained within the Menu did not come with it.

The last steps you will need to make to correctly pass the BackColor properties over to the schedule forms involve altering the code under the form_load subroutines of these schedules along with the code under their corresponding menu options on frmControlPanel. Begin by deleting the code under frm(schedule name)_load subroutine that we recently used to attempt to pass the color property. Specifically, delete the:

```
Dim x As New frmControlPanel
me.BackColor = x.pnlBackColor(0-3).BackColor
```

Here the 0-3 will correspond to your code across the four different schedule forms.

Now return to frmControlPanel and change the code under the menu option *mnuVI* so that it now reads as the following for frmVI:

```
Dim x as New frmVI()
x.BackColor = me.pnlBackColor2.BackColor
x.Visible = True
x.mdiParent = me
me.gbBackColor.Visible = False
```

This code first generates a new instance of frmVI called *x*, and alters the form's BackColor property to the value of the Parent form (*me*) to the existing BackColor of pnlBackColor2. Next it makes *x*, or frmVI, visible, changes it to a Child form, and hides the GroupBox gbBackColor from the Parent form.

Alter the remaining three menu options related to the other three schedule forms. The code under the menu option for frmFI should now read:

```
Dim x as New frmFI()
x.BackColor = me.pnlBackColor3.BackColor
x.Visible = True
x.mdiParent = me
me.gbBackColor.Visible = False
```

The code under the menu option for frmFR should now read:

```
Dim x as New frmFR()
x.BackColor = me.pnlBackColor1.BackColor
x.Visible = True
x.mdiParent = me
me.gbBackColor.Visible = False
```

The code under the menu option for frmVR should now read:

```
Dim x as New frmVR()
x.BackColor = Me.pnlBackColor0.BackColor
x.Visible = True
```

```
x.mdiParent = me
me.gbBackColor.Visible = False
```

Run the program and see if it works. Make sure your ppnlBackColor#s line up with the right schedule. If so, you should be able to pass the pnlBackColor BackColor property to your schedule form. Once done with that specific schedule, click on the "X" in the top right corner of the form to close it. Now go back to your menu, and select *Control Panel,* to once again reveal the GroupBox allowing you to alter BackColors. Make some modifications, and check out another schedule form to make sure it passed the BackColor property there too. If you do not close the schedule form before clicking on the *Control Panel* option in the Menu, you will see the GroupBox pop up on top of your schedule form. There are ways to safeguard against this, like making the Control Panel option Enabled = False, until a schedule has been completed. You could also make that option Visible = False. Program "fool proofing" like this can sometimes be just as challenging as creating the program itself. When doing so, look at all the possible ways a subject might be able to disrupt the flow of the program and put safeguards in place to eliminate potential problems.

Now suppose we want to allow the user to change the picture for the reinforcement stimulus. Open frmControlPanel, add a GroupBox, change the name property to *gbReinforcer,* change the text property to *Reinforcer:* and then resize gbReinforcer so you can work in it. As with gbBackColor, we will need four Labels and four Buttons. We will also need a PictureBox to hold the Image property instead of the Panel object. Add a Label to gbReinforcer, change the name to lblReinforcer0, and change the text to read *FI.* Add an PictureBox to gbReinforcer, change the BorderStyle property to *Fixed Single,* change SizeMode property to *StretchImage,* and change the name property to *imgReinforcer0.* Finally, add a Button to gbReinforcer, change the name to *butReinforcer0,* and change the text to "...".

We need three more of each object in gbReinforcer, so select all three objects while holding down the Ctl-key. Position the mouse pointer on each object and click. Once all three are highlighted, select *Copy,* and then select *Paste.* Remember that you must have the GroupBox selected in order to paste the objects into it. Repeat this process two more times so that you again have four Buttons, PictureBoxes, and Labels. Change the Label texts to correspond with the schedule forms. Position the objects and size the GroupBox to the same size as gbBackColor. Also change the name properties so that they mirror what you did above in your gbBackColor using sufixes 0-3.

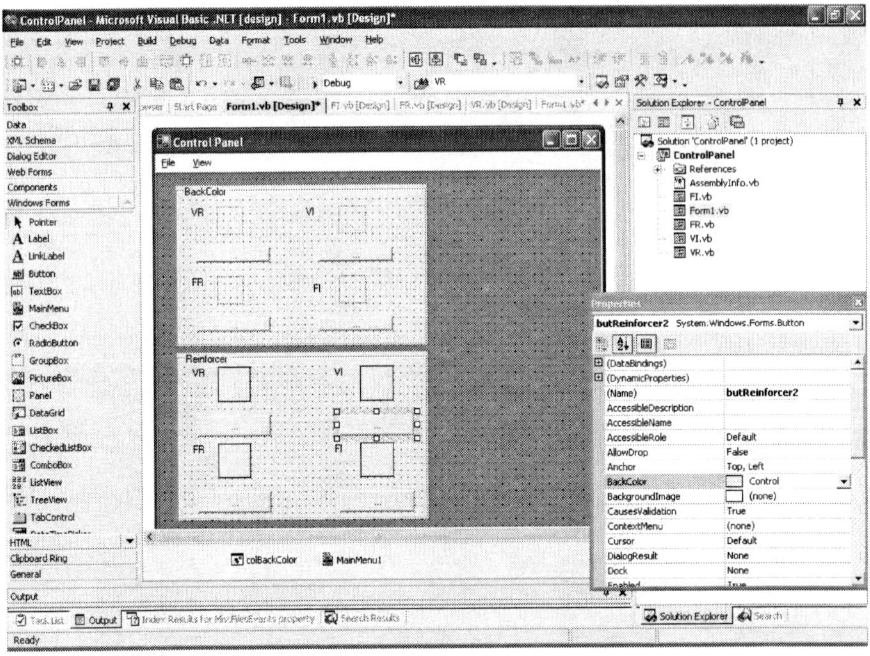

Figure 4.5 displays an image of the control panel now with reinforcer options.

We now need to enter some code to open a dialog box that will allow us to browse through image files. Double-click on any of the butReinforcer buttons to enter edit mode. Change the subroutine from "butReinforcer(0-3)"_click to "butReinforcer_click." In other words, get rid of the suffix after butReinforcer. This is done because this Button array that you are going to create will be designed to handle all four of the butReinforcer objects. Now add the other three Buttons' names to the end of the "Handles" section of the subroutine as you did before for butBackColor. It should now read:

```
Private Sub…Handles butReinforcer0.click,
   butReinforcer1.click, butReinforcer2.click,
   butReinforcer3.click
```

Return to the form layout and add the control named *OpenFileDialog* to your frmControlPanel. Note that it dropped below your form and is now sitting next to your colBackcolor dialog box. Change the name of this OpenFileDialog box to *ofReinforcer*. Return to your butReinforcer subroutine. Finally add the following code under the butReinforcer_click (By Val…butReinforcer3.click) subroutine:

```
ofReinforcer.ShowDialog()
```

```
Dim x as Button
x = CType(sender, Button)
If x.Name = "butReinforcer0" Then imgReinforcer0.Image()
   = Image.FromFile(ofReinforcer.FileName)
If x.Name = "butReinforcer1" Then imgReinforcer1.Image()
   = Image.FromFile(ofReinforcer.FileName)
If x.Name = "butReinforcer2" Then imgReinforcer2.Image()
   = Image.FromFile(ofReinforcer.FileName)
If x.Name = "butReinforcer3" Then imgReinforcer3.Image()
   = Image.FromFile(ofReinforcer.FileName)
```

Run the program and see if your images load correctly into your imgReinforcer PictureBoxes.

Now return to frmControlPanel and note the code under the menu option mnuFI as the following for frmFI:

```
Dim x as New frmFI()
x.BackColor = me.pnlBackColor3.BackColor
x.Visible = True
x.mdiParent = me
me.gbBackColor.Visible = False
```

What you need to do here is add a couple lines of code that are similar to the BackColor code. The new subroutine for under the mnuFI event on frmControlPanel should now read:

```
Dim x as New frmFI()
x.BackColor = me.pnlBackColor3.BackColor
x.imgFI.Image = me.imgReinforcer3.Image
x.Visible = True
x.mdiParent = me
me.gbBackColor.Visible = False
me.gbReinforcer.Visible = False
```

The first new line of code instructs VB.NET to place whatever image is located on the Parent form's (me) imgReinforcer PictureBox, and make it equal to the imgFI that is located on frmVI (x). The second new line of code makes the GroupBox for reinforcer options on the Parent form invisible. Repeat the editing of your code under the remaining mnu(FR, VR, & VI) subroutines to incorporate these two new lines of code. *Make sure to change the names of img(schedule name) and imgReinforcer(0-3) to correspond to your specific schedule.* Run the program. Add images to gbReinforcer. View each form to see if the correct reinforcer appears after you have met criteria. Exit the program.

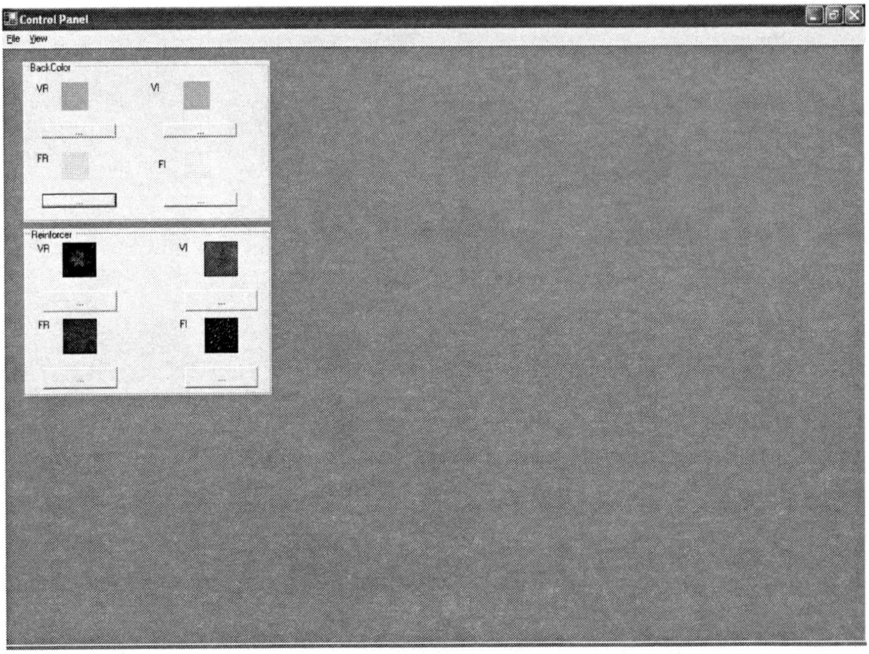

Figure 4.6 displays an image of the control panel with images and colors loaded.

So far we have learned to change properties using dialog boxes. Now we will add a GroupBox to frmControlPanel so the user can change some of the reinforcement parameters using TextBoxes.

Start by adding another GroupBox to frmControlPanel. Change the name to gbSchedule. Change the text to *Schedule*, then add four Labels corresponding to the schedule forms to gbSchedule, name them *lblFI, FR, VI* and *VR,* respectively, and change their text properties accordingly. Add a TextBox object, rename it *txtSch0,* change the text property to " ", and create a total of 20 TextBoxes named txtSch0 through txtSch19 within fraSchedule. All of the TextBox text properties should be changed to blank.

Next add five Labels to the top of gbSchedule so that they give meaning to the series of TextBoxes. Change the name of the Label placed above txtSch0 to lblPoints and its Text property to Points. Change the name of the Label placed above txtSch4 to lblClicks and its Text property to Clicks. Change the name of the Label placed above txtSch8 to lblInterval and its Text property to Interval-s. Change the name of the Label placed above txtSch12 to lblRange and its Text property to Range. Change the name of the Label placed above txtSch16 to lblRfers and its Text property to Total Refers. Position the first four of txtSch(0-3) to the right of the corresponding form Labels. Make sure the suffix values indexes are matched starting with 0. Place txtSch4 to the right of txtSch0 and place txtSch(5 to 7) below txtSch4. Start the next column with txtSch(8 to 11) and the next column with txtSch(12 to 15) and finally txtSch(16 to19) for the last column. Make absolutely sure that the suffixes are in sequence by clicking on each one and checking the name in the properties box. Some of the txtSch boxes should never have a value. For example a user should not be able to enter a value for number of clicks for frmFI. For TextBoxes that will not use a value, change the enabled property to *false* so a value cannot be entered. *Use Figure 4.7 as your guide.* So that it is clear to the user that these boxes are not functional (and are just being used as place holders) change the BackColor to a different color. Run the program. See how you can enter values into the active txtSchedule boxes and not the disabled ones. Exit the program.

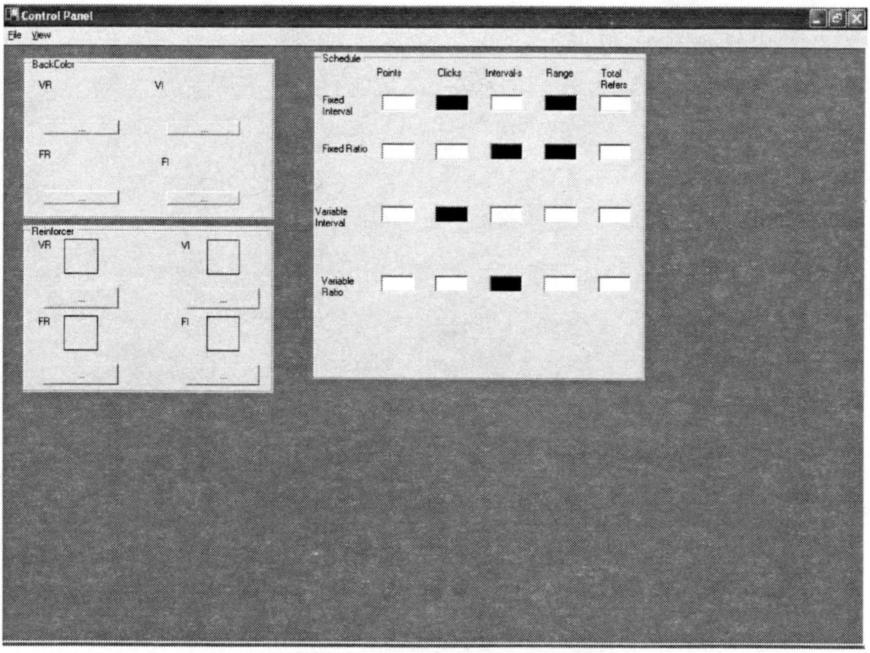

Figure 4.7 displays an image of the control panel with parameter options.

We now have to pass these parameters to the respective forms. To do this we need to carefully keep track of the txtSch suffix values so that we pass the correct information to the correct schedule forms with the use of additional variables. First go to frmFI, and enter the edit mode. Add the following declarations under the section `Inherits System.Windows.Forms.Form`:

```
Public vPoints As Integer
Public vTimeB As Integer
Public vTotalClicks As Integer
```

```
Dim vClickCount As Integer
Dim vReinforcer As Integer
```

Also change the code:

```
If VB.Timer - vTime > 15 Then
```
to
```
If VB.Timer - vTime > vTimeB Then
```

Also change:

```
txtFI = txtFI.Text + 5
```
to
```
txtFI = txtFI.Text + vPoints
```

Delete

```
If txtFI > 49 then End
```

Under Private Sub imgFI_Click() and before your existing code, type:

```
vReinforcer = vReinforcer + 1
If vReinforcer >= vTotalClicks Then
vClickCount = 0
imgFI.Visible = False
me.Hide
End If
```

And under mnuFI on frmControlPanel add the following code directly below x.imgFI.Image = me.imgReinforcer(0=3).Image:

```
x.vTotalClicks = me.txtSch16.Text
x.vPoints = me.txtSch0.Text
x.vTimeB = me.txtSch8.Text
```

Note: the suffix numbers of the txtSch objects may differ depending on your layout. Also add at the bottom of this subroutine the code to hide the Schedule GroupBox:

```
me.gbSchedule.Visible = False
```

Run your FI form. It should work properly.

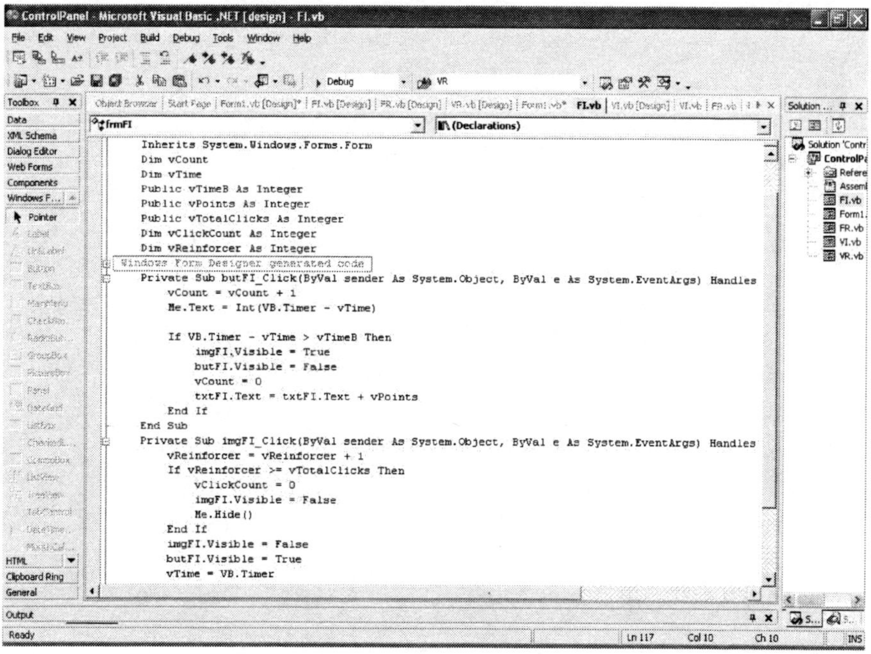

Figure 4.8 shows the new FI code.

The process will be quite similar on your existing three schedule forms, but not exactly. So follow these steps closely. Go to the edit mode on your frmFR form. Type the following declarations under `Inherits System.Windows.Forms.Form`:

```
Public vPoints As Integer
Public vClicks As Integer
Public vTotalClicks As Integer
Dim vClickCount As Integer
Dim vReinforcer As Integer
```

You might notice that we have replaced vTime with vClicks. This is because the variable vTime is used to hold the interval value we entered in our control panel. The "interval" is not used in the ratio schedule, so we have created a different variable, vClicks. vClicks will be used to store the value of the response ratio that is required on that schedule.

Change the following code:

```
If vCount > 9 Then
```

to

```
If vCount = vClicks Then
```

Also change:

```
txtFR.Text = txtFR.Text + 5
```
to
```
txtFR.Text = txtFR.Text + vPoints
```

Delete

```
If txtFR.Text > 49 then End
```

Under Private Sub imgFR_Click(), type the following before the existing code:

```
vReinforcer = vReinforcer + 1
If vReinforcer >= vTotalClicks Then
vClickCount = 0
imgFR.Visible = False
me.Hide
End If
```

and under mnuFR_click on frmControlPanel directly under x.imgFR.Image = me.imgReinforcer(0-3).Image add:

```
x.vTotalClicks = me.txtSch17.Text
x.vPoints = me.txtSch1.Text
x.vClicks = me.txtSch5.Text
```

Also add the following at the bottom of this subroutine:

```
me.gbSchedule.Visible = False
```

Double check your txtSch suffixes depending on your layout.

You will make some additional changes in order for your VI form to recognize the range of time values associated with the variable interval. Begin by adding the following code under `Inherits System.Windows.Forms.Form` on your VI form.

```
Public vPoints As Integer
Public vTimeB As Integer
Public vTotalClicks As Integer
Dim vClickCount As Integer
Public vRange As Integer
Dim vReinforcer As Integer
```

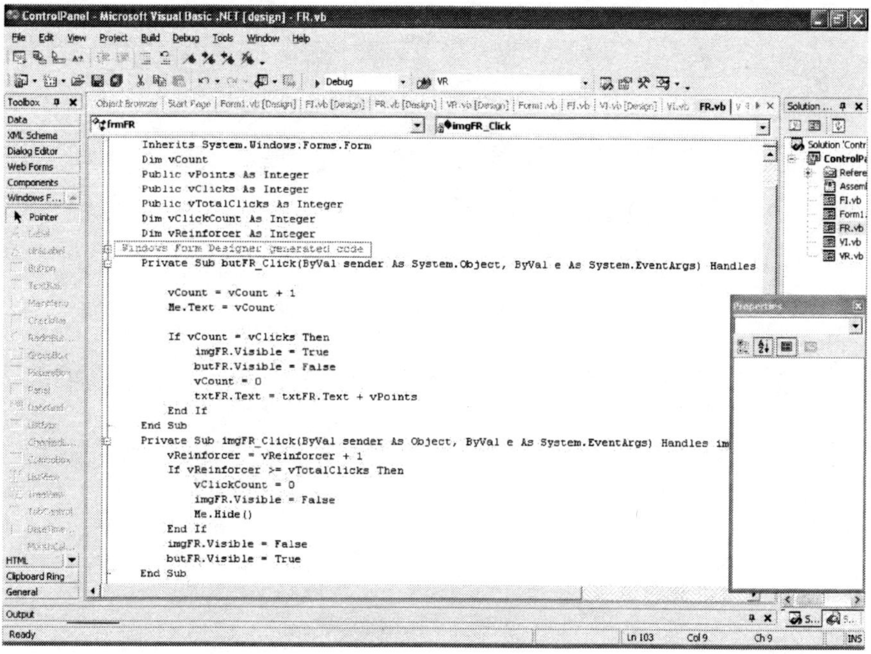

Figure 4.9 shows the new FR code.

Change

```
txtVI.Text = txtVI.Text + 5
```

to

```
txtVI.Text = txtVI.Text + vPoints
```

Under Private Sub imgVI_Click(), type the following before the existing code:

```
vReinforcer = vReinforcer + 1
If vReinforcer >= vTotalClicks Then
vClickCount = 0
imgVI.Visible = False
me.Hide
End If
```

Delete

```
If txtVI.Text > 49 then End
```

And under mnuVI_click on frmControlPanel directly below x.imgVI.Image = me.Reinforcer2.Image, add the following code:

```
x.vTotalClicks = me.txtSch18.Text
x.vRange = me.txtSch14.Text
x.vPoints = me.txtSch2.Text
x.vTimeB = me.txtSch10.Text
```

At the bottom of this subroutine add the following code necessary for the GroupBox of the Schedule parameters to disappear:

```
me.gbSchedule.Visible = False
```

Lastly, under Sub rand_number() on frmVI delete the following code:

```
vRand = Int(Rnd() * 11) + 5
```

And add:

```
vRand = Int(Rnd() * (vRange + 1)) + vTimeB - ((vRange + 1)
   / 2)
```

This modification was done because we need to subtract out the half of the range from the time interval entered as the range on the control panel. For example, if you enter a variable range value of 6, the above equation takes 6 and divides it by 2 – so you have a range of +/- 3 on each end of the value you entered as the interval. Run your VI form. It should work properly.

The final form we need to modify is the VR form. Start your modifications by adding the following Dim statements under `Inherits System.Windows.Forms.Form`.

```
Public vPoints As Integer
Public vClicks As Integer
Public vTotalClicks As Integer
Dim vClickCount As Integer
Public vRange As Integer
Dim vReinforcer As Integer
```

Change

```
txtVR.Text = txtVR.Text + 5
```

to

```
txtVR.Text = txtVR.Text + vPoints
```

Under Private Sub imgVR_Click(), type the following before the existing code:

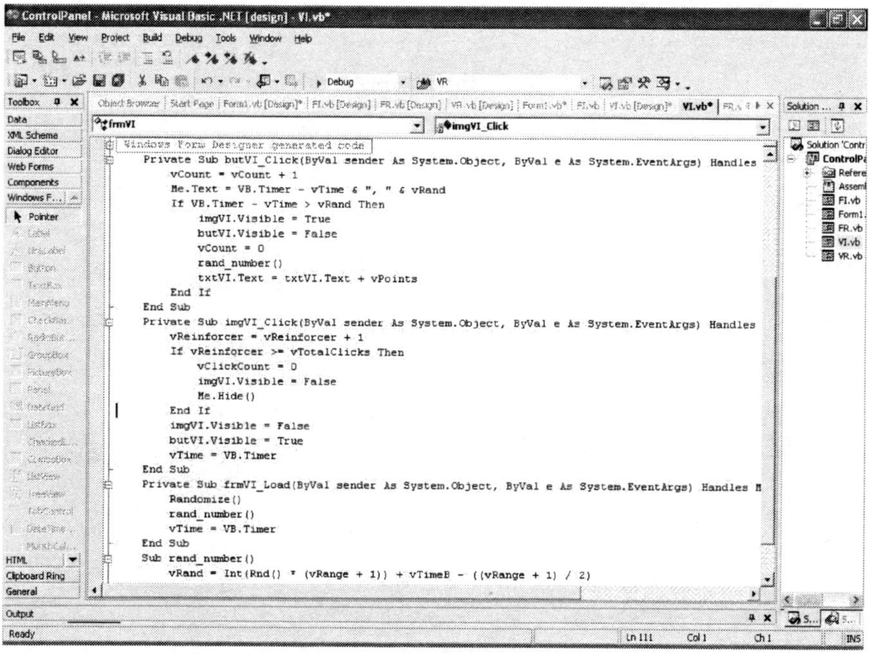

Figure 4.10 shows the new VI code.

```
vReinforcer = vReinforcer + 1
If vReinforcer >= vTotalClicks Then
vClickCount = 0
imgVR.Visible = False
me.Hide
End If
```

Delete

```
If txtVR.Text > 49 then End
```

And under mnuVR_click on frmControlPanel add the following code directly under x.imgVR.Image = me.imgReinforcer0.Image:

```
x.vTotalClicks = me.txtSch19.Text
x.vRange = me.txtSch15.Text
x.vPoints = me.txtSch3.Text
x.vClicks = me.txtSch7.Text
```

At the end of this subroutine also add:

```
me.gbSchedule.Visible = Flase
```

Lastly, under Sub rand_number() on frmVR delete the following code:

```
vRand = Int(Rnd() * 7) + 7
```

And add:

```
vRand = Int(Rnd() * vRange + 1) + vClicks - (vRange + 1 /
   2)
```

Run your VR form. It should work properly.

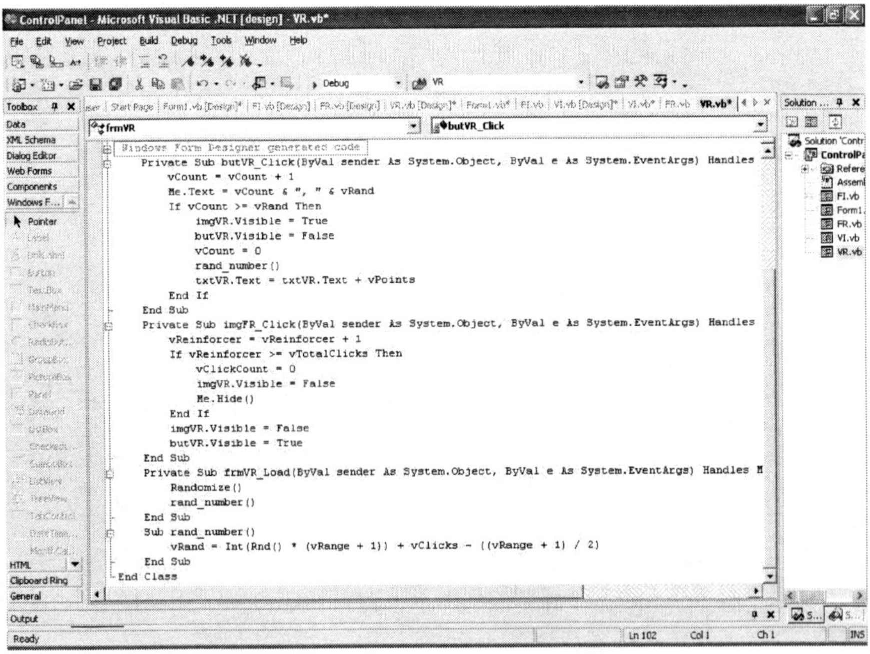

Figure 4.11 shows the new VR code.

Finaly add the following code under mnuControlPanel on frmControlPanel to reveal the gbSchedule and gbReinforcer GroupBoxes from the menu:

```
me.gbReinforcer.Visible = True
me.gbSchedule.Visible = True
```

You should now have a working program that allows users to input response, reinforcement, and interval parameters. It should also allow you to have different screen colors and reinforcers associated with each schedule of reinforcement. This type of program can be useful for classroom demonstrations of schedules of reinforcement or serve as the backbone for your own schedule research.

We made a large number of changes to the frmControlPanel. The following lists this Form's code in its entirety:

```
Private Sub butBackColor_Click(ByVal sender As
   System.Object, ByVal e As System.EventArgs) Handles
   butBackColor0.Click, butBackColor1.Click,
   butBackColor2.Click, butBackColor3.Click
colBackColor.ShowDialog()
Dim x As Button
x = CType(sender, Button)
If x.Name = "butBackColor0" Then pnlBackColor0.BackColor
   = colBackColor.Color
If x.Name = "butBackColor1" Then pnlBackColor1.BackColor
   = colBackColor.Color
If x.Name = "butBackColor2" Then pnlBackColor2.BackColor
   = colBackColor.Color
If x.Name = "butBackColor3" Then pnlBackColor3.BackColor
   = colBackColor.Color
End Sub

Private Sub mnuVI_Click(ByVal sender As System.Object,
   ByVal e As System.EventArgs) Handles mnuVI.Click
Dim x As New frmVI()
x.BackColor = Me.pnlBackColor2.BackColor
x.imgVI.Image = Me.imgReinforcer2.Image
x.vTotalClicks = Me.txtSch18.Text
x.vRange = Me.txtSch14.Text
x.vPoints = Me.txtSch2.Text
x.vTimeB = Me.txtSch10.Text
x.Visible = True
x.MdiParent = Me
Me.gbBackColor.Visible = False
Me.gbReinforcer.Visible = False
Me.gbSchedule.Visible = False
End Sub

Private Sub mnuFI_Click(ByVal sender As System.Object,
   ByVal e As System.EventArgs) Handles mnuFI.Click
Dim x As New frmFI()
x.BackColor = Me.pnlBackColor3.BackColor
```

```
x.imgFI.Image = Me.imgReinforcer3.Image
x.vTotalClicks = Me.txtSch16.Text
x.vPoints = Me.txtSch0.Text
x.vTimeB = Me.txtSch8.Text
x.Visible = True
x.MdiParent = Me
Me.gbBackColor.Visible = False
Me.gbReinforcer.Visible = False
Me.gbSchedule.Visible = False
End Sub

Private Sub mnuFR_Click(ByVal sender As System.Object,
   ByVal e As System.EventArgs) Handles mnuFR.Click
Dim x As New frmFR()
x.BackColor = Me.pnlBackColor1.BackColor
x.imgFR.Image = Me.imgReinforcer1.Image
x.vTotalClicks = Me.txtSch17.Text
x.vPoints = Me.txtSch1.Text
x.vClicks = Me.txtSch5.Text
x.Visible = True
x.MdiParent = Me
Me.gbBackColor.Visible = False
Me.gbSchedule.Visible = False
Me.gbReinforcer.Visible = False
End Sub

Private Sub mnuVR_Click(ByVal sender As System.Object,
   ByVal e As System.EventArgs) Handles mnuVR.Click
Dim x As New frmVR()
x.BackColor = Me.pnlBackColor0.BackColor
x.imgVR.Image = Me.imgReinforcer0.Image
x.vTotalClicks = Me.txtSch19.Text
x.vRange = Me.txtSch15.Text
x.vPoints = Me.txtSch3.Text
x.vClicks = Me.txtSch7.Text
x.Visible = True
x.MdiParent = Me
Me.gbBackColor.Visible = False
Me.gbReinforcer.Visible = False
Me.gbSchedule.Visible = False
End Sub
```

```
Private Sub mnuControlPanel_Click(ByVal sender As
   System.Object, ByVal e As System.EventArgs) Handles
   mnuControlPanel.Click
Me.gbBackColor.Visible = True
Me.gbReinforcer.Visible = True
Me.gbSchedule().Visible = True
End Sub

Private Sub mnuExit_Click(ByVal sender As System.Object,
   ByVal e As System.EventArgs) Handles mnuExit.Click
End
End Sub

Private Sub butReinforcer_Click(ByVal sender As
   System.Object, ByVal e As System.EventArgs) Handles
   butReinforcer0.Click, butReinforcer1.Click,
   butReinforcer2.Click, butReinforcer3.Click
ofReinforcer.ShowDialog()
Dim x As Button
x = CType(sender, Button)
If x.Name = "butReinforcer0" Then imgReinforcer0.Image()
   = Image.FromFile(ofReinforcer.FileName)
If x.Name = "butReinforcer1" Then imgReinforcer1.Image()
   = Image.FromFile(ofReinforcer.FileName)
If x.Name = "butReinforcer2" Then imgReinforcer2.Image()
   = Image.FromFile(ofReinforcer.FileName)
If x.Name = "butReinforcer3" Then imgReinforcer3.Image()
   = Image.FromFile(ofReinforcer.FileName)

End Sub
End Class
```

The programming route we took to hook all four schedule forms up to a control panel was done in a roundabout fashion. This may seem unusual for a text to create a program this way, but it was done deliberately. Every time you create a program, you will change you mind, add options, and delete certain variables. It will never be a straight shot from beginning to end. Therefore, we attempted to illustrate this sporadic adventure to you. If you successfully completed this chapter – you will surely agree.

What other additions might you make to the control panel? How would you go about them? If you were to write this program from scratch how different would it look from the one we just completed? Would it have instructions? Would it have a form at the end thanking the participant for their help? Would it write data to a file? If so what? Would it save the changes inputted on the control panel?

As you can see there are numerous modifications we could make with this program - far too many to be covered in this book. However the tools you have learned and will learn later on in this book will allow you to make the modifications above and many more we haven't thought of yet.

Chapter 5: Advanced Topics

Overview

Chapter 5 is designed to get you acquainted with some of the more advanced features ofVisual Basic.NET and their application within multimedia. While we use the term "advanced" this does not mean it will require more skill or computer saviness than what was necessary to complete previous chapters. What we mean by "advanced" is that Chapter 5 will allow you to enhance your program in many desirable ways beyond simple parameters. For example, what if you want to add your own voice to the program? Or, what if you want your get your data to write to a text file or a spreadsheet? Or, what about using a video clip as a stimulus? All of these questions will be answered in Chapter 5.

Variable Types

VB.NET has the ability to use several variable types such as Variant, Binary, String, Integer, Short, and Long. We have already been using some variables in our VB.NET programming, namely Integers. In some program languages it is critical to accurately define the variable you will be using in your program. Not so with VB.NET. VB.NET allows the user to define a variable as a Variant. Variants can later be assigned by VB.NET to a variety of variable types depending on how they are being used in the program. Binary variables can hold a value of 0 or 1 only. String variables are used to hold non-numeric values such as letters or letters and numbers combined. Integer variables are numeric, but round down any decimal value. However,Short and Long variables will hold decimal values.

Variable types are assigned when the variable is declared. We have already declared variables in our previous schedule of reinforcement programs. To declare a variable we use the Dim statement. For example to declare a variable called vStop to hold an integer value, you simply would type the line:

```
Dim vStop as Integer
```

If we wanted vStop to hold a string of characters, we would declare the variable by typing:

```
Dim vStop as String
```

And so on. The default for VB.NET is Variant. If a variable is not declared, VB.NET will assign it as Variant by default. Remember this point. Declaring your variables incorrectly will often result in your program not running correctly.

Minmizing Typos

Another problem with variables is that we often misspell them when we are programming. For example if you accidentally typed *vStob* rather than *vStop* the program would not do what you wanted it to and it could cause you to waste a considerable amount of time trouble shooting and debugging your program. The last thing you want to add to your list of chores is spell checking your entire program. One way to prevent this is by using the *Option Explicit On* statement at the top of each form.

Levels of Variables

Perhaps the most important issue regarding variables in VB.NET is the variable hierarchy. Variables can be Public, Form Level, or Local. Variables can be declared in a Module, at the top of the form, and within a subroutine. Depending on where you declare your variable some may take precedence over others. Generally, variables in the module take precedence over variables declared at the form level. Variables at the form level generally take precedence over variables declared at the subroutine level. The best way to deal with these issues at present is to avoid using the same variable names. Also, variables used at the subroutine level cannot be used at the form level. And variables used at the form level are difficult to use at the module or multiform level. We have been using the construct of assigning a *v* to our form level variables. For example *vStop*, *vGo*, and *vCount.* You might want to use the letter *p* to indicate global or module level variables. For example *pStop*, *pGo*, and *pCount* to make completely different variables but with similar names. For variables declared only in the subroutines, also called the local level, you might want to use the simple algebraic variables such as *x*, *r*, and *i*. If you follow these simple constructs you will be able to keep better track of your variables and others will be able to follow your code if they happen across it at a later date.

The choice of variable type is an important issue in programming as the type of variable you assign will determine how much space the computer assigns or reserves for that variable. While VB.NET is very tolerant, and computers are faster and more efficient every year, the type of variable you use is not that much of a concern when designing simple programs. Yet as you construct larger projects or if you decide to develop commercial programs, variable declaration can become very important.

The last issue you may wish to consider when constructing variables is if they should hold values across forms. One application this may occur with is a point counter. If you have multiple forms, yet wish the subject to retain his/her current point total across those forms (as when switching from Phase 1 to Phase 2 of an experiment) the variable will need to be Public in order for VB.NET to retain the relevant information. In this case, do not declare your variable on the form, but rather declare it in a module as will be discussed in Chapter 8.

Input/Output – Reading and Writing Data from Text Files

Input Files

We have already discussed how to get data from the participant through the keyboard using frames and textboxes. Another way to enter data is by using text files. This allows us to create a program parameter before running the program, and the computer will simply access this set of parameters during run time, and adjust the experiment accordingly.

Open a new standard Windows Project and name it *Variable*. Rename the form *frmVariable* and change the text property to *Variable*. Now we need to create a text file. Microsoft provides a text editor called *NotePad* with its software. If you have *NotePad*, open it using the Windows® start button usually located at the lower left of the monitor. Select the *Programs* option, next select *Accessories*, and finally *NotePad*. With *NotePad* open type the number 10 then press *Enter* to write on a new line. Type the number 55, then on a new line type 23. Save the file on the C-Directory as *C:\Variable.txt* and close *NotePad*.

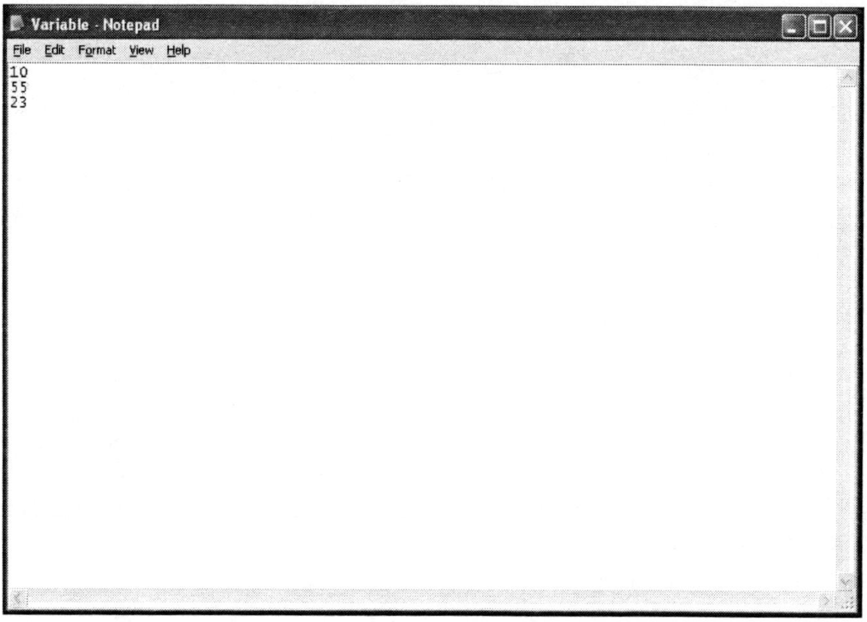

Figure 5.1 shows the input file for the Variable program.

Return to project *Variable* and change the WindowState property to *Maximized*. Afterwards, open the VB.NET code editor by double-clicking on your form. What we want to do is read each line of *Variable.txt* to a variable. So to do this we must first declare a variable that will hold the data found in our *Variable.txt* data file. In the editor, place the cursor above all existing code. Then type:

```
Option Explicit On
```

Next reposition the cursor below the line of code "InheritsSystem.Vindows.Forms.Form" and type:

```
Dim vReadFile as Integer
```

This will declare a variable vReadFile as an Integer to declare the variable. Under the frmVariable_Load() subroutine type:

```
FileOpen (1, "c:\Variable.txt", OpenMode.Input)
```

This tells the computer the name and location of the file to open, that the file will be used to read from as input and that from now on we will refer to that file by its alias "#1." From now on we refer to the file Variable.txt as #1 (BTW: we could use any name for an alias) when we are programming. We now need some code to read in a line from the text file and assign it to vReadFile. We also need to assign the code to an event. Let's use a Timer object to accomplish this task.

Add a Timer to frmVariable, rename it *tmrVariable*, change the Enabled property to *True*, and change the interval property to 5000 (ms) so that every 5 seconds it will read in a new number. Double-click in tmrVariable to enter edit mode. Type the following code into the timer subroutine.

```
Input (1, vReadFile)
me.Text = vReadFile
```

This will allow the program to read the first line and then to display that value in the text section of our form. Change your window state property of your form to *Maximized.* Now run the program after you change the Startup object. Notice that every 5 seconds (5000ms) a new number is displayed until the end of the file is reached and then we get an error message.

End of File Statements

We could have included an error handler to eliminate our error message, but there is a better way to do this with the End of File (EOF) statement and an If / Then statement. Therefore, add the additional code under your Timer object after Private Sub tmrVariable_Timer() so the entire subroutine lookks like this:

```
If Not EOF(1) Then
Input (1, vReadFile)
```

```
me.Text = vReadFile
Else
File Close (1)
End
End If
```

Notice too that we have added a line of code to close the input file when the EOF is reached. Run the program. Your error should disappear, and the program should end at the end of file.

Output Files

Now, suppose we want to write values to a different text file. In other words, we want an output file that writes some type of data to it. Say we want to read a value in from *Variable.txt*, multiply it by 10 and divide it by 2, then write the output to a file called *TimesFive.txt*. First we would have to open *TimesFive.txt* and then each time vReadFile is updated, that value is read into an equation and then written to *TimesFive.txt*.

To open the output file type the following line in the frmVariable_Load() subroutine:

```
FileOpen (2,"c:\TimesFive.txt", OpenMode.Output)
```

You can put this code above or below the other open statement.

Notice that we are having the computer open a file that currently does not exist on our computer. This was done purposely. VB.NET will create the file the first time we run the program. The next step is to make the calculation after it is read from *Variable.txt*. To do this, type the following code below the Input (1, vReadFile) line in the tmrVariable subroutine:

```
x = vReadFile * 10 / 2
```

To get the value of *x* to write to *TimesFive.txt*, type the following code on the line immediately below equation we just wrote:

```
WriteLine (2, x)
```

Because we are using a variable in the subroutine, we must declare it at the beginning of the subroutine by typing:

```
Dim x
```

Now include a close statement for file #2 under the existing Close #1 statement by typing the following:

```
FileClose (2)
```

The timer subroutine should look like this:

```
If Not EOF(1) Then
Dim x
Input (1, vReadFile)
   x = vReadFile * 10 / 2
   Write (2, x)
me.Text = vReadFile
Else
FileClose (1)
FileClose (2)
End
End If
```

Run the program. When the program ends, open *TimesFive.txt* using the *NotePad* text editor. You should see three lines with 50, 275, and 115. Close *NotePad.*

Now suppose you want to write the input values vReadFile to *TimesFive.txt.* To do this, change the `Write (2, x)` statement to:

```
WriteLine (2, vReadFile, x)
```

Run the program and then open *TimesFive.txt* using *NotePad.* Notice that the program added a comma between each value. Most importantly, notice that the old information in the file has been overwritten! This is because output files are always overwritten each time they are opened. To instruct VB.NET to append the new data below the existing data, change the open statement for the output file to read:

```
FileOpen (2, "c:\TimesFive.txt", OpenMode.Append)
```

Here the Append text is replacing the Output text. Append and Output are two different types of data file writing procedures and you can select between them depending on your research purposes. Run the program. Open *TimesFive.txt* using *NotePad* and notice that the new values have been appended to the file.

Adding a Header to Your Data File

When you append data to a file, it is a good idea to divide the output by using headers. Headers usually contain information about the program, the programmer, and the data. Below is an example of a header that might be found in a program. Add the following code in the Private Sub frmVariable_Load ( ) under the two FileOpen statements.

```
WriteLine (2, "*****************************************")
WriteLine (2, "This program was written by: (Put your name
   here)")
WriteLine (2, "The date is", Date.Now)
WriteLine (2, "****************************************")
```

The Date.Now function will return the current date and time to your computer. Make sure you include the appropriate quotation marks. Make sure this code is located below the open statement for file 2. Also make sure you use commas in the header after the file alias, and that you use quotes before and after Text or Literals. Run the program and then open the output file. The header separates your data sets and provides you with additional information.

Just as we combined Literals with other types of information, we can combine our output with literals. For example, change your output code under the Timer to:

```
WriteLine (2, "Input = ", vReadFile, "Output = ",x)
```

Try running the program now. Notice that VB.NET maintains the comma between the literal and the input/output values. This is a good thing. Some programs such as Microsoft Excel can import data and use the commas to separate individual fields. If you were to import TimesFive.txt there would be four separate columns. There should be two columns with numbers and two columns with the literals.

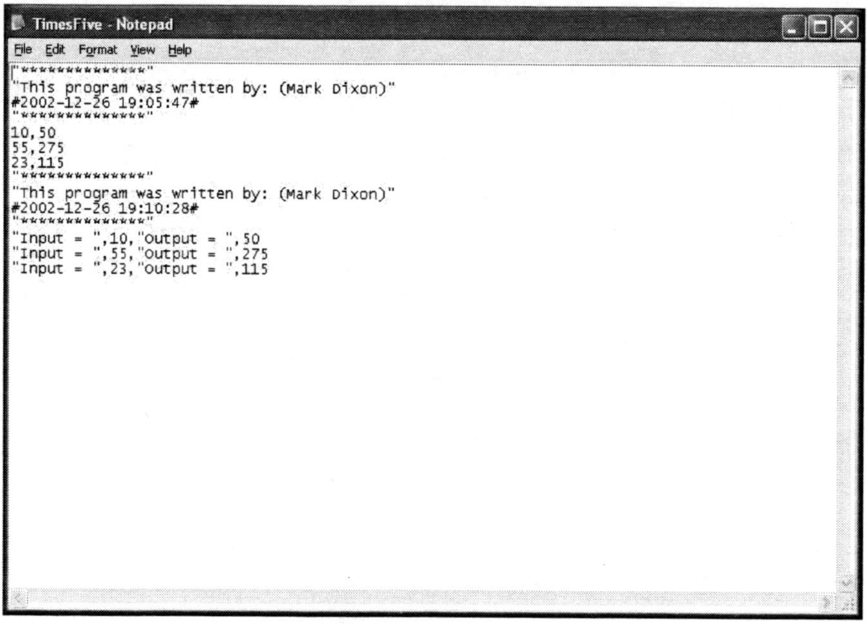
TimesFive - Notepad
File Edit Format View Help

```
"****************"
"This program was written by: (Mark Dixon)"
#2002-12-26 19:05:47#
"****************"
10,50
55,275
23,115
"****************"
"This program was written by: (Mark Dixon)"
#2002-12-26 19:10:28#
"****************"
"Input = ",10,"Output = ",50
"Input = ",55,"Output = ",275
"Input = ",23,"Output = ",115
```

Figure 5.2 shows the output file for the Variable program.

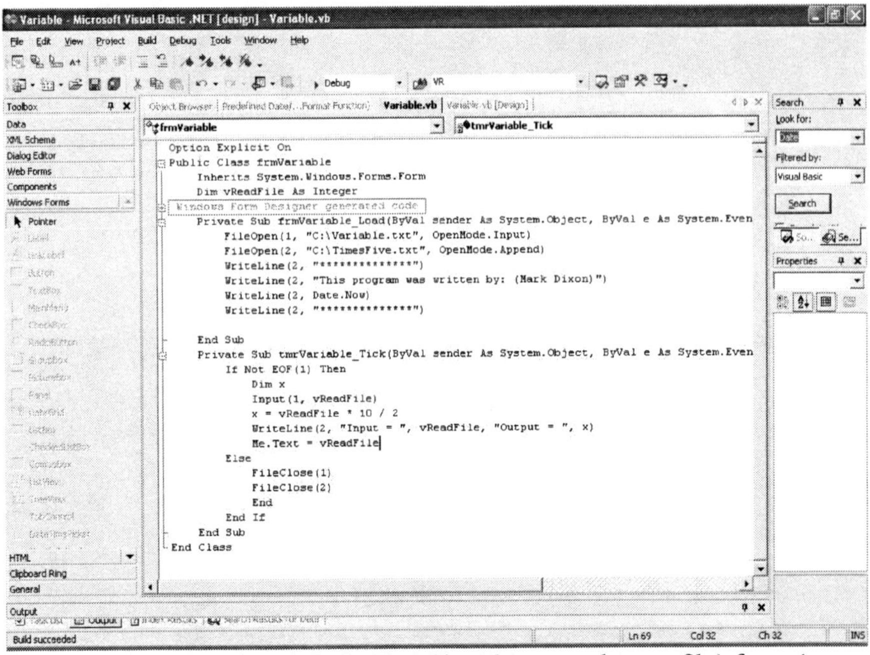

Figure 5.3 displays the code for frmVariable with input and output file information.

Multimedia Control (AxMediaPlayer) and Common Dialogue Control

Overview

So far we have shown you how to add sound to the programs using the Beep function and how to add pictures to the programs using the PictureBox object. VB.NET has advanced abilities to play sound files such as .wav and to play animated graphic files such as .avi or .mpeg. In this next section we will write a program to open a sound file and play it using the Windows Media Player. To use the Windows Media Player object you MUST have a SOUND CARD.

Open a new project and name it *Multimedia*. Rename the form to *frmMultimedia*, change the text property to *Multimedia*, and change the WindowState to *Maximized*.

Adding the Windows Media Player Object

If your toolbox does not contain the Windows Meida Player object (most of them will not), you can add it by right clicking the toolbox and selecting *Customize Toolbox*. Once the Com Components dialog box appears locate "Windows Media Player" and check the box to its left. Click OK to make it appear in the toolbox.

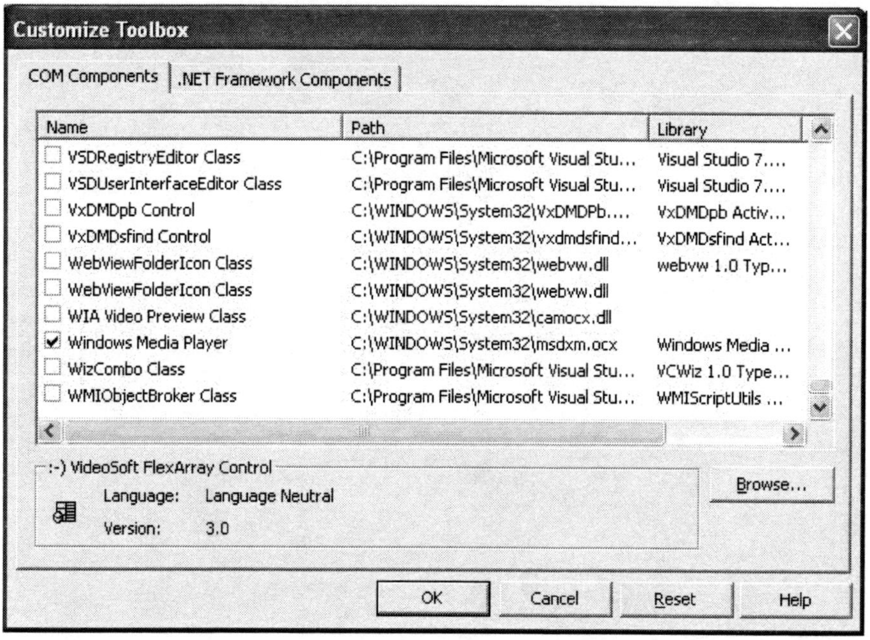

Figure 5.4 displays the customize toolbox menu for adding components to the toolbar.

If your computer does not have an option for Windows Media Player Control, you will need to click on the *browse* button. You will be sent to the windows system files. Now, locate the file name

```
c:\Windows\System32\msdxm.ocx
```

Once done, click, add. The Windows Media Player Control should now be an option for you to add. If for some reason your system files do not include msdxm.ocx, you will need to obtain the file via the Microsoft web site or from a friend.

Now double-click on the Media Player object to add it to the new project. Change the Media Player Visible property to *False* and the Name to *wmp1*.

Adding the Microsoft Common Dialogue Control

In order to select an audio file to play, we will need to add an OpenFileDialog Object. This Object will be already located in your toolbox by default. When you attempt to place it on your form, it will drop below much like the Timer object does. Now rename the OpenFileDialog1 control, *ofdMultimedia*.

We will also need to add a TextBox object named txtMultimedia, and a Button named butMultimedia. Change the text in butMultimedia and txtMultimedia to "...".

We will need to write some code to activate the OpenFileDialog object to butMultimedia so that we can browse for .wav files. Double-click butMultimedia and add the following code under Private Sub cmdMultimedia_Click()

```
ofdMultimedia.ShowDialog()
txtMultimedia.Text = ofdMultimedia.FileName
```

Now we need to add another Button. Do so, and rename it butPlay. Also change the text to *Play*.

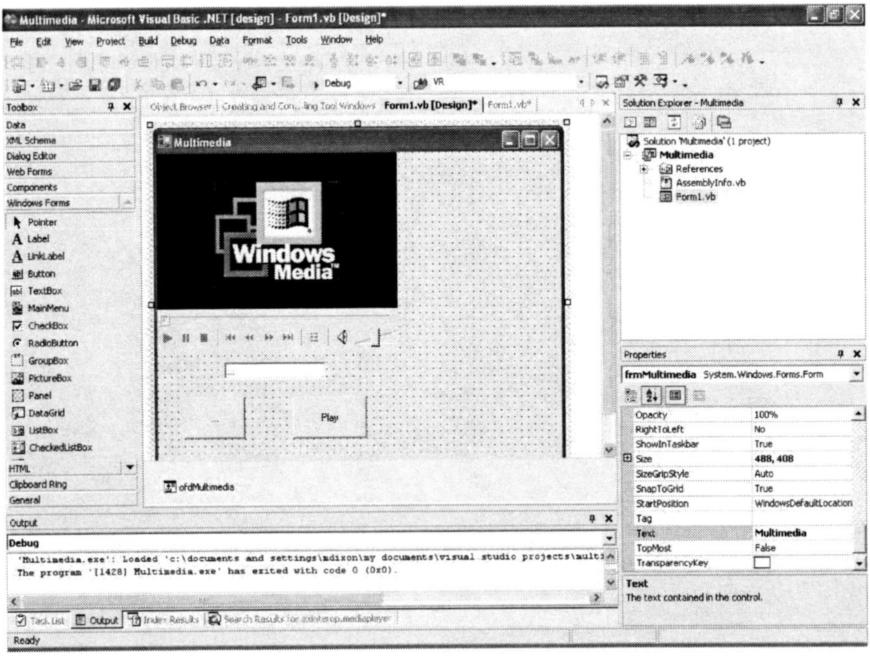

Figure 5.5 displays a possible screen configuration for the Multimedia application.

Next we need to enter the following under the butPlay_Click() subroutine to play our .wav selection: (note there is a number 1 after the word wmp – not a letter L).

```
wmp1.FileName = txtMultimedia.text
wmp1.Play()
```

Now move the cursor to the top of the Edit menu and type:

```
Option Explicit On
```

Run your program, click on the "..." Button and browse for a media file. Now you should have a program that, during run time, allows you to select an audio or video file of various formats including .wav, .mid, .avi, etc., with one button, and play that .wav file with another button.

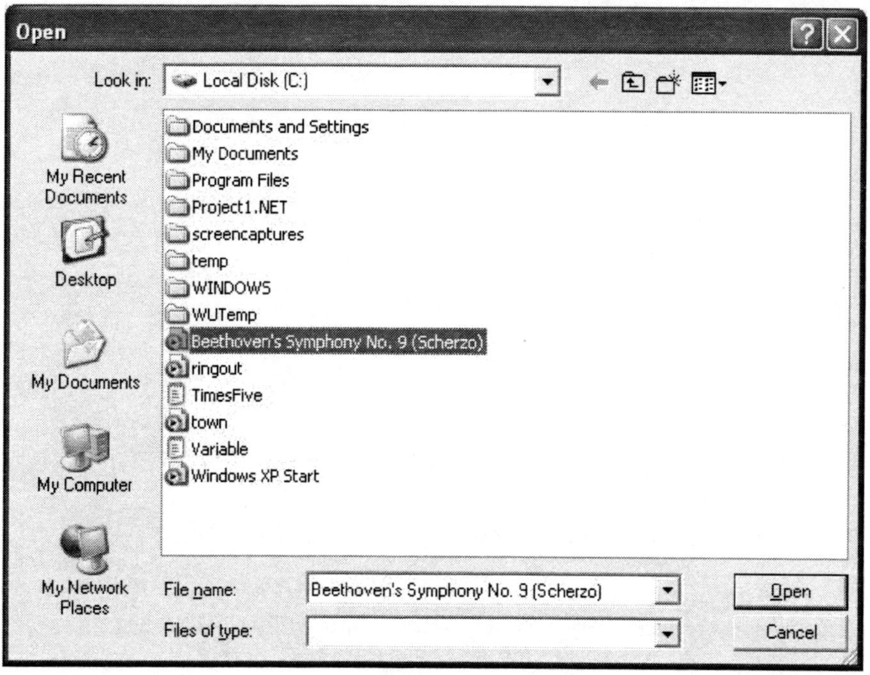

Figure 5.6 shows the window for choosing your multimedia during runtime application.

Experimenter Selected Media Files

Another method of playing media files that is useful when doing research is for the files to be pre-selected before runtime. This way a subject would simply click on a button, and it would result in the playing of the media file. Such files may serve as either discriminative or consequential stimuli. To do this, we will need to modify the current program. Add a new Button. Leave it named as Button 1. Under Private SubButton 1_Click ( ), type:

```
wmp1.FileName = "c:\windows\media\Chimes.wav"
(note: you can put any media file directory and name you
   want here)
wmp1.Play()
```

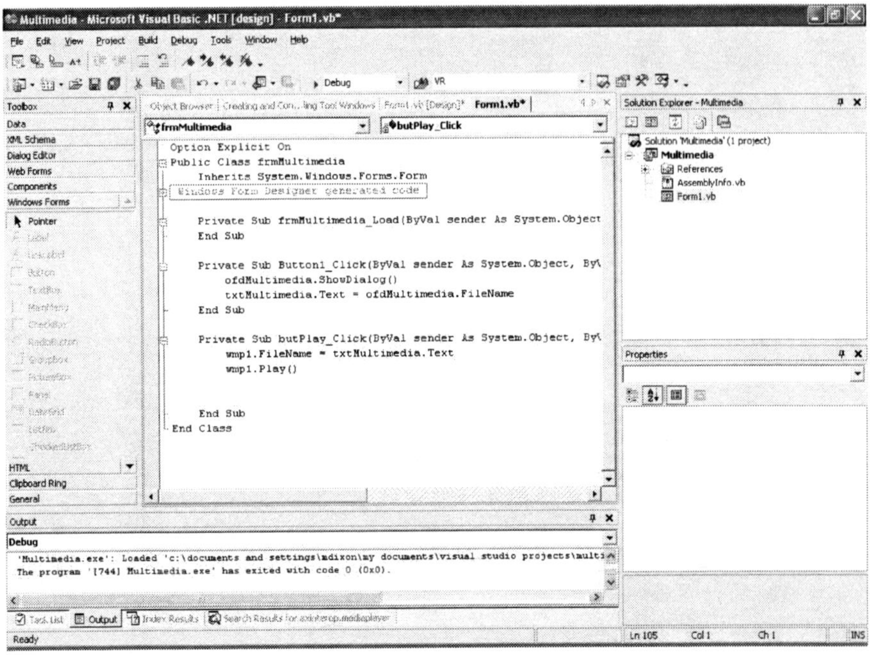

Figure 5.7 displays the code for creating a Multimedia program.

Your program now will contain features that you no longer need. Like the TextBox and the Button with the "..." text, and the Button with the "Play" text. Actually, if you click on these Buttons during runtime, you may get error messages. So, just click on these two Buttons and txtMultimedia when the program is not running and hit delete. They disappear. Go into the edit mode and delete their associated code. Now you should be left with only your new Button1 that plays your favorite .wav file, the Windows Media Player, and the ofdMultimedia.

If you want more than one Button to play media files, say one per Button, you can repeat the above steps *x* more times. Now, create two new Buttons, and copy the code from Button1 to the new buttons. Change the .wav file for each of the Buttons and you are done.

There are many features for the Windows Media Player and we cannot cover them all here in this book. We recommend you consult the VB.NET language reference guide included with the program for more features. There are also many very sophisticated commercially available visual basic books on game programming. When you use the Windows Media Player to play media files, the code above is generally sufficient. In later chapters we will write code for complex matching-to-sample programs that will use the Windows Media Player in a slightly different way.

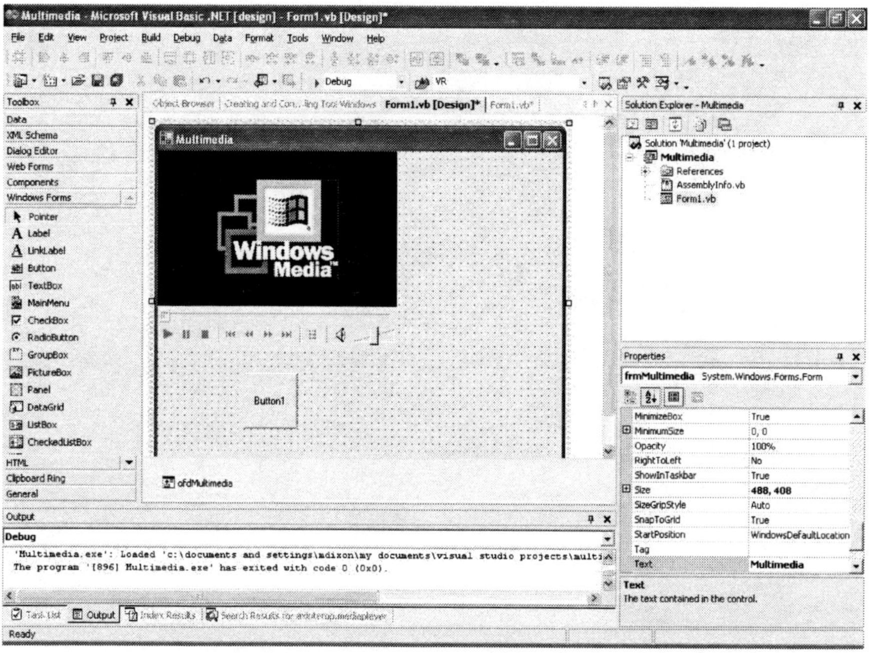

Figure 5.8 shows a possible screen configuration for when the experimenter selects media files.

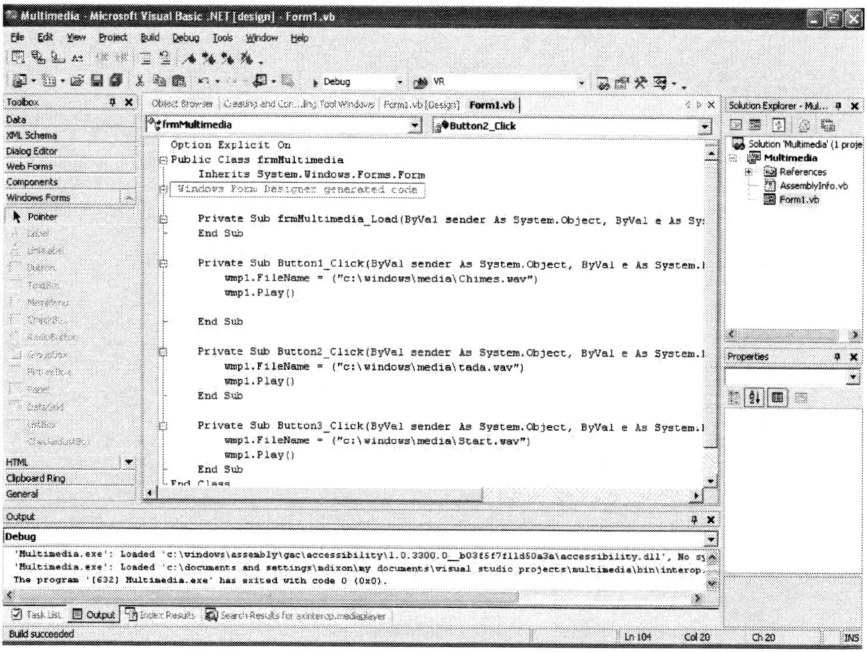

Figure 5.9 shows the code for creating 3 Buttons that play different sounds.

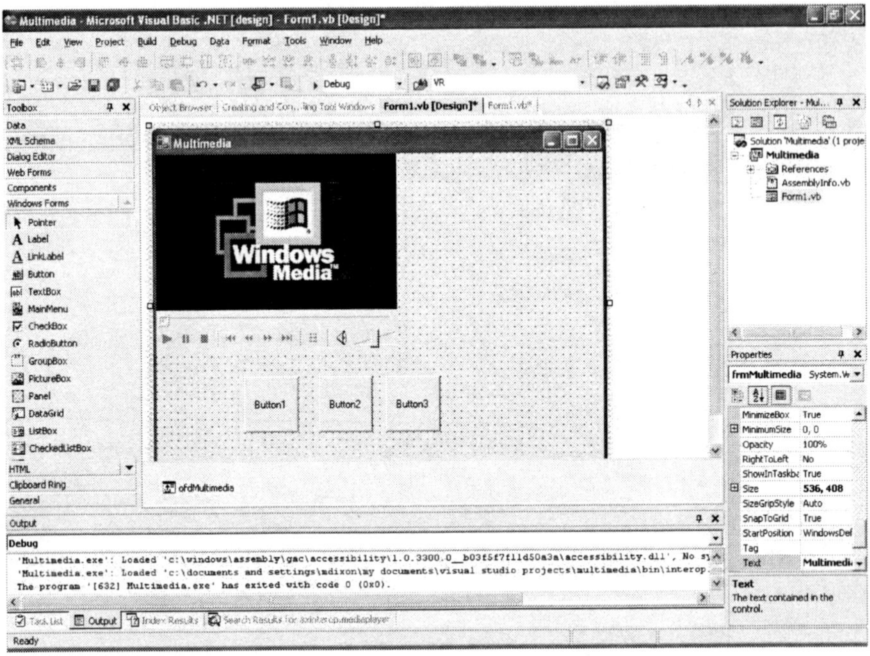

Figure 5.10 shows a screen configuration for the 3 Buttons that play different sounds.

Chapter 6: Behavior Observation and Data Recording

Overview

The Human Observer

Until now this book has dealt with the designing of human operant experiments that consisted of both the computerization of the apparatus and the data collection system. It has been assumed that the setting of your experiment is a laboratory room equipped with a computer and monitor that the subject interacts with. Yet, the purpose of this chapter is to teach you how to create a stand-alone data collection program that would be useful for the observation of human behavior in natural or applied settings.

Many times the preparations we design for research are not capable of incorporating into a computer interface. Much of the applied behavior analytic research occurring today does not lend itself to total atomization. For example, one can not provide attention or extinction to a subject via the computer interface. One can not conduct a descriptive or functional analysis by placing a client displaying any one of a variety of problematic behaviors on the computer. The recording of these naturally occurring behaviors such as aggression, verbal abuse, depression, or self-stimulation can not be captured automatically by the computer because the subject is not directly interacting with the computer. The only way such behaviors can be recorded is via the human observer with the subject's interaction in a naturalistic environment. Many times this human observer records data on these types of behaviors using a pencil and paper. There are many parameters of data collection that might be recorded including response frequency, latency, intensity, duration, or topography. While pencil and paper systems work well when observers are well trained, they are often time consuming, and labor intensive. Many companies offer their own version of an automated data collection system to aid the human observer in his/her data collection activity. Yet, these systems cost money, are static in nature, and may become obsolete before justifying the price paid.

Many excellent resources exist for behavioral psychologists interested in learning more about data collection (c.f. Bellack & Hersen, 1998). Those readers interested in learning more about the utility of automated data collection systems may wish to explore Kahng and Iwata (1998). For a step by step programming guide to handheld computerized data collection use Microsoft Visual Tools for the Pocket PC, see Dixon, (in press).

In this chapter we will incorporate some of the earlier techniques of file inputting and outputting, variable creations, and using multiple forms to create a user friendly, very dynamic data collection system. With the examples in this chapter you should be able to collect a wide range of data in a variety of ways in a very short time period. The biggest benefit of designing such a system is that it allows for you the human observer to customize your system to the specific experiment or clinical observation at hand.

Control Panel

Form Interface

A simple yet efficient means of constructing a control panel is by using a separate form with Buttons serving as options to link various types of data collection together in one program. For example, you may wish to have a data collection system that can be used for duration and latency recording, yet also incorporate the ability to collect frequency type data. Here we would create a separate form for each type of data collection and link the various types of data collection together via the control panel.

To begin creating this control panel, open VB.NET and create a new project. Name the project "Data Collection" . Change the name of the form to "frmControl", change the text to "Control Panel", and change the Startup object to frmControl. In this chapter's example we will create a system that will collect duration/frequency, time sampling, frequency, and descriptive analysis data. Therefore, add four separate Buttons to frmControl and change their text to correspond to the four types of data collection. Also change their names from Buttons1-4, to butDuration, butTS, butFreq, and butDA.

You might also wish to add a simple greeting or brief instruction onto the control panel form. Therefore, add a Label, change the name to lblInstructions, and change the text to "Welcome to the Data Collection Assistant. Please select the type of data you would like to record from the options below." Alter the font properties for a better design.

Now that your control panel template is in an appropriate layout, a few lines of simple code will take the user to their desired type of data collection. Yet, before we create these code links of hiding one form and displaying another, let's create the actual various data collection forms.

Duration and Latency Recording

Form Overview

Insert a new Windows form into your project and rename it frmDuration. Add a Label to the form that displays to the user that this is the correct form for collecting duration and latency data. Change the name of the Label to lblInstructions and change the text to "Duration and Latency Recording."

Starting and Stopping Timers

The most basic components of this form consist of two Buttons that will start and stop the computer timers when clicked, which will generate the duration and latency data. Therefore add two Buttons separately to your frmDuration and change

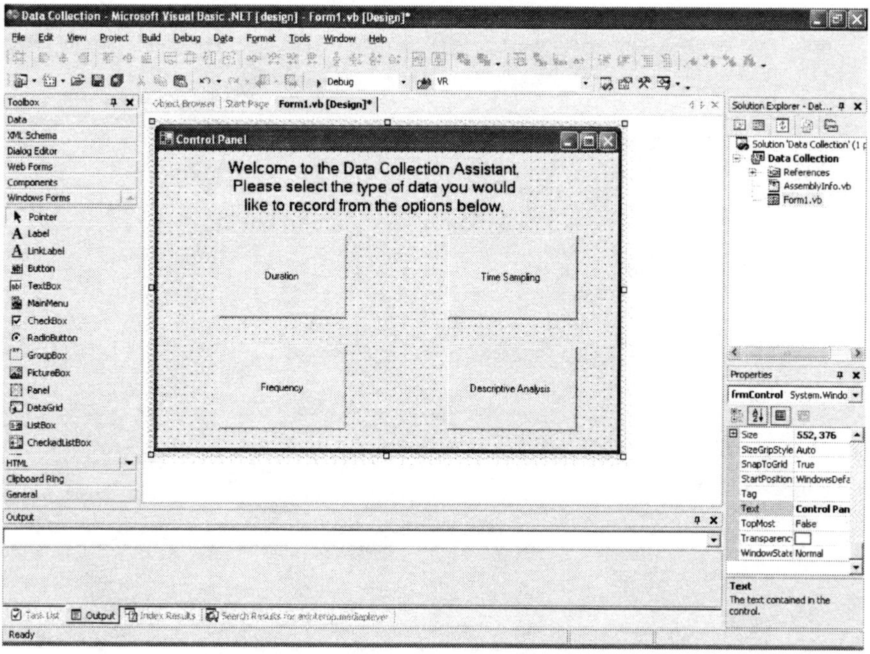

Figure 6.1 displays a possible form layout for the control panel of the data collection system.

their names to butStart and butStop. Because you will want the user to see the actual duration and latency values as they are generated, add two TextBoxes and change their names to txtDuration and txtLatency. Change their text property so they are blank. You may also wish to add a Label above each TextBox so the user easily identifies them. Therefore, add two Labels and change their names to lblDuration and lblLatency and position them directly above their associated TextBoxes. Also change their text property to *Duration* and *Latency* respectively.

Note there is a tool in the toolbox called a *Panel.* Add this tool to your form and initially cover all of your existing Buttons, Textboxes, and Labels with it. Next, with the right mouse button, click on the panel and select *Send to Back.* Finally change the BorderStyle property of the Panel to *Fixed Single.*

Identifying and Creating an Output File

Because many different users might use the data collection program in a variety of situations, it makes a lot of sense to allow the user to specify the name and location of the data output file. There are many ways to do this, yet a very simple way is via a TextBox the user inputs the file name and extension. Therefore, simply add a TextBox and change the name to txtFile. Change the text property to "Enter your data file here." To further aid the user in entering the data file name and location, add a Label directly to the left of this TextBox, change the name to lblFile, and change the text to "What data file do you want to create? Ex. a:\john.txt."

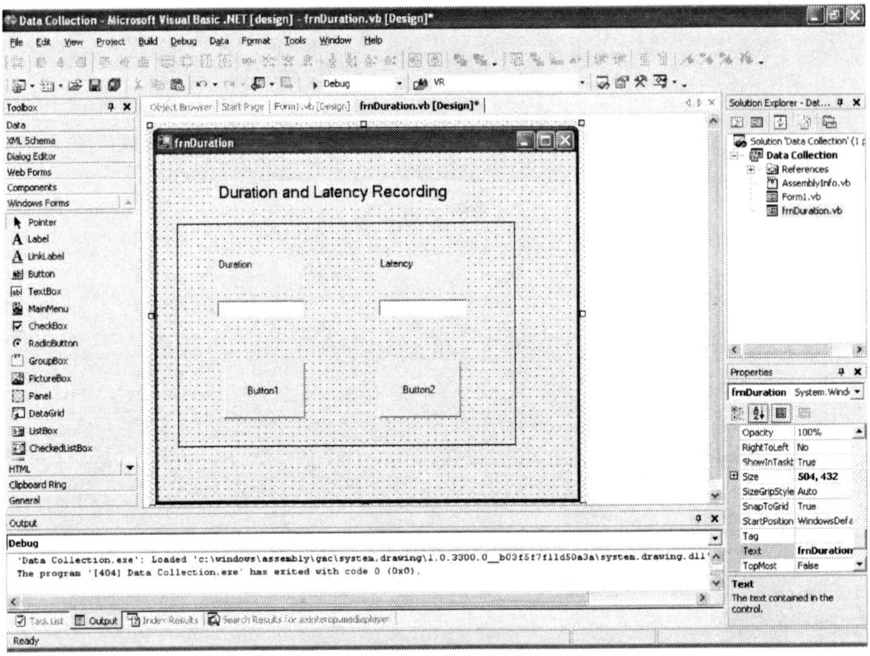

Figure 6.2 displays the initial layout for the duration and latency data collection form.

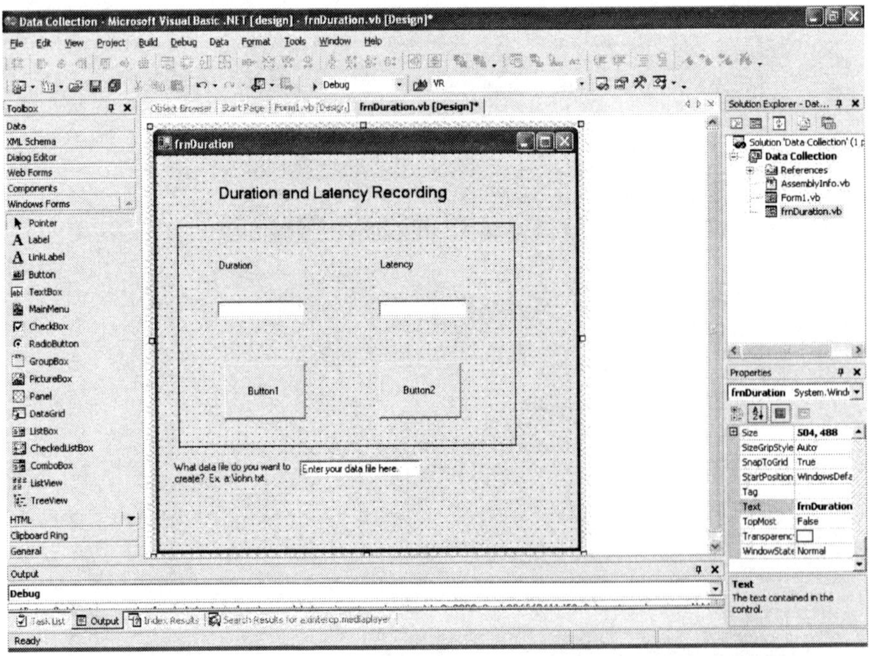

Figure 6.3 displays frmDuration with the addition of the user output file objects.

Reducing Errors

It is often the case that programs are designed less than "fool proof" for a user. This means that users might click on a wrong Button or select an incorrect option and crash the program. Take for example the current form. If the user clicks on butStart before selecting an output file, duration data will be computed; yet it will not be recorded into a file for later analysis. One way to minimize the risk of run-time errors on the part of your user is to make possible incorrect response options invisible or disabled until the "optimal" time for them to be available to the user. With this form, the optimal time for the user to click on butStart is after a data output file has been specified. Therefore change the *Enabled* properties of butStart and butStop to *False*. It probably makes sense to also change their text properties from Button1 and Button2 to *Start* and *Stop* respectively. Add a new Button, change the name to butBegin, the text to *Begin*, and place it next to the TextBox txtFile. This Button will kick in the data output file and change your butStart and butStop enabled properties to *True*. To do this, add the following code under the butBegin Button:

```
butStart.Enabled = True
butStop.Enabled = True
butBegin.Visible = False
FileOpen (2, txtFile.Text, OpenMode.Append)
```

Using TextBoxes to Track Client and Staff Names

If a relatively small number of users will be using the data system, or if you wish to track the user of the system for a given time period, you may wish to incorporate additional TextBoxes into your program. In the case of our data collection system let's assume we want to track user name and client name. The latter referring to the person we are collecting data on. To incorporate the TextBoxes for these purposes, add one to your form from the toolbox. Change the name from Textbox1 to txtClient and the text to blank. Now add a second TextBox and change the name to txtStaff and the text to blank. Next add Labels above these TextBoxes to orient the user as to their function. Name these two labels lblStaff and lblClient, change their text properties accordingly,and position them directly above their corresponding TextBoxes.

Lastly add a new Button somewhere towards the bottom of the form that will allow the user to terminate the data collection program. Change the name of this Button to butEnd and the text to *End.*

Linking the Form Functions Together

Because the user will only need to write the client name and staff name once to file, this information would be best generated via butBegin. This Button is present upon the form loading, and since it disappears after it is clicked (via the "butBegin.Visible = False" code) it will only write this information once. Therefore,

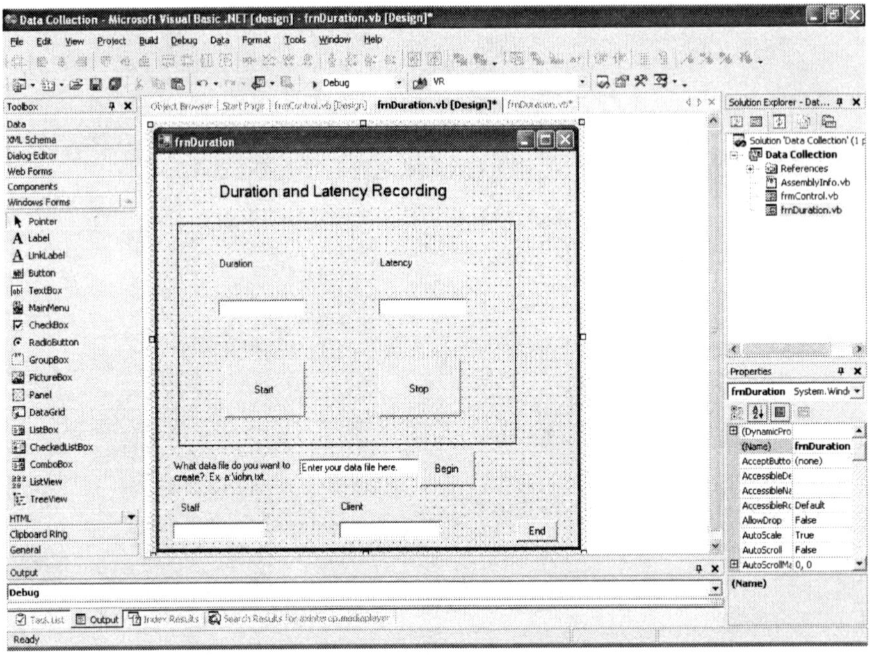

Figure 6.4 displays a possible layout of the Duration form for data collection.

add the following line of code under the butBegin Button after the previously written code.

```
WriteLine (2, txtStaff.Text, txtClient.Text)
```

In order for the computer to generate duration and latency measures when the butStart and butStop buttons are clicked by the user, Visual Basic's *Timer* function will need to be used. The Timer function is a command of code that captures the clock time of your computer. Unfortunately this clock time is a number corresponding to the *number of seconds after midnight*. This time is pretty irrelevant for most programming purposes. Yet, there is an easy transition of this value into a meaningful number. By capturing the clock time at point A, and again at point B, we can then subtract value at point A from the value at point B and obtain the difference in seconds. Using this conceptualization, the time from clicking on the start Button to clicking on the stop Button can create a *duration* measure. Therefore, add the following code under butStart:

```
WriteLine (2, txtDuration.Text, txtLatency.Text)
vTime1 = VB.Timer
txtLatency.Text = VB.Timer - vTime3
```

What the above code does is first write the current time and date to the data output file followed by the time values placed in the txtDuration and txtLatency TextBoxes. The first time this Button is clicked, these values will be blank. Yet, using the next line of code, this will soon change. vTime1 = VB.Timer places the current computer clock time into a variable called vTime1. This value will be held until the butStop Button is clicked to compute duration. The third line of code places the current computer clock time minus the value of a variable called vTime3. vTime3 will be 0 upon the first run through of the subroutine because it will be created upon clicking on the butStop Button to compute latency. As a result, this value will be simply the computer clock time and will appear in txtLatency.

In order to capture latency we need to obtain a value for vTime3. We also need to calculate the time from the clicking of butStart to butStop, or duration. Therefore, add the following code under butStop:

```
vTime2 = VB.Timer - vTime1
txtDuration.Text = vTime2
vTime3 = VB.Timer
```

What the above code does is calculate a value for vTime2 which will be placed in txtDuration. vTime2 is based on the current computer clock time minus the clock time when the butStart Button was clicked (i.e. vTime1). The next line of code places this value in txtDuration. The third line of code creates a value for vTime3. This value is used as described above for computing latency. Before running the program and testing your code writing skills, remember to declare your vTime1, vTime2, and vTime3 variables under the `Inherits System.Windows.Form3.Form` section of the editor. To do so, type the following code:

```
Dim vTime1
Dim vTime2
Dim vTime3
```

Next place the cursor above all existing code and type:

```
Option Explicit On
```

Finally type the shorthand recognition for the VB.Timer code directly under Option Explicit On:

```
Imports VB = Microsoft.VisualBasic
```

An Exit Option

In addition to ending your program, the butEnd Button should close the data output file. This will allow for subsequent users to run the program and create their own data file without the difficulty possibly encountered if a previous file is still open. Therefore add the following code under butEnd:

```
FileClose(2)
End
```

The last step to complete is to link frmDuration to the control panel (frmControl). To do this add the following code to frmControl's butDuration:

```
Dim x as New frmDuration()
x.Show()
me.Visible() = False
```

Run the program and check your progress after you change the Startup object.

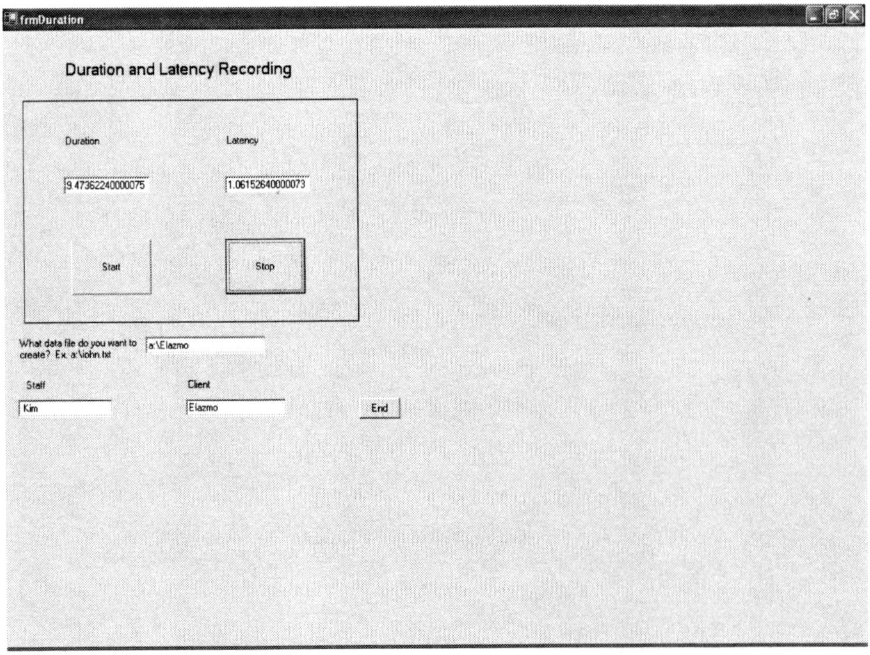

Figure 6.5 displays the run time display of frmDuration.

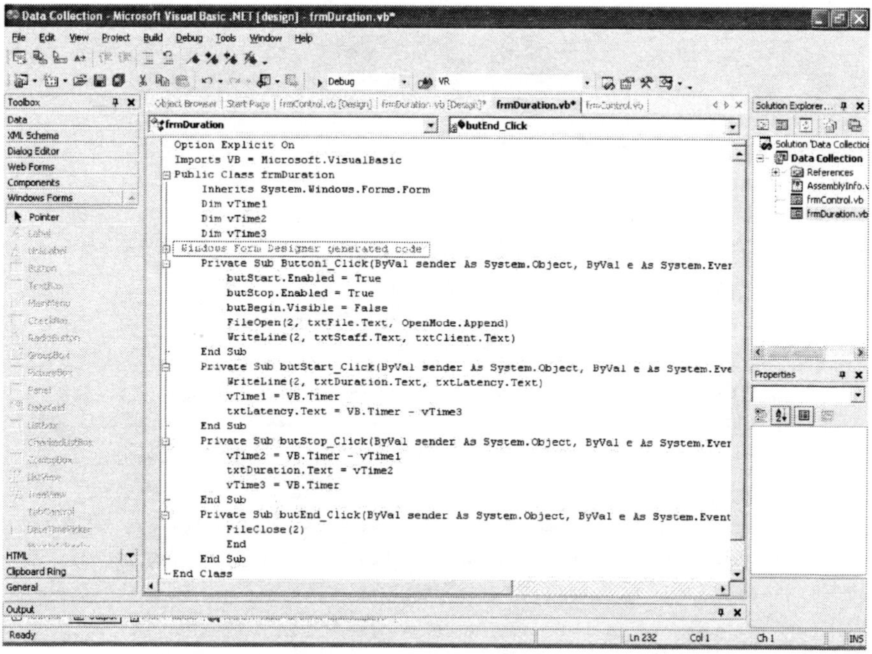

Figure 6.6 displays the programming code of frmDuration.

Time Sampling Recording

Form Overview

Insert a new Windows form into your project and rename it frmTS. Change the text property to frmTS. Add a Label to the form that displays to the user that this is the correct form for collecting time sampling data. Change the name of the Label to lblInstructions and change the text to "Time Sampling Recording." Alter font and TextAlign properties for a more custom look.

The most basic components of this form consist of an output data file TextBox, a TextBox indicating the duration of time between samplings, and responses for the user to select from during these time samplings.

Create the file TextBox by adding a new TextBox and changing the name to txtFile. Change the text to blank. Next place a Label to the left of txtFile named lblFile and change the text to "Enter your data file here."

Time sampling data collection requires specific intervals of time to elapse before the user records a response indicating that the behavior has occurred during the last interval of time or that the behavior is occurring right now (as in the case of momentary time sampling). In order for Visual Basic.NET to "prompt" the user following the elapsing of certain intervals of time, we will need to use the Timer object. The Timer object is different from the timer function described above which only grabs the current computer clock time. The Timer object is in essence a counter that will perform a variety of actions upon its enabling. What we want this object to do is prompt the user to make a response following the elapsing of an interval of time. Therefore, add a Timer object from the toolbar and place it on your form. Note that it drops below the form. This is fine because the Timer is invisible during runtime. Change the name to tmrInterval and its enabled property to *false*. While we could pre-set the interval of time during the programming process by changing tmrInterval's interval property to X, it would make more sense to allow the user to do this during run time. As a result, the time interval could vary across each running of the program.

Timer Customization

To allow for the customization of the Timer's interval, add a new TextBox, change the name to txtInterval and the text property to blank. Next add a new Label box, change the name to lblInterval, and the text property to "Time Interval (sec)." The txtInterval will allow the user to input a desired time interval for their recording purposes and the lblInterval will orient that user to the TextBox. In order for the Timer object to obtain the value entered into the TextBox, as well as for Visual Basic.NET to create the data file specified in txtFile, we need an event to happen. So, as before in the previous form we will have the user click on a Button to activate these parameters. Add a new Button, change the name to "butBegin" and the text to "Begin." Place the following code under butBegin:

```
butBegin.Enabled = False
FileOpen (2, txtFile.Text, OpenMode.Append)
WriteLine (2, Date.Now, txtInterval.Text)
vInterval = txtInterval.Text
tmrInterval.Interval = vInterval * 1000
tmrInterval.Enabled = True
```

This code first disables the butBegin Button so that this data is only generated once. Second, it opens/creates the text file that is specified in txtFile for Append. Third, it creates a variable entitled vInterval and makes its value equal to the value inputted into txtInterval. Fourth, it alters the tmrInterval interval property to equal the value of vInterval multiplied by 1000. This calculation is done because values entered into txtInterval are in milliseconds and the computer needs to recalculate them into seconds. Lastly, the tmrInterval is enabled, or turned on. Now that it is turned on, we need to make it do something once the interval has elapsed.

Because we just created a variable entitled vInterval this will need to be declared on the form so that VB.NET recognizes it. Therefore, type the following code under the `Inherits System.Windows.Forms.Form` section of the editor:

```
Dim vInterval
```

Now at the top of the editor type:

```
Option Explicit On
```

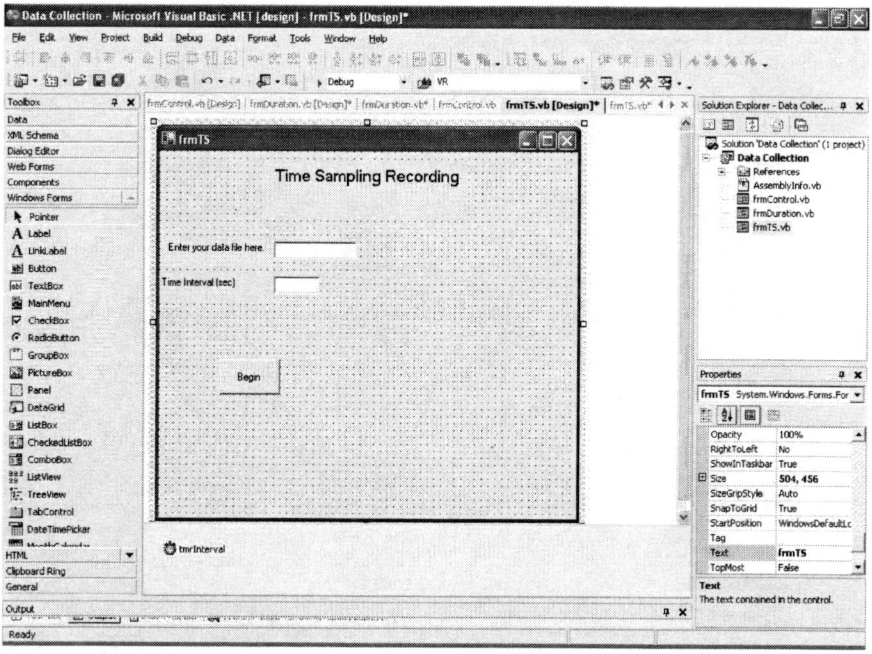

Figure 6.7 displays a possible graphical layout of the data output file, Timer object, and "Begin" Button.

Timer Prompted Responding

Let's move forward with having the user make one of two response options after the interval has elapsed. A *yes* or a *no* response regarding the occurrence of a behavior. We will want the computer to record the response, and reinitiate the Timer so that the interval will start over again. Begin by adding two new Buttons, and changing one's name to butYes and the other's name to butNo. Now change butYes's text to *Yes* and butNo's text to *No*.

Standing alone these Buttons could have a variety of meanings to the user of the program. This is good because many types of questions could be posed, allowing for a more diverse program. For example one may wish to assess "Is the behavior of interest occurring right now?" or "Has the behavior of interest occurred since the last interval?" or even "Has the behavior become more severe since the last interval?" To orient the user to the specific functions of the butYes and butNo Buttons, add a Label object, change the name to lblPrompt, and change the text to your desired question. For purposes of this example, let's make the text read "Is the behavior occurring right now?" Change the visible property to *False* because we will want the prompt to be displayed only following the completion of the tmrInterval's interval. Go ahead and also change butYes and butNo's visible property to *False* because we do not want the user to click on them immediately when the form loads.

To link the *Yes / No* Buttons to the behavior of the Timer, display lblPrompt, as well as have appropriate responses write to the data file, add the following code under butYes:

```
WriteLine (2, "yes")
tmrInterval.Enabled = True
lblPrompt.Visible = False
butYes.Visible = False
butNo.Visible = False
```

And the following code under butNo:

```
WriteLine (2, "no")
tmrInterval.Enabled = True
lblPrompt.Visible = False
butYes.Visible = False
butNo.Visible = False
```

Lastly, add the following code under tmrInterval:

```
Beep
lblPrompt.Visible = True
butYes.Visible = True
butNo.Visible = True
tmrInterval.Enabled = False
```

Let's start with the code under the Timer. The first line simply generates an audible tone for the user to orient himself/herself to the fact that it is now time to record data. The second line makes the lblPrompt object visible. The next two lines make the *Yes* and *No* response options visible. The last line turns the Timer's enabled function to *False*. In other words, it stops the Timer.

The code under the *Yes* and *No* response option buttons do a variety of similar things. First, they write to the data output file either an actual *Yes* or a *No* textual response. You may wish to add to this line of data by including time and date (using the Date.Now functions described above), or the number of intervals that have elapsed from the beginning of the data collection session (using a variable that adds by one each time the timer interval has completed). Next the code tells VB.NET to make the lblPrompt visible property *False* as well as the butYes and butNo buttons. These properties are changed so that the prompt is not always displayed on the

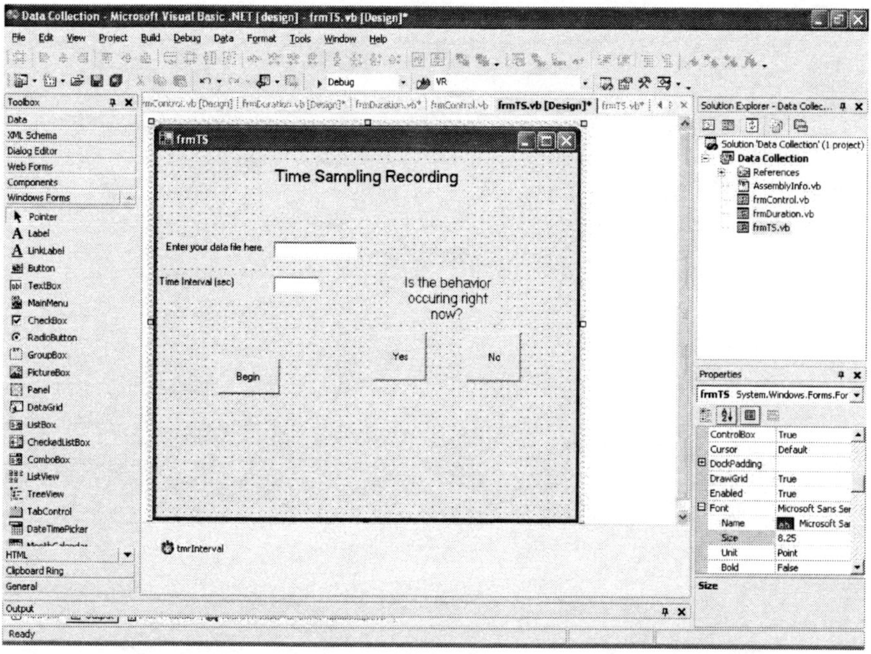

Figure 6.8 displays the status of the form following the elapsing of the Timer's interval.

computer screen and so that responses are not made on the Yes and No buttons prior to the completion of the next interval of time. Finally, the last line of code restarts tmrInterval to start the beginning of the next interval.

As with the Duration form, add an *End* Button to terminate data collection, along with the necessary code to link frmTS to the control panel. To do so, add the following code under frmControl's butTS:

```
Dimx as New frmTS()
x.Show()
me.Visible = False
```

Run the program and check your progress.

Frequency Recording

Form Overview

Insert a new Windows form into your project and rename it frmFrequency. Add a Label to the form that displays to the user that this is the correct form for collecting frequency data. Change the name of the Label to lblInstructions, change the text to *Frequency Recording*, and alter font and TextAlign properties.

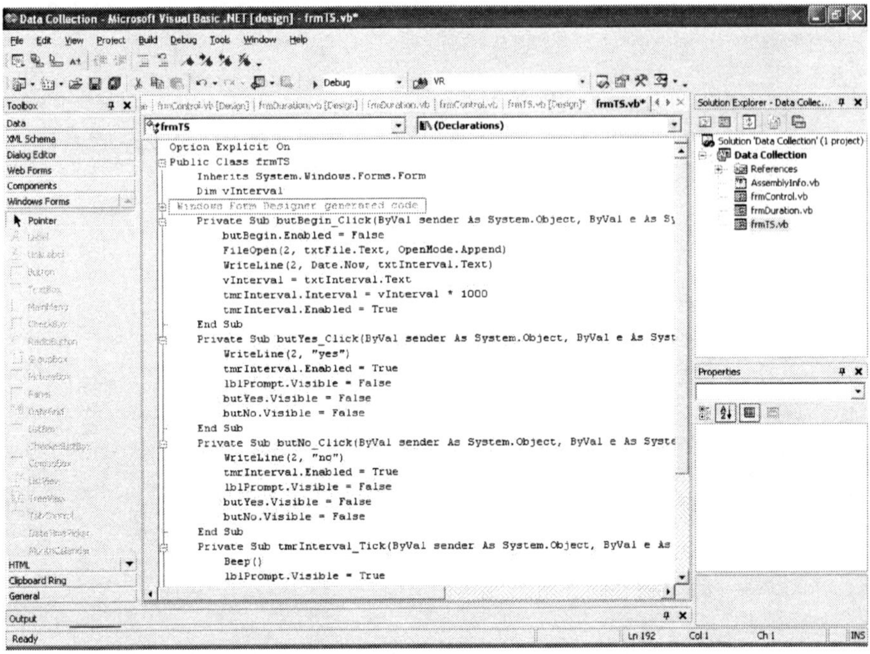

Figure 6.9 displays the majority of code found under frmTS.

The most basic components this form consists of are a series of Buttons that add occurrences of targeted behaviors when clicked upon. This is easily accomplished with Buttons and corresponding variables. While you could already craft such a form incorporating the existing information found in this chapter, let's add some additional sophistication to the program via a data input file.

Data Input File

Using a data input file for observational recording allows for any variety of parameters to be loaded into the computer program during run time instead of being manually entered by the user. The input file can save time as well as add a greater degree of diversity into your data collection program. Take for example our current frequency data collection form. A user may wish to track the frequency of a variety of target behaviors of a given client. Yet, that user might work with 10 or so different clients each with their own set of targeted behaviors. The amount of time spent inputting each client's information increases along with the number of clients. Designing a data collection system that can handle such changing demands on the user is paramount.

To incorporate the input data file into our program, add a TextBox, change the name to txtInput and the text property to blank. Next add a Label to the left of the TextBox, change the name to lblInput and the text to "Enter data file to input here. Type directory, data file, and extension. Ex. a:\pete.txt." This is a rather long Label text, but it crucial that the user input this specific information in order for the program to access his/her data file correctly.

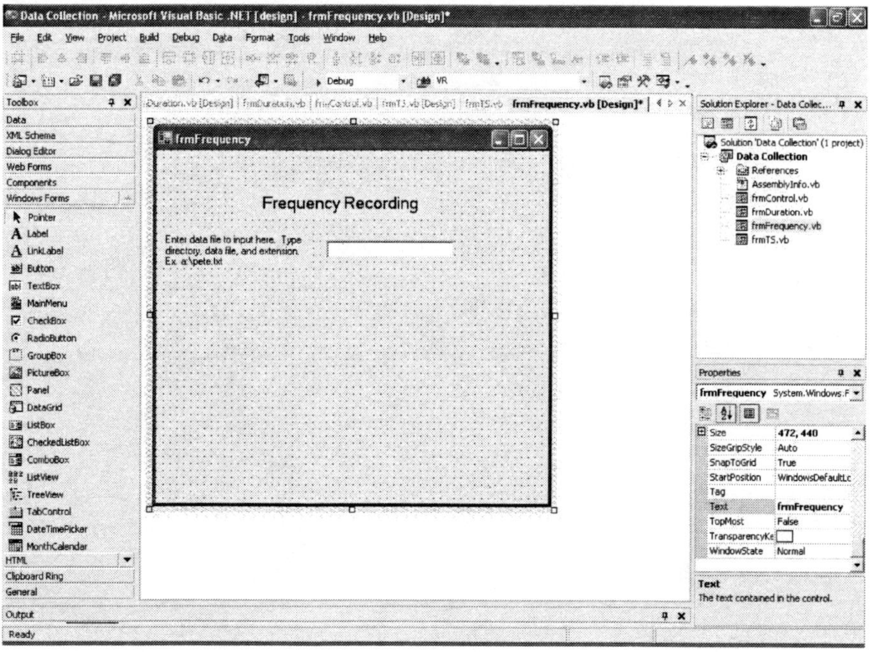

Figure 6.10 shows frmFrequency along with the lblInput and txtInput objects.

We will also need a Button to create the event which accesses the data file and brings that information into Visual Basic.NET. Therefore, add a Button, change its name to butDatain an its text to "Load Data File." Place the following code under butDatain to open the desired data file:

```
FileOpen (1, txtInput.Text, OpenMode.Input)
```

Designing the Input File

Next we need to determine what type of information we would like to store in our data input file, and create the corresponding objects and code in Visual Basic.NET to interact with that information. For purposes of illustration, let's say we would like to have the client's name and up to six targeted behaviors stored in our data file. This will require that we have information separated by commas in our data file such as: "Pete, physical-aggression, SIB, hair-pulling, threats, request, in-seat." Create such a file yourself by opening Microsoft Notepad or Wordpad, which come standard with Microsoft Windows, type the above sequence, and save it as a text file named "pete.txt" to your a-drive. Make sure you add the "-" between words for a multiple word behavior like *hair-pulling*. Close your text editor program and return to Visual Basic.NET.

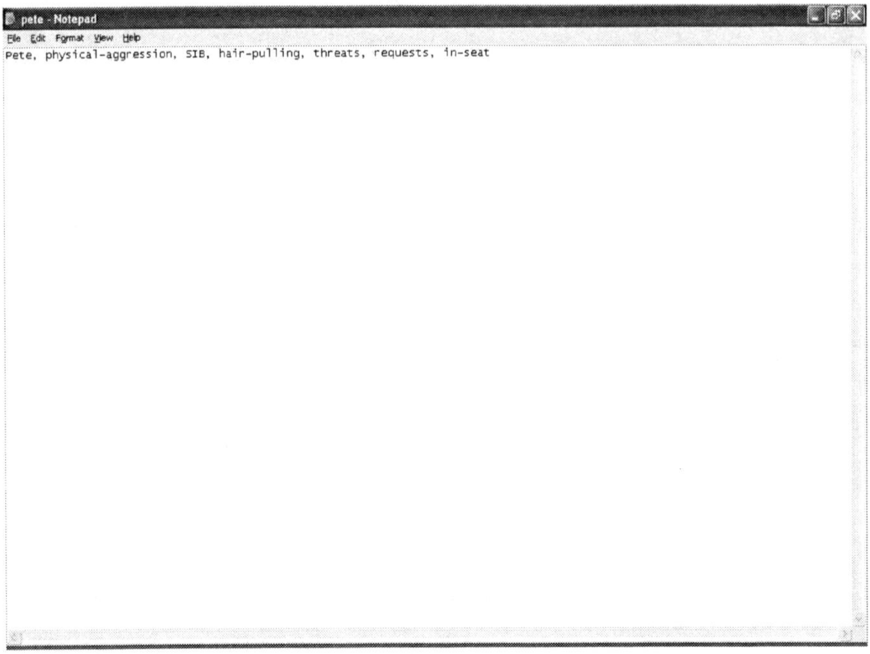

Figure 6.11 shows the correct format of the pete.txt data input file.

Creating the Response Recorders

Because the data input file has the client's name and up to six identified behaviors to be frequency recorded, let's create a TextBox that displays client name and six Buttons to correspond to each of the behaviors. Start by adding a TextBox to your frmFrequency form, change the name to txtName, and change the text property to blank. Next add a Label, change the name to lblName, and change the text to "Client Name." Now add six separate Buttons to your form to correspond to the six target behaviors. Change their names to butBeh1 through butBeh6 and all their text to blank. Finally add six new Labels and place them directly above your newly added Buttons. These labels will be used to display the current frequency of each identified behavior. Change the names of these labels to lblBeh1 through lblBeh6 and change all their text to blank. You might also change their BorderStyle property to "Fixed Single".

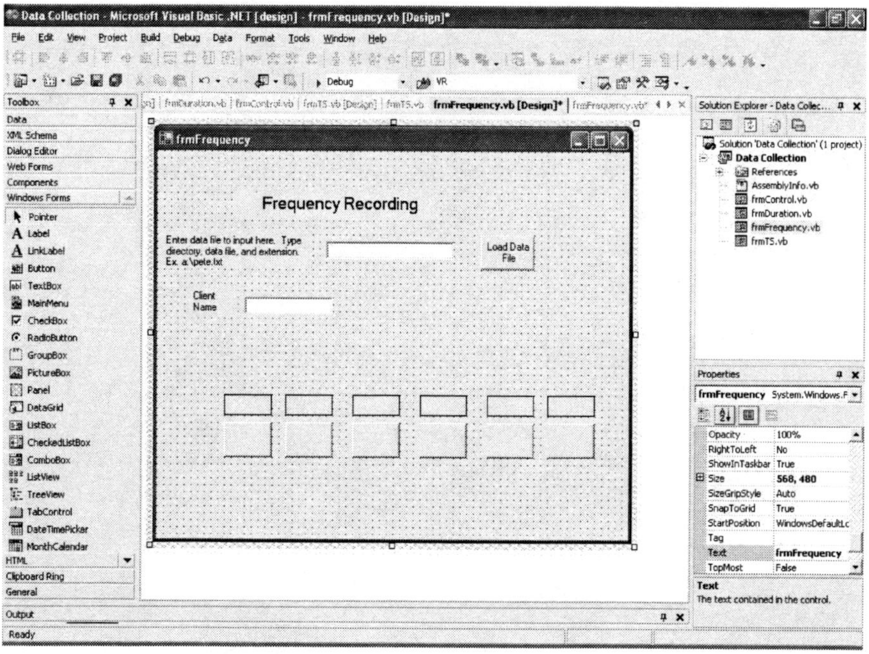

Figure 6.12 shows a possible layout of the newly added command buttons and labels.

Customization for Less than X Response Options

Earlier we specified that the program would collect information on *up to* six targeted behaviors. If numbers less than six are found in the data file an error might occur during run time if certain precautions are not made. There are many ways to accomplish the safeguarding against such errors. A very simple way is to have a *dummy* target behavior that if placed in the input file corresponds to the absence of a target behavior. For example, the pete.txt file would now read: "Pete, physical aggression, SIB, x, x, x, x." Here the dummy target behavior is x, indicating that there really are only two behaviors we wish to record for Pete: physical aggression and SIB. Using these dummy behaviors, we can alter the properties of the butBeh3-butBeh6 buttons so that they do not record any information when clicked upon. Let's begin this process by adding the following code to the "butDatain" Button:

```
Input (1, vName)
Input (1, vB1)
Input (1, vB2)
Input (1, vB3)
Input (1, vB4)
Input (1, vB5)
Input (1, vB6)
```

```
txtName.Text = vName
butBeh1.Text = vB1
If vB2 = "x" Then
butBeh2.Enabled = False
Else
butBeh2.Text = vB2
End If
If vB3 = "x" Then
butBeh3.Enabled = False
Else
butBeh3.Text = vB3
End If
If vB4 = "x" Then
butBeh4.Enabled = False
Else
butBeh4.Text = vB4
End If
If vB5 = "x" Then
butBeh5.Enabled = False
Else
butBeh5.Text = vB5
End If
If vB6 = "x" Then
butBeh6.Enabled = False
Else
butBeh6.Text = vB6
End If
```

This code first loads the information found in the text input file into a series of seven variables. The first variable is called vName and the following six are called vB1-vB6 (short for behaviors 1-6). Remember that you need to declare such variables under the `Inherits System.Windows.Forms.Form` section of the editor with:

```
Dim vName, vB1, vB2, vB3, vB4, vB5, vB6
```

At the top of the editor add:

```
Option Explicit On
```

After loading the information found in the text file into these variables, VB.NET places the first variable's text into txtName. Next it places the second variable's text (the first target behavior) into the text of butBeh1. Afterwards it checks to see if there are any more behaviors that are to be recorded. It does so by checking to see if the variable has a value of *x*. If it does, it disables the corresponding butBeh Button, but if not, it places that information into the text of butBeh Button and leaves the enable property equal to true. This last series of steps is repeated for the remaining four variables (vB3-vB6).

Variables to Track Frequency

Now with the input file information properly loaded into the Buttons, we are ready to link the Buttons (butBeh1-6) to variables that will keep track of behavior frequency. What will be necessary here are a series of integer variables, each corresponding to a target behavior that increases in value each time the butBeh Button is clicked by the user. To create this series of integer variables, add the following code in the `Inherits System.Windows.Forms.Form` section of the editor:

```
Dim vFB1, vFB2, vFB3, vFB4, vFB5, vFB6 as Integer
```

Here each vFB corresponds to each behavior that will be recorded. Next, add the following code under each of the corresponding butBeh Buttons changing the lblBeh and vFB numbers with each:

```
vFB1 = vFB1 + 1
lblBeh1.Text = vFB1
```

You should now have the necessary code for frequency counts of up to six independent behaviors.

Handling Recording Errors

While this last code adds the total frequencies of each behavior as desired, it is quite plausible that the user will make a mistake, click on the wrong button, or double-click and add too many instances of a behavior than desired. There are many ways we could handle this problem, from simply flagging the error in the text file, to subtracting an instance of behavior using code like: vFB = vFB - 1 . The option is up to you if the possibility of error seems important enough to safegauard your program against. Let's attempt to solve the problem in a pretty straightforward way via an error button.

Begin by adding a new Button, renaming it butError, and changing the text to *Error*. Next create a new variable called *vError* by adding the following code to the `Inherits System.Windows.Forms.Form` section of the editor:

```
Dim vError
```

Using the vError variable we can control the behavior of the vFB1 – vFB6 variables to either add one or subtract one when the butError Button is clicked. To

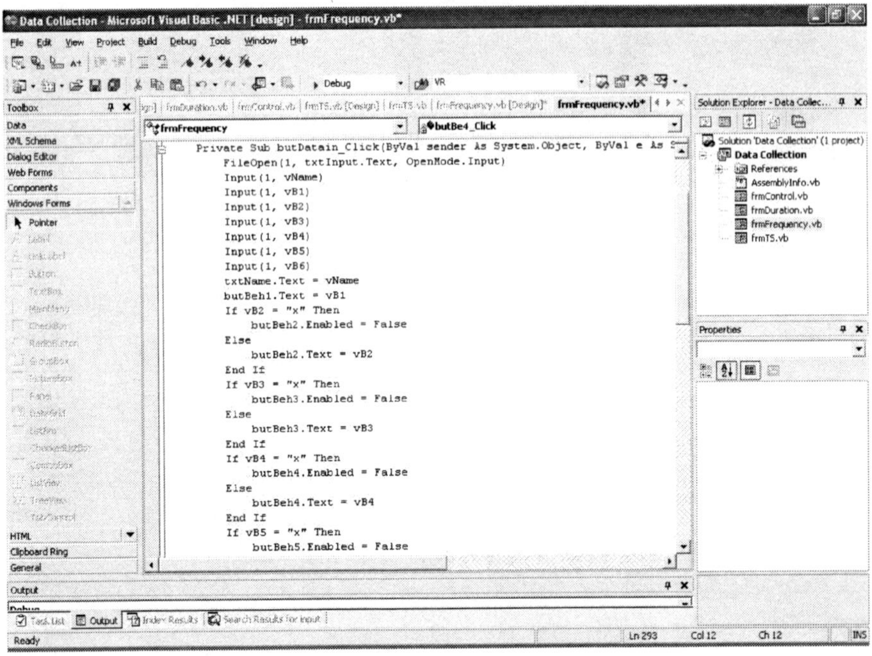

Figure 6.13 displays highlights of the necessary code to record behavior frequency.

do this we can make the value of vError equal to one when it is clicked on and then use an If-Then-Else statement under each butBeh Button to add or subtract 1 from the corresponding vFB. Begin by adding the following code under butError:

```
vError = vError + 1
```

This code will add a value of 1 to the vError variable. Next go ahead and add the following code under each of the butBeh Buttons before the existing vFB1-6 = vFB1-6 + 1 code. Remember to change the FB(number):

```
If vError = 1 Then
vFB1 = vFB1 - 1
vError = 0
Else
```

Finish this If-Then-Else statement with the required *End If* following the previously existing vFB1-6 = vFB1-6 +1. Your finalized subroutine should look like the following for butBeh1 and change only in the 1-6 value across your other butBeh Buttons:

```
If vError = 1 Then
```

```
vFB1 = vFB1 - 1
vError = 0
Else
vFB1 = vFB1 + 1
End If
lblBeh1.Text = vFB1
```

This additional code creates a means for errors to be corrected before they are written to file. By turning vError's value to 1, any subsequent click on a butBeh Button will subtract 1 from the current value of vFB. This is what the "If vError = 1" code will do. Immediately after this subtraction, vError is changed back to 0. Now if any additional clicks are made on butBeh buttons, 1 will be added to the total vFB variable, as before. Subtractions will only occur if vError is turned back to 1 by clicking on butError.

Data Output Using Timers

Next we need to deal with data collection output. Because we are collecting frequency data, the easiest way to handle this is for all accumulated frequencies to write to file when the data collection session is over. While this will accomplish a macro analysis of frequency, a user may wish to see subtle changes in frequencies as the session progresses. To do this we can incorporate a Timer object that automatically writes data to file every time that Timer's interval has elapsed. By making the interval repeat over and over again at a pre-specified time period, we will be able to have moment-by-moment frequency data for our subject.

Begin by adding a new Timer object to your form and changing the name to tmrData. Because we do not want the timer to kick in upon form load, change the enabled property to false. Add the following code under the tmrData subroutine:

```
WriteLine (2, vFB1, vFB2, vFB3, vFB4, vFB5, vFB6)
```

This code will simply write the values of our six behaviors to the data file. Along with the addition of this timer, we need to add code to open the data file we wish to write to. Plus, since we do not want to write data until the session actually begins, we need to have the user initiate the beginning of the session. As before, this task is easily accomplished via a Button.

Add a new Button to your form, change the name to butBegin, and the text to *Begin*. Add the following code under this Button:

```
tmrData.Enabled = True
WriteLine (2, vFB1, vFB2, vFB3, vFB4, vFB5, vFB6)
```

Now the Timer will write to file following the completion of the pre-specified interval placed in its interval property. Plus, frequency data for all six variables will write to file immediately upon initiating the program. Obviously, these values should initially be 0.

As before in our frmDuration and frmTS forms, we will want the user to control the name and location of the data output file. Add a TextBox, change the name to txtDataout, and the text property to blank. Next, add a Label to the left of this TextBox, change the name to lblDataout, and the text to "Enter data file to OUTPUT here. Type directory, data file, and extension. Ex. a:\firstsession.txt."

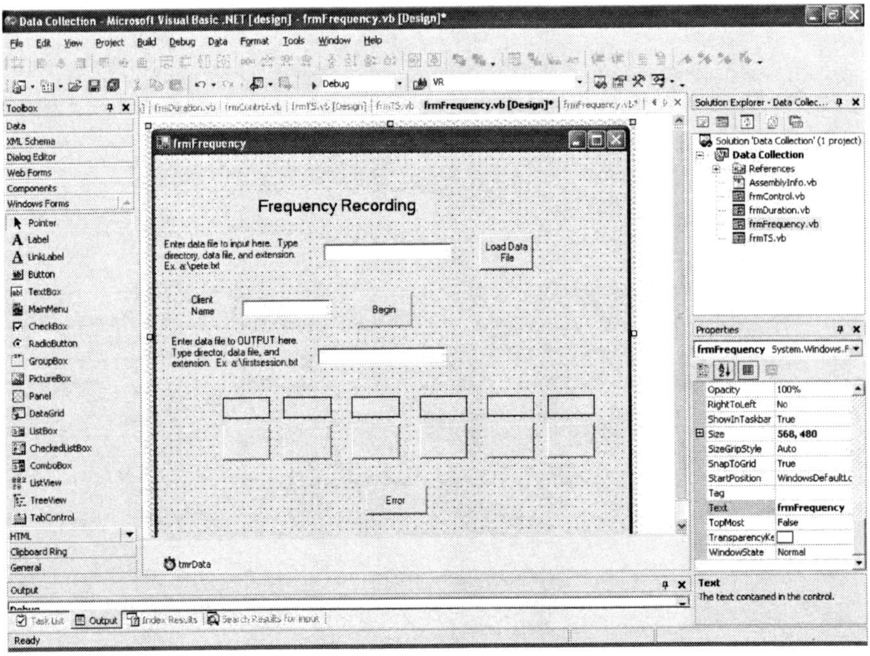

Figure 6.14 displays a possible layout of frmFrequency with data output file information.

To add user control over the interval of time between data recording to the output file, simply add a TextBox, change its name to txtInterval, and the text to blank. Now add a Label to the left of this TextBox and change the name to lblInterval and its text to "Write data every X seconds." Alter the code under the butBegin Button to read:

```
tmrData.Interval = txtInterval.Text * 1000
tmrData.Enabled = True
FileOpen (2, txtDataout.Text, OpenMode.Output)
WriteLine (2, Date.Now, "data record=",
      txtInterval.Text)
WriteLine (2, vB1, vB2, vB3, vB4, vB5, vB6)
```

This code first takes the value entered in txtInterval, multiplies it by 1000 (to get seconds), and places it in the interval property of tmrData. Now the data file will write every time this interval elapses. Next, the code kicks in the timer or turns it on with *Enabled=True.* The code then opens or creates the data file in the directory and with the name specified in the txtDataout TextBox. After the file is open, the time and date are written followed by noting what interval of time was specified in txtInterval. Lastly, the values of all the vB1-6 variables are written to the text file.

Before we finish up here though, think about how you will get the program to stop writing data to file. This task could be accomplished via an *Exit* button containing *FileClose(2)* code. Yet, the same function is possible with the addition of another Timer, one that would keep track of session length. This feature will also ensure that data are not recorded for longer periods of time than desired. Keeping session length exactly the same interval may be critical for comparisons across sessions.

To accomplish this feat, just add another TextBox and Timer. First, add the TextBox, change the name to txtSession, and the txt to blank. Second, add a label, change the name to lblSession, and the text to "Session Length." Now add the Timer and change the name to tmrSession. Place the following code under the new Timer to close the program, plus write the data to file one last time:

```
WriteLine (2, vFB1, vFB2, vFB3, vFB4, vFB5, vFB6)
End
```

To hook up the desired session length to this timer, add the following code under butBegin:

```
tmrSession.Interval = txtSession.Text * 1000
tmrSession.Enabled = True
```

That should do it. Add another Button to prematurely terminate the session called butEnd and add the code:

```
End
```

Finally, add the following code to frmControl's butFreq Button to link this form to your control panel:

```
Dim x as New frmFrequency()
x.Show()
me.Visible = False
```

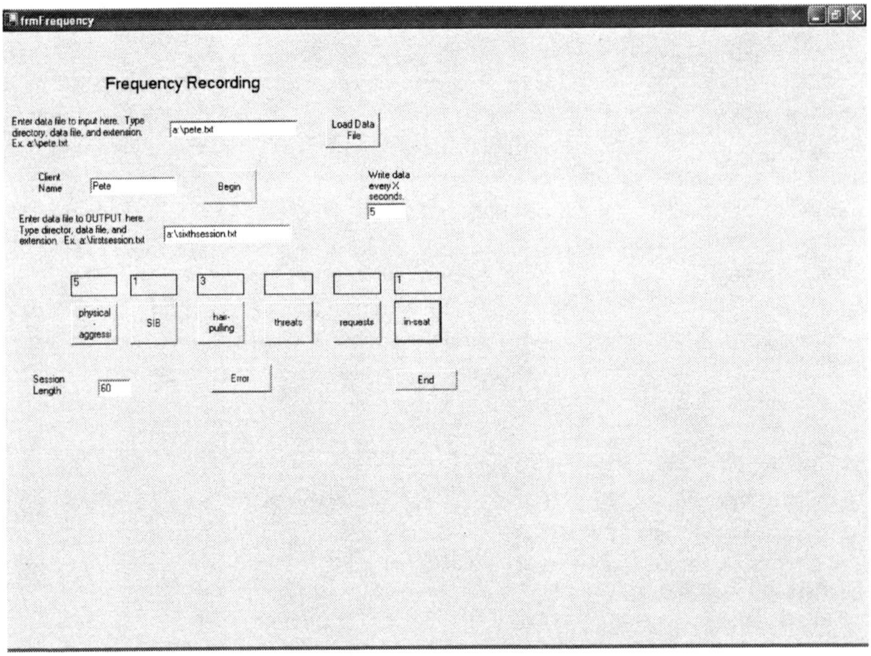

Figure 6.15 shows the resulting final graphical interface for frmFrequency.

Descriptive Analysis Recording

Form Overview

Insert a new Windows form into your project and rename it frmDA. Add a Label to the form that displays to the user that this is the correct form for collecting Descriptive Analysis data. Change the name of the Label to lblInstructions and change the text to "Descriptive Analysis Recording." Also change the Font and TextAlign properties to suit your style.

The most basic components of this form consist of a series of ComboBoxes that contain a list of options for the user to select from regarding antecedents, behaviors, and consequences. This is easily accomplished by adding three separate ComboBoxes to frmDA and changing their names to cbAnt, cbBeh, and cbCon. Next change the text property of each of these boxes to *Antecedent*, *Behavior*, and *Consequence* respectively.

ComboBox Items

To add options to the cbAnt, double-click on the *Item* property of the box in the properties window. Double-click on the (collections)... text and a little blank box will appear. Type your first possible antecedent here and press enter. You will have to repeat this step for each additional antecedent. Once done, click on cbBeh and do the same for behaviors. Finally, click on cbCon to add options to the

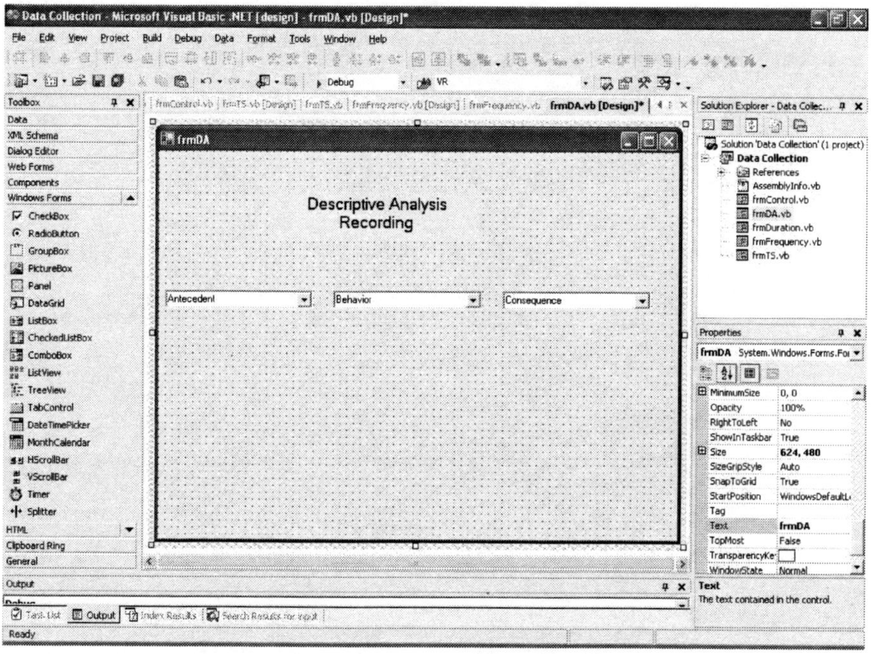

Figure 6.16 displays a possible layout of frmDA.

consequence ComboBox. Predetermining these options will reduce the amount of effort your data recorder would need to emit to type all this information in by hand. A great feature of the Combo Box is that if an option is not provided, the user could actually type in a customized novel option during the running of the program. Planning ahead for the most probable response options will keep this activity to a minimum.

A few other features we will need to add to this form to make it functional are a TextBox specifying where the data output file will go and a Button that writes the ComboBox information to that file. First, add the TextBox, change the name to txtData, and the text to blank. Next, add a Label to the left of this TextBox, change the name to lblData, and the text to "Data File Name: ex. a:\mary.txt." Now add a Button directly below the txtData object that opens / creates the text file. Change the name of this Button to butBegin and the text to "Begin." Place the following code under the butBegin button:

```
FileOpen (5, txtData.Text, OpenMode.Append)
butBegin.Visible = False
```

This code will first open or create the data file, and second remove the butBegin Button so that it does not accidentally get clicked on again.

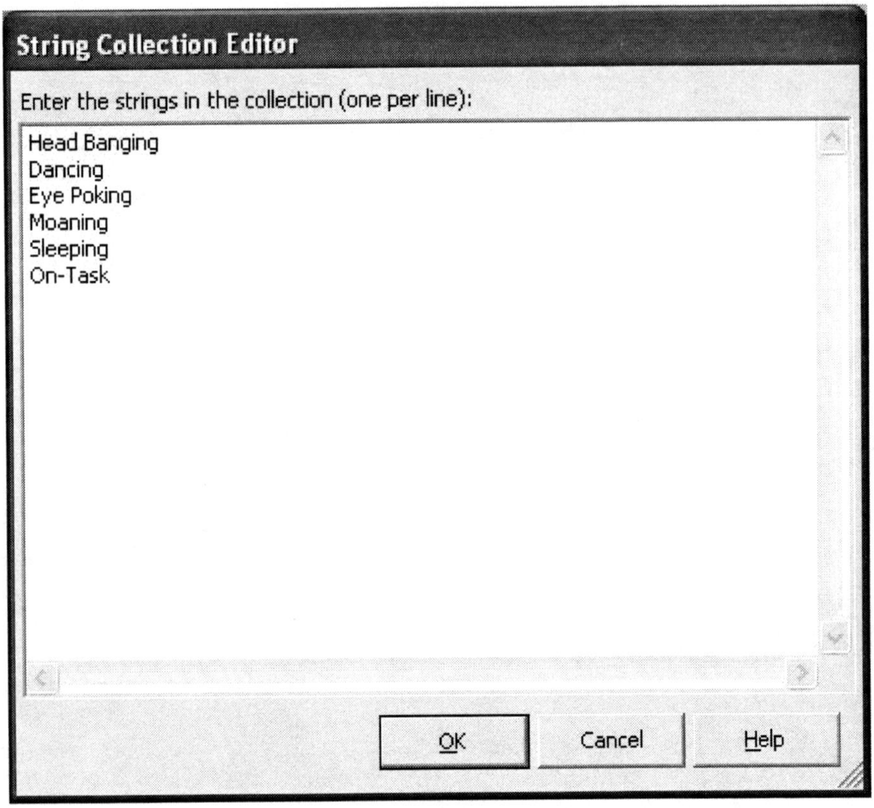

Figure 6.17 shows how the items are added to the ComboBoxes.

The last step for this form is to add another Button, this time to record the options selected in the ComboBoxes to the data output file. To accomplish this, add a Button, change the name to butRecord, and the text to "Record Information." Under this command button, add the following code:

```
WriteLine (5, Date.Now, cbAnt.Text, cbBeh.Text,
      cbCon.Text)
```

With this code, your form for Descriptive Analysis should be functional. Keep in mind you might want to add TextBoxes for client and staff names, a Timer for session length, or an End Button.

Link the frmDA to your frmControl by placing the following code under frmControl's but DA button:

```
Dim x as New frmDA()
x.Show()
me.Visible = False
```

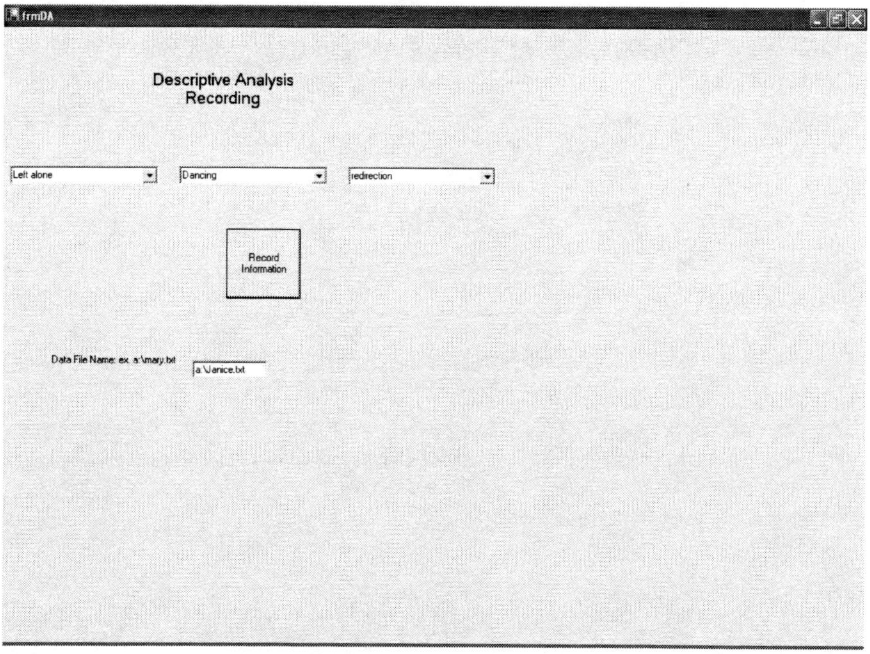

Figure 6.18 displays frmDA during run time.

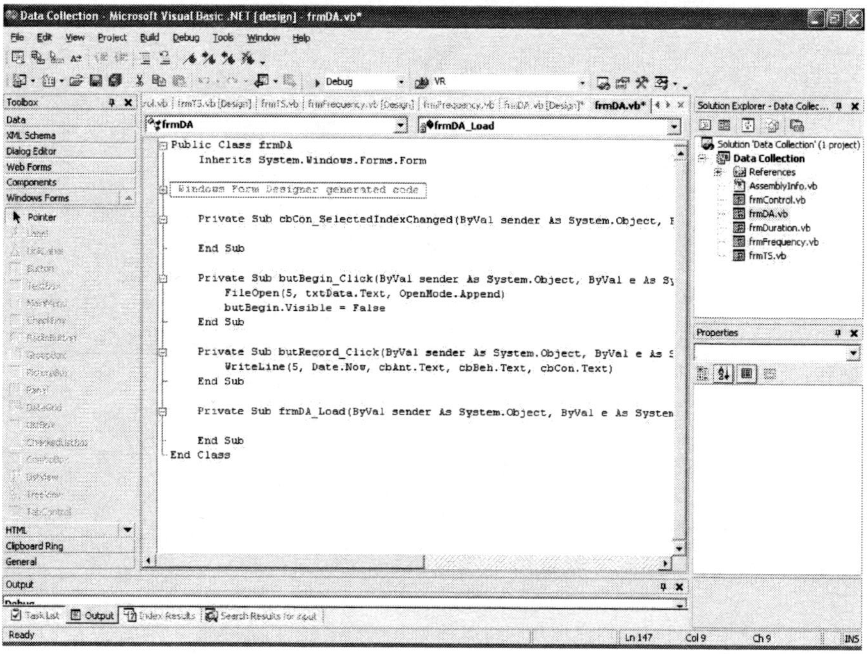

Figure 6.19 displays the necessary code for frmDA.

Our computerized data collection program should be complete. Run the program and check your progress. There are endless additional features that could be added to the program. Hopefully we have provided you an example that demonstrates the diversity in data collection options Visual Basic.NET has to offer, and the framework for designing your own optimal program.

References

Bellack, A. S., & Hersen, M. (1998). *Behavioral assessment* (4th Ed). New York: Allyn & Bacon.

Dixon, M. R. (in press). Creating your own portable data collection system with Microsoft Embedded Visual Tools for the Pocket PC. *Journal of Applied Behavior Analysis.*

Kahng, S., & Iwata, B. A. (1998). Computerized systems for collecting real-time observational data. *Journal of Applied Behavior Analysis, 31*, 253-261.

Chapter 7: Matching to Sample

Creating a Stimulus Equivalence Program

A research preparation often used in behavior analysis to study human language and concept formation is called "matching to sample." In a matching to sample procedure, one stimulus, called the sample, is usually presented at the top of the computer screen while two or more stimuli, called comparisons, are presented directly below the sample. The subject is either shaped or instructed to make a "match" between the object at the top of the screen with one at the bottom of the screen. This is technically called conditional discrimination learning. The matching to sample preparation is useful for teaching colors, words, or identity relations among stimuli, and can be used for more complex learning preparations such as stimulus equivalence. In this latter type of matching to sample preparation, certain relations between the sample and the comparison stimuli are trained via differential reinforcement for correct responses, while other novel stimuli relations are simply tested without reinforcement to assess if they have "emerged" from a specific training history. For more information about research using the Match to Sample procedure to examine stimulus equivalence see Green and Saunders, (1998).

Assuming a general understanding of the methodology, here is what a basic outline for a matching to sample program used for stimulus equivalence research might consist of:

1. Create the stimulus classes with three member classes (3 classes) for a total of nine stimuli. Label each class A, B, and C. Label each specific stimulus A1, A2, A3, etc.
2. Arrange stimuli placement on the computer screen (with PictureBoxes) for the sample and comparison stimuli.
3. Program A-B conditional discrimination training. Start with a block of 18 trials, but make the trial number into a variable to allow for customization of the number of trials later on if desired. Ensure that all stimuli are displayed 6 times as samples in a random sequence. Ensure that all comparison stimuli are also randomized in terms of their placement.
4. Develop protocol to check if a response criterion has or has not been met. Initially set criteria at 16 out of 18 trials in a given block of trials. Create a variable that will add trial numbers until it gets to 18 and then at that time check to see if the number correct is 16 or greater. If so, go on to the next type of training (A-C), if not send back to restart A-B training with another block of 18 trials. As with the number of trials, make the criterion a variable to allow for customization.
5. Program A-C conditional discrimination training. Use the same methods as above for randomization and criterion. If responding is less than

specified criterion, repeat this phase, and do not go back to A-B training.

6. Program Mixed A-B / A-C training. Simply mix the types of trials from A-B and A-C together. Start off with 36 trials and a criterion of 32. If criterion is met, go on to testing phases. If criterion is not met, repeat only this phase.
7. Program various tests for derived relations in the absence of any type of reinforcement.
   a. Reflexivity test of A-A, B-B, and C-C relations. Start with 27 trials containing 3 presentations of each sample but allow for customization.
   b. Symmetry test of B-A and C-A relations. Start off with 36 trials containing 18 presentations of B-A and 18 presentations of C-A each but allow for customization.
   c. Transitivity test of B-C relations. Start with 18 trials of B-C presentations with each B stimulus serving as a sample 6 times for but allow for customization.
   d. Equivalence test of C-B relations. Start with 18 trials of C-B presentations with each C stimulus serving as a sample 6 times for but allow for customization.
8. Create programming routine to write a various amount of information to a data file on every trial. This information will include sample stimulus, comparison stimulus selected, correct comparison (if not selected), and response time from sample presentation to comparison selection.

While this is a list of what the program must do, there is more than one way to make it do these things. We have decisions to make about the look and feel of the program and we have to anticipate the research needs that are not outlined above. For example, do we need a control panel? Are there any additional parameters the researcher will want to change? What would these be? Are there any object properties the researcher will want to change during run time? What would these be? Are there going to be instructions to the participant? If so will the instructions be in the beginning of the program, at the end, or both? By now you might be able to anticipate these questions and others, plus you might even be able to respond to these questions using your programming ability.

Rather than using a control panel we will design this program so the researcher can pass parameters and object properties to the program during run time using an input file, similar to the input files designed in Chapters 5 and 6.

Program Requirements

1. Creating the Stimuli

You as the programmer will first need to decide what the stimuli will be. Common forms of visual stimuli may be arbitriay shapes, pictures of faces, or drawings of objects. Auditory simuli could also be utilized, by adding .wav or MP3 files. In this chapter's example, we will stick with all visual stimuli. Because you may wish to add, delete, or modify stimuli at a later date, we will design this program to allow stimuli parameters to be loaded during run time via a data input file. This is a nice feature, because it lets the user change stimuli prior to the program running without modifying any existing computer code to do so.

At this point, open a text editor such as NotePad, and create a new text file, call it M2S.txt (for Match to Sample) and save it in the directory where you will store the program files you are about to write. Your current text file will be blank. That is ok for now. Let's also create a directory structure of "c:\programming\M2S" and put the blank text file there. Close NotePad.

The program requirements above note that the stimuli should consist of three 3-class members. Therefore, you will need nine image files: A1, A2, A3; B1, B2, B3; C1, C2, C3. For programming purposes the images can be of anything, but it is easier for now during program construction if you make your own images as simple letters and numbers using the Paint program provided with Windows. This will allow for you to pre-test the program without having to recall which abstract stimuli were related to each other. When the program is completed, you can easily replace these "test" stimuli with actual stimuli.

Locate the Paint program and open it on your computer. Once the Paint program is open, select *Image* then *Attributes* from the main menu. Change the width and height to 75 pixels. You can then use the text tool to type *A1* and save it as *a1.bmp* in the same directory as your text file (c:\programming\M2S). This way the image will literally be that of *A1*. Again, using the image of A1 will allow you to track the program when you are writing it. Now create the other eight images and save them to the same directory. Close Microsoft Paint.

2. Configure the Forms

The next programming requirement refers to arranging the stimuli configuration. We have some decisions to make about the number of form(s) we will want to use for the program. Open Visual Basic.NET and create a new project named M2S and change the location of the project to your c:\programming\M2S directory. Let's make the first form of this project an instructions form. Change the name property to *frmIns1*, the WindowState to *Maximized*, and the form Text to *Instructions*. Add a Label named *lblIns1* and size lblIns1 to fit the form based on how detailed you instructions may be. You may have to make adjustments after you run the program and see how everything lines up during run time. Add a Button and change the Name property to *butBegin*, and change the Text property to *Begin*.

Go back to NotePad and reopen M2S.txt. On the first line of the document type the line:

```
INSTRUCTIONS, This is where the instructions will go.
```

Note: type your instructions on the same line. Do not start a new line or press the ENTER button until you have completed your instructions. Also make sure the word *Instructions* is in all capital letters.

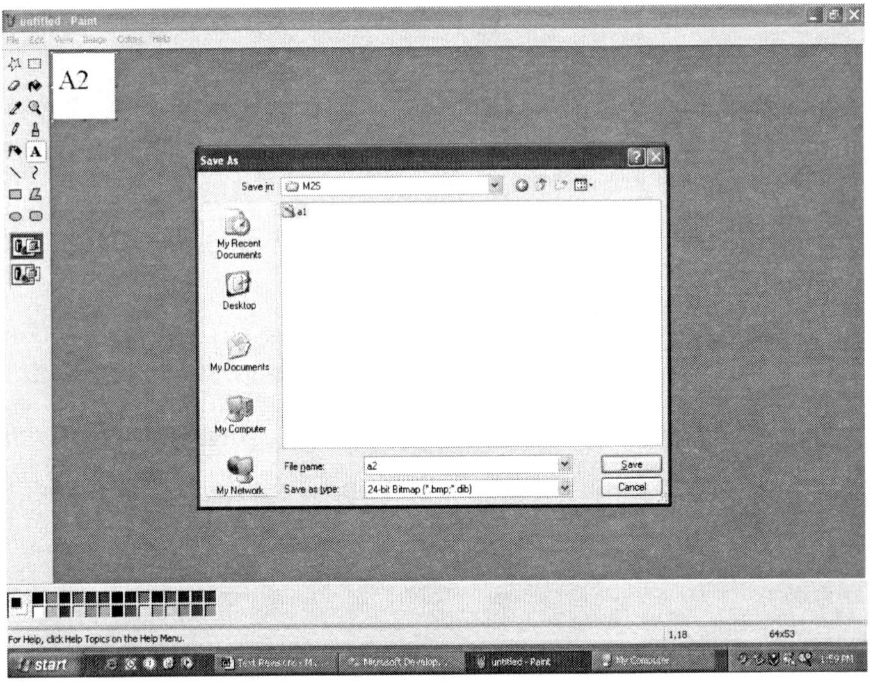

Figure 7.1 displays the A2 stimulus being created in Microsoft Paint.

Your text file should look like this:

```
INSTRUCTIONS, This is where the instructions will go.
```

Save and close the M2S.txt text file. *frmIns1* will be the first form to open, therefore we need to tell this form to open the input file M2S.txt when it is loaded. Also, we want it to read in the instructions, and display those instructions lblIns1. Double-click on the form, not on the Label or the Button, enter the edit mode, and type the following code in the Private Sub frmIns1_Load subroutine:

```
FileOpen(1, "C:\programming\M2S\M2S.txt",
OpenMode.Input)
Input(1, vHeader)
Input(1, vInstructions)
lblIns1.Text = vInstructions
```

Notice that we are using C:\programming\M2S to tell the computer to look for the text file in the same directory as the application or program. Because we are using this directory, all of the files used for this program have to be located in that same directory. We also need to declare two variables, vHeader and vInstructions. Under Inherits System Windows.Forms.Form in the VB.NET editor, type:

```
Dim vHeader As String
Dim vInstructions As String
```

And above the line Public Class frmIns1, type the following:

```
Option Explicit On
```

Run the program after you change the Startup object. You should see the instructions.

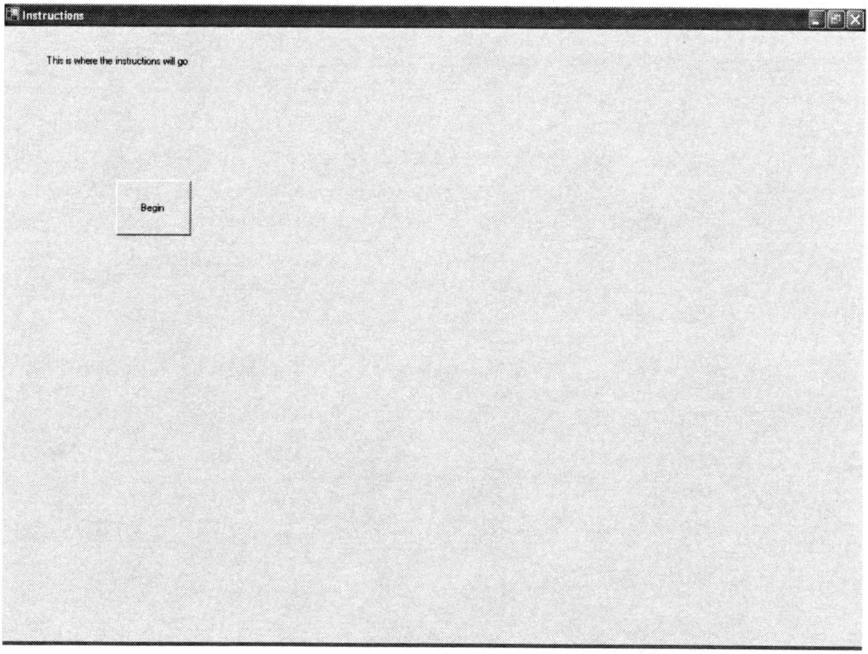

Figure 7.2 shows the instructions screen for the M2S program.

We now need to create a form for the main program. Add a new form by selecting *Project* and then *Add Windows Form* from the Main Menu. Change the name property to *frmM2S*, make the Text blank. Change the WindowState to *Maximized*. This form should load after the participant reads the instructions. To do this, go to frmIns1 and double-click on *butBegin* to enter edit mode. In the butBegin_Click subroutine type:

```
Dim x As New frmM2S
```

```
x.show()
me.Hide()
```

Run the program to make sure the change worked. Remember that by opening a new form before closing an old form prevents flicker. Close the program and go back to frmM2S. We now need to add PictureBoxes for the stimuli to appear in during run time. Specifically, we need one box for the sample stimulus and three boxes for the comparison stimuli. Add a PictureBox, change the name property to *picM2S0* and set the SizeMode property to StretchImage. Make the height and size property equal because the images that were designed in the Paint program were square.

Now make a control array by copying *picM2S0* and pasting it 3 times. You should now change the suffixes of the three added PictureBoxes to picM2S1, picM2S2, and picM2S3. Make *picM2S0* the sample stimulus by placing it at the top of the screen, and make the others sample stimuli by placing them below the sample stimulus. We now need to link up the four picM2S PictureBoxes together into an array. This process is identical to the procedure used in Chapter 2. Start by double-clicking on picM2S0 and enter the edit mode. At the end of the line Private Sub picM2S0_Click(ByVal sender As System.Object, ByVal e As System.EventArgs) Handles picM2SO.Click add the following additional code:

```
,picM2S1.Click, picM2S2.Click, picM2S3.Click
```

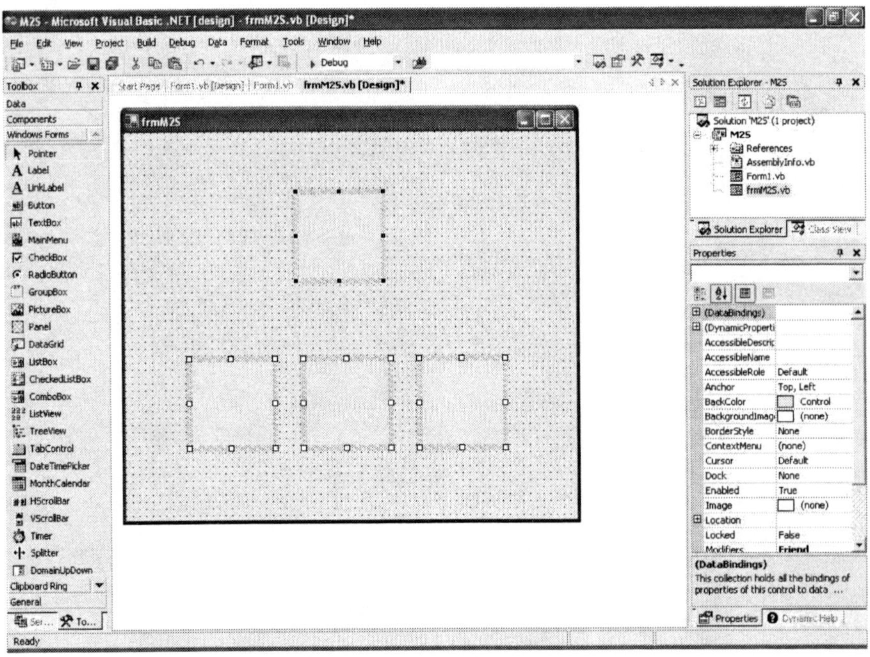

Figure 7.3 displays the screen layout with PictureBox arrays.

3. Training w/ Reinforcement

Recall that the type of reinforcement was not specified in the above outline. Reinforcement may take the form of points added to a counter, an audible noise, or a visual display of a smiley face. Let's use audio clips for reinforcement because the creation of a point counter was discussed in previous chapters. Let's have a relatively positive sounding audio clip for a correct response and a negative sounding audio clip for an incorrect response. The audio files should be brief so the participant does not have to wait for them to finish playing before making the next response.

For purposes of illustration, let's use "c:\windows\media\chimes.wav" for correct responses and "c:\windows\media\chord.wav" for incorrect responses. (Note: If your computer does not have these files in this specific directory you will need to use other files. For simplicity of following along with this chapter's example, you should create files with these names in this directory). Since the researcher may want to change the audio files later down the road or across sets of participants, let's add a few lines to our text file to say where the .wav files are located. Therefore, at the bottom of the M2S.txt file type:

```
CORRECT, "c:\windows\media\chimes.wav"
INCORRECT, "c:\windows\media\chord.wav"
```

Make sure that you capitalize the letters in your file names and directories where appropriate.

Let us next consider the following distribution of stimuli combination for A-B training where the first letter/number represents the sample stimulus and the three subsequent letter/number combinations represent the comparison stimuli: A1 - **B1**, B2, B3; A2 - B1, **B2**, B3; A3 - B1, B2, **B3.** As you can see, there are three basic combinations with the correct answers indicated in **bold**. Although the requirements from the above outline called for 18 trials, let's just start with three to make sure everything works. Therefore, add the following lines to your text file:

```
TRIAL1,A1,B1,B2,B3
TRIAL2,A2,B2,B1,B3
TRIAL3,A3,B3,B1,B2
END,,,,
```

The text file should now look like:

```
INSTRUCTIONS, This is where the instructions will go.
CORRECT, "c:\windows\media\chimes.wav"
INCORRECT, "c:\windows\media\chord.wav"
TRIAL1, A1,B1,B2,B3
TRIAL2, A2,B2,B1,B3
```

```
TRIAL3, A3,B3,B1,B2
END,,,,
```

Here the text TRIAL indicates a new trial. The number represents the trial number. The first stimulus represents the sample and will be loaded into picM2S0. The next stimulus represents the correct answer and will be loaded into picM2S1. And the other two stimuli will be loaded into picM2S2 and picM2S3 respectively. END,,,, signals the end of the trials (the four commas are used for place holders). Save the changes to M2S.txt, and go back to edit mode of frmM2S.

You will need to generate a number of string variables in order for VB.NET to recognize this input file information and convert it into code. Therefore, declare the following variables as String vHeader, vPos, vNeg and declare a variable array called vStimuli(0 to 3) as String by typing the following code under the Inherits System.Windows.Forms.Form:

```
Dim vHeader As String
Dim vPos As String
Dim vNeg As String
Dim vStimuli (3) As String
```

And above the line Public Class frmM2S, type the following:

```
Option Explicit On
```

Now go back to the form design mode of frmM2S and double-click on the form. Under the Private Sub frmM2S_Load subroutine, we need to read in the name of the reinforcement stimuli by adding the following lines of code:

```
Input(1, vHeader)
Input(1, vPos)
Input(1, vHeader)
Input(1, vNeg)
```

The code for the reinforcers is in place, but we still need to read in additional stimuli information. The vStimuli variable needs to hold four values and these values of vStimuli can correspond with the suffix values of the picM2S PictureBoxes for simplicity. Since we want all this information to load into the program immediately upon the form loading, and not wait for the participant to respond first, all this information must be inputted during the *form load*. To do so, just create a subroutine called *Load_Stimuli*. Do this by typing:

```
Sub Load_Stimuli()
```

A new subroutine will be created called *Load_Stimuli.* In this subroutine type:

```
Dim i
Input(1, vHeader)
Input(1, vStimuli(0))
Input(1, vStimuli(1))
Input(1, vStimuli(2))
Input(1, vStimuli(3))
For i = 0 To 3
picM2S0.Image = Image.FromFile("c:\programming\M2S\" &
   vStimuli(0) & ".bmp")
picM2S1.Image = Image.FromFile("c:\programming\M2S\" &
   vStimuli(1) & ".bmp")
picM2S2.Image = Image.FromFile("c:\programming\M2S\" &
   vStimuli(2) & ".bmp")
picM2S3.Image = Image.FromFile("c:\programming\M2S\" &
   vStimuli(3) & ".bmp")
Next i
```

The subroutine will read the stimuli values (A1, B1, etc.), append the file path to the beginning of the file name, and then add the file type (.bmp). The program then assigns the new values to the PictureBoxes using the For/Next statement. To have the program call on the subroutine, add the following code at the end of the Form_Load() Subroutine (before the *End Sub* of course):

```
Load_Stimuli
```

You may have noticed that as the program is currently designed, the correct response is always placed in the first position of the comparison row. This will be altered shortly. Also, note that in the case of our first trial, *B1* should be the correct response. However nothing happens when we click on *B1* just yet. We need to hook up the audio files. To do so add the Windows Media Player to frmM2S, set the Visible property to *False* and change the name to *wmp1*. Refer to Chapter 5 if you do not recall the specific steps for adding the Windows Media Player.

Double-click on one of the PictureBoxes to start a subroutine in edit mode. When the participant clicks on the PictureBox with the suffix value of 1 (the correct answer) we want the computer to play vPos. When the participant clicks in a PictureBox with the suffix value of 2 or 3, we want to play vNeg. We can accomplish this using an *If Then - Else* statement. Under the picM2S0_Click() subroutine type the following code:

```
Dim buttonClicked As PictureBox
buttonClicked = CType(sender, PictureBox)
```

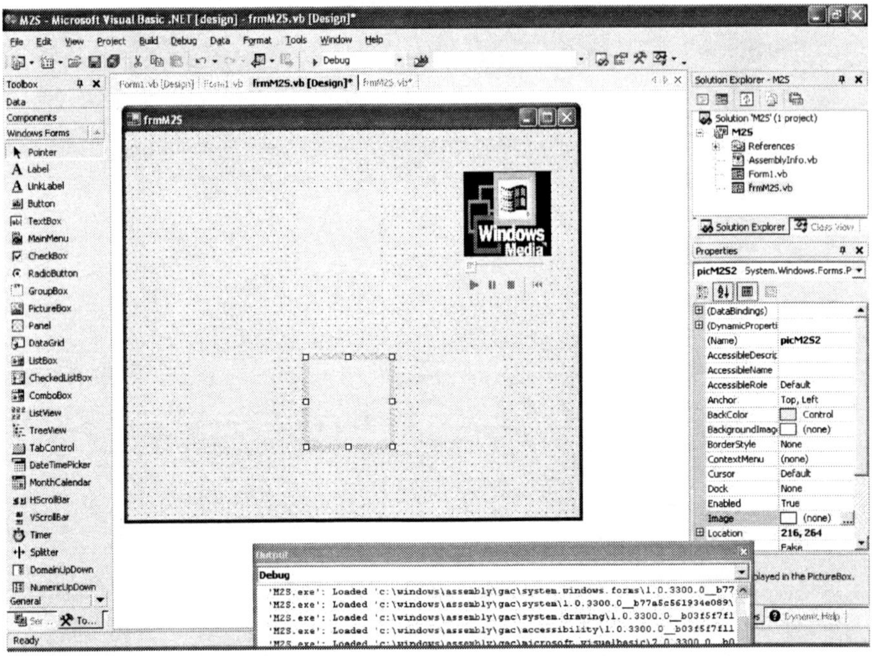

Figure 7.4 shows a screen configuration of the PictureBoxes and Windows Media Player.

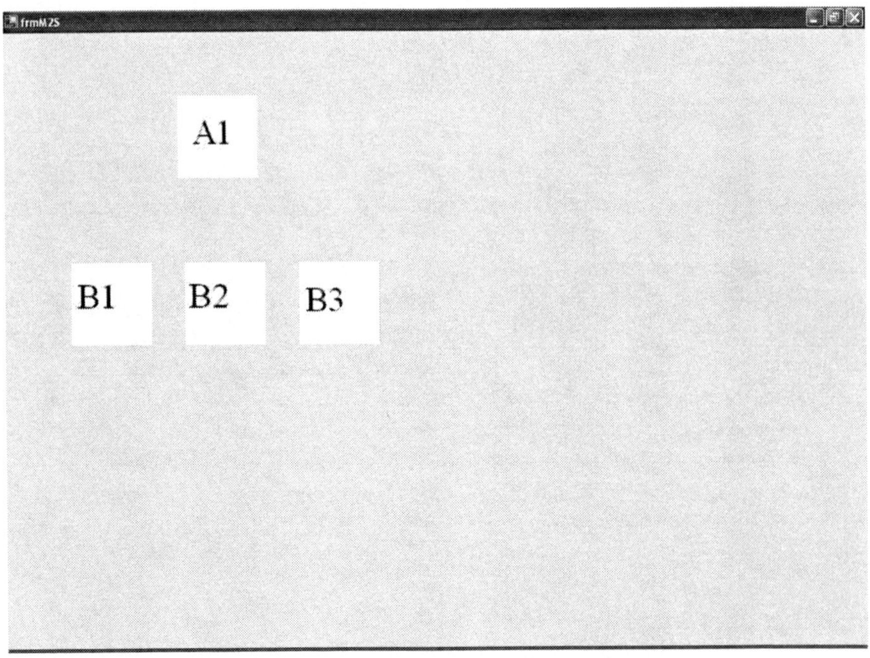

Figure 7.5 shows the PictureBoxes during runtime with stimuli loaded.

```
If buttonClicked.Name = picM2S1.Name() Then
wmp1.FileName = vPos
wmp1.Play()
Else
If buttonClicked.Name = picM2S2.Name() Or
   buttonClicked.Name = picM2S3.Name Then
wmp1.FileName = vNeg
wmp1.Play()
End If
End If
```

Here is how the code works. First this code keeps track of which Button was clicked using the buttonClicked variable and CType command. Once it stores the specific Button name (vM2S(0-3)) that was clicked, it checks to see which of the "If-Then-Else" conditions has been satisfied. If picM2S1 was clicked, it opens the Media Player and plays the positive .wav file we placed in the text file. If picM2S1 was not clicked, the code checks to see if either picM2S(2 or 3) was clicked. If so, the negative .wav file. If picM2S0 is clicked, nothing happens, which is good since, this is the sample stimulus.

Let's take this a step further. After we click on the comparison stimuli, we want the next trial to appear. To do this we just need to call on the Load_Stimuli() subroutine we created. Add the following line of code at to the end of both sections of the If-Then-Else code:

```
Load_Stimuli
```

The new subroutine should look like the following:

```
Dim buttonClicked As PictureBox
buttonClicked = CType(sender, PictureBox)
If buttonClicked.Name = picM2S1.Name() Then
wmp1.FileName = vPos
wmp1.Play()
Load_Stimuli()
Else
If buttonClicked.Name = picM2S2.Name() Or buttonClicked.Name
   = picM2S3.Name Then
wmp1.FileName = vNeg
wmp1.Play()
Load_Stimuli()
End If
End If
```

Run the program again. Notice that the stimuli changes after each response. We only have three lines of stimuli, thus the program ends abruptly because it has reached the end of the text file. This will be changed when we add more lines of stimuli configurations to the input file.

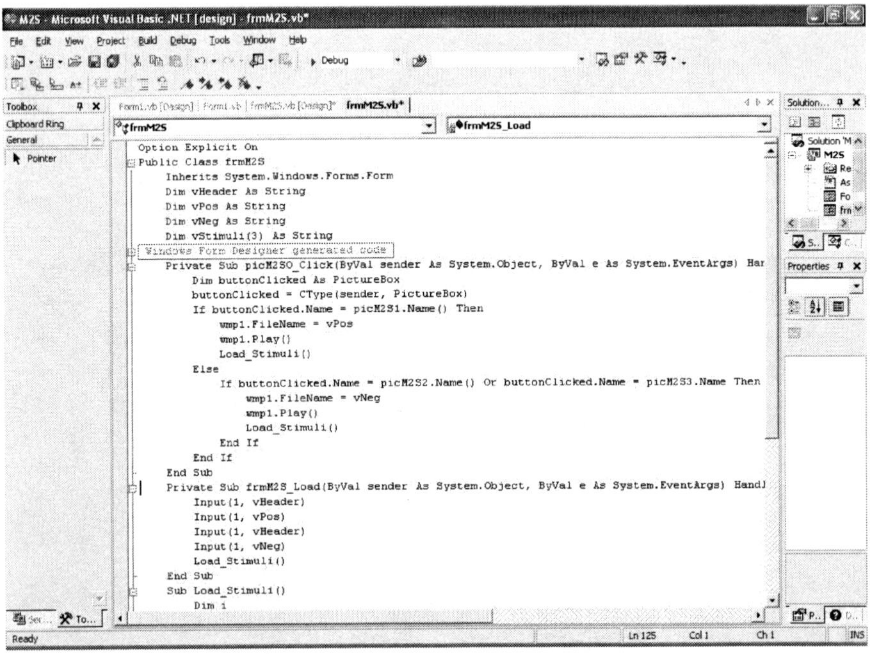

Figure 7.6 shows the code for loading the different trials into the M2S program.

We still haven't finished all of the requirements of #3 in the earlier outline, but we are making progress. The stimuli still need randomized placement across trials. This is rather easy because we know how to generate a random string of three numbers without replacement. So type the following anywhere in the text editor:

```
Sub Randomize_Stimuli_Position()
```

This will create a new subroutine called Randomize_Stimuli_Position. Under this new routine now type:

```
Randomize()
Dim r
r = Int(6 * Rnd() + 1)

Select Case r
```

```
Case 1
picM2S1.Image = Image.FromFile("c:\programming\M2S\" &
   vStimuli(1) & ".bmp")
picM2S2.Image = Image.FromFile("c:\programming\M2S\" &
   vStimuli(2) & ".bmp")
picM2S3.Image = Image.FromFile("c:\programming\M2S\" &
   vStimuli(3) & ".bmp")

Case 2
picM2S1.Image = Image.FromFile("c:\programming\M2S\" &
   vStimuli(3) & ".bmp")
picM2S2.Image = Image.FromFile("c:\programming\M2S\" &
   vStimuli(1) & ".bmp")
picM2S3.Image = Image.FromFile("c:\programming\M2S\" &
   vStimuli(2) & ".bmp")

Case 3
picM2S1.Image = Image.FromFile("c:\programming\M2S\" &
   vStimuli(2) & ".bmp")
picM2S2.Image = Image.FromFile("c:\programming\M2S\" &
   vStimuli(3) & ".bmp")
picM2S3.Image = Image.FromFile("c:\programming\M2S\" &
   vStimuli(1) & ".bmp")

Case 4
picM2S1.Image = Image.FromFile("c:\programming\M2S\" &
   vStimuli(1) & ".bmp")
picM2S2.Image = Image.FromFile("c:\programming\M2S\" &
   vStimuli(3) & ".bmp")
picM2S3.Image = Image.FromFile("c:\programming\M2S\" &
   vStimuli(2) & ".bmp")

Case 5
picM2S1.Image = Image.FromFile("c:\programming\M2S\" &
   vStimuli(3) & ".bmp")
picM2S2.Image = Image.FromFile("c:\programming\M2S\" &
   vStimuli(2) & ".bmp")
picM2S3.Image = Image.FromFile("c:\programming\M2S\" &
   vStimuli(1) & ".bmp")

Case 6
```

```
picM2S1.Image = Image.FromFile("c:\programming\M2S\" &
   vStimuli(2) & ".bmp")
picM2S2.Image = Image.FromFile("c:\programming\M2S\" &
   vStimuli(1) & ".bmp")
picM2S3.Image = Image.FromFile("c:\programming\M2S\" &
   vStimuli(3) & ".bmp")
End Select

picM2S0.Image.FromFile("c:\programming\M2S\" & vStimuli(0)
   & ".bmp")
```

There are three parts to this subroutine. First, we use the Randomize statement to generate a string of random numbers to be used in during running of the program. Second, we declare the variable r to use to hold the random number we generate on each trial. Third, we generate a random number between 1 and 6. The reason for the 1 to 6 range is because there are 6 possible combinations of comparison stimuli arrangements. They are B1, B2, B3; B1, B3, B2; B2, B3, B1; B2, B1, B3; B3, B1, B2; and B3, B2, B1. Using the random number placed into the variable "r", we can create a Select Case statement to distribute the stimuli into their respective PictureBoxes. Because vStimuli(0) is always the sample, and our sample stimulus in the data file will always be listed first, we can just have one line of code that always puts vStimuli(0) into picM2S0 and not repeat it throughout each Select Case.

To link this subroutine up to the program, add the following text at the end of the Private Sub frmM2S_Load() (i.e. below Load_Stimuli()):

```
Randomize_Stimuli_Position()
```

Also place this code below the Load_Stimuli()line found in the two different locations the Private Sub picM2SO_Click subroutine. Placing the code here allows for a new random number and stimuli positioning to occur each time a comparison stimulus is clicked upon.

Run the program and check your progress.

Fixing One Problem Often Creates a New One

You may have noticed that now that you solved the randomization problem, you created another problem. The Media Player now plays vPos every time you click on picM2S1 regardless if this is the correct response or not. This is not good and will need to be fixed.

To fix this problem we need to create a variable that can be used to track where vStimuli(1) is no matter where our random number generator places it. Once we know where vStimuli(1) is, we can check to see if it is sitting in the PictureBox that the participant just clicked on. Two things need to happen here. First, we need to place a value in this new tracking variable when the stimuli are loaded into the PictureBoxes. Second, we need to edit the Media Player code to play the vPos .wav file only if our tracking variable is a specific value. Let us start by creating a new variable called vTrack. Declare this variable under the Inherits System.Windows.Forms.Form section by typing:

```
Dim vTrack
```

Add the following line of code at the end of the Select Case 1 section of the Randomize_Stimuli_Position()subroutine:

```
vTrack = 1
```

This code will inform Visual Basic.NET that vStimuli(1) is sitting in the first comparison position (i.e. picM2S1). The new Select Case 1 section of code should look like:

```
Case 1
picM2S1.Image = Image.FromFile("c:\programming\M2S\" &
   vStimuli(1) & ".bmp")
picM2S2.Image = Image.FromFile("c:\programming\M2S\" &
   vStimuli(2) & ".bmp")
picM2S3.Image = Image.FromFile("c:\programming\M2S\" &
   vStimuli(3) & ".bmp")
vTrack = 1
```

Add the following line of code at the end of the Select Case 2 section of the Randomize_Stimuli_Position()subroutine:

```
vTrack = 2
```

Add the following line of code at the end of the Select Case 3 section of the Randomize_Stimuli_Position()subroutine:

```
vTrack = 3
```

Add the following line of code at the end of the Select Case 4 section of the Randomize_Stimuli_Position()subroutine:

```
vTrack = 1
```

Add the following line of code at the end of the Select Case 5 section of the Randomize_Stimuli_Position()subroutine:

```
vTrack = 3
```

Add the following line of code at the end of the Select Case 6 section of the Randomize_Stimuli_Position()subroutine:

```
vTrack = 2
```

The logic should be easy to follow by this time. Now the code to kick in the Media Player needs to be altered. Begin by editing the line of code which currently states:

```
If buttonClicked.Name = picM2S1.Name Then
```

to read

```
If buttonClicked.Name = picM2S1.Name And vTrack = 1 Or
   buttonClicked.Name = picM2S2.Name And vTrack = 2 Or
   buttonClicked.Name = picM2S3.Name And vTrack = 3 Then
```

This is all one long line of code but it is not as scary as it might seem. This code is nothing more than a giant If-Then statement that can be satisfied in three different ways. Because this statement takes care of playing the vPos .wav file if the conditions are satisfied, anything else should kick in the vNeg .wav file. Therefore, delete the line of code which currently states:

```
If buttonClicked.Name = picM2S2.Name Or buttonClicked.Name
   = picM2S3.Name Then
```

and the corresponding *End If.*

One last problem that has now arisen is that without this line of code, clicks on picM2S0 (the sample stimulus) can kick in the next trial. We do not want this to happen. Actually we never want anything to happen when a participant clicks on picM2S0. To remove anything ever occurring when picM2S0 is clicked, simply remove the section of code:

```
picM2S0.Click
```

from the first line of the Private Sub picM2S0_Subroutine. The edited first line of this subroutine should now read:

```
Private Sub picM2SO_Click(ByVal sender As System.Object,
ByVal e As System.EventArgs) Handles picM2S1.Click,
picM2S2.Click, picM2S3.Click
```

Run the program and check your progress. Everything should work fine up to this point. As a matter of fact, as the program stands, you have a working conditional discrimination computer program.

A "Debriefing" Form

Once you finish the three trials the program ends abruptly. This is because we are not taking advantage of the END,,,, command in the text file. Let's make it so that when the program reads the END,,,, command it shows a final form with some debriefing information. Add a new form, change the name property to frmIns2, change the text property to *Thank You*, and change the WindowState to maximized. Add the following text below the "Input(1, vStimuli(3))" line in the Load_Stimuli() subroutine on frmM2S:

```
If vHeader = "END" Then
Dim x As New frmIns2()
x.Show()
Me.Close()
Else
```

Add the following line after the "Next i" line in that same subroutine:

```
End If
```

and delete the automatically added *End If* that was inserted above *For i=0 to 3*. Also edit your M2S.txt file so the last line reads:

```
END, A1,A1,A1,A1
```

The entire Load_Stimuli () subroutine should look as follows:

```
Dim i
Input(1, vHeader)
Input(1, vStimuli(0))
Input(1, vStimuli(1))
Input(1, vStimuli(2))
Input(1, vStimuli(3))
If vHeader = "END" Then
Dim x As New frmIns2()
x.Show()
Me.Close()
Else
For i = 0 To 3
```

```
picM2S0.Image = Image.FromFile("c:\programming\M2S\" &
   vStimuli(0) & ".bmp")
picM2S1.Image = Image.FromFile("c:\programming\M2S\" &
   vStimuli(1) & ".bmp")
picM2S2.Image = Image.FromFile("c:\programming\M2S\" &
   vStimuli(2) & ".bmp")
picM2S3.Image = Image.FromFile("c:\programming\M2S\" &
   vStimuli(3) & ".bmp")
Next i
End If
```

The commas served us well earlier, but now we need to put actual stimuli in these place holders to avoid getting an error when we run the program. This is just another little picky aspect of Visual Basic.NET. While the A1 stimuli are never actually seen by the participant (or you while you test the program), they need to be "virtually" placed into the Load_Stimuli () subroutine before frmM2S can shut itself down (i.e. Hide). You can try running the program without the four A1s just for fun to see the error that would occur.

So far we have developed the program to read instructions and present them to the participant. Open .wav files and play them differentially for correct or incorrect responses. Read in stimuli trials and randomize placement of the comparison stimuli, and display an instruction screen when the trials have been complete.

Requirement #3 specifies that each sample is presented 6 times, a total of 18 trials. As with most of the programming decisions, there are several ways to accomplish this requirement. For now let's just enter all 18 trials by cutting the three existing trials in M2S.txt and pasting them back in 5 times. Obviously you could make different arrangements of trial sequences, but just stick to this cut and paste method now for illustrative purposes. Change the number in the TRIAL header to increment up to 18. Save the changes to the text file. Your text file should now look like this:

```
INSTRUCTIONS, This is where the instructions will go.
CORRECT, "c:\windows\media\chimes.wav"
INCORRECT, "c:\windows\media\chord.wav"
TRIAL1, A1,B1,B2,B3
TRIAL2, A2,B2,B1,B3
TRIAL3, A3,B3,B1,B2
TRIAL4, A1,B1,B2,B3
TRIAL5, A2,B2,B1,B3
TRIAL6, A3,B3,B1,B2
TRIAL7, A1,B1,B2,B3
TRIAL8, A2,B2,B1,B3
TRIAL9, A3,B3,B1,B2
```

```
TRIAL10, A1,B1,B2,B3
TRIAL11, A2,B2,B1,B3
TRIAL12, A3,B3,B1,B2
TRIAL13, A1,B1,B2,B3
TRIAL14, A2,B2,B1,B3
TRIAL15, A3,B3,B1,B2
TRIAL16, A1,B1,B2,B3
TRIAL17, A2,B2,B1,B3
TRIAL18, A3,B3,B1,B2
END, A1,A1,A1,A1
```

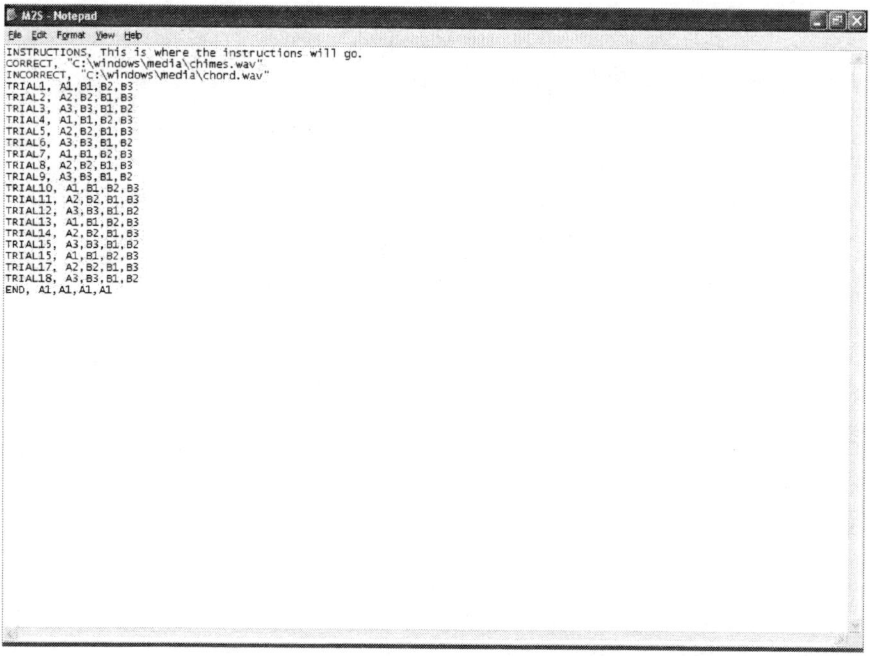

Figure 7.7 displays the Notepad document with all 18 trials.

Try running the program and see if it goes through all 18 trials. As you may have guessed, you could enter as many trials as you wanted. The program will continue to display the stimuli until it reaches the END,,,, command.

Keep in mind that we wanted to randomize the presentation of the trials each time the program runs. Right now the trials are being presented in the order that we wrote them in the input file. While randomization may be important here, other times when you may be assessing behavior across a sequence of specific contingency arrangements the existing code would do fine. Randomization of these trials can be a bit tricky, but we know how to make a random string of number between 1 and

18. We also know about variable arrays and how they can hold multiple amounts of information.

Basically we need to create something programmers often call a "lookup table" for our stimuli trials. For example, once we generate a random string of numbers from 1 to 18 (that correspond to our trial types), we can look at the first number and then display the stimuli in that particular row. So if the first number was 7, then we would display the stimuli listed in TRIAL7 of our data input file. If the random number generated was 11, we would display the stimuli listed in TRIAL 11, and so on.

What would be useful here is something called a two dimensional array. VB.NET has the capability to use multidimensional arrays, but they are difficult keep track of, therefore we recommend using a two dimensional array and only when needed. The two dimensional array can be read like a spreadsheet that has rows listed from 0 to 17 and columns listed from 0 to 3.

We will also need to modify our code by declaring a two dimensional array to hold the trial information. Then we need to have VB.NET read in the information from the text file stopping at the END,,,, command. Also, we need to create a random string of numbers from 1 to 18 including a one dimensional array to hold these values. Lastly we will need a third variable to keep track of the trial we are on. Once all 18 trials have been displayed, the program needs to end or goes on to the next task.

Before we begin changing all this code in our M2S project, let's write a pilot program to see how this works. Creating small little side programs like this are helpful because they allow you to test new routines as well as not disrupt the existing and so far correctly working main program. When creating larger scale programs, the last thing you want to do is find out that the past five hours of programming does not work correctly, and you can not remember how to get back to the point that did work five hours ago.

Save your current project and open a new one called *Pilot*. Rename the form to *frmPilot* and change the location of the files to C:\programming. Change the Text property to *Pilot*, and change the WindowState to Maximized. Add a Label to frmPilot. Change the name property to *lblPilot*, and the BorderStyle to *FixedSingle*. Copy and paste lblPilot to create the array. We need an array of 4, so paste the Label 3 times. Double-click on the first of your Labels, enter the Edit mode and add `Label1.Click, Label2.click, Label3.click` after `Handles lblPilot.click` as detailed earlier in this chapter for picM2S0-3. We will also need a Button to advance the trials. Add a Button to frmPilot, change the name property to *butNext*, and the Text property to *Next*. That should do it. Code is also needed to open the file and advance the trials. Then we need to read the trial information into a two dimensional array, and create a random string of numbers. This all has to happen before the form appears, so it needs be located in the Form_Load() subroutine.

But before we get there, let's declare the necessary variables. As mentioned earlier, a two dimensional array is needed to hold the trial information, Dim vTrials((18), (3)). Also a one dimensional array is needed to hold the random number string: Dim vRandNumber(18) As Integer, and we will need a variable to keep track of the actual trial number: Dim vCounter As Integer. Place all of this under the Inherits System.Windows.Forms.form statement by typing the following code:

```
Dim vTrials((18), (3))
Dim vRandNumber(18) As Integer
Dim vCounter As Integer
```

Now under the Form_Load() subroutine you will need to declare a couple of variables we will be using and add some code to open the text file. Go back to the frmPilot design window, double-click on the form, enter the edit mode and type the following after Private Sub frmPilot_Load()

```
Dim i, r, x, y
FileOpen(1, "C:\programming\M2S\M2S.txt", OpenMode.Input)
```

There are three rows of information we are not currently interested in, specifically that code pertaining to the instructions and the two .wav files. We can advance past these by entering the following code under the last line you typed:

```
For i = 1 To 3
Input (1, x)
Input (1, y)
Next i
```

Also, go back and edit your M2S.txt file so that the INSTRUCTIONS line only has 1 word ("This") after the word INSTRUCTIONS. You can change back your instructions to "This is where the instructions will go." later after finishing this little side Pilot project.

We now need to read in the next 18 lines containing trial information. We don't want to read in the header, so we will use the *x* variable as a place holder.

```
For i = 1 To 18
Input(1, x)
Input(1, vTrials(i, 0))
Input(1, vTrials(i, 1))
Input(1, vTrials(i, 2))
Input(1, vTrials(i, 3))
Next i
```

Finally, we need to generate our random numbers using the following code:

```
Randomize()
For i = 1 To 18
r = Int(18 * Rnd() + 1)
If vRandNumber(r) < 1 Then
vRandNumber(r) = i
Else
i = i - 1
End If
Next i
```

You may recall that this is the same type of randomization routine we explained in an earlier section of the book. The completed Form_Load() subroutine should look like this:

```
Dim i, r, x, y
FileOpen(1, "C:\programming\M2S\M2S.txt", OpenMode.Input)
For i = 1 To 3
Input(1, x)
Input(1, y)
Next i
For i = 1 To 18
Input(1, x)
Input(1, vTrials(i, 0))
Input(1, vTrials(i, 1))
Input(1, vTrials(i, 2))
Input(1, vTrials(i, 3))
Next i
Randomize()
For i = 1 To 18
r = Int(18 * Rnd() + 1)
If vRandNumber(r) < 1 Then
vRandNumber(r) = i
Else
i = i - 1
End If
Next i
```

Both arrays should now be loaded. Run the program and see if you have any errors. Nothing will happen if you click on the *Next* Button because we have yet to add some code. But the absence of errors means you have typed in the above code properly.

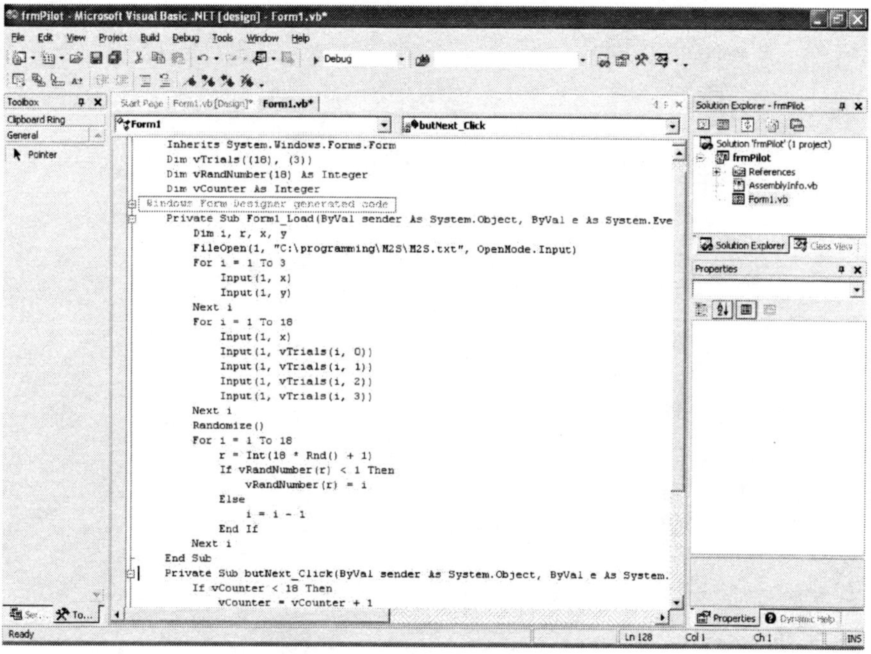

Figure 7.8 shows the code for frmPilot.

Stop the program and double-click on butNext to enter edit mode at the butNext_Click() subroutine. When we click on butNext, we can use an IF statement to ensure we don't advance past the 18th trial, as well as keep track of the trial number. We can also watch the trials advance using me.Text = vCounter. Add the following four lines of code under *butNext* to load the trial information in the Labels:

```
If vCounter < 18 Then
vCounter = vCounter + 1
me.Text = vCounter
lblPilot.Text = vTrials(vCounter, 0)
Label1.Text = vTrials(vCounter, 1)
Label2.Text = vTrials(vCounter, 2)
Label3.Text = vTrials(vCounter, 3)
End If
```

Run the program and see if it works. Notice that the trials are not yet randomized. To do this we need to make a small modification to the Label objects' vTrials(vCounter, 0) code. Specifically it needs to include our random number. Therefore, change the code to look like this:

```
If vCounter < 18 Then
```

```
vCounter = vCounter + 1
Me.Text = vCounter
lblPilot.Text = vTrials(vRandNumber(vCounter), 0)
Label1.Text = vTrials(vRandNumber(vCounter), 1)
Label2.Text = vTrials(vRandNumber(vCounter), 2)
Label3.Text = vTrials(vRandNumber(vCounter), 3)
End If
```

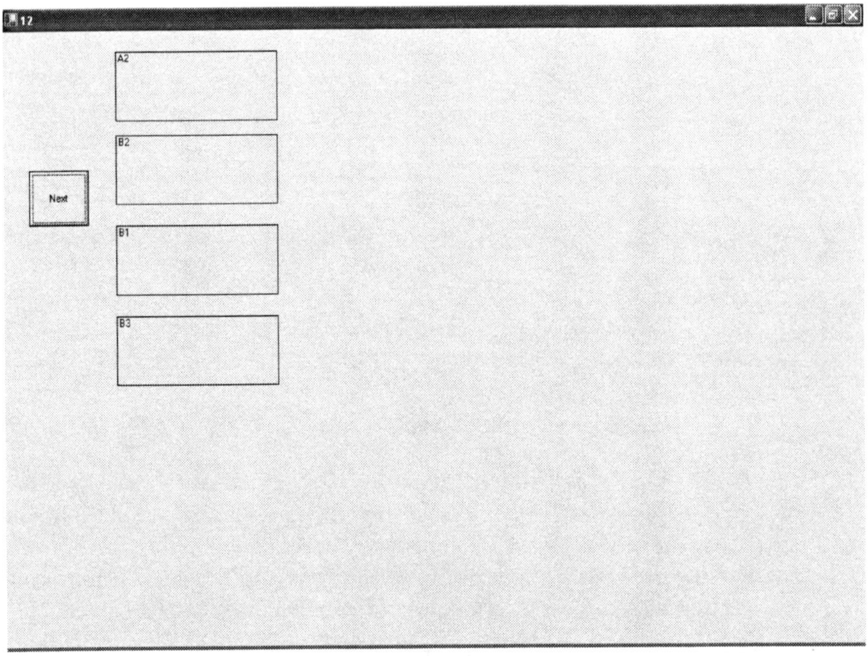

Figure 7.9 displays the Pilot program during runtime.

The trials should now be randomized because we are using the array with the random numbers to indicate which trial stimuli to use. It should work fine.

Now let's transplant the code back into the M2S project. Save the Pilot project and open the M2S project. Locate your mouse cursor in the Solution Explorer on the upper right of the screen, highlight M2S, and right-click to display the pop-up menu. Select *Add*, then *Add Existing Item.* Now select frmPilot from the M2S directory. Note: Your frmPilot may still say *Form1*, depending on how you saved it initially. If it does still say *Form1* (you can check when the Pilot project is still open by looking in the Solution Explorer) you must first, reclose the M2S project, go back, open Pilot project and save frmPilot correctly. This will add the form to your project so you can copy and paste code as needed. We need to copy the code under the Form_Load() subroutine from frmPilot to frmM2S. The Form_Load() code in frmM2S is getting rather busy. We can make a subroutine with the code from frmPilot and then simply run the subroutine from the Form_Load() subroutine of M2S.

To start a subroutine, double-click on frmM2S to enter edit mode, move the mouse to the last line of the editor (before *End Class*), and type:

```
Sub Load_Random_Trials
```

Press the return key if you have not already done so. VB.NET will make the subroutine for you. Copy and paste the code written in frmPilot under the Form_Load() subroutine into the Load_Random_Trials() subroutine. Now type the followingbelow the Load_Stimuli code in frmM2S_Load() subroutine:

```
Load_Random_Trials
```

Remember that there was a For/Next statement in frmPilot to advance past the first three lines in the text file. This is no longer needed in the frmM2S project, so remark out the following four lines using the ':

```
'FileOpen(1, "C:\programming\M2S\M2S.txt", OpenMode.Input)
'For i = 1 To 3
'Input(1, x)
'Input(1, y)
'Next i
```

Now copy and paste all the code from under frmPilot's butNext to a new sub routine on frmM2S. Create this new subroutine by typing the following on the last line of the editor (before *End Class*):

```
Sub Show_Rand_Stim
```

Now place the code here. First, copy the code from frmPilot under butNext to this new subroutine. Next, move the vCounter = vCounter + 1 statement from the middle of the subroutine to the beginning of the subroutine. The subroutine should look like this:

```
Sub Show_Rand_Stim()
vCounter = vCounter + 1
If vCounter < 18 Then
Me.Text = vCounter
lblPilot.Text = vTrials(vRandNumber(vCounter), 0)
Label1.Text = vTrials(vRandNumber(vCounter), 1)
Label2.Text = vTrials(vRandNumber(vCounter), 2)
```

```
Label3.Text = vTrials(vRandNumber(vCounter), 3)
End If
End Sub
```

Next the program will need to read the trial information into the PictureBoxes and not the labels used when we built the little side program on frmPilot. Plus we will need to declare the variable vTrials that we used on frmPilot now on our frmM2S. First, copy the variables declared under Inherits System.Windows.Forms.Form in frmPilot to Inherits System.Windows.Forms.Form in frmM2S. Since the two dimensional array (vTrials(18),(3)) will be replacing the one dimensional array (vStimuli(3)), remark out the Dim vStimuli(3) by placing an apostrophe before the line of code. Your new variable declarations on your frmM2S should now look like this:

```
Dim vTrack
Dim vHeader As String
Dim vPos As String
Dim vNeg As String
'Dim vStimuli(3) As String
Dim vTrials((18),(3))
Dim vRandNumber(18) As Integer
Dim vCounter As Integer
```

Second, edit your Label code so that the data can be read into the PictureBoxes instead. As your code currently stands, you have a Select Case that is being used to generate random numbers for the random placement of comparison stimuli in picM2S1-3, as well as the two dimensional array that holds and displays random trials. You will be able to control for order and positioning effects of the comparison stimuli by merging these two components together: the random trial presentations coupled with random positioning of the comparison stimuli. To accomplish this feat we need to change the stimuli presentation code under the Select Case. What we can use here is the code from frmPilot's butNext Button that now resides in a subroutine called Show_Rand_Stim. Let's combine the two by changing the code under your Select Case statements to read the like the following:

```
Case 1
picM2S0.Image = Image.FromFile("c:\programming\M2S\" &
   vTrials(vRandNumber(vCounter), 0) & ".bmp")
picM2S1.Image = Image.FromFile("c:\programming\M2S\" &
   vTrials(vRandNumber(vCounter), 1) & ".bmp")
picM2S2.Image = Image.FromFile("c:\programming\M2S\" &
   vTrials(vRandNumber(vCounter), 2) & ".bmp")
```

```
picM2S3.Image = Image.FromFile("c:\programming\M2S\" &
   vTrials(vRandNumber(vCounter), 3) & ".bmp")
vTrack = 1
```

You should be able to see what we did here was replace the previous picM2S0-3 = code that specified a specific stimulus from our recently deceased "vStimuli" variable and replaced it with code that now specifies a stimulus that is selected using our vRandNumber, vTrials, and vCounter variables we created on frmPilot. Edit the remaining 5 Cases of this subroutine so that the entire subroutine looks as follows:

```
Sub Randomize_Stimuli_Position()
Randomize()
Dim r
r = Int(6 * Rnd() + 1)

Select Case r
Case 1
picM2S0.Image = Image.FromFile("c:\programming\M2S\" &
   vTrials(vRandNumber(vCounter), 0) & ".bmp")
picM2S1.Image = Image.FromFile("c:\programming\M2S\" &
   vTrials(vRandNumber(vCounter), 1) & ".bmp")
picM2S2.Image = Image.FromFile("c:\programming\M2S\" &
   vTrials(vRandNumber(vCounter), 2) & ".bmp")
picM2S3.Image = Image.FromFile("c:\programming\M2S\" &
   vTrials(vRandNumber(vCounter), 3) & ".bmp")
vTrack = 1
Case 2
picM2S0.Image = Image.FromFile("c:\programming\M2S\" &
   vTrials(vRandNumber(vCounter), 0) & ".bmp")
picM2S1.Image = Image.FromFile("c:\programming\M2S\" &
   vTrials(vRandNumber(vCounter), 2) & ".bmp")
picM2S2.Image = Image.FromFile("c:\programming\M2S\" &
   vTrials(vRandNumber(vCounter), 1) & ".bmp")
picM2S3.Image = Image.FromFile("c:\programming\M2S\" &
   vTrials(vRandNumber(vCounter), 3) & ".bmp")
vTrack = 2
Case 3
picM2S0.Image = Image.FromFile("c:\programming\M2S\" &
   vTrials(vRandNumber(vCounter), 0) & ".bmp")
picM2S1.Image = Image.FromFile("c:\programming\M2S\" &
   vTrials(vRandNumber(vCounter), 3) & ".bmp")
```

```
picM2S2.Image = Image.FromFile("c:\programming\M2S\" &
   vTrials(vRandNumber(vCounter), 2) & ".bmp")
picM2S3.Image = Image.FromFile("c:\programming\M2S\" &
   vTrials(vRandNumber(vCounter), 1) & ".bmp")
vTrack = 3
Case 4
picM2S0.Image = Image.FromFile("c:\programming\M2S\" &
   vTrials(vRandNumber(vCounter), 0) & ".bmp")
picM2S1.Image = Image.FromFile("c:\programming\M2S\" &
   vTrials(vRandNumber(vCounter), 1) & ".bmp")
picM2S2.Image = Image.FromFile("c:\programming\M2S\" &
   vTrials(vRandNumber(vCounter), 3) & ".bmp")
picM2S3.Image = Image.FromFile("c:\programming\M2S\" &
   vTrials(vRandNumber(vCounter), 2) & ".bmp")
vTrack = 1
Case 5
picM2S0.Image = Image.FromFile("c:\programming\M2S\" &
   vTrials(vRandNumber(vCounter), 0) & ".bmp")
picM2S1.Image = Image.FromFile("c:\programming\M2S\" &
   vTrials(vRandNumber(vCounter), 2) & ".bmp")
picM2S2.Image = Image.FromFile("c:\programming\M2S\" &
   vTrials(vRandNumber(vCounter), 3) & ".bmp")
picM2S3.Image = Image.FromFile("c:\programming\M2S\" &
   vTrials(vRandNumber(vCounter), 1) & ".bmp")
vTrack = 3
Case 6
picM2S0.Image = Image.FromFile("c:\programming\M2S\" &
   vTrials(vRandNumber(vCounter), 0) & ".bmp")
picM2S1.Image = Image.FromFile("c:\programming\M2S\" &
   vTrials(vRandNumber(vCounter), 3) & ".bmp")
picM2S2.Image = Image.FromFile("c:\programming\M2S\" &
   vTrials(vRandNumber(vCounter), 1) & ".bmp")
picM2S3.Image = Image.FromFile("c:\programming\M2S\" &
   vTrials(vRandNumber(vCounter), 2) & ".bmp")
vTrack = 2
End Select
'picM2S0.Image.FromFile("c:\programming\M2S\" & vStimuli(0)
& ".bmp")
```

Now that we have capitalized on the code image location code used in Show_Rand_Stim, we can delete the following four lines and the If-Then statement:

```
lblPilot.Text = vTrials(vRandNumber(vCounter), 0)
Label1.Text = vTrials(vRandNumber(vCounter), 1)
Label2.Text = vTrials(vRandNumber(vCounter), 2)
Label3.Text = vTrials(vRandNumber(vCounter), 3)
```

We will no longer need the line of code used to display the trial count in the Text of frmPilot: me.Text=vCounter so delete that too. All that should now remain in Show_Rand_Stim is: vCounter=vCounter + 1. Because we want to activate the Show_Rand_Stim subroutine when the form loads and when the participant clicks on the PictureBox, add that line of code in both subroutines. In other words, add the following code BOTH in the Private Sub frmM2S_Load( ) and two places in Private Sub picM2S0_Click subroutine. Make sure you position this code between the Load_Stimuli() and the Randomize_Stimuli_Presentation() code in each location:

```
Show_Rand_Stim
```

Again, make sure the above code is positioned above Randomize_Stimuli_Presentation() and below the Load_Stimuli() lines.

Because we reconfigured the code to generate the presentation of stimuli in random order, you do not need the form to use the Load_Stimuli subroutine anymore. That subroutine would only load trials in the order they were written in the file. Therefore, delete that entire subroutine along with the Load_Stimuli code written under Private Sub frmM2S_Load( ) and Private Sub picM2S0_Click(). You could simply just remark out the above code too and get the same result.

One last revision needs to be made before we run the program and check to see if this big change actually will work. Now that the correct comparison stimulus is randomized, it does not always wind up being presented in picM2S1. Our code for playing our "reinforcing" .wav file assumes that it does. Therefore change the two lines of code which checks to see which picM2S Button has been clicked along with which vTrack value was generated by our Select Case to:

```
If buttonClicked.Name = picM2S1.Name() And vTrack = 1 Or
   buttonClicked.Name = picM2S2.Name() And vTrack = 2
   Or buttonClicked.Name = picM2S3.Name And vTrack = 3
   Then
And
Else
If buttonClicked.Name = picM2S2.Name() Or buttonClicked.Name
   = picM2S1.Name() Or buttonClicked.Name = picM2S3.Name
   Then
```

Run the program. That should take care of requirement #3 (Finally!). The resulting code of your frmM2S form should read as follows:

```
Option Explicit On
Public Class frmM2S
Inherits System.Windows.Forms.Form
Dim vTrack
Dim vHeader As String
Dim vPos As String
Dim vNeg As String
'Dim vStimuli(3) As String
Dim vTrials((18), (3))
Dim vRandNumber(18) As Integer
Dim vCounter As Integer

Private Sub picM2SO_Click(ByVal sender As System.Object,
   ByVal e As System.EventArgs) Handles picM2S1.Click,
   picM2S2.Click, picM2S3.Click
Dim buttonClicked As PictureBox
buttonClicked = CType(sender, PictureBox)
If buttonClicked.Name = picM2S1.Name() And vTrack = 1 Or
   buttonClicked.Name = picM2S2.Name() And vTrack = 2 Or
   buttonClicked.Name = picM2S3.Name And vTrack = 3 Then
wmp1.FileName = vPos
wmp1.Play()
'Load_Stimuli()
Show_Rand_Stim()
Randomize_Stimuli_Position()
Else
If buttonClicked.Name = picM2S2.Name() Or buttonClicked.Name
   = picM2S1.Name() Or buttonClicked.Name = picM2S3.Name
   Then
wmp1.FileName = vNeg
wmp1.Play()
'Load_Stimuli()
Show_Rand_Stim()
Randomize_Stimuli_Position()
End If
End If
End Sub

Private Sub frmM2S_Load(ByVal sender As System.Object,
   ByVal e As System.EventArgs) Handles MyBase.Load
Input(1, vHeader)
Input(1, vPos)
```

```
Input(1, vHeader)
Input(1, vNeg)
'Load_Stimuli()
Load_Random_Trials()
Show_Rand_Stim()
Randomize_Stimuli_Position()
End Sub

Sub Randomize_Stimuli_Position()
Randomize()
Dim r
r = Int(6 * Rnd() + 1)

Select Case r
Case 1
picM2S0.Image = Image.FromFile("c:\programming\M2S\" &
   vTrials(vRandNumber(vCounter), 0) & ".bmp")
picM2S1.Image = Image.FromFile("c:\programming\M2S\" &
   vTrials(vRandNumber(vCounter), 1) & ".bmp")
picM2S2.Image = Image.FromFile("c:\programming\M2S\" &
   vTrials(vRandNumber(vCounter), 2) & ".bmp")
picM2S3.Image = Image.FromFile("c:\programming\M2S\" &
   vTrials(vRandNumber(vCounter), 3) & ".bmp")
vTrack = 1
Case 2
picM2S0.Image = Image.FromFile("c:\programming\M2S\" &
   vTrials(vRandNumber(vCounter), 0) & ".bmp")
picM2S1.Image = Image.FromFile("c:\programming\M2S\" &
   vTrials(vRandNumber(vCounter), 2) & ".bmp")
picM2S2.Image = Image.FromFile("c:\programming\M2S\" &
   vTrials(vRandNumber(vCounter), 1) & ".bmp")
picM2S3.Image = Image.FromFile("c:\programming\M2S\" &
   vTrials(vRandNumber(vCounter), 3) & ".bmp")
vTrack = 2
Case 3
picM2S0.Image = Image.FromFile("c:\programming\M2S\" &
   vTrials(vRandNumber(vCounter), 0) & ".bmp")
picM2S1.Image = Image.FromFile("c:\programming\M2S\" &
   vTrials(vRandNumber(vCounter), 3) & ".bmp")
picM2S2.Image = Image.FromFile("c:\programming\M2S\" &
   vTrials(vRandNumber(vCounter), 2) & ".bmp")
picM2S3.Image = Image.FromFile("c:\programming\M2S\" &
   vTrials(vRandNumber(vCounter), 1) & ".bmp")
```

```
vTrack = 3
Case 4
picM2S0.Image = Image.FromFile("c:\programming\M2S\" &
   vTrials(vRandNumber(vCounter), 0) & ".bmp")
picM2S1.Image = Image.FromFile("c:\programming\M2S\" &
   vTrials(vRandNumber(vCounter), 1) & ".bmp")
picM2S2.Image = Image.FromFile("c:\programming\M2S\" &
   vTrials(vRandNumber(vCounter), 3) & ".bmp")
picM2S3.Image = Image.FromFile("c:\programming\M2S\" &
   vTrials(vRandNumber(vCounter), 2) & ".bmp")
vTrack = 1
Case 5
picM2S0.Image = Image.FromFile("c:\programming\M2S\" &
   vTrials(vRandNumber(vCounter), 0) & ".bmp")
picM2S1.Image = Image.FromFile("c:\programming\M2S\" &
   vTrials(vRandNumber(vCounter), 2) & ".bmp")
picM2S2.Image = Image.FromFile("c:\programming\M2S\" &
   vTrials(vRandNumber(vCounter), 3) & ".bmp")
picM2S3.Image = Image.FromFile("c:\programming\M2S\" &
   vTrials(vRandNumber(vCounter), 1) & ".bmp")
vTrack = 3
Case 6
picM2S0.Image = Image.FromFile("c:\programming\M2S\" &
   vTrials(vRandNumber(vCounter), 0) & ".bmp")
picM2S1.Image = Image.FromFile("c:\programming\M2S\" &
   vTrials(vRandNumber(vCounter), 3) & ".bmp")
picM2S2.Image = Image.FromFile("c:\programming\M2S\" &
   vTrials(vRandNumber(vCounter), 1) & ".bmp")
picM2S3.Image = Image.FromFile("c:\programming\M2S\" &
   vTrials(vRandNumber(vCounter), 2) & ".bmp")
vTrack = 2
End Select
'picM2S0.Image.FromFile("c:\programming\M2S\" & vStimuli(0)
   & ".bmp")
End Sub

Sub Load_Random_Trials()
Dim i, r, x, y
'FileOpen(1, "C:\programming\M2S\M2S.txt", OpenMode.Input)
'For i = 1 To 3
'Input(1, x)
'Input(1, y)
'Next i
```

```
For i = 1 To 18
Input(1, x)
Input(1, vTrials(i, 0))
Input(1, vTrials(i, 1))
Input(1, vTrials(i, 2))
Input(1, vTrials(i, 3))
Next i
Randomize()
For i = 1 To 18
r = Int(18 * Rnd() + 1)
If vRandNumber(r) < 1 Then
vRandNumber(r) = i
Else
i = i - 1
End If
Next i
End Sub

Sub Show_Rand_Stim()
vCounter = vCounter + 1
End Sub
```

All should run just fine, except for when you finish trial 18. We deleted our code that closes frmM2S and shows frmIns2. Add the following code at the beginning of the Randomize_Stimuli_Position() subroutine (above the Select Case) to correct the problem:

```
If vCounter > 18 Then
Dim x As New frmIns2()
Me.Hide()
x.Show()
Else
```

Delete the automatically added *End If* that was inserted after *Else* and add the line:

```
End If
```

at the bottom of the subroutine (after "End Select" and before "End Sub").

4. Mastery Criterion

You may recall that requirement 4 of the outline stated that a criterion must be met by the participant before the program should advance to the next phase (A-C training). Specifically 16 out of 18 trials of A-B training must be correct. We can add a great degree of flexibility to the program if we allow a line in the text file to enable the user to change this criterion across participants or experiments. Open your M2S.txt file using Notepad or another text editor and just before the line beginning TRIAL1, and just below the INCORRECT, insert a new line and add:

```
CRITERION, 16
```

Also, retype your instructions in the first line.

Save the changes and close the text file. Declare a new variable to store the criterion value: something like vCriterion As Integer, as well as add code to read in the criterion just below the second input statement under the Form_Load() subroutine. Therefore, in the declarations of your frmM2S, add:

```
Dim vCriterion As Integer
```

And under the Sub Form Load() after the line Input(1, vNeg) add the following:

```
Input (1, vHeader)
Input (1, vCriterion)
```

Now that the criterion is stored in the computer, the computer needs a way to check and see if the criterion is met. For this we will have to create another variable that holds the number of correct responses made for each trial. Let's name it *vCorrect*. At the end of the trial, the program compares the value in vCriterion with vCorrect. And if vCriterion is greater than vCorrect (If vCriterion>vCorrect then) then it will go on to the next phase, otherwise it will repeat the phase.

Therefore add to the general declaration the following code:

```
Dim vCorrect As Integer
```

We will have to add a line of code within the existing subroutine that plays the positive .wav file so it also makes increments of vCorrect increase by 1. We can also monitor the number of correct responses during programming by writing the value of vCorrect to the Text of frmM2S. Therefore add the following code under the wp1.Filename=vPos, wp1.Play() portion and above the Show_Rand_Stim() portion of Private Sub picM2S0_Click:

```
vCorrect = vCorrect + 1
me.Text = vCorrect
```

Now we need to add code into the Randomize_Stimuli_Position subroutine to either repeat the previous phase or advance to the next one.
Edit the first section of the subroutine so that it appears like:

```
If vCounter > 18 Then
If vCriterion < vCorrect Then 'ADDED NOW
Dim x As New frmIns2()
Me.Hide()
x.Show()
Else 'ADDED NOW
Start_Over_Again()'ADDED NOW
End If 'ADDED NOW
Else
Randomize()
```

The modifications are placed in the subroutine that is already checking to see if the phase is over (*If vCounter > 18 Then*). Thus if the condition is met (i.e. vCounter is greater than 18) the program checks to see if the performance criterion has been met using a "Nested IF/ELSE statement." If the criterion is less than the number of correct responses then the computer proceeds. In this case it displays frmIns2 which thanks the participant. However, if the criterion is NOT met, the participant has to start the phase over again.

Starting over again is not too difficult. We already have several subroutines in place that we can recycle. We will just have to reinitialize (set back to zero) some of our variables. Let's begin by writing a new subroutine called Start_Over_Again. So, type, Sub Start_Over_Again() on the last line in the editor before *End Class*. Then type the following code within that subroutine:

```
Dim i, r
For i = 1 To 18
vRandNumber(i) = 0
Next i
vCounter = 0
vCorrect = 0
For i = 1 To 18
r = Int(18 * Rnd + 1)
If vRandNumber(r) < 1 Then
vRandNumber(r) = i
Else
i = i - 1
End If
Next i
```

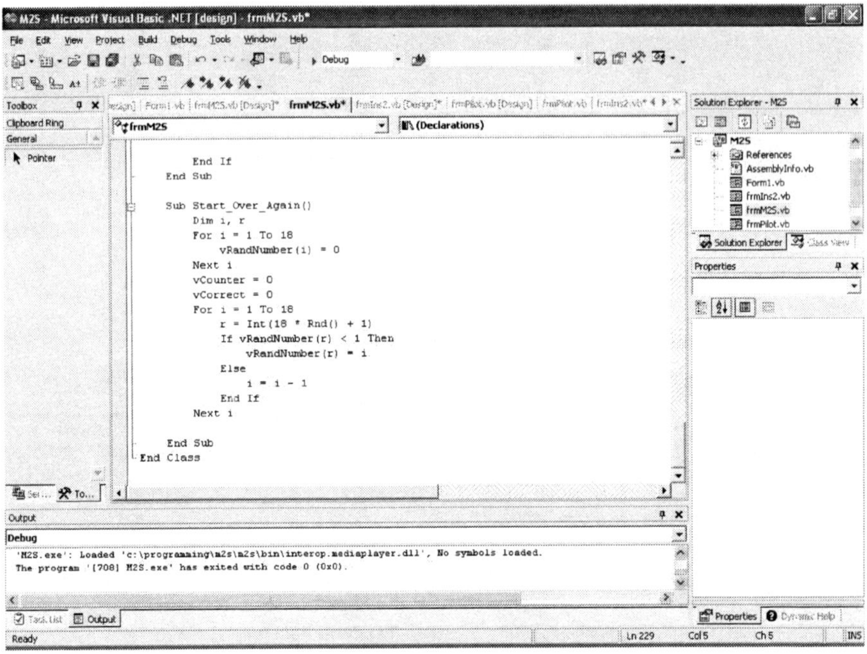

Figure 7.10 shows the newly added Start_Over_Again subroutine.

Run the program and try to click on all of the correct comparison stimuli. The caption bar should count up to 18 and the program will show the final instruction form. Now run the program again and miss 1 of the comparisons. The frmM2S text should count up to 17 and then show the final instruction form. So far we have met criterion. Let's run the program and miss two correct responses.

After running the program you may decide that it would be nice to have a Button on frmIns2 that closes the program. Add a Button named *butEnd*, change the Text to *End*, and type the following under the Private Sub butEnd_Click() subroutine before `Dim x As New frmM2S():`

```
Close
End
```

The *Close* command will close any existing file, and the *End* command will terminate the program. Also you may have noticed that the Text with the variable information only refreshes when a correct response is made. Go to the picM2S0_Click subroutine, delete the line: me.Text=vCorrect. Then add the following line directly above the line *End Sub* (of this subroutine):

```
me.Text = "Criterion = " & vCriterion & " Correct =
   " & vCorrect & " Trial# = " & vCounter
```

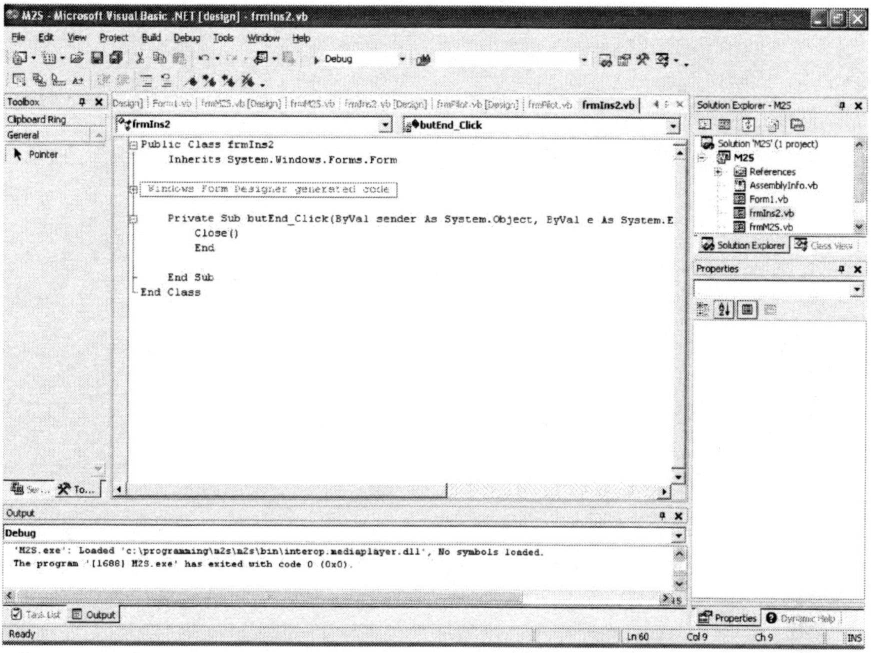

Figure 7.11 shows the code to end the program when frmIns2 is shown.

Now we can get new trial information even when we make an incorrect response. Of course you would remark out this line of code so the participants are not able to monitor their progress when the program is finalized.

Now run the program and ensure the changes worked. We have now finished meeting Requirement #4. Although the requirement is met, let's add something useful here. Let's have VB.NET open a new text file and write the number criterion, number correct and the current phase. Start by going to the code level of frmIns1. Add the following code to open a text file in the Append mode and write a header with the current date and time to that file at the bottom of the frmIns1_Load() subroutine:

```
FileOpen(2, "C:\programming\M2S\M2S_OUT.txt",
   OpenMode.Append)
WriteLine(2, "**************************")
WriteLine(2, Date.Now)
WriteLine(2, "**************************")
```

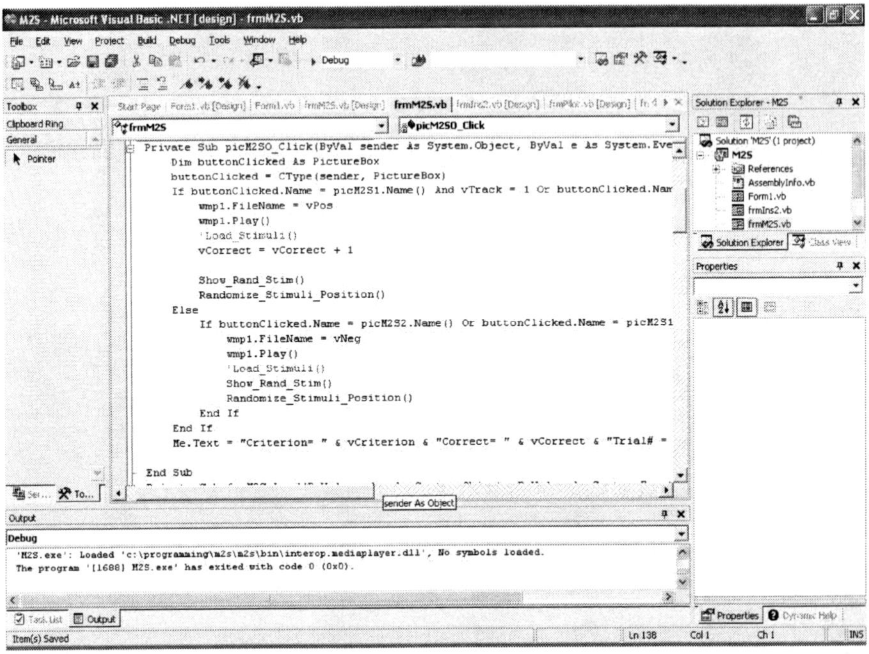

Figure 7.12 shows the code for the newly edited picM2S0_Click subroutine.

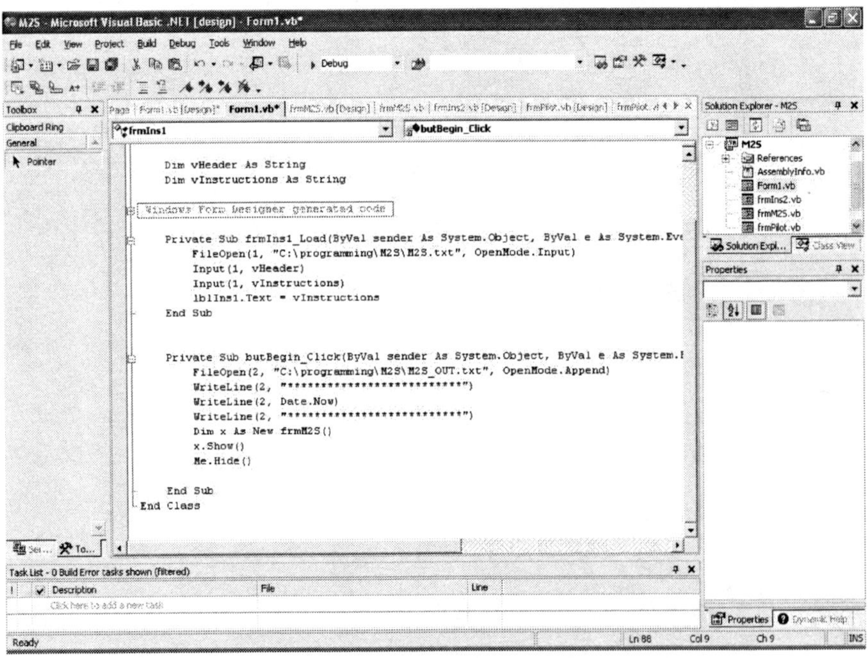

Figure 7.13 shows the newly added file output information of frmIns1.

Next, we will want to write the phase number to this data output file too. To do this we need to initially build the code in frmM2S, and then add it to the data file output information. We can add a line to our input text file using NotePad just below the INSTRUCTIONS command and just above the CORRECT command:

```
PHASE, 1
```

Save and close the text file. Finally, we can declare a new variable called vPhase on the frmM2S form by adding the following line of code under the Inherits System.Windows.Forms.Form statement:

```
Dim vPhase As Integer
```

The phase information we are storing is located before the other input information in the text file, therefore add the following line of code to read in this information above all the other input statements in the frmM2S_Load() subroutine:

```
Input (1, vHeader)
Input (1, vPhase)
```

Run the program, check the data output file M2S_OUT.txt and make sure the date and time are written correctly.

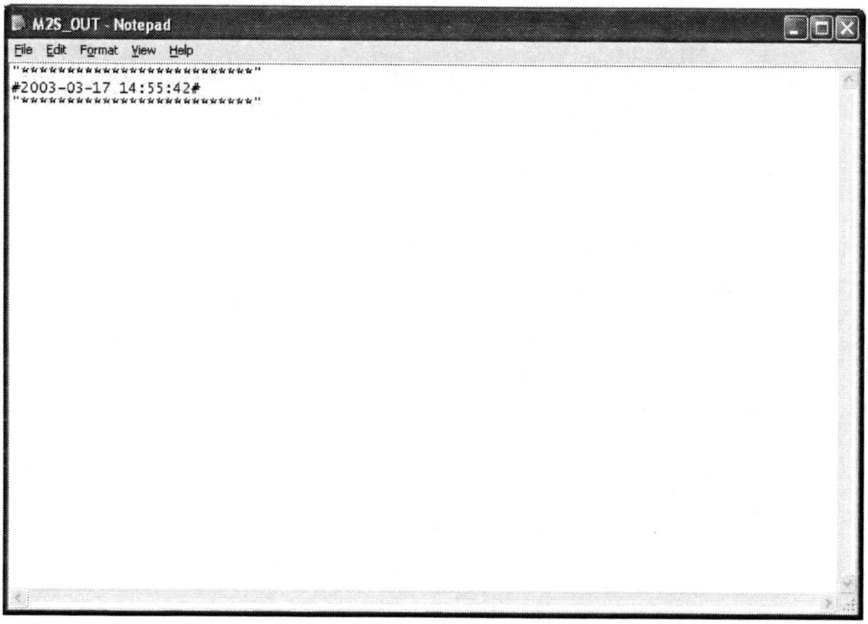

Figure 7.14 displays the correct output file information.

Streamlining Your Code

As you might be thinking, this subroutine, even this entire program in general is getting rather busy. We can streamline the code by reorganizing it into a series of independent subroutines. Let's create a subroutine for the input information called Input_Trial_Information by typing Sub Input_Trial_Information on the last line of the editor (before *End Class*), and then moving the input information there by cutting and pasting the code from frmM2S_Load(). The new Input_Trial_Information subroutine should look like this:

```
Sub Input_Trial_Information()
Input(1, vHeader)
Input(1, vPhase)
Input(1, vHeader)
Input(1, vPos)
Input(1, vHeader)
Input(1, vNeg)
Input(1, vHeader)
Input(1, vCriterion)
End Sub
```

Now add the necessary code to trigger the new subroutine when the form loads. Type the following at the top of frmM2S_Load():

```
Input_Trial_Information
```

The entire frmM2S_Load subroutine should now look like this:

```
Private Sub frmM2S_Load()
Input_Trial_Information()
Load_Random_Trials()
Show_Rand_Stim()
Randomize_Stimuli_Position()
End Sub
```

Run the program to ensure no changes were made that disrupt the working of the program. After this test, you should finish up creating the output file. A good place to write phase information is where the program checks to see if criterion has been met. In our program, this point is during the `Randomize Stimuli_Position()` subroutine. Edit the subroutine to look like this:

```
Sub Randomize_Stimuli_Position()
If vCounter > 18 Then
If vCriterion < vCorrect Then
```

```
Dim x As New frmIns2()
Me.Hide()
x.Show()
Else
WriteLine(2, "Phase =" & vPhase, "Criterion = " &
   vCriterion, "Correct = " & vCorrect)
Start_Over_Again()
End If
Else
Randomize()
Dim r
r = Int(6 * Rnd() + 1)

Select Case r
Case 1
picM2S0.Image = Image.FromFile("c:\programming\M2S\" &
   vTrials(vRandNumber(vCounter), 0) & ".bmp")
picM2S1.Image = Image.FromFile("c:\programming\M2S\" &
   vTrials(vRandNumber(vCounter), 1) & ".bmp")
picM2S2.Image = Image.FromFile("c:\programming\M2S\" &
   vTrials(vRandNumber(vCounter), 2) & ".bmp")
picM2S3.Image = Image.FromFile("c:\programming\M2S\" &
   vTrials(vRandNumber(vCounter), 3) & ".bmp")
vTrack = 1
Case 2
picM2S0.Image = Image.FromFile("c:\programming\M2S\" &
   vTrials(vRandNumber(vCounter), 0) & ".bmp")
picM2S1.Image = Image.FromFile("c:\programming\M2S\" &
   vTrials(vRandNumber(vCounter), 2) & ".bmp")
picM2S2.Image = Image.FromFile("c:\programming\M2S\" &
   vTrials(vRandNumber(vCounter), 1) & ".bmp")
picM2S3.Image = Image.FromFile("c:\programming\M2S\" &
   vTrials(vRandNumber(vCounter), 3) & ".bmp")
vTrack = 2
Case 3
picM2S0.Image = Image.FromFile("c:\programming\M2S\" &
   vTrials(vRandNumber(vCounter), 0) & ".bmp")
picM2S1.Image = Image.FromFile("c:\programming\M2S\" &
   vTrials(vRandNumber(vCounter), 3) & ".bmp")
picM2S2.Image = Image.FromFile("c:\programming\M2S\" &
   vTrials(vRandNumber(vCounter), 2) & ".bmp")
picM2S3.Image = Image.FromFile("c:\programming\M2S\" &
   vTrials(vRandNumber(vCounter), 1) & ".bmp")
```

```
vTrack = 3
Case 4
picM2S0.Image = Image.FromFile("c:\programming\M2S\" &
   vTrials(vRandNumber(vCounter), 0) & ".bmp")
picM2S1.Image = Image.FromFile("c:\programming\M2S\" &
   vTrials(vRandNumber(vCounter), 1) & ".bmp")
picM2S2.Image = Image.FromFile("c:\programming\M2S\" &
   vTrials(vRandNumber(vCounter), 3) & ".bmp")
picM2S3.Image = Image.FromFile("c:\programming\M2S\" &
   vTrials(vRandNumber(vCounter), 2) & ".bmp")
vTrack = 1
Case 5
picM2S0.Image = Image.FromFile("c:\programming\M2S\" &
   vTrials(vRandNumber(vCounter), 0) & ".bmp")
picM2S1.Image = Image.FromFile("c:\programming\M2S\" &
   vTrials(vRandNumber(vCounter), 2) & ".bmp")
picM2S2.Image = Image.FromFile("c:\programming\M2S\" &
   vTrials(vRandNumber(vCounter), 3) & ".bmp")
picM2S3.Image = Image.FromFile("c:\programming\M2S\" &
   vTrials(vRandNumber(vCounter), 1) & ".bmp")
vTrack = 3
Case 6
picM2S0.Image = Image.FromFile("c:\programming\M2S\" &
   vTrials(vRandNumber(vCounter), 0) & ".bmp")
picM2S1.Image = Image.FromFile("c:\programming\M2S\" &
   vTrials(vRandNumber(vCounter), 3) & ".bmp")
picM2S2.Image = Image.FromFile("c:\programming\M2S\" &
   vTrials(vRandNumber(vCounter), 1) & ".bmp")
picM2S3.Image = Image.FromFile("c:\programming\M2S\" &
   vTrials(vRandNumber(vCounter), 2) & ".bmp")
vTrack = 2
End Select
End If
```

While you don't want to go overboard on writing subroutines, subroutines make your code easier to follow in part due to the descriptive nature of the subroutine names.

Let's see if the output file works. Run the program and make some incorrect responses before you meet criterion. Close the program and look for the output file in the C:\programming\M2S directory. You should see a header with the time and date, plus the trial information. From observation of your data output file you will discover that your newly added phase and criterion information is only written for blocks of trials where you did not meet criterion. Look at the code in Figure 7.15

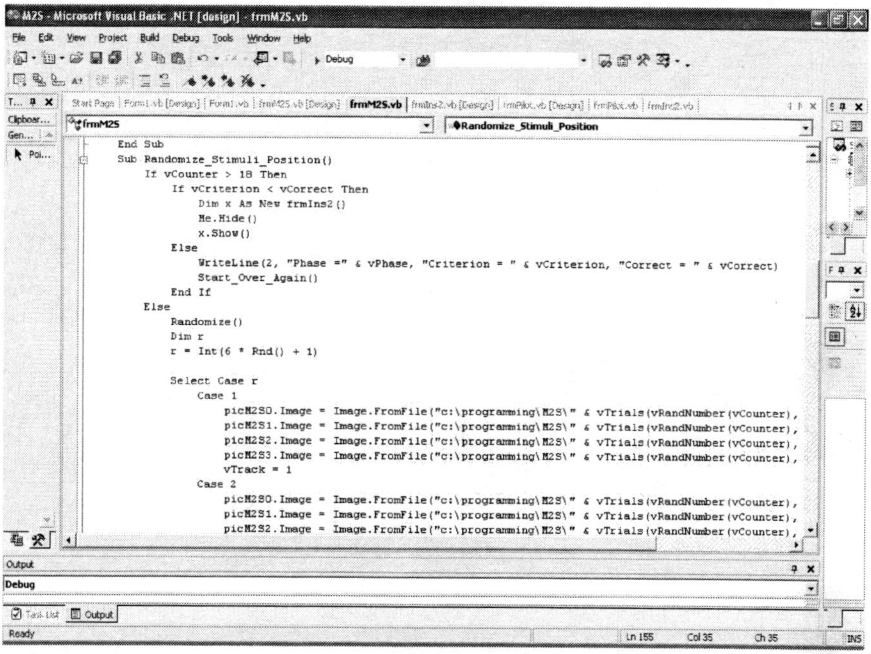

Figure 7.15 displays the edited section of the Randomize_Stimuli_Position() subroutine after it has been reorganized.

to figure out why this occurred. The `WriteLine(2, "Phase =" & vPhase, "Criterion = " & vCriterion, "Correct = " & vCorrect)` code only is read if vCriterion is not met. To have these data write to the output file regardless of vCriterion, add the identical line of code above Dim x as New frmIns2. Rerun the program, make at least 3 errors during the first 18 trials, and then make only 1 error on the next 18 trials. Check the output file. It should look like Figure 7.16.

You may have noticed a "bug" or flaw in the program. Is everything being presented correctly? Is everything being recorded correctly? If you can't find it don't worry we will point it out and fix it later.

5. A-C Training

Requirement #5 is for A-C training similar to the A-B training, however if the participant fails to meet criterion, A-B should not be repeated.

The first order of business is to open M2S.txt (our input file) and modify it to include A-C trials. We can copy and paste the PHASE, CORRECT, INCORRECT, AND CRITERION information and paste this at the end of the input file (remember to change the phase number information from 1 to 2). As with the A-B trials, type in the first three lines, (TRIAL1, A1, C1, C2, C3; TRIAL2, A2, C2, C1, C3; TRIAL3, A3, C3, C1, C2) then copy and paste. Then change the TRIAL information to

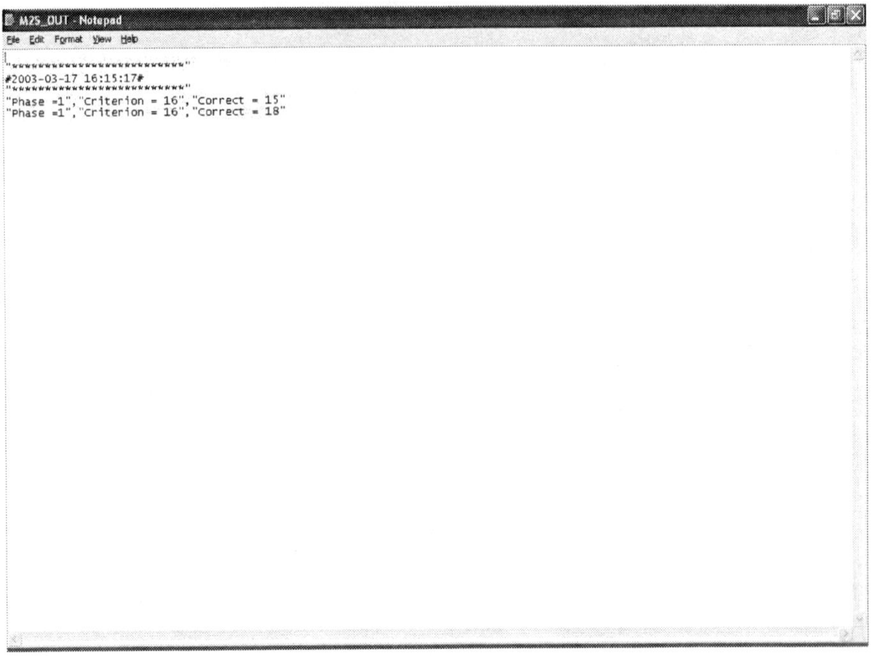

Figure 7.16 displays the M2S_OUT.txt file after correcting the WriteLine statement placement.

increment by 1. Remove the END,,,, command from the bottom of Phase1 and move it to the bottom of Phase2. Save the changes and the input file should be complete. Your new text file should look like this:

```
INSTRUCTIONS, This is where the instructions will go.
PHASE, 1
CORRECT, "c:\windows\media\chimes.wav"
INCORRECT, "c:\windows\media\chord.wav"
CRITERION, 16
TRIAL1,A1,B1,B2,B3
TRIAL2,A2,B2,B1,B3
TRIAL3,A3,B3,B1,B2
TRIAL4,A1,B1,B2,B3
TRIAL5,A2,B2,B1,B3
TRIAL6,A3,B3,B1,B2
TRIAL7,A1,B1,B2,B3
TRIAL8,A2,B2,B1,B3
TRIAL9,A3,B3,B1,B2
TRIAL10,A1,B1,B2,B3
TRIAL11,A2,B2,B1,B3
```

```
TRIAL12,A3,B3,B1,B2
TRIAL13,A1,B1,B2,B3
TRIAL14,A2,B2,B1,B3
TRIAL15,A3,B3,B1,B2
TRIAL16,A1,B1,B2,B3
TRIAL17,A2,B2,B1,B3
TRIAL18,A3,B3,B1,B2
PHASE, 2
CORRECT, "c:\windows\media\chimes.wav"
INCORRECT, "c:\windows\media\chord.wav"
CRITERION, 16
TRIAL1,A1,C1,C2,C3
TRIAL2,A2,C2,C1,C3
TRIAL3,A3,C3,C1,C2
TRIAL4,A1,C1,C2,C3
TRIAL5,A2,C2,C1,C3
TRIAL6,A3,C3,C1,C2
TRIAL7,A1,C1,C2,C3
TRIAL8,A2,C2,C1,C3
TRIAL9,A3,C3,C1,C2
TRIAL10,A1,C1,C2,C3
TRIAL11,A2,C2,C1,C3
TRIAL12,A3,C3,C1,C2
TRIAL13,A1,C1,C2,C3
TRIAL14,A2,C2,C1,C3
TRIAL15,A3,C3,C1,C2
TRIAL16,A1,C1,C2,C3
TRIAL17,A2,C2,C1,C3
TRIAL18,A3,C3,C1,C2
END,A1,A1,A1,A1
```

Rather than showing frmIns2 when criterion is met for Phase 1, we want to present the trials for Phase 2. Modify the code at that point in the Randomize_Stimuli_Position() subroutine. Right now this code shows frmIns2 once vCriterion < vCorrect. This works fine for an experiment with one phase, but not for the current experiment with multiple phases. A simple edit of this code will allow you to present subsequent phases without needing to use multiple forms. While multiple forms are possible here, they can become rather cumbersome with many different experimental conditions. The choice is yours. We will show you how to use just frmM2S for all training and testing conditions because it is the cleanest way to write the program.

Begin by declaring a new variable that will be used to hold information found in our "END, A1, A1, A1, A1" line from the text input file. Specifically, add the following line of code to the rest of the Dim statements found on frmM2S under the Inherits System.Windows.Forms.Form:

```
Dim vCheckEnd as Integer
```

Open your M2S.txt data input file in Notepad and change that useless "A1, A1, A1, A1" portion of the code to something we can use to determine if the program is completed or not. Rewrite the last line of your M2S.txt to read:

```
END, 0
```

Next, cut and paste this newly written line of text between the CRITERION line of A-B training and the first line of the trials (i.e. TRIAL1, A1, B1, B2, B3). Do the same for the A-C training phase except this time change the 0 to a 1 as shown below.

```
END, 1
```

Now the data file contains specific information, either a 0 or 1, which can be used to signal to VB.NET if there are more phases of trials that are to be presented to the participant or if the program should terminate. The resulting M2S.txt file should look identical to Figure 7.17. Close your M2S.txt file and return to Visual Basic.

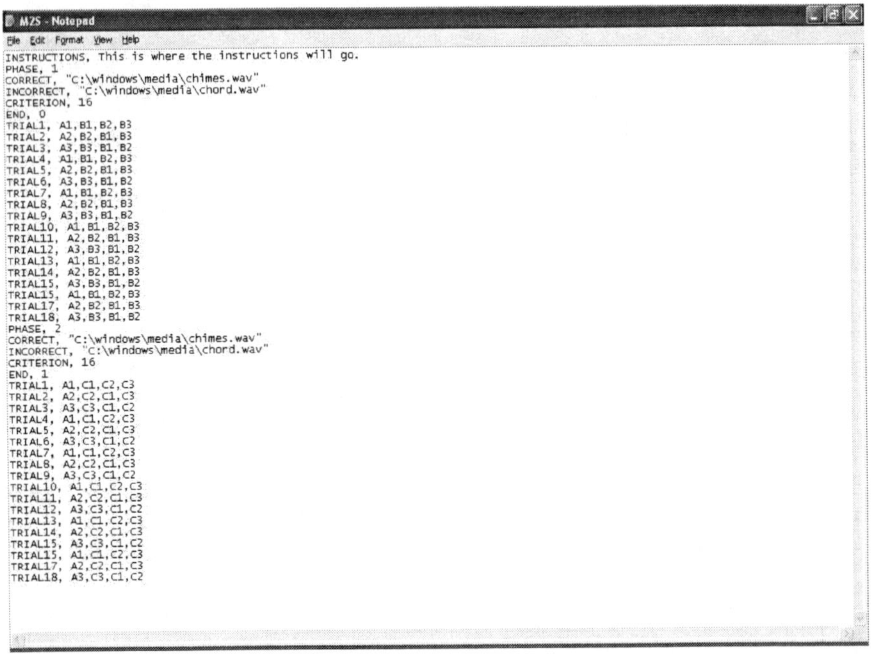

M2S - Notepad

File Edit Format View Help

```
INSTRUCTIONS, This is where the instructions will go.
PHASE, 1
CORRECT, "C:\windows\media\chimes.wav"
INCORRECT, "C:\windows\media\chord.wav"
CRITERION, 16
END, 0
TRIAL1, A1,B1,B2,B3
TRIAL2, A2,B2,B1,B3
TRIAL3, A3,B3,B1,B2
TRIAL4, A1,B1,B2,B3
TRIAL5, A2,B2,B1,B3
TRIAL6, A3,B3,B1,B2
TRIAL7, A1,B1,B2,B3
TRIAL8, A2,B2,B1,B3
TRIAL9, A3,B3,B1,B2
TRIAL10, A1,B1,B2,B3
TRIAL11, A2,B2,B1,B3
TRIAL12, A3,B3,B1,B2
TRIAL13, A1,B1,B2,B3
TRIAL14, A2,B2,B1,B3
TRIAL15, A3,B3,B1,B2
TRIAL15, A1,B1,B2,B3
TRIAL17, A2,B2,B1,B3
TRIAL18, A3,B3,B1,B2
PHASE, 2
CORRECT, "C:\windows\media\chimes.wav"
INCORRECT, "C:\windows\media\chord.wav"
CRITERION, 16
END, 1
TRIAL1, A1,C1,C2,C3
TRIAL2, A2,C2,C1,C3
TRIAL3, A3,C3,C1,C2
TRIAL4, A1,C1,C2,C3
TRIAL5, A2,C2,C1,C3
TRIAL6, A3,C3,C1,C2
TRIAL7, A1,C1,C2,C3
TRIAL8, A2,C2,C1,C3
TRIAL9, A3,C3,C1,C2
TRIAL10, A1,C1,C2,C3
TRIAL11, A2,C2,C1,C3
TRIAL12, A3,C3,C1,C2
TRIAL13, A1,C1,C2,C3
TRIAL14, A2,C2,C1,C3
TRIAL15, A3,C3,C1,C2
TRIAL15, A1,C1,C2,C3
TRIAL17, A2,C2,C1,C3
TRIAL18, A3,C3,C1,C2
```

Figure 7.17 displays the correctly edited M2S.txt data input file.

Add the following lines of code at the bottom of your Input_Trial_Information() subroutine to acquire the newly added END statements and their associated values:

```
Input(1, vHeader)
Input(1, vCheckEnd)
```

The reason why we shifted that crazy END statement to the beginning of each phase instead of the end, is because all the other Input information preceded the randomization and presentation of that phase's trials. Shifting END right after the CRITERION line streamlines when VB.NET accesses the text file for variable values.

The final step here to incorporate the A-C trials is to edit the Randomize_Stimuli_Position subroutine section that pertains to vCriterion. Edit this portion of the subroutine to read as follows (the Select Case statements are not shown here because no changes are made to them):

```
If vCounter > 18 Then
If vCriterion < vCorrect Then
WriteLine(2, "Phase =" & vPhase, "Criterion = " & vCriterion, "Correct = " &
    vCorrect)
If vCheckEnd = 1 Then
Dim x As New frmIns2()
Me.Hide()
x.Show()
End If
If vCheckEnd = 0 Then
Dim x As New frmM2S()
x.Show()
Me.Hide()
End If
Else
WriteLine(2, "Phase =" & vPhase, "Criterion = " & vCriterion, "Correct = " &
    vCorrect)
Start_Over_Again()
End If
Else
Randomize()
Dim r
r = Int(6 * Rnd() + 1)
```

Essentially what this code does is check to see if 18 trials have elapsed. If they have, it next checks if the criterion has been met. If it has, 1) data are written to the output file, 2) it checks to see if vCheckEnd is equal to 1. This would signify the end of the experiment. If vCheckEnd is equal to 1, then frmIns2 is shown. Yet, if vCheckEnd is equal to 0, more trials need to be presented. VB.NET should move on down the data input file, and bring in the new trials and their related information. Essentially, the program should start again, only now with the next phase of trials. Instead of showing the frmIns2 form, we simply reshow, or reload, the same frmM2S form. The whole process starts again, but now with the next set of trials! Run the program; meet the criterion in A-B, than A-C training should start. At this point fail the A-C criterion initially, than pass it. The program should run without a hitch, and eventually display frmIns2. Check your M2S_OUT.txt file to check out your performance. This should take care of requirement #5.

6. Mixed Training

Requirement #6 requests that 36 mixed trials of A-B and B-C be randomly presented. This is just like requirement #5 except that there is two times the number of trials. Our arrays are set for 18 and the FOR/NEXT statements are set for 18 as well. As they stand, only phases with 18 trials or less will work correctly in the program. To customize this feature to allow for more than 18 trials per phase, you will need to make a few code and input file adjustments. Start off by opening M2S.txt and under the PHASE command for phase 1 and 2 add the following new command:

```
NUMBEROFTRIALS, 18
```

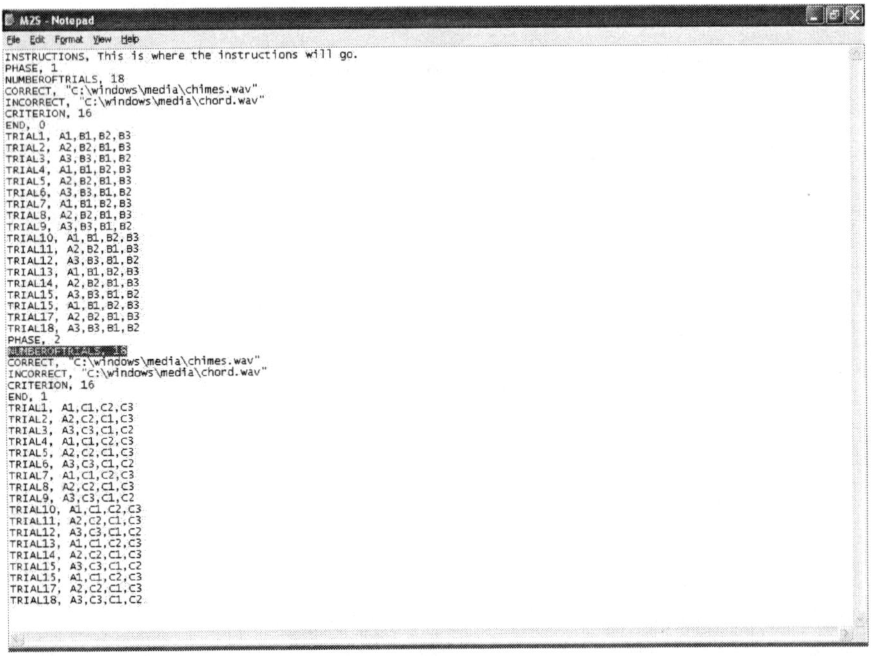

Figure 7.18 shows the M2S text file after adding the new command: NUMBEROFTRIALS.

The NUMBEROFTRIALS, 18 will change to 36 for the mixed trials in phase 3. But don't do the mixed trials just yet, because we need to make sure the changes work with what we just did to the input file. Save your changes to the text file and return to frmM2S. Declare a new variable on this form as follows:

```
Dim vNumberTrials as Integer
```

Add the following input lines under the Input_Trial_Information() subroutine right under the vPhase line:

```
Input(1, vHeader)
Input(1, vNumberTrials)
```

The Input_Trial_Information() subroutine should now look like this:

```
Sub Input_Trial_Information()
Input(1, vHeader)
Input(1, vPhase)
Input(1, vHeader)
Input(1, vNumberTrials)
Input(1, vHeader)
Input(1, vPos)
Input(1, vHeader)
Input(1, vNeg)
Input(1, vHeader)
Input(1, vCriterion)
Input(1, vHeader)
Input(1, vCheckEnd)
End Sub
```

We can't easily change the size of variable arrays during run time, but we can adjust them to the largest size we anticipate using. Remember this point if you designed larger sets of training or testing pahses in your own research. Therefore change:

```
Dim vTrials((18),(3))
Dim vRandNumber(18) As Integer
```

to read:

```
Dim vTrials((36),(3))
Dim vRandNumber(36) As Integer
```

We also need to change the following code in the Randomize_Stimuli_Presentation() subroutine:

```
If vCounter > 18 Then
```
to
```
If vCounter > vNumberTrials Then
```

Now if the number of trials is greater than 18 the program won't check the criterion early. Similarly change all of the FOR/NEXT statements throughout the form that read:

```
For i = 1 To 18
```

to read

```
For i = 1 To vNumberTrials
```

Also change the two random functions that read:

```
r = Int(18 * Rnd + 1)
```

to read

```
r = Int(vNumberTrials * Rnd + 1).
```

Run the program a few times making different criterion for the two phases and see if the changes worked.

Now we can add the mixed trials for requirement #6. Open the input file. Select rows 2 to 7 and copy and paste them at the end of the file. Change the PHASE to 3, NUMBEROFTRIALS to 36. We will use the same .wav files and set the criterion at 32 (twice the previous criterion). We must change the END command in phase 3, to a 1 and to a 0 in Phase 2. Now copy the A-B trials and paste them at the bottom of the input file. Do the same with the A-C trials. Renumber to change the trial headers to read 1-36. Save the input file. Run the program.

7.Test Trials

Requirement #7a indicates that the trials for testing should provide no feedback. Open the input file and copy the lines from *Phase 3* to *End,1* and paste it at the bottom of the input file and make the following changes:

```
PHASE, 4
NUMBEROFTRIALS, 27
CORRECT, "c:\windows\media\nothing.wav"
INCORRECT, "c:\windows\media\nothing.wav"
```

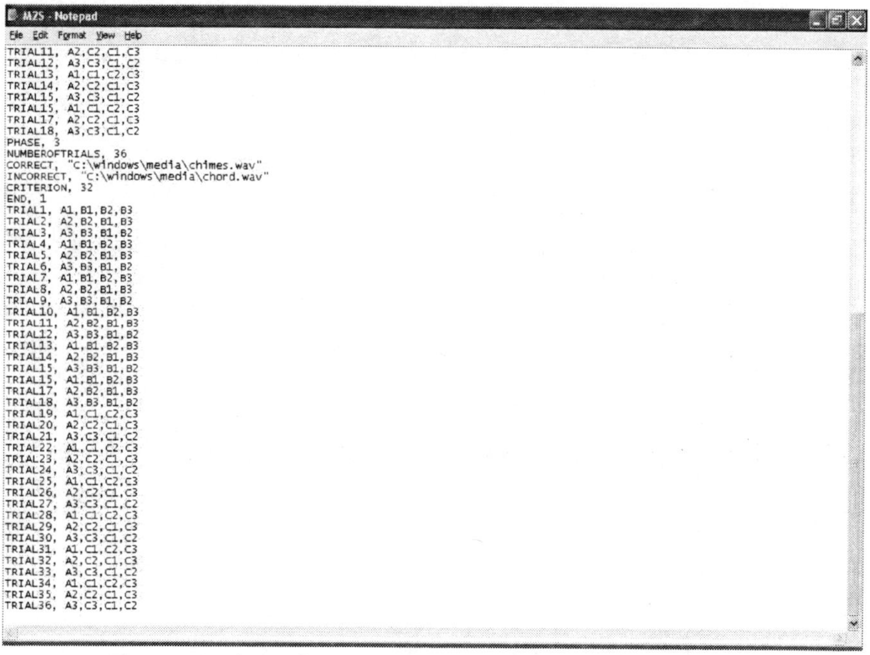

```
TRIAL11, A2,C2,C1,C3
TRIAL12, A3,C3,C1,C2
TRIAL13, A1,C1,C2,C3
TRIAL14, A2,C2,C1,C3
TRIAL15, A3,C3,C1,C2
TRIAL15, A1,C1,C2,C3
TRIAL17, A2,C2,C1,C3
TRIAL18, A3,C3,C1,C2
PHASE, 3
NUMBEROFTRIALS, 36
CORRECT, "C:\windows\media\chimes.wav"
INCORRECT, "C:\windows\media\chord.wav"
CRITERION, 32
END, 1
TRIAL1, A1,B1,B2,B3
TRIAL2, A2,B2,B1,B3
TRIAL3, A3,B3,B1,B2
TRIAL4, A1,B1,B2,B3
TRIAL5, A2,B2,B1,B3
TRIAL6, A3,B3,B1,B2
TRIAL7, A1,B1,B2,B3
TRIAL8, A2,B2,B1,B3
TRIAL9, A3,B3,B1,B2
TRIAL10, A1,B1,B2,B3
TRIAL11, A2,B2,B1,B3
TRIAL12, A3,B3,B1,B2
TRIAL13, A1,B1,B2,B3
TRIAL14, A2,B2,B1,B3
TRIAL15, A3,B3,B1,B2
TRIAL15, A1,B1,B2,B3
TRIAL17, A2,B2,B1,B3
TRIAL18, A3,B3,B1,B2
TRIAL19, A1,C1,C2,C3
TRIAL20, A2,C2,C1,C3
TRIAL21, A3,C3,C1,C2
TRIAL22, A1,C1,C2,C3
TRIAL23, A2,C2,C1,C3
TRIAL24, A3,C3,C1,C2
TRIAL25, A1,C1,C2,C3
TRIAL26, A2,C2,C1,C3
TRIAL27, A3,C3,C1,C2
TRIAL28, A1,C1,C2,C3
TRIAL29, A2,C2,C1,C3
TRIAL30, A3,C3,C1,C2
TRIAL31, A1,C1,C2,C3
TRIAL32, A2,C2,C1,C3
TRIAL33, A3,C3,C1,C2
TRIAL34, A1,C1,C2,C3
TRIAL35, A2,C2,C1,C3
TRIAL36, A3,C3,C1,C2
```

Figure 7.19 shows the M2S text file with the Mixed training section.

```
CRITERION, -1
END, 1
```

Notice that there are new .wav files specified for this text phase called *nothing.wav*. To remove the auditory feedback you need to "trick" VB.NET into playing a soundless .wav file. Go to the *Accessories* Program Group on your computer's operating system, select *Entertainment* and then select *Sound Recorder*. Make your soundless *nothing* .wav file by pressing the *Record* Button once, and then quickly pressing the *Stop* Button. Save the file as *nothing.wav* in the c:\windows\media directory, then close the Sound Recorder.

Also notice that criterion is set to –1. This is because there is no criterion. Because of the way we wrote the code, the number correct has to be greater than the criterion. If for some reason the participant does not make a correct choice, then the number correct would not be greater than the criterion. So –1 it is. Change the END command in phase 3 to END, 0 so the program will continue to run. Now add the trials for phase 4 – Reflexivity. A1-A1, A2-A2, etc. The first nine trials should look like this:

```
TRIAL1, A1,A1,A2,A3
TRIAL2, A2,A2,A1,A3
TRIAL3, A3,A3,A1,A2
```

```
TRIAL4, B1,B1,B2,B3
TRIAL5, B2,B2,B1,B3
TRIAL6, B3,B3,B1,B2
TRIAL7, C1,C1,C2,C3
TRIAL8, C2,C2,C1,C3
TRIAL9, C3,C3,C1,C2
```

Now copy and paste in two more sections to make 27 trials. Remember to change the TRIAL headers. Run the program. You can see that as the number of trials grows, the more effort it is to test and trouble shoot your program. If the program runs and there is no feedback during the testing trials, requirement #7a should be met.

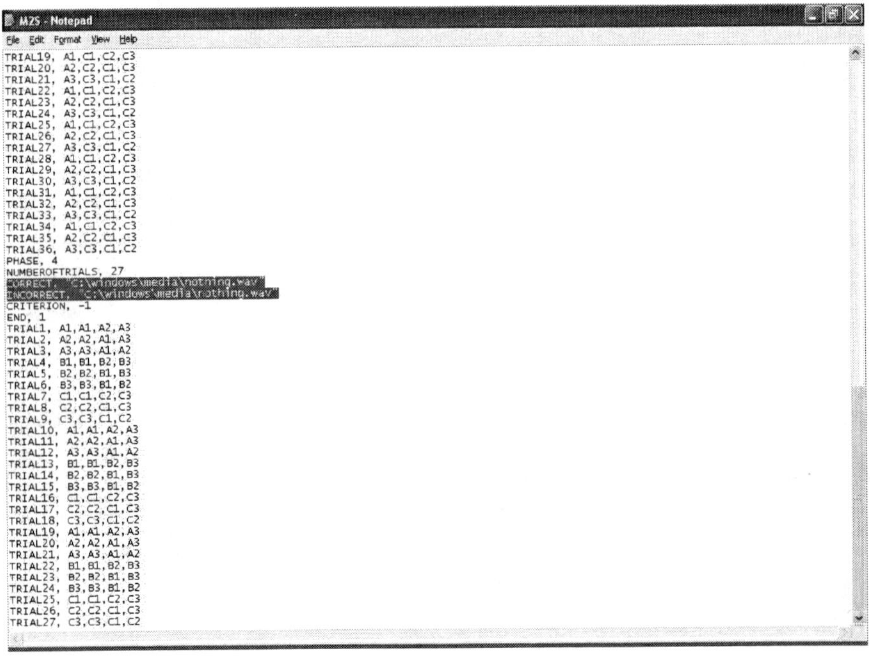


```
TRIAL19, A1,C1,C2,C3
TRIAL20, A2,C2,C1,C3
TRIAL21, A3,C3,C1,C2
TRIAL22, A1,C1,C2,C3
TRIAL23, A2,C2,C1,C3
TRIAL24, A3,C3,C1,C2
TRIAL25, A1,C1,C2,C3
TRIAL26, A2,C2,C1,C3
TRIAL27, A3,C3,C1,C2
TRIAL28, A1,C1,C2,C3
TRIAL29, A2,C2,C1,C3
TRIAL30, A3,C3,C1,C2
TRIAL31, A1,C1,C2,C3
TRIAL32, A2,C2,C1,C3
TRIAL33, A3,C3,C1,C2
TRIAL34, A1,C1,C2,C3
TRIAL35, A2,C2,C1,C3
TRIAL36, A3,C3,C1,C2
PHASE, 4
NUMBEROFTRIALS, 27
CORRECT, "C:\windows\media\nothing.wav"
INCORRECT, "C:\windows\media\nothing.wav"
CRITERION, -1
END, 1
TRIAL1, A1,A1,A2,A3
TRIAL2, A2,A2,A1,A3
TRIAL3, A3,A3,A1,A2
TRIAL4, B1,B1,B2,B3
TRIAL5, B2,B2,B1,B3
TRIAL6, B3,B3,B1,B2
TRIAL7, C1,C1,C2,C3
TRIAL8, C2,C2,C1,C3
TRIAL9, C3,C3,C1,C2
TRIAL10, A1,A1,A2,A3
TRIAL11, A2,A2,A1,A3
TRIAL12, A3,A3,A1,A2
TRIAL13, B1,B1,B2,B3
TRIAL14, B2,B2,B1,B3
TRIAL15, B3,B3,B1,B2
TRIAL16, C1,C1,C2,C3
TRIAL17, C2,C2,C1,C3
TRIAL18, C3,C3,C1,C2
TRIAL19, A1,A1,A2,A3
TRIAL20, A2,A2,A1,A3
TRIAL21, A3,A3,A1,A2
TRIAL22, B1,B1,B2,B3
TRIAL23, B2,B2,B1,B3
TRIAL24, B3,B3,B1,B2
TRIAL25, C1,C1,C2,C3
TRIAL26, C2,C2,C1,C3
TRIAL27, C3,C3,C1,C2
```

Figure 7.20 shows the M2S text file with the Reflexivity Phase added.

Requirement #7b is a test for Symmetry. This will involve the B-A and C-A relations each presented six times. There will be 18 trials, no feedback, and again no criterion. Therefore, copy and paste the command header and make the necessary changes in the input file as before. The header and the first six trials of our symmetry test should look like this:

```
PHASE, 5
NUMBEROFTRIALS, 18
```

```
CORRECT, "c:\windows\media\nothing.wav"
INCORRECT, "c:\windows\media\nothing.wav"
CRITERION, -1
END, 1
TRIAL1, B1,A1,A2,A3
TRIAL2, B2,A2,A1,A3
TRIAL3, B3,A3,A1,A2
TRIAL4, C1,A1,A2,A3
TRIAL5, C2,A2,A1,A3
TRIAL6, C3,A3,A1,A2
```

Make sure to change the End statement of Phase 4 from 1 to 0. Save your changes then run the program.

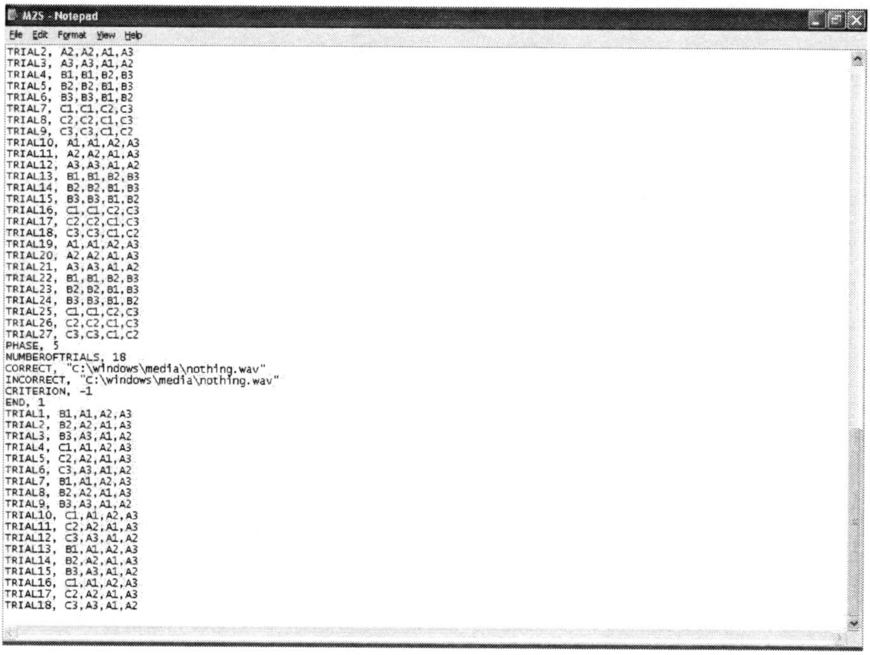

Figure 7.21 shows the M2S text file with the Symmetry Test trials.

Requirement #7c is a test for Transitivity involving B-C relations. There will be 18 trials with each relation tested 6 times, no feedback, and no criterion. The first few lines of the input file should look like this:

```
PHASE, 6
NUMBEROFTRIALS, 18
CORRECT, "c:\windows\media\nothing.wav"
```

```
INCORRECT, "c:\windows\media\nothing.wav"
CRITERION, -1
END, 1
TRIAL1, B1,C1,C2,C3
TRIAL2, B2,C2,C1,C3
TRIAL3, B3,C3,C1,C2
```

Make sure to change END, 1 in the previous phase to END, 0. Save your changes then run the program.

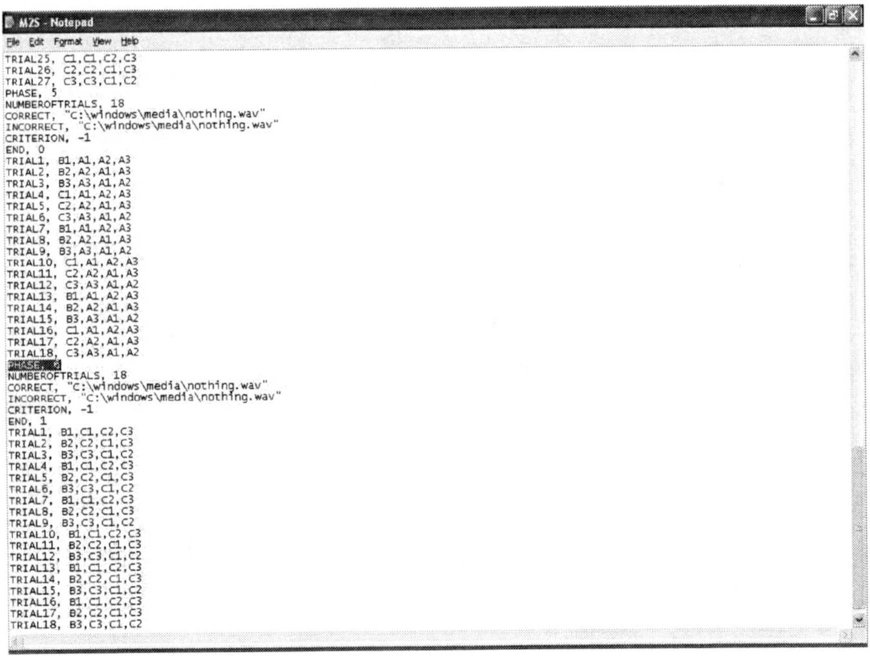

```
M2S - Notepad
File Edit Format View Help
TRIAL25, C1,C1,C2,C3
TRIAL26, C2,C2,C1,C3
TRIAL27, C3,C3,C1,C2
PHASE, 5
NUMBEROFTRIALS, 18
CORRECT, "C:\windows\media\nothing.wav"
INCORRECT, "C:\windows\media\nothing.wav"
CRITERION, -1
END, 0
TRIAL1, B1,A1,A2,A3
TRIAL2, B2,A2,A1,A3
TRIAL3, B3,A3,A1,A2
TRIAL4, C1,A1,A2,A3
TRIAL5, C2,A2,A1,A3
TRIAL6, C3,A3,A1,A2
TRIAL7, B1,A1,A2,A3
TRIAL8, B2,A2,A1,A3
TRIAL9, B3,A3,A1,A2
TRIAL10, C1,A1,A2,A3
TRIAL11, C2,A2,A1,A3
TRIAL12, C3,A3,A1,A2
TRIAL13, B1,A1,A2,A3
TRIAL14, B2,A2,A1,A3
TRIAL15, B3,A3,A1,A2
TRIAL16, C1,A1,A2,A3
TRIAL17, C2,A2,A1,A3
TRIAL18, C3,A3,A1,A2
PHASE, 6
NUMBEROFTRIALS, 18
CORRECT, "C:\windows\media\nothing.wav"
INCORRECT, "C:\windows\media\nothing.wav"
CRITERION, -1
END, 1
TRIAL1, B1,C1,C2,C3
TRIAL2, B2,C2,C1,C3
TRIAL3, B3,C3,C1,C2
TRIAL4, B1,C1,C2,C3
TRIAL5, B2,C2,C1,C3
TRIAL6, B3,C3,C1,C2
TRIAL7, B1,C1,C2,C3
TRIAL8, B2,C2,C1,C3
TRIAL9, B3,C3,C1,C2
TRIAL10, B1,C1,C2,C3
TRIAL11, B2,C2,C1,C3
TRIAL12, B3,C3,C1,C2
TRIAL13, B1,C1,C2,C3
TRIAL14, B2,C2,C1,C3
TRIAL15, B3,C3,C1,C2
TRIAL16, B1,C1,C2,C3
TRIAL17, B2,C2,C1,C3
TRIAL18, B3,C3,C1,C2
```

Figure 7.22 displays the Transitivity test in the M2S text file.

Requirement #7d is a test for Equivalence. Here the C-B relations will be presented. There will be 18 trials with each relation tested 6 times, no feedback, and no criterion. The header and the first three lines of the trials should look like this:

```
PHASE, 7
NUMBEROFTRIALS, 18
CORRECT, "c:\windows\media\nothing.wav"
INCORRECT, "c:\windows\media\nothing.wav"
CRITERION, -1
END, 1
```

```
TRIAL1, C1,B1,B2,B3
TRIAL2, C2,B2,B1,B3
TRIAL3, C3,B3,B1,B2
```

Make sure to change END, 1 in the previous phase to END, 0. Save your changes then run the program. This should conclude all of the requirements for #7. All of the testing is complete.

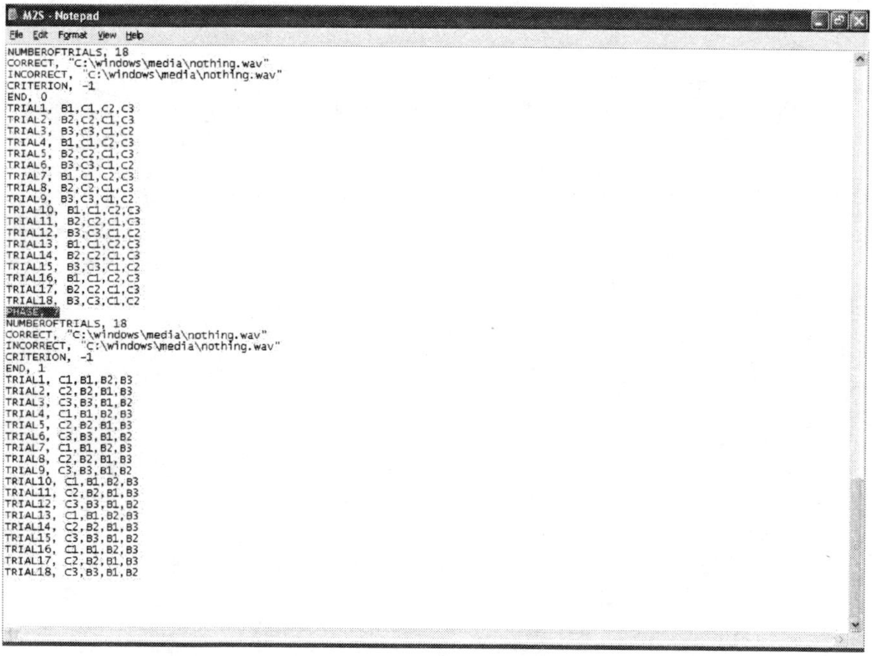

```
M2S - Notepad
File Edit Format View Help
NUMBEROFTRIALS, 18
CORRECT, "C:\windows\media\nothing.wav"
INCORRECT, "C:\windows\media\nothing.wav"
CRITERION, -1
END, 0
TRIAL1, B1,C1,C2,C3
TRIAL2, B2,C2,C1,C3
TRIAL3, B3,C3,C1,C2
TRIAL4, B1,C1,C2,C3
TRIAL5, B2,C2,C1,C3
TRIAL6, B3,C3,C1,C2
TRIAL7, B1,C1,C2,C3
TRIAL8, B2,C2,C1,C3
TRIAL9, B3,C3,C1,C2
TRIAL10, B1,C1,C2,C3
TRIAL11, B2,C2,C1,C3
TRIAL12, B3,C3,C1,C2
TRIAL13, B1,C1,C2,C3
TRIAL14, B2,C2,C1,C3
TRIAL15, B3,C3,C1,C2
TRIAL16, B1,C1,C2,C3
TRIAL17, B2,C2,C1,C3
TRIAL18, B3,C3,C1,C2
PHASE, 7
NUMBEROFTRIALS, 18
CORRECT, "C:\windows\media\nothing.wav"
INCORRECT, "C:\windows\media\nothing.wav"
CRITERION, -1
END, 1
TRIAL1, C1,B1,B2,B3
TRIAL2, C2,B2,B1,B3
TRIAL3, C3,B3,B1,B2
TRIAL4, C1,B1,B2,B3
TRIAL5, C2,B2,B1,B3
TRIAL6, C3,B3,B1,B2
TRIAL7, C1,B1,B2,B3
TRIAL8, C2,B2,B1,B3
TRIAL9, C3,B3,B1,B2
TRIAL10, C1,B1,B2,B3
TRIAL11, C2,B2,B1,B3
TRIAL12, C3,B3,B1,B2
TRIAL13, C1,B1,B2,B3
TRIAL14, C2,B2,B1,B3
TRIAL15, C3,B3,B1,B2
TRIAL16, C1,B1,B2,B3
TRIAL17, C2,B2,B1,B3
TRIAL18, C3,B3,B1,B2
```

Figure 7.23 displays the Equivalence test in the M2S text file.

8. Data Output

Requirement #8 regards writing data to an output file. We have already created code that writes summary data after each phase, however more reporting detail is usually desired. Requirement #8 specifically requests:

For each trial indicate the sample stimulus and the comparison stimulus chosen.

For each trial indicate the response latency (the time the sample stimulus was displayed and the time a comparison stimulus was chosen).

And total number of trials correct (we have already done this).

One way to satisfy this requirement is to capitalize on the information already being written into the Text bar of frmM2S. By adding a few more pieces of information to this existing code we can have a comprehensive data record which updates every trial.

One piece of information that currently is lacking in the me.Text is if a specific response is correct or wrong. Right now, we have values of vCorrect, but those values could be displayed more usefully. Therefore, add a new variable to the form by typing:

```
Dim vAnswer as String
```

Using this new variable we can produce a textual note that signals if the response made by the participant was correct or incorrect on every trial. We shall come back to vAnswer shortly. For now though edit the existing me.Text= code so that it reads as follows:

```
Me.Text = "Phase= " & vPhase & "Criterion= " & vCriterion
   & "Correct= " & vCorrect & "Trial# = " & vCounter &
   vTrials(vRandNumber(vCounter), 0) &
   vTrials(vRandNumber(vCounter), 1) & vAnswer & Date.Now
```

This is all one big long line of code, but it provides a really nice small amount of information in the Text bar. It now includes the newly created vAnswer variable, the stimulus presented as the sample, the stimulus that is the correct comparison, the phase in effect, and the time and date.

Cut this newly written line from its' current position and paste it into two different places under picM2S0_Click. The reason why we are shifting the code here is because we want the information to update immediately after the participant makes a response. This is especially true for the Date.Now function. Paste the above code as follows into the picM2S0_Click subroutine() and add the two new lines of code pertaining to generating a string for vAnswer. The new subroutine should now look like:

```
Dim buttonClicked As PictureBox
buttonClicked = CType(sender, PictureBox)
If buttonClicked.Name = picM2S1.Name() And vTrack = 1 Or
   buttonClicked.Name = picM2S2.Name() And vTrack = 2 Or
   buttonClicked.Name = picM2S3.Name And vTrack = 3 Then
wmp1.FileName = vPos
wmp1.Play()
'Load_Stimuli()
vCorrect = vCorrect + 1
vAnswer = "Correct"
```

```
Me.Text = "Phase= " & vPhase & "Criterion= " & vCriterion
   & "Correct= " & vCorrect & "Trial# = " & vCounter &
   vTrials(vRandNumber(vCounter), 0) &
   vTrials(vRandNumber(vCounter), 1) & vAnswer & Date.Now

Show_Rand_Stim()
Randomize_Stimuli_Position()
Else
If buttonClicked.Name = picM2S2.Name() Or buttonClicked.Name
   = picM2S1.Name() Or buttonClicked.Name = picM2S3.Name
   Then
wmp1.FileName = vNeg
wmp1.Play()
'Load_Stimuli()
vAnswer = "Wrong"
Me.Text = "Phase= " & vPhase & "Criterion= " & vCriterion
   & "Correct= " & vCorrect & "Trial# = " & vCounter &
   vTrials(vRandNumber(vCounter), 0) &
   vTrials(vRandNumber(vCounter), 1) & vAnswer & Date.Now
Show_Rand_Stim()
Randomize_Stimuli_Position()
End If
End If
```

Run the program and see your changes appear in the Text bar of frmM2S. There is a lot of information here, but you can sort out what is useful to you when running your own experiments.

Now that me.Text is displaying the data you wish to record, the next step is to place this information into M2S_OUT.txt. Add the following line under BOTH locations you just placed the me.Text = ... code:

```
WriteLine(2, "Phase= " & vPhase, "Criterion= " & vCriterion,
   "Correct= " & vCorrect, "Trial# = " & vCounter,
   vTrials(vRandNumber(vCounter), 0),
   vTrials(vRandNumber(vCounter), 1), vAnswer, Date.Now)
```

Run the program and check your data output file. It should look similar to a section displayed in Figure 7.25.

You might notice a little bit of a problem here with your data output file as well as that displayed in Figure 7.25. Examine the line of data written after the first 18 trials. There are errors in it including the trial number's value is zero. Now look 18 trials down the data file and note that there were 19 responses made in a block of trials that should have been 18. Yep, the programming bug has raised its ugly head.

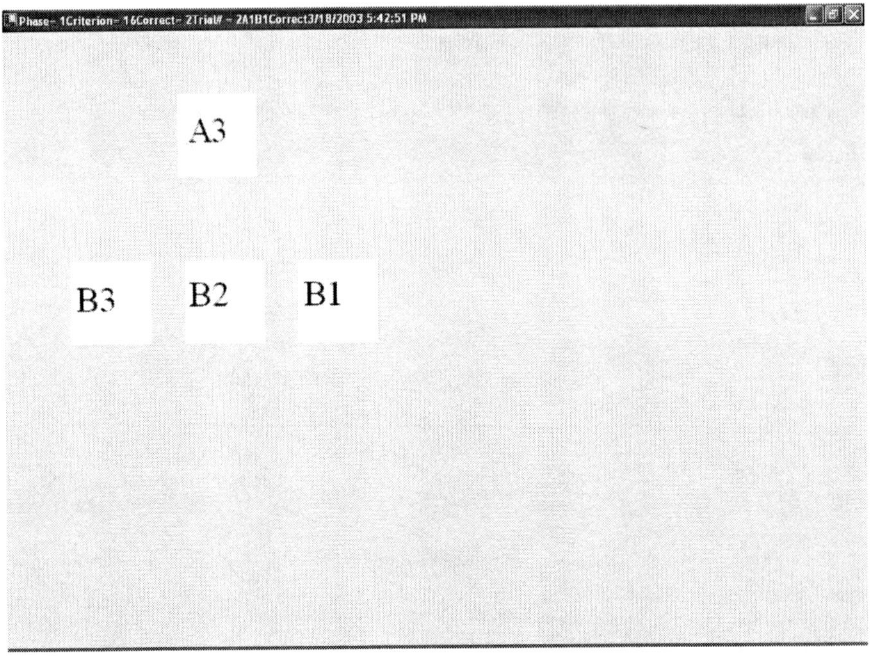

Figure 7.24 displays the revisions to me.Text as they appear during run time.

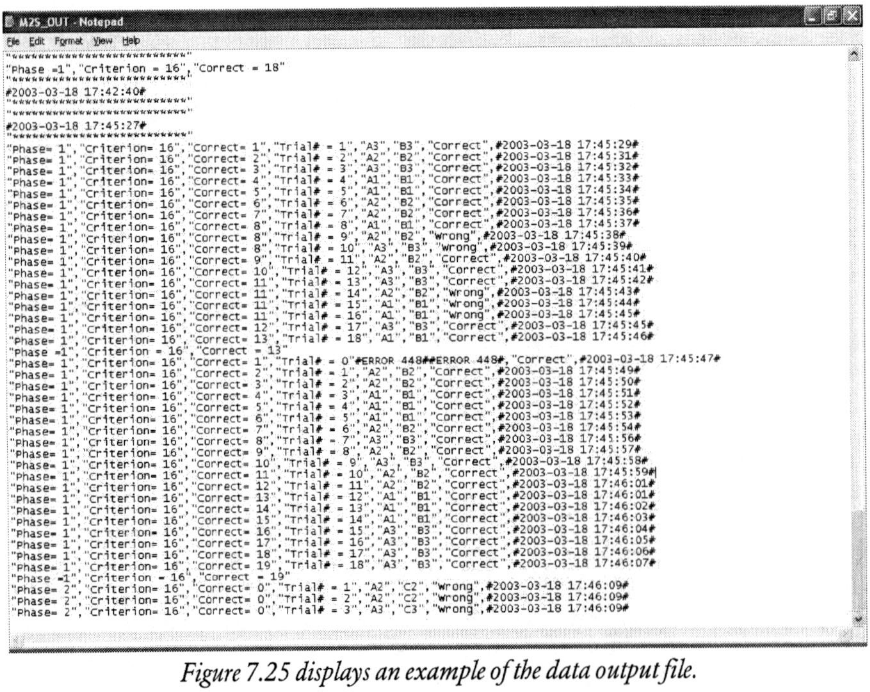

```
M2S_OUT - Notepad
File Edit Format View Help
"***************************"
"Phase =1","Criterion = 16","Correct = 18"
"***************************"
#2003-03-18 17:42:40#
"***************************"
"***************************"
#2003-03-18 17:45:27#
"***************************"
"Phase= 1","Criterion= 16","Correct= 1","Trial# = 1","A3","B3","Correct",#2003-03-18 17:45:29#
"Phase= 1","Criterion= 16","Correct= 2","Trial# = 2","A2","B2","Correct",#2003-03-18 17:45:31#
"Phase= 1","Criterion= 16","Correct= 3","Trial# = 3","A3","B3","Correct",#2003-03-18 17:45:32#
"Phase= 1","Criterion= 16","Correct= 4","Trial# = 4","A1","B1","Correct",#2003-03-18 17:45:33#
"Phase= 1","Criterion= 16","Correct= 5","Trial# = 5","A1","B1","Correct",#2003-03-18 17:45:34#
"Phase= 1","Criterion= 16","Correct= 6","Trial# = 6","A2","B2","Correct",#2003-03-18 17:45:35#
"Phase= 1","Criterion= 16","Correct= 7","Trial# = 7","A2","B2","Correct",#2003-03-18 17:45:36#
"Phase= 1","Criterion= 16","Correct= 8","Trial# = 8","A1","B1","Correct",#2003-03-18 17:45:37#
"Phase= 1","Criterion= 16","Correct= 8","Trial# = 9","A2","B2","Wrong",#2003-03-18 17:45:38#
"Phase= 1","Criterion= 16","Correct= 8","Trial# = 10","A3","B3","Wrong",#2003-03-18 17:45:39#
"Phase= 1","Criterion= 16","Correct= 9","Trial# = 11","A2","B2","Correct",#2003-03-18 17:45:40#
"Phase= 1","Criterion= 16","Correct= 10","Trial# = 12","A3","B3","Correct",#2003-03-18 17:45:41#
"Phase= 1","Criterion= 16","Correct= 11","Trial# = 13","A3","B3","Correct",#2003-03-18 17:45:42#
"Phase= 1","Criterion= 16","Correct= 11","Trial# = 14","A2","B2","Wrong",#2003-03-18 17:45:43#
"Phase= 1","Criterion= 16","Correct= 11","Trial# = 15","A1","B1","Wrong",#2003-03-18 17:45:44#
"Phase= 1","Criterion= 16","Correct= 11","Trial# = 16","A1","B1","Wrong",#2003-03-18 17:45:45#
"Phase= 1","Criterion= 16","Correct= 12","Trial# = 17","A3","B3","Correct",#2003-03-18 17:45:45#
"Phase= 1","Criterion= 16","Correct= 13","Trial# = 18","A1","B1","Correct",#2003-03-18 17:45:46#
"Phase =1","Criterion = 16","Correct = 13"
"Phase= 1","Criterion= 16","Correct= 1","Trial# = 0"#ERROR 448##ERROR 448#,"Correct",#2003-03-18 17:45:47#
"Phase= 1","Criterion= 16","Correct= 2","Trial# = 1","A2","B2","Correct",#2003-03-18 17:45:49#
"Phase= 1","Criterion= 16","Correct= 3","Trial# = 2","A2","B2","Correct",#2003-03-18 17:45:50#
"Phase= 1","Criterion= 16","Correct= 4","Trial# = 3","A1","B1","Correct",#2003-03-18 17:45:51#
"Phase= 1","Criterion= 16","Correct= 5","Trial# = 4","A1","B1","Correct",#2003-03-18 17:45:52#
"Phase= 1","Criterion= 16","Correct= 6","Trial# = 5","A1","B1","Correct",#2003-03-18 17:45:53#
"Phase= 1","Criterion= 16","Correct= 7","Trial# = 6","A2","B2","Correct",#2003-03-18 17:45:54#
"Phase= 1","Criterion= 16","Correct= 8","Trial# = 7","A3","B3","Correct",#2003-03-18 17:45:56#
"Phase= 1","Criterion= 16","Correct= 9","Trial# = 8","A2","B2","Correct",#2003-03-18 17:45:57#
"Phase= 1","Criterion= 16","Correct= 10","Trial# = 9","A3","B3","Correct",#2003-03-18 17:45:58#
"Phase= 1","Criterion= 16","Correct= 11","Trial# = 10","A2","B2","Correct",#2003-03-18 17:45:59#
"Phase= 1","Criterion= 16","Correct= 12","Trial# = 11","A2","B2","Correct",#2003-03-18 17:46:01#
"Phase= 1","Criterion= 16","Correct= 13","Trial# = 12","A1","B1","Correct",#2003-03-18 17:46:01#
"Phase= 1","Criterion= 16","Correct= 14","Trial# = 13","A1","B1","Correct",#2003-03-18 17:46:02#
"Phase= 1","Criterion= 16","Correct= 15","Trial# = 14","A1","B1","Correct",#2003-03-18 17:46:03#
"Phase= 1","Criterion= 16","Correct= 16","Trial# = 15","A3","B3","Correct",#2003-03-18 17:46:04#
"Phase= 1","Criterion= 16","Correct= 17","Trial# = 16","A3","B3","Correct",#2003-03-18 17:46:05#
"Phase= 1","Criterion= 16","Correct= 18","Trial# = 17","A3","B3","Correct",#2003-03-18 17:46:06#
"Phase= 1","Criterion= 16","Correct= 19","Trial# = 18","A3","B3","Correct",#2003-03-18 17:46:07#
"Phase =1","Criterion = 16","Correct = 19"
"Phase= 2","Criterion= 16","Correct= 0","Trial# = 1","A2","C2","Wrong",#2003-03-18 17:46:09#
"Phase= 2","Criterion= 16","Correct= 0","Trial# = 2","A2","C2","Wrong",#2003-03-18 17:46:09#
"Phase= 2","Criterion= 16","Correct= 0","Trial# = 3","A3","C3","Wrong",#2003-03-18 17:46:09#
```

Figure 7.25 displays an example of the data output file.

Debugging

Solving the Problems in Your Program One Step at a Time

We had told you earlier that there was a bug in the program and would deal with it later. The problem was that trial 18 was being recorded twice. This was not preventing the program from running, but it does present a problem now that we are trying to write the data to file. Computer programming bugs can sometimes take hours, days, or weeks to find and solve. Do not become discouraged when attempting to identify and fix problems that arise in your program. They will occur and they will take some time to "debug." The bug that is currently in the M2S project took us over 30 hours to fix when we designed this program initially. It will take you 3 seconds to fix it. The dissimilarity in time illustrates the difference between being a contingency shaped versus a rule-governed programmer. Spend some time attempting to figure out where the bug is before reading on.

The best way to potentially identify bugs in your program is to track the values of your variables step by step as your program goes through the code. This may appear hard to do in Visual Basic.NET because the graphical interface covers up your code when running and everything happens so fast. A complete running through of all your code might take the computer less than a millisecond. There are others way though to track your variable values. We have been using one all along in this chapter. It is via the me.Text display at the top of your screen. Although we did not place all our variables within this display, you easily could do so when encountering bugs in your program. Another way to track the values of your variables is to create a series of TextBoxes on the side of your form that you write the variable values into each time the values are loaded. When you run the program you can watch the values within these TextBoxes change correctly or incorrectly at the moment they are generated. After finding the bug(s), simply delete the TextBoxes from the form or make them Visible = False.

Now back to our current bug. The problem that we are experiencing here only appears to happen when a given criterion is not met and the participant is "recycled" through the same phase of the experiment again. This should be your first clue. Something is wrong with the code that reinitiates the same phase again. The relevant code begins when the participant clicks on picM2S(1-3) which is found in the picM2S0_Click subroutine. Look now at the code which becomes read by VB.NET if the responses are correct or incorrect. We know that the .wav files are playing correctly so this is not the problem. However, there are directions here to start the Randomize_Stimuli_Presentation subroutine which will then check to see if the criterion is met or not. Here is where the problem begins. When the criterion is not met, there are directions to go to the Start_Over_Again subroutine. This subroutine is only accessed when a criterion is not achieved, and our error is only occurring when a criterion is not achieved. The problem must lay here.

Take a good look at this subroutine. What does it actually do?

```
Sub Start_Over_Again()
Dim i, r
For i = 1 To vNumberTrials
vRandNumber(i) = 0
Next i
vCounter = 0
vCorrect = 0
For i = 1 To vNumberTrials
r = Int(vNumberTrials * Rnd() + 1)
If vRandNumber(r) < 1 Then
vRandNumber(r) = i
Else
i = i - 1
End If
Next i
End Sub
```

First it declares the letters i and r to be used as variables only within this subroutine. Next it clears out the previous values of i and r that were used to hold the random trial and position information from our two dimensional array. When starting the phase of trials over again we wanted to clear out the values from the "used" trials that had already been presented to the participant. We also reset some variables back to 0; specifically vCounter and vCorrect. Think about what each of these variables do. vCorrect tracks the frequency of correct responses made during a given. Shifting this value back to 0 appears to be logically correct. Now look at vCounter. This variable tracks the trial number the participant is on. Shifting this value back to 0 means that the next trial presented to the participant will be trial 0, when in fact it should really be trial 1. Here is the bug. The value of vCounter should be reset to 1 and not 0. Change the code accordingly and run the program. The bug should be fixed. Edit this subroutine so that:

```
vCounter = 0
```

is changed to:

```
vCounter = 1
```

Summary

There are many ways to build upon this working matching to sample program. You can put any stimuli you create into the program. Simply delete the images you currently have, and replace them with your new images (keeping the same file names of course). If you want to add more stimuli than the 9 we used here, all you need to do is change the names in the data input file and the size of some of the variables. If you want to add more trials or longer phases you just need to change the array sizes and the variable ranges. You can add entirely different sets of stimuli by adding another frmM2S with different stimuli and having this form show instead of the debriefing instructions. You could change the background colors during certain phases. You could add a point counter to track obtained reinforcers. You could use video clips as reinforcing or punishing stimuli. The possibilities are endless.

We took you on a pretty windy road to get to the end of this chapter's program. There were many detours and even some dead ends. It was done purposely to illustrate a programmer's real travel route from start to finish. In case you missed any of the subtle changes that we made throughout the chapter, here is the frmM2S code in its entirety:

```
Option Explicit On
Public Class frmM2S
Inherits System.Windows.Forms.Form
Dim vTrack
Dim vHeader As String
Dim vPos As String
Dim vNeg As String
'Dim vStimuli(3) As String
Dim vTrials((36), (3))
Dim vRandNumber(36) As Integer
Dim vCounter As Integer
Dim vCriterion As Integer
Dim vCorrect As Integer
Dim vPhase As Integer
Dim vCheckEnd As Integer
Dim vNumberTrials As Integer
Dim vAnswer As String

Private Sub picM2SO_Click(ByVal sender As System.Object,
   ByVal e As System.EventArgs) Handles picM2S1.Click,
   picM2S2.Click, picM2S3.Click

Dim buttonClicked As PictureBox
buttonClicked = CType(sender, PictureBox)
If buttonClicked.Name = picM2S1.Name() And vTrack = 1 Or
   buttonClicked.Name = picM2S2.Name() And vTrack = 2 Or
   buttonClicked.Name = picM2S3.Name And vTrack = 3 Then
wmp1.FileName = vPos
wmp1.Play()
'Load_Stimuli()
```

```
vCorrect = vCorrect + 1
vAnswer = "Correct"
Me.Text = "Phase= " & vPhase & "Criterion= " & vCriterion
   & "Correct= " & vCorrect & "Trial# = " & vCounter &
   vTrials(vRandNumber(vCounter), 0) &
   vTrials(vRandNumber(vCounter), 1) & vAnswer & Date.Now
WriteLine(2, "Phase= " & vPhase, "Criterion= " & vCriterion,
   "Correct= " & vCorrect, "Trial# = " & vCounter,
   vTrials(vRandNumber(vCounter), 0),
   vTrials(vRandNumber(vCounter), 1), vAnswer, Date.Now)
Show_Rand_Stim()
Randomize_Stimuli_Position()
Else
If buttonClicked.Name = picM2S2.Name() Or buttonClicked.Name
   = picM2S1.Name() Or buttonClicked.Name = picM2S3.Name
   Then
wmp1.FileName = vNeg
wmp1.Play()
'Load_Stimuli()
vAnswer = "Wrong"
Me.Text = "Phase= " & vPhase & "Criterion= " & vCriterion
   & "Correct= " & vCorrect & "Trial# = " & vCounter &
   vTrials(vRandNumber(vCounter), 0) &
   vTrials(vRandNumber(vCounter), 1) & vAnswer & Date.Now
WriteLine(2, "Phase= " & vPhase, "Criterion= " & vCriterion,
   "Correct= " & vCorrect, "Trial# = " & vCounter,
   vTrials(vRandNumber(vCounter), 0),
   vTrials(vRandNumber(vCounter), 1), vAnswer, Date.Now)
Show_Rand_Stim()
Randomize_Stimuli_Position()
End If
End If
End Sub

Private Sub frmM2S_Load(ByVal sender As System.Object,
   ByVal e As System.EventArgs) Handles MyBase.Load
Input_Trial_Information()
Load_Random_Trials()
Show_Rand_Stim()
Randomize_Stimuli_Position()
End Sub

Sub Randomize_Stimuli_Position()
```

```
If vCounter > vNumberTrials Then
If vCriterion < vCorrect Then
WriteLine(2, "Phase =" & vPhase, "Criterion = " &
   vCriterion, "Correct = " & vCorrect)
If vCheckEnd = 1 Then
Dim x As New frmIns2()
Me.Hide()
x.Show()
End If
If vCheckEnd = 0 Then
Dim x As New frmM2S()
x.Show()
Me.Hide()
End If
Else
WriteLine(2, "Phase =" & vPhase, "Criterion = " &
   vCriterion, "Correct = " & vCorrect)
Start_Over_Again()
End If
Else
Randomize()
Dim r
r = Int(6 * Rnd() + 1)

Select Case r
Case 1
picM2S0.Image = Image.FromFile("c:\programming\M2S\" &
   vTrials(vRandNumber(vCounter), 0) & ".bmp")
picM2S1.Image = Image.FromFile("c:\programming\M2S\" &
   vTrials(vRandNumber(vCounter), 1) & ".bmp")
picM2S2.Image = Image.FromFile("c:\programming\M2S\" &
   vTrials(vRandNumber(vCounter), 2) & ".bmp")
picM2S3.Image = Image.FromFile("c:\programming\M2S\" &
   vTrials(vRandNumber(vCounter), 3) & ".bmp")
vTrack = 1
Case 2
picM2S0.Image = Image.FromFile("c:\programming\M2S\" &
   vTrials(vRandNumber(vCounter), 0) & ".bmp")
picM2S1.Image = Image.FromFile("c:\programming\M2S\" &
      vTrials(vRandNumber(vCounter), 2) & ".bmp")
picM2S2.Image = Image.FromFile("c:\programming\M2S\" &
   vTrials(vRandNumber(vCounter), 1) & ".bmp")
```

```
picM2S3.Image = Image.FromFile("c:\programming\M2S\" &
   vTrials(vRandNumber(vCounter), 3) & ".bmp")
vTrack = 2
Case 3
picM2S0.Image = Image.FromFile("c:\programming\M2S\" &
   vTrials(vRandNumber(vCounter), 0) & ".bmp")
picM2S1.Image = Image.FromFile("c:\programming\M2S\" &
   vTrials(vRandNumber(vCounter), 3) & ".bmp")
picM2S2.Image = Image.FromFile("c:\programming\M2S\" &
   vTrials(vRandNumber(vCounter), 2) & ".bmp")
picM2S3.Image = Image.FromFile("c:\programming\M2S\" &
   vTrials(vRandNumber(vCounter), 1) & ".bmp")
vTrack = 3
Case 4
picM2S0.Image = Image.FromFile("c:\programming\M2S\" &
   vTrials(vRandNumber(vCounter), 0) & ".bmp")
picM2S1.Image = Image.FromFile("c:\programming\M2S\" &
   vTrials(vRandNumber(vCounter), 1) & ".bmp")
picM2S2.Image = Image.FromFile("c:\programming\M2S\" &
   vTrials(vRandNumber(vCounter), 3) & ".bmp")
picM2S3.Image = Image.FromFile("c:\programming\M2S\" &
   vTrials(vRandNumber(vCounter), 2) & ".bmp")
vTrack = 1
Case 5
picM2S0.Image = Image.FromFile("c:\programming\M2S\" &
   vTrials(vRandNumber(vCounter), 0) & ".bmp")
picM2S1.Image = Image.FromFile("c:\programming\M2S\" &
   vTrials(vRandNumber(vCounter), 2) & ".bmp")
picM2S2.Image = Image.FromFile("c:\programming\M2S\" &
   vTrials(vRandNumber(vCounter), 3) & ".bmp")
picM2S3.Image = Image.FromFile("c:\programming\M2S\" &
   vTrials(vRandNumber(vCounter), 1) & ".bmp")
vTrack = 3
Case 6
picM2S0.Image = Image.FromFile("c:\programming\M2S\" &
   vTrials(vRandNumber(vCounter), 0) & ".bmp")
picM2S1.Image = Image.FromFile("c:\programming\M2S\" &
   vTrials(vRandNumber(vCounter), 3) & ".bmp")
picM2S2.Image = Image.FromFile("c:\programming\M2S\" &
   vTrials(vRandNumber(vCounter), 1) & ".bmp")
picM2S3.Image = Image.FromFile("c:\programming\M2S\" &
   vTrials(vRandNumber(vCounter), 2) & ".bmp")
vTrack = 2
```

```
End Select

End If

End Sub
Sub Load_Random_Trials()
Dim i, r, x, y

For i = 1 To vNumberTrials
Input(1, x)
Input(1, vTrials(i, 0))
Input(1, vTrials(i, 1))
Input(1, vTrials(i, 2))
Input(1, vTrials(i, 3))
Next i
Randomize()
For i = 1 To vNumberTrials
r = Int(vNumberTrials * Rnd() + 1)
If vRandNumber(r) < 1 Then
vRandNumber(r) = i
Else
i = i - 1
End If
Next i
End Sub

Sub Show_Rand_Stim()
vCounter = vCounter + 1
End Sub

Sub Start_Over_Again()
Dim i, r
For i = 1 To vNumberTrials
vRandNumber(i) = 0
Next i
vCounter = 1
vCorrect = 0
For i = 1 To vNumberTrials
r = Int(vNumberTrials * Rnd() + 1)
If vRandNumber(r) < 1 Then
vRandNumber(r) = i
Else
i = i - 1
```

```
End If
Next i

End Sub
Sub Input_Trial_Information()
Input(1, vHeader)
Input(1, vPhase)
Input(1, vHeader)
Input(1, vNumberTrials)
Input(1, vHeader)
Input(1, vPos)
Input(1, vHeader)
Input(1, vNeg)
Input(1, vHeader)
Input(1, vCriterion)
Input(1, vHeader)
Input(1, vCheckEnd)

End Sub
```

References

Green, G., & Saunders, R. R. (1998). Stimulus equivalence. In K. A. Lattal & M. Perone (Eds.) *Handbook of research methods in human operant behavior*. Plenum Press: New York.

Chapter 8: Complex Schedules and Data Exportation

Beyond the Simple Schedule

Many of the contemporary research questions being asked by human operant researchers can not be answered using just simple schedules of reinforcement. Such questions involve response allocations on concurrently available schedules, sensitivity (or insensitivity) to programmed contingencies on mixed or multiple schedules, and the effects of negative reinforcement or punishment conditions on behavior. For example, you may wish to examine behavior when a subject is exposed to a differential reinforcement of low rate schedule and then compare it to when he/she is exposed to a negative reinforcement schedule for high rates. This could be done using a multiple or mixed schedule with a different Visual Basic.NET Windows Form being utilized for each schedule component. You might also wish to examine whether a subject allocates his responses proportional to the relative rates of reinforcement obtained across two response options in a concurrent choice paradigm. Here one Windows Form could house both response options, and using two different Buttons, you could link the two different schedules together. There are many ways to build upon the simple schedules of reinforcement that we presented in Chapters 3 and 4. In this chapter we will show you a couple of ways you can do so. At the same time, we will teach you the important process of transferring your output data into a spreadsheet of analysis.

Data analysis is often a labor intensive process. It often can take just as long to analyze the data as it can to acquire it. By taking some preventative measures at the beginning of your program, you can design data output files that can be easily read into spreadsheets or databases for analysis. By haphazardly writing your data output code while programming, you will spend hours reworking or reentering your data into an acceptable format for the spreadsheet or other program to read. In Chapters 5, 6, and 7 we integrated data output files into our programs. We checked the workability of the output files by popping open Notepad or Word. Some programs you design may produce data that are sufficiently analyzed using a word processor. Others will require more in-depth analysis and graphing. We will construct examples of these latter types of programs in this chapter as we design a few complex schedules of reinforcement.

Building a Multiple Schedule of Negative Reinforcement

Creating the Interface

Multiple schedules are nothing more than two or more simple schedules of reinforcement that are alternated in presentation to the participant following the elapsing of a given amount of time or a given number of reinforcers contacted. Each schedule has a discriminative stimulus associated with it which allows for responding to come under discriminative control. In a sense the two (or more) schedules and their associated discriminative stimuli actually flip-flop in presentation. For example, after 10 minutes of responding to a VR schedule with an orange colored screen background, the participant may be presented with a VI schedule with a red colored screen background in which to respond. After another 10 minutes, the VR schedule returns. This process repeats over and over again until a steady state of responding has occurred, or a pre-determined amount of schedule presentations have been made.

Let us begin creating a multiple schedule of reinforcement which contains one component that is a Fixed-Ratio (FR) schedule and another component that is a Differential Reinforcement of Low Rate (DRL). We discussed the Fixed-Ratio schedule contingencies in Chapter 3, but have not mentioned what a DRL schedule consists of yet. As the name "low rate" suggests, this schedule provides reinforcement for responding at a low rate, or at a slow pace. In the working example, we will use pre-set values for these schedules as we did in Chapter 3. Specifically we will use a FR-3 and a DRL-1. Here however, as opposed to previous chapters, the schedules will be negative reinforcement schedules, whereby the participant will *avoid* point loss by emitting behavior consistent with the parameters of the schedule component in place at a given time. Programmers who wish to construct a more customizable version of a multiple schedule could adapt a control panel to this chapter's program as was presented in Chapter 4.

Start by opening Visual Basic.NET and creating a new Windows Application Project entitled *Multiple*. Change the name of the form to frmFR and the text to FR. This form will serve as the Fixed Ratio form. Now click on *Project* from the main menu, and select the option *Add Windows Form*, change the name to frmDRL, and click *Open*.

The text of the newly added form will appear as *frmDRL* automatically, therefore alter the text property so that it reads *DRL* instead. Visual Basic.NET will automatically change the Text property of the form to match its Name property when it is added to the Project. This new form will serve as the DRL form. As noted above, each schedule component in a multiple schedule has a distinctive discriminative stimulus associated with it. This stimulus might consist of a PictureBox with different pictures, a Label object with various textual characters, or a variation in screen BackColor. Here we will alter the forms' background colors to serve as the discriminative stimuli. Select frmFR from the Solution Explorer window by double-clicking on it, and change the BackColor property of this form to a shade of green. Now select *frmDRL* from the Solution Explorer window and change the BackColor property of this form to a shade of red. The colors are arbitrary and can be altered to suit your own color preferences if you wish.

At this time we may wish to alter some additional properties of both forms to make them suitable for actual participants. First, change the WindowState properties to *Maximized*. Second, change the MinimizeBox properties to *False*. This will keep

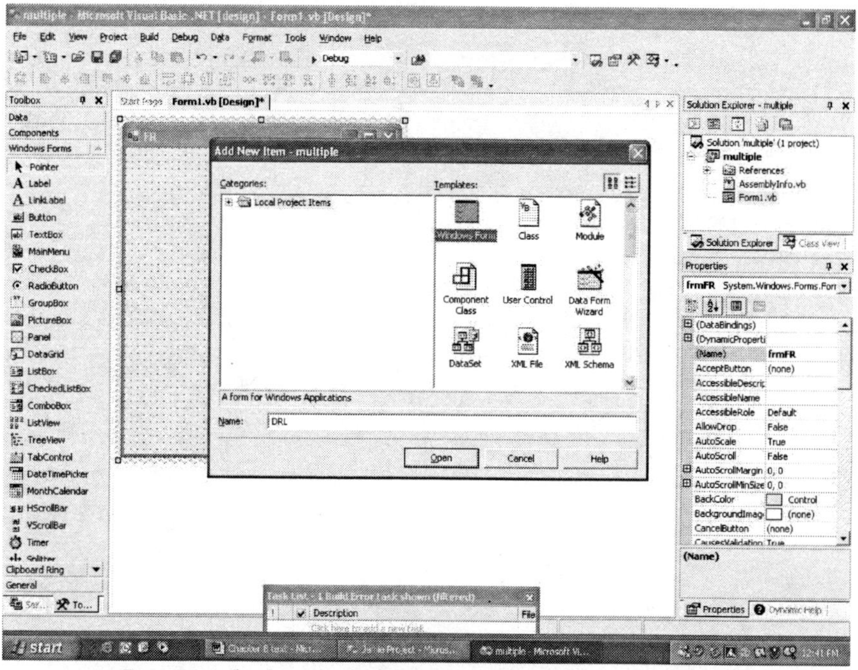

Figure 8.1 displays the dialog box used for inserting a second form into the Multiple Project.

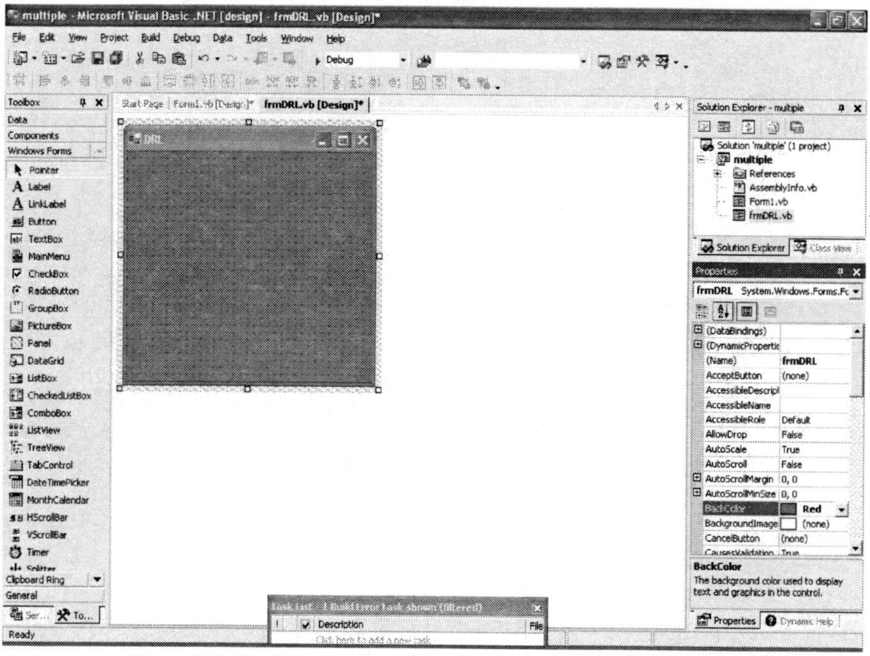

Figure 8.2 displays the altered BackColor properties of frmDRL.

the participant from being able to minimize the forms when the program is running. Third, change the MaximizeBox properties to *False*. This will have a similar effect whereby the participant can not alter form size and then re-maximize the form during program running. Change the StartUp object to the frmFR form and run the program to check your progress.

You might have discovered that while a participant can not minimize or maximize the form, they can still "close" the form while it is running using the small box in the top right hand corner. We can remove this box too, by changing the ControlBox property of our forms to *False*. Yet, if we do, we too will have trouble terminating the program while it is being constructed. Save this last safeguard for later, once the program is up and running and ready for real participants.

The next step will be to add a response operanda for the participant. Select a Button object and place it onto your FR form. Position the Button in the middle of the form, change its name to *butResponse*, and its Text to blank. You may also wish to alter the BackColor property of this Button because it will be the same color as the form's BackColor property by default. Make a similar Button on your DRL form, change its name also, to *butResponse*, and its Text to *blank*. You may be curious how you were able to change both of these Button objects to the same Name (butResponse) without VB.NET delivering you an Error message. The reason why is because while the objects do in fact have the same name, they reside on different forms. As a result, there is no problem. If the FR form is running, then the Button on frmFR is accessed and if the DRL form is running, then the Button on frmDRL is accessed. Even if both forms are running simultaneously, VB.NET can keep track of which Button refers to which form and access them accordingly.

Now add a TextBox to each form that will be used to display points to the participant. Change the name of these TextBoxes to *txtPoints* and the text property to *blank*. Also add a Label above the TextBoxes, change the name to *lblPoints* and the text to *Points*.

Code for the FR Schedule Component

The backbone of this form needs to be a Timer object which will occasionally check to see if the FR has been meet within a given amount of time. This schedule might more accurately be conceptualized as Differential Reinforcement of High Rates (DRH). However, it does lack a specific interresponse interval contingency. Therefore, for ease of discrimination while programming it will be simply referred to as a FR. The function of this "given amount of time" is to generate relatively high rates of responding, and compare and contrast these rates to the hopefully lower rates of responding that are inherent in a DRO schedule. Also, because we are using a negative reinforcement contingency with this schedule component, we need to specify an allotted amount of time we allow the participant to respond before we take away or subtract points from their point total.

For ease of illustration, we will use a 3 second time period in which we want to see three responses made by the participant. In other words, we want a rate of about

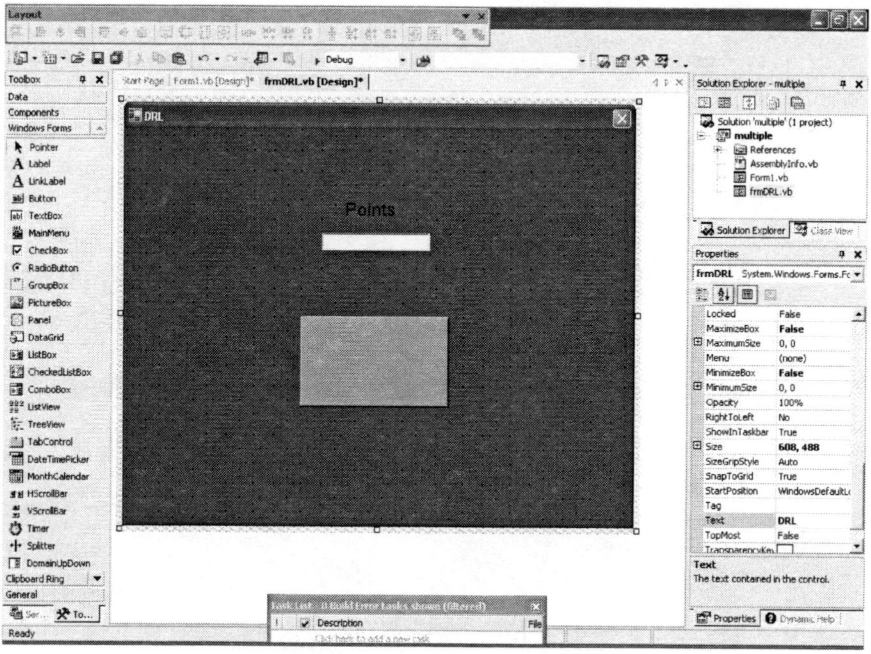

Figure 8.3 displays the DRL form with the addition of Button, TextBox, and Label objects.

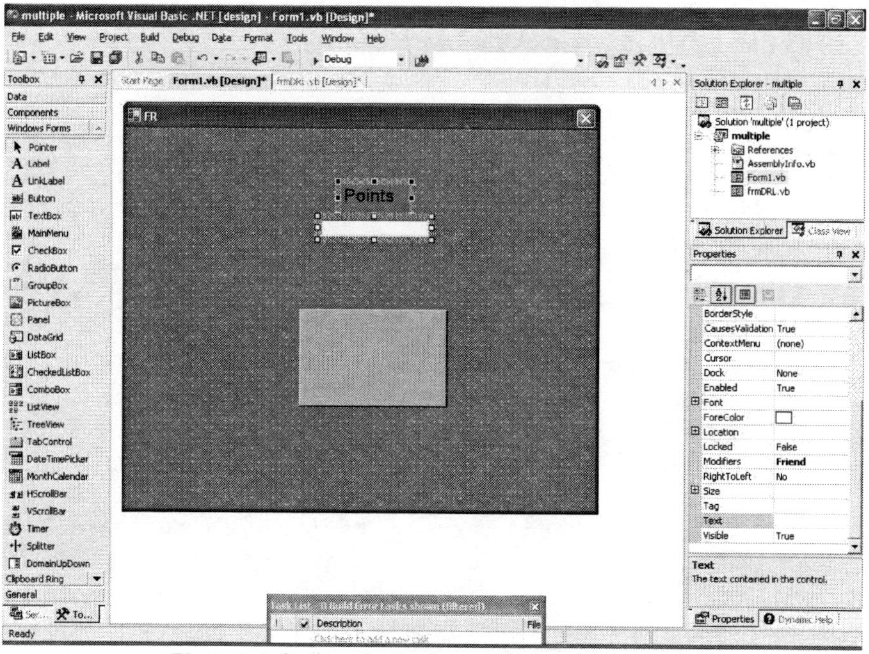

Figure 8.4 displays the FR form with the addition of the Button, TextBox, and Label objects.

1/sec. To develop code for this contingency, we need to do a couple of things. First, we need a variable that will keep track of each participant response on the Button object. Second we need the Timer to kick in every three seconds and see if the responses are at least 3. Your specific programming needs may differ from the parameters we will use as an example here, but customization will only require you to change the values from 3 seconds to X seconds and from 3 responses to X responses. Plus you already should know how to create a control panel for even further modifications.

Add a Timer object to frmFR and rename it *tmrCheck*. Change the Enabled property to *True* and change the Interval property to 3000. Now when the form loads, the Timer will automatically begin ticking away and upon the elapsing of 3000 milliseconds (3 seconds), any code we place under the Timer will activate. Double-click on tmrCheck and enter the edit mode. Place the following code under Private Sub tmrCheck_Tick():

```
If vClicks < 3 Then 'FR 3 THEN AVOID POINT LOSS
vPoints = vPoints - 1
txtPoints.Text = vPoints
End If
vClicks = 0
```

What we have created here is a little If-Then statement which states that if a variable named vClicks (we still need to declare this variable), is less than 3, take away a value of 1 from a variable named vPoints. If the value of vClicks is greater than 3, VB.NET skips this If-Then statement and jumps down to the next line of code which resets vClicks to 0. Now as the next 3 second interval begins, the value of vClicks has been reset to allow for rechecking of the above If-Then statement upon the completion of the next interval.

Let us now declare vClicks under the Inherits System.Windows.Forms.Form line of code by typing:

```
Dim vClicks As Integer
```

Declaring vPoints on the other hand is a little bit more tricky. Pretend we declare it as we did for vPoints. What will happen when this component of the multiple schedule terminates and the DRO component starts? How will the value of vPoints transfer across the forms? As you may recall, using multiple forms in a project requires you to create a new instance of the form each time it is presented on the computer screen. If you create this new instance, the value of vPoints which is located in the txtPoints object on frmFR will be blank when frmDRO appears! The way around this problem is to use a Module to hold the value of vPoints. This Module is just another object that sits within your Multiple project and stores values of variables that are to be recognized over and above the single form level. Because we want our points to remain constant across the two components of the multiple schedule, we can declare the variable of vPoints here on the Module instead of on the individual forms.

Begin by adding a Module to your project by selecting the text "Multiple" in your Solution Explorer window and right clicking on this text. A popup menu will appear. Select the option "Add" and then the sub-option "Add Module." You can change the name of the Module if you like or leave it as Module1. More complicating programming may require multiple modules, but you will probably never need to use more than one.

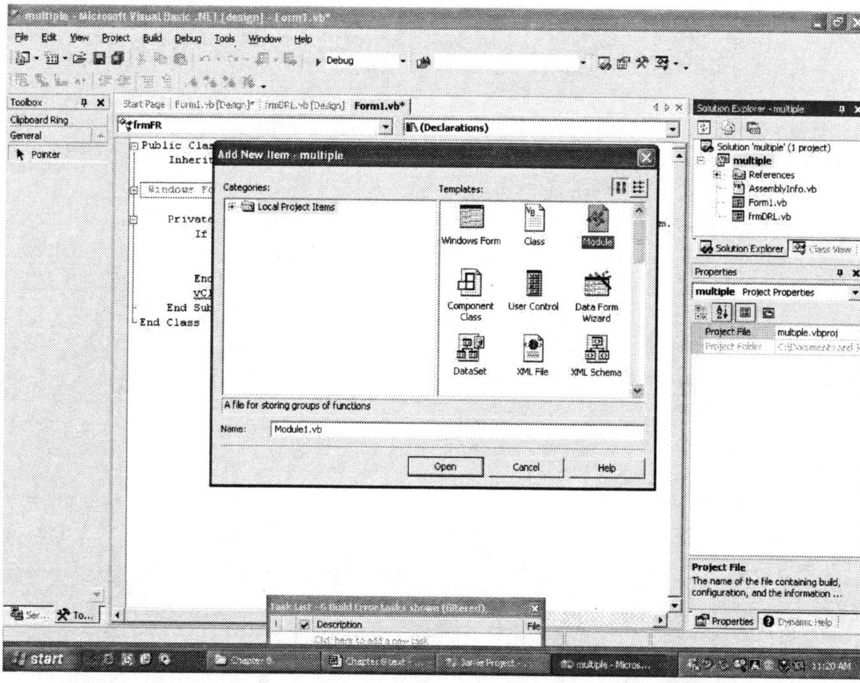

Figure 8.5 displays the popup dialog box for adding a Module to the Multiple Project.

Declaring the vPoints variable on the new Module is rather simple. First double-click on the new Module which has been added to your Solution Explorer window. You will automatically enter the edit mode for the Module, because the Module has no visible components which appear during run time. Rather the Module is nothing more than a virtual container that holds information. Under the text `Module Module1`, type the following declaration:

```
Public vPoints
```

That is it: very simple. Remember during our discussion of variables in Chapter 5, that a variable spanning beyond a single form should be declared using the "Public" declaration rather than the "Dim" declaration.

Return to frmFR and double-click on the butResponse object to enter the edit mode. Here we need to add the necessary code to increase values of vClicks each time the Button is clicked upon. Therefore, add the following code under Private Sub butResponse_Click

```
vClicks = vClicks + 1
```

Run the program and test your progress. The FR form should open, and if you don't click fast enough on the Button, negative points will start accumulating in the txtPoints TextBox.

One small issue at this time is that the points in txtPoints start off at 0, actually they are displayed as a blank box, when the program loads. This may or may not be desirable. If it is not, you can start the program with a different value of vPoints than the default 0 when the form loads. The easy thing to do is to make vPoints = 100 or some other value. Yet, a problem arises when you begin the alternations of the FR and DRL forms in the multiple schedule. If each time you load the form, the value of vPoints resets to 100, participants will be extremely confused. Here is how to get around this problem. Begin by typing the following text under the Private Sub frmFR_Load()

```
If vSwitch = 0 Then vPoints = 100 'TO SET THE INITIAL POINT
   VALUE
txtPoints.Text = vPoints
```

The first line of code contains an If – Then statement which states if a variable called vSwitch = 0 (we still need to declare this variable) then make the value of vPoints = 100. The second line of code states to display the value of vPoints in the txtPoints TextBox. The new variable vSwitch can be used to count successive presentations of the multiple schedule's components. So once the FR component is completed, vSwitch will go from 0 to 1. If vSwitch is sitting at 0 right now, and it will be when the program is first started, turn vPoints to 100. Afterwards, vSwitch will never be 0 again, and VB.NET passes this If – Then statement and just moves down to the next one and places the value of the Public variable, vPoints, into txtPoints.

Declare vSwitch on your Module1 not on your FR or DRL forms because we will use this variable across forms to track the number of presentations of each component of the schedule. To declare vSwitch type:

```
Public vSwitch
```

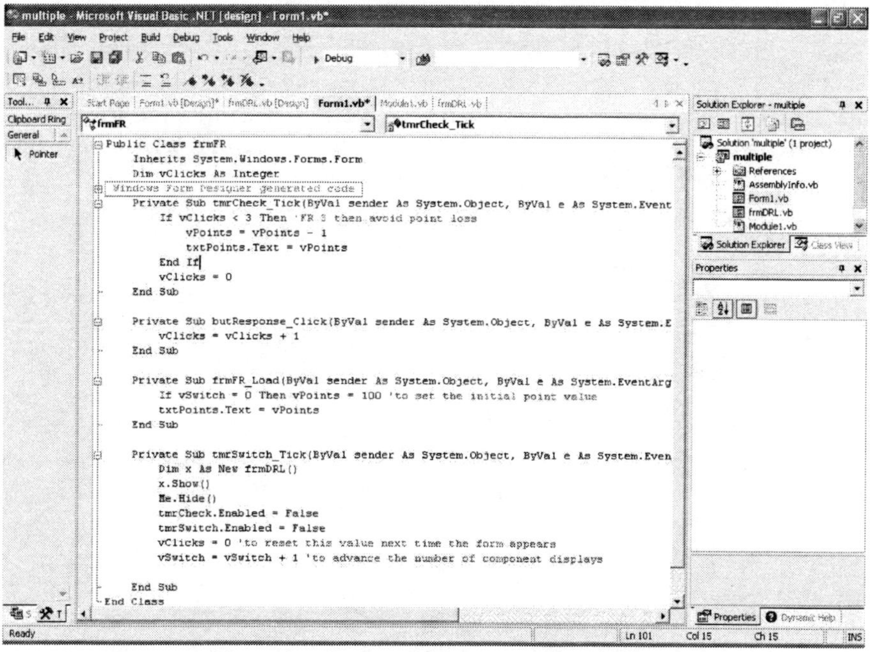

Figure 8.6 displays the correct code for frmFR.

All that is left to do on this form now is to add another Timer that will close this schedule component (and this FR form) and open the DRL form and initiate those contingencies. Begin by adding a Timer object and renaming it tmrSwitch. Also change the enabled property to True and the Interval property to 30000 (or 30 seconds). The 30000 millisecond interval will be used for the desired length of exposure to this component of the multiple schedule. You can change the interval to meet your own needs later. Finally add the following code under tmrSwitch:

```
Dim x As New frmDRL()
x.Show()
Me.Hide()
tmrCheck.Enabled = False
tmrSwitch.Enabled = False
vClicks = 0 'TO RESET THIS VALUE NEXT TIME THE FORM
   APPEARS
vSwitch = vSwitch + 1 'TO ADVANCE THE NUMBER OF
   COMPONENT DISPLAYS
```

This code generates a new instance of form frmDRL and shows the form while hiding the existing FR form (called *me*). Next both Timers are shut down so they do not continue to run while the DRL form is in action. The variable vClicks is also reset to 0 so that the next time frmFR is loaded it is not containing old values of vClicks, and a value of one is added to variable vSwitch. We can use this increasing value of vSwitch to eventually terminate the entire program with an If – Then vSwitch type statement. Run the program and check your progress. If done correctly, after 30 seconds of responding on frmFR, frmDRL should appear. Not much happens after this, but adding some code will fix it.

Code for the DRL Schedule Component

Much of the code used in the FR form can be recycled on the DRL form. Begin with the Private Sub frmDRL_Load subroutine and type (or copy and paste from frmFR) the following:

```
txtPoints.Text = vPoints
```

You will not need to add the other line of code found in the Private Sub frmFR_Load subroutine that set the initial value of vPoints to 100 because by now, vPoints will have a participant specific value after their exposure to the first component of the schedule.

The code under butResponse is the same for this form as it was on frmFR. Therefore copy and paste the following code from butResponse on frmFR to butResponse on frmDRL under the Private butResponse_Click subroutine:

```
vClicks = vClicks + 1
```

Also declare this variable under the Inherits System.Windows.Forms.Form line in the code editor by typing:

```
Dim vClicks As Integer
```

As with the FR form, we will again need two Timers on the DRL form. The first Timer will check the rate of responding to ensure it is within our DRL contingencies, and the second Timer will control the total amount of time the DRL component is presented. Add the first of the two Timers and change the name to tmrCheck, the enabled property to True, and the Interval property to 3000 (for 3 seconds). For demonstration purposes, we will program a DRL schedule where only 1 response must occur within a three second time interval in order to avoid point loss. Therefore, add the following code under the Private Sub tmrCheck_Tick subroutine:

```
If vClicks <> 1 Then
vPoints = vPoints - 1
txtPoints.Text = vPoints
End If
vClicks = 0
```

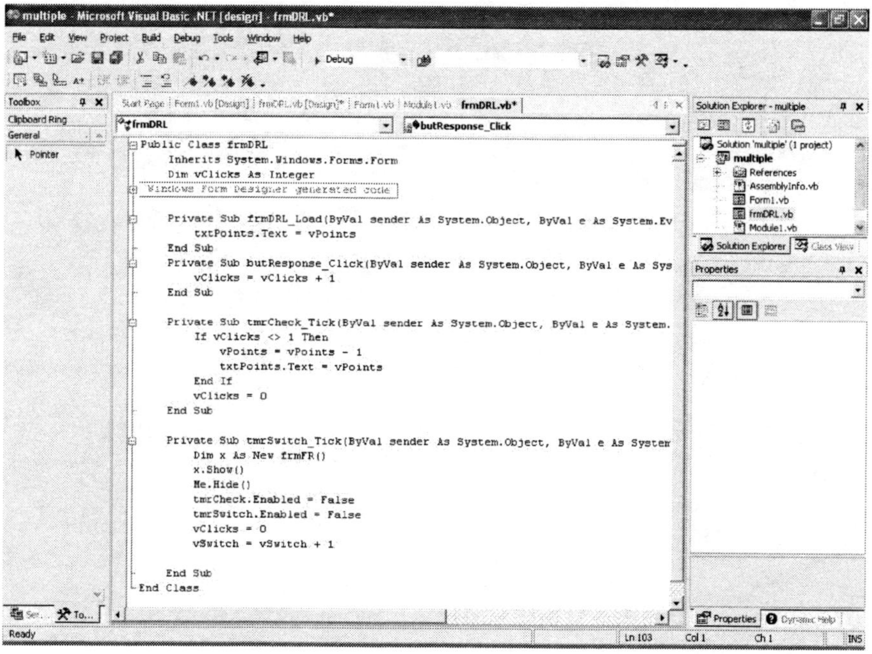

Figure 8.7 displays the correct code for frmDRL.

The first section of code, the If – Then statement, checks to see if the value of vClicks is not equal to 1. If the value is anything greater than 1 or less than 1, one point will be subtracted from vPoints and displayed in the txtPoints TextBox. After the elapsing of the 3 second interval, regardless of whether points were subtracted or not, vClicks are then reset back to 0 as the next interval begins.

Add the second Timer to frmDRL and rename it tmrSwitch as you did before on the second Timer you added to frmFR. Change the Enabled property to True and the Interval property to 30000 milliseconds. Double-click on tmrSwitch and enter the edit mode. Type the following code under Private Sub tmrSwitch_Click:

```
Dim x As New frmFR()
x.Show()
Me.Hide()
tmrCheck.Enabled = False
tmrSwitch.Enabled = False
vClicks = 0
vSwitch = vSwitch + 1
```

This code operates identically as its counterpart did on the FR form. Specifically, it generates a new instance of form frmFR and shows the form while hiding the existing DRL form (called *me*). The Timers are then shut down so they do not continue to run while the FR form is in action. The variable vClicks is also reset to 0 so that the next time frmFR is loaded it is not containing old values of vClicks, and the value of one is added to the variable vSwitch. Run the program and check your progress. If all goes well you will have a working multiple schedule of negative reinforcement with one component consisting of a FR (or DRH) schedule and another component consisting of a DRL schedule.

Enhancing the Multiple Schedule with Data Collection, Writing to an Output File, and Generating a Cumulative Record

There are a variety of different ways we could write to file the response data that are being collected with our multiple schedule. We could store values of vClick and write them to file at the end of the experiment. We could also write vClicks each time the butResponse is clicked for a molecular level analysis. We could create another Timer with an interval of x seconds specifically for writing data to file. Finally we could tie into the existing tmrCheck Timer and have it write to file upon completing its interval, which in this case is 3 seconds for both components. For illustration purposes, we shall do the last of these options and add data output code under the existing tmrCheck Timers. Begin with frmFR by double-clicking on tmrCheck and adding the following code above the line vClicks=0 of the Private Sub tmrCheck_Tick subroutine:

```
WriteLine(1, vSwitch, vClicks, vPoints)
```

The new subroutine should look like:

```
If vClicks < 3 Then 'FR 3 THEN AVOID POINT LOSS
vPoints = vPoints - 1
txtPoints.Text = vPoints
End If
WriteLine(1, vSwitch, vClicks, vPoints)
vClicks = 0
```

This line of code writes the values of vSwitch and vClicks to a text file with an alias name called "1". It also writes the current point total to the same file. Add the exact code under the tmrCheck Timer on the DRL form, this time under vClicks=0.

We have not yet opened a file for the data to be written into, so we need to do so. The most logical place is right along with the code that sets the initial value of vPoints to 100 on frmFR. Therefore, add the following code under the existing If vSwitch = 0 Then vPoints = 100 code that is in the Private Sub frmFR_Load subroutine:

```
If vSwitch = 0 then FileOpen(1, "C:\data.txt",
   OpenMode.Append)
```

This code will open the file with a name of "data" in the c:\ directory and it will remain open until the program is terminated or additional code under an "Exit" Button or a Timer closes it. The data output raises another question: how long will the program run? You could design the program to terminate once a steady state of responding has been met. This could be assessed by creating an If – Then statement with code such that if no more than X number of points were subtracted from vPoints for a given number of vSwitch the program would end. You could also design the program to terminate regardless of responding patterns after x number of component presentations. In this example we will do the latter. The program will terminate after 10 presentations of both components of the multiple schedule. Therefore, add the following code under the Private Sub frmFR_Load subroutine:

```
If vSwitch > 10 then
FileClose(1)
End
```

Keep in mind that if you want the program to end after an odd number of vSwitch presentations (like 3, 9, 25), you will need to place the above code under the frmDRL Private Sub frmDRL_Load subroutine instead. Run the program, check your progress, and after 10 sequences the program should end. Afterwards, find your data file in the C:\ directory and check out your data using NotePad. It should look similar to Figure 8.8.

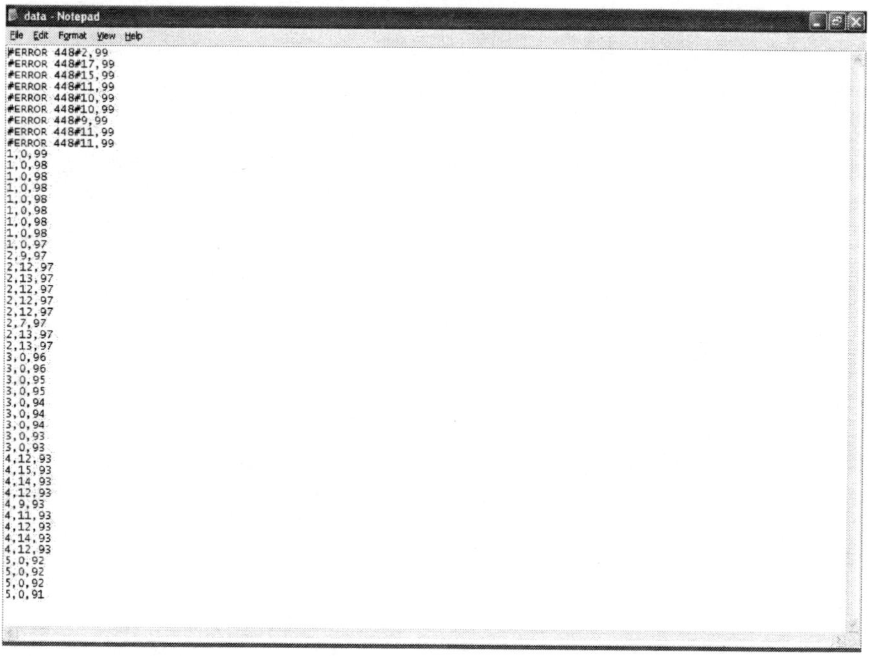

Figure 8.8 displays an illustrative example of the resulting data file.

From observation of the data file in Figure 8.8 you will notice that an error message (#ERROR 448#) was written in the vSwitch spot of the data file instead of the value 0. This will occur every time you have a variable with a value of 0. It is just another VB.NET flaw. So, before you save your data for analysis you might want to replace these error lines with the 0 value. Besides the error at the beginning of the file, all the desired data has been written. Researchers can now examine relative response rates on the multiple schedule. You could enhance this data file with more detail regarding which component is in effect when. Perhaps the values of vSwitch are not as important as naming the actual schedule component. If so, you could delete the vSwitch section of the data writing code and replace it with *FR* on frmFR and *DRL* on frmDRL. Another way to enhance the data file would be to generate values of a variable which continue to increase every time butResponse is clicked but not reset the way vResponse is. Doing so could allow for the creation of a cumulative record of responding. If we create such a cumulative variable it would need to be added to the Module rather than the form because it would span across forms the same way that vPoints does.

Add a variable to your Module entitled vCumm that will increase in value every time either butResponse Buttons are clicked upon. To do this add the following declaration code to Module1.

```
Public vCumm
```

Now add the following code under both butResponse Buttons directly below the existing code vClicks = vClicks + 1:

```
vCumm = vCumm + 1
```

Finally, alter the data file output code to include the vCumm values each time data are written to file. The new code under the tmrCheck Timers for both forms should now read:

```
WriteLine(1, vSwitch, vClicks, vCumm, vPoints)
```

Run the program and check your data file output to ensure it includes the new vCumm variable values. From observation of the data file you can see that it appears vCumm values are being recorded properly. Look a little closer though and examine the values of vClicks when the DRL schedule is operating. All the values are 0, regardless of how many clicks you actually made during that time period. Go back and examine your code on the DRL where vClicks is reset to 0. Do you see anything suspicious? Below is the existing subroutine:

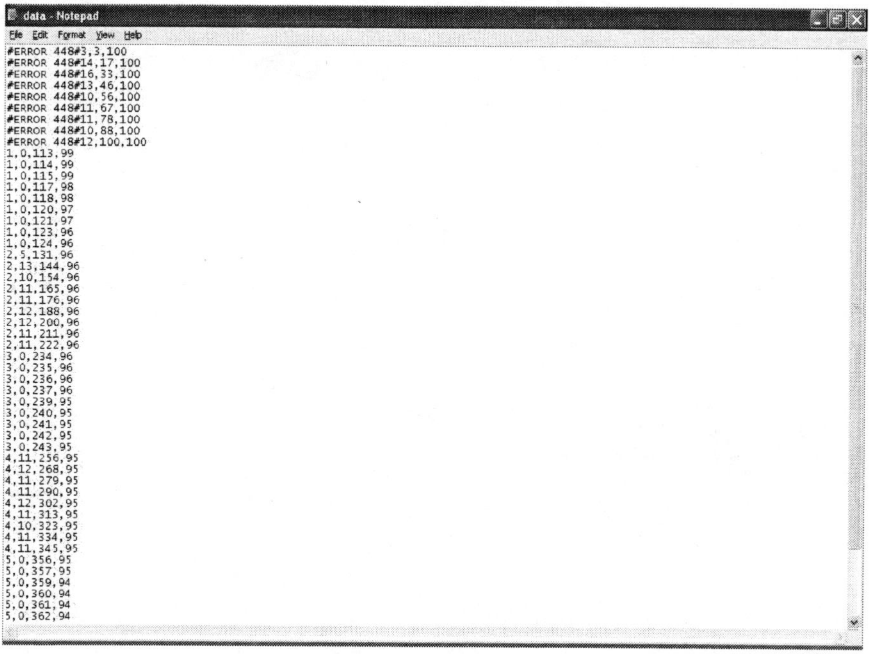

Figure 8.9 displays an illustrative example of the resulting data file with the addition of vCumm.

```
Private Sub tmrCheck_Tick(ByVal sender As System.Object,
   ByVal e As System.EventArgs) Handles tmrCheck.Tick
If vClicks <> 1 Then
vPoints = vPoints - 1
txtPoints.Text = vPoints
End If
vClicks = 0
WriteLine(1, vSwitch, vClicks, vCumm, vPoints)
End Sub
```

From examination above, you might notice that we have made the value of vClicks = 0 before we write the values to file in the next WriteLine statement. That is our problem! To fix it, just reverse these two lines of code, and then all should work properly. Run the program and check the data file. Everything should now work properly except that crazy error in the data file when vSwitch is still at 0.

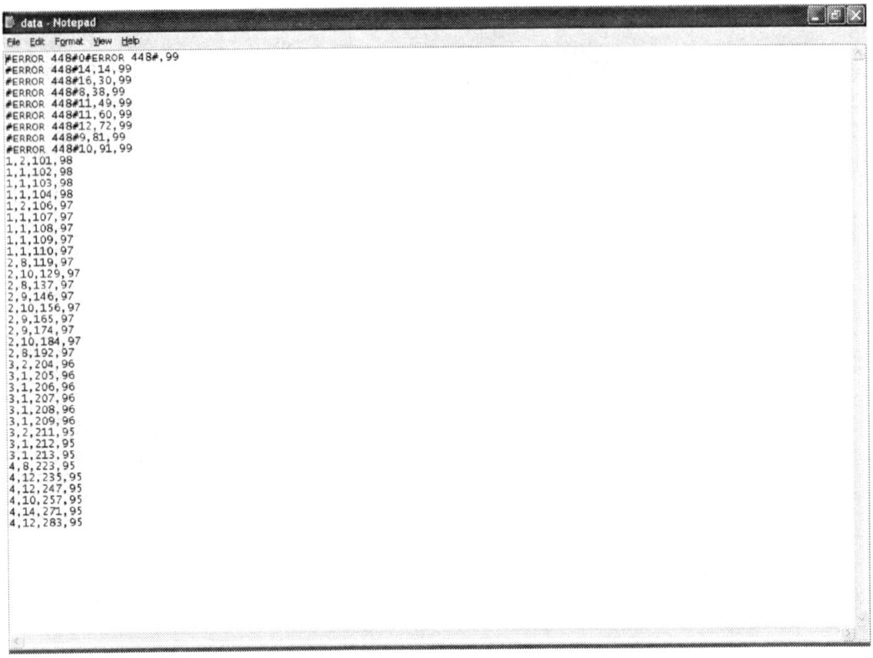

Figure 8.10 displays the data file output after correcting the code error that made all values of vClicks equal 0 on the DRL component.

Transferring the Data File into Excel for Analysis

Locating the File

Until now we have viewed our data file in Notepad or another text editor. This is fine for some data collection applications, but other applications that may lead to complex graphs and data analyses are better examined and manipulated in spreadsheets like Microsoft Excel. The process will be similar in other spreadsheets, but we will provide you with an example using Excel because it is the most commonly used program. Before getting your data into Excel, you will need to tell Excel what type of file it is and how you want it configured. This sounds more complicated than it really is. In fact, the process is very easy and can open up endless analysis possibilities for you.

Before opening Excel, figure out what directory your data file is in. If you have been following along with this chapter's example, it should be in the C:\ directory. Open up the file in Notepad, and fix that error written when vSwitch was 0. Change these errors to 0s and save and close the file.

The Transfer Process

Open Microsoft Excel. A blank worksheet should appear similar to that shown in Figure 8.11. Click on the File option found in the main toolbar on the left hand side. Select the *Open* option, and an open file dialogue box will appear. Change the *Files of Type* option from *All Microsoft Excel Files* to *All Files* using the downward arrow to the right of this option. Now browse through your directories until you find the *data.txt* file you created in the above example. Select the data.txt file and click on *Open*. Figure 8.12 displays the open file dialogue box.

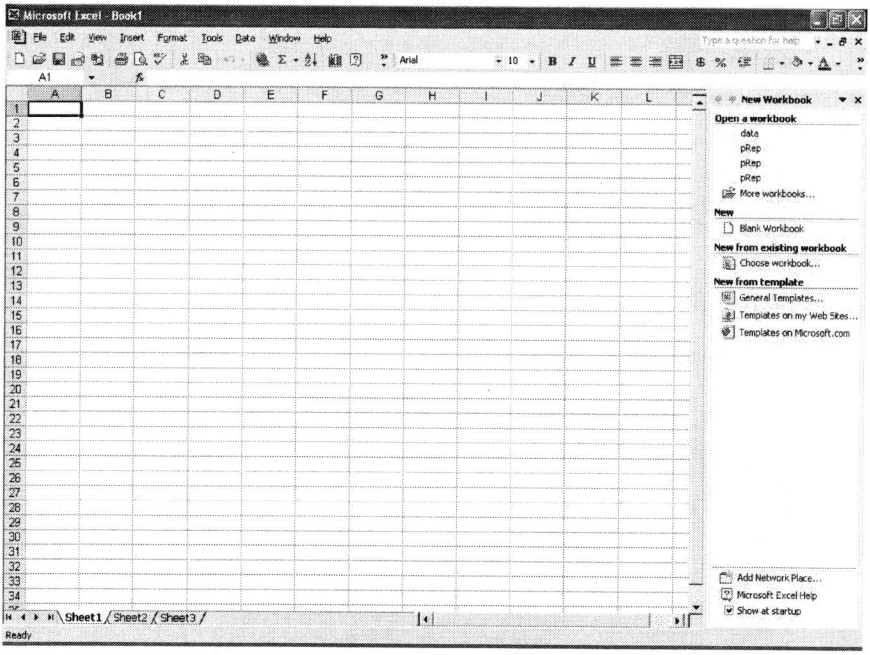

Figure 8.11 displays a blank worksheet in Microsoft Excel.

The next screen which appears is probably a little less familiar than the previous ones. This new screen is a dialogue box called the *Text Import Wizard.* An example of this dialogue box is displayed in Figure 8.13. The dialogue box contains a variety of information which is used to help Excel understand the type of file you are trying to place within it. The first section of the dialogue box asks you to tell Excel if your data are *Delimited* or *Fixed Width*.

Data that are *delimited* means that different sections of the data that are on each line of the file are separated by a *delimiter* or a textual character – in our case a comma. Data that are *fixed width* means that different sections of the data that are on each line of the file are separated by a set number of spaces. Our data file fits the first category, delimited, so select that option if it is not already. The next question that Excel wants you to answer is at what row should Excel start importing your data. This is an outstanding feature, because you might not want to start importing your data into Excel at row 1 of the data.txt file every time. This is especially the case when using

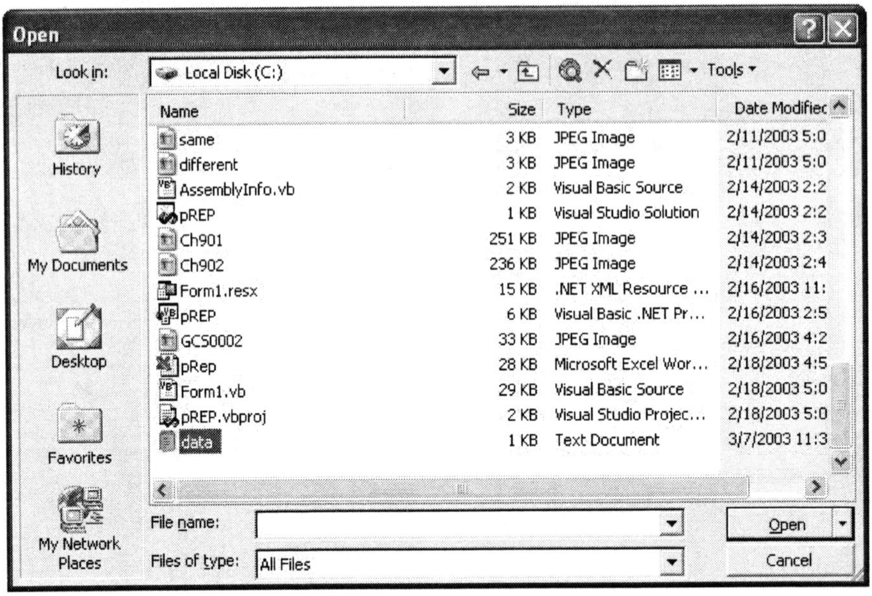

Figure 8.12 displays the open file dialogue box, the change made to "Files of Type", and the selection of "data.txt".

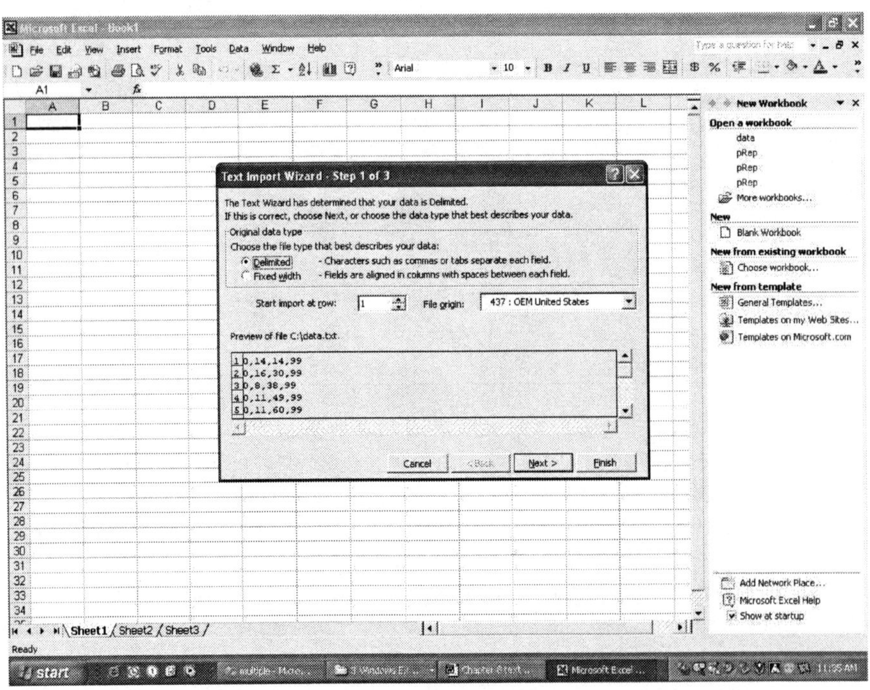

Figure 8.13 displays the first screen of the Text Import Wizard used to open a text file in Excel.

an appended data file, as we have been using, which keeps a running archive of all participants that we have run in the experiment. For now, let us assume you want to start importing the data at row 1, so leave this option as is, and click on the *Next* button. The second screen of the Text Import Wizard asks you to supply more information.

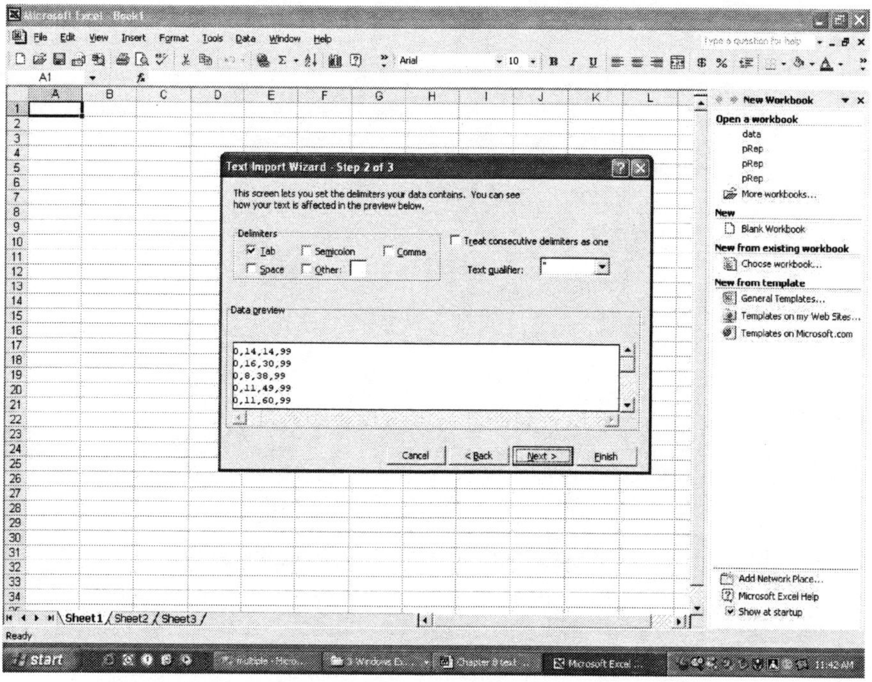

Figure 8.14 displays the second screen of the Text Import Wizard used to open a text file in Excel.

Because you selected the *Delimited* option on the previous screen, Excel now wants to know what specific type of delimiter was used to separate the data fields. The default selection is a *Tab*. We used a *Comma* to separate our data, so change this option accordingly. As soon as you make this change, Excel draws vertical lines through your data columns as depicted in Figure 8.15.

At this point, click on the *Next* button to advance to the final screen of the Text Import Wizard. This last screen asks you if you wish to convert any of your data to dates, or dates to values, or text to other types of characters. Such alterations do not apply to our data file, so just click on the *Finish* button.

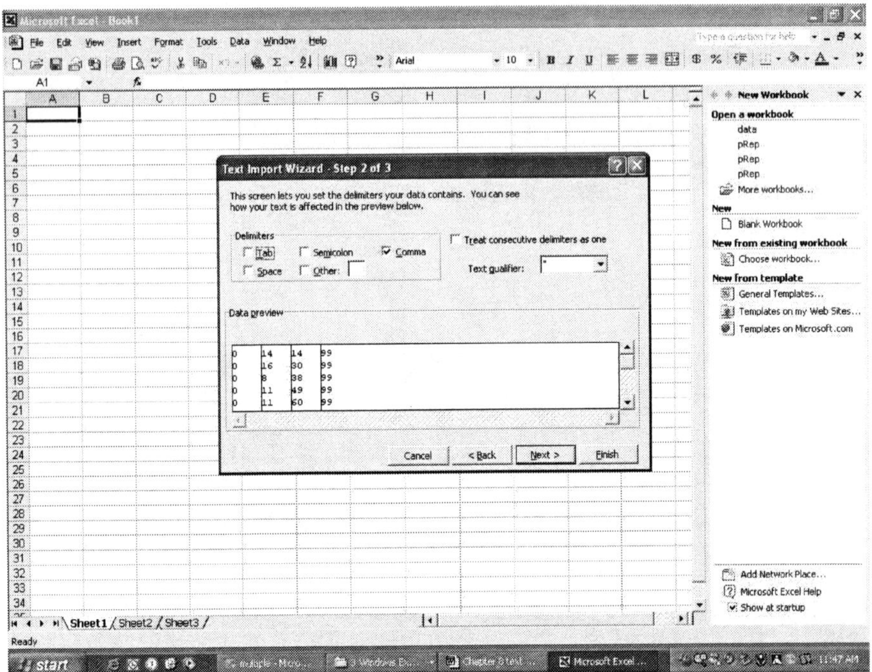

Figure 8.15 displays the second screen of the Text Import Wizard following the selection of "Comma" delimiter.

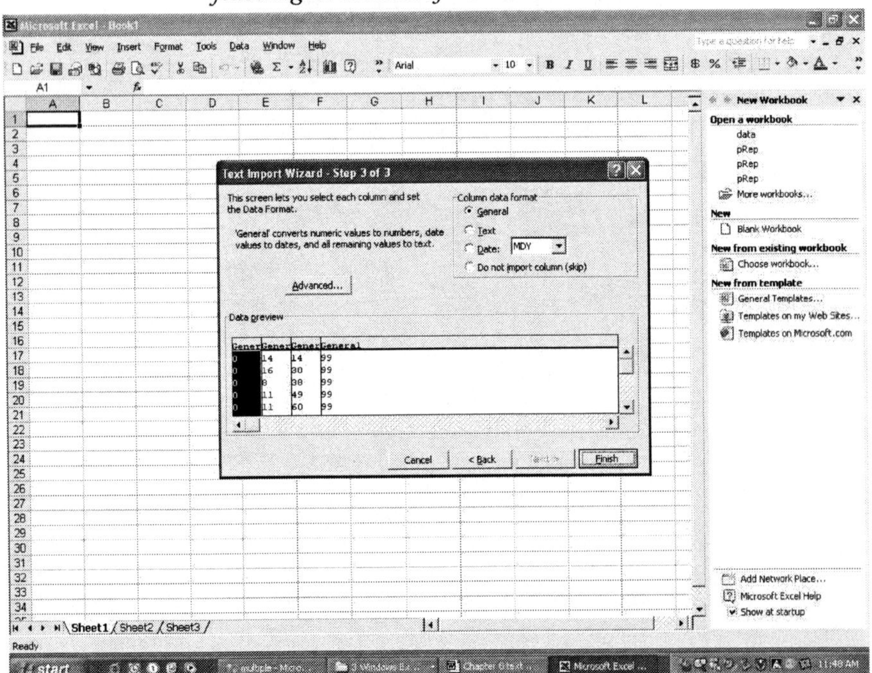

Figure 8.16 displays the final screen of the Text Import Wizard allowing you to transpose data from numbers to dates or dates to numbers.

Once you click on the *Finish* button, the Text Import Wizard goes away and you return to the main Excel program. Your data.txt data are magically entered into the Excel worksheet for endless data analysis as displayed in Figure 8.17.

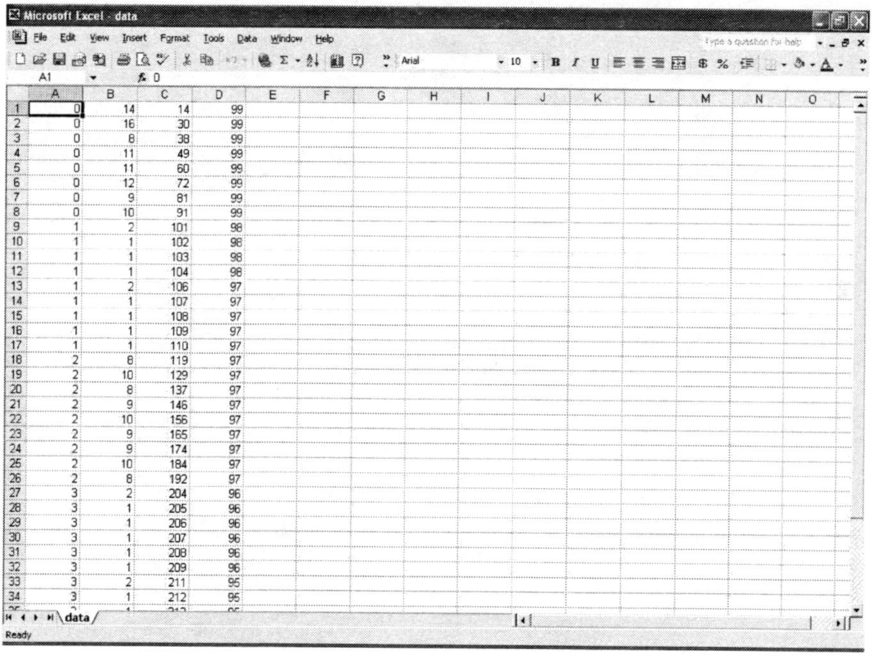

Figure 8.17 displays the Excel worksheet containing data.txt.

While the purpose of this book is not to teach you how to graph in Excel, a quick illustration will be provided to show you how truly easy this feat is to accomplish. To create a cumulative record from our data.txt file, highlight the first column of data containing the values of vSwitch. Once this column is highlighted correctly, press and hold down the *Ctrl* key and highlight the third column of data containing the values of vCumm. If done correctly, both columns should be highlighted as displayed in Figure 8.18.

With these columns highlighted, you can release the depression of the Ctrl key, and select the *Insert* option from the main menu. Now select *Chart* from the submenu, and another *Wizard* will appear. This time it is the *Chart Wizard* as shown in Figure 8.19.

There are many different types of charts to choose from. The most appropriate one for our type of data is the *Line* chart. Select this option and press the *Next* key. The next screen of the Wizard, as displayed in Figure 8.20, asks you to customize your chart in a variety of ways. Many of these customizations are beyond the scope of this book. Interested readers should acquire an additional text on Microsoft Excel. At this point, simply press the *Next* button.

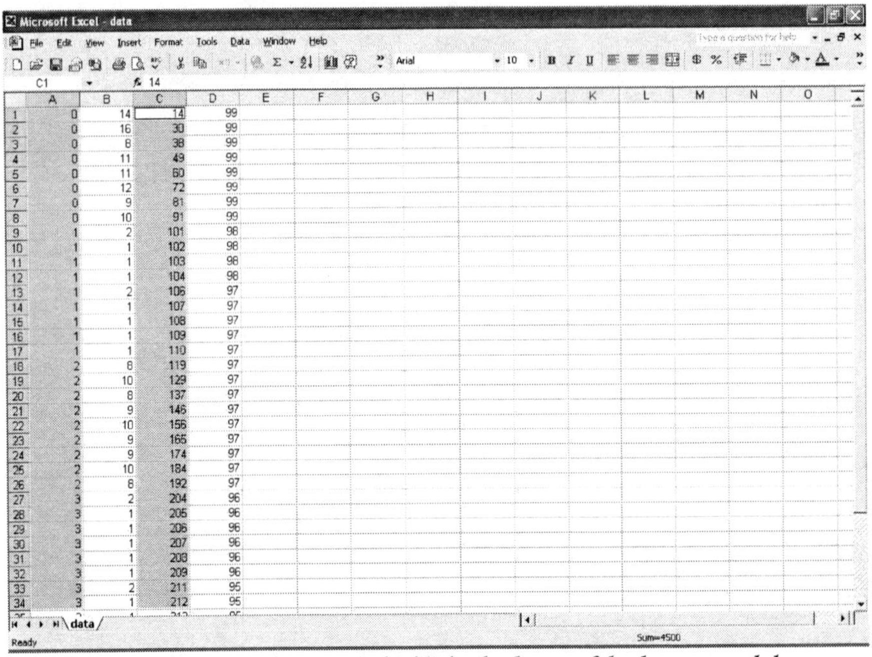

Figure 8.18 displays the correctly highlighted columns of the data.txt worksheet.

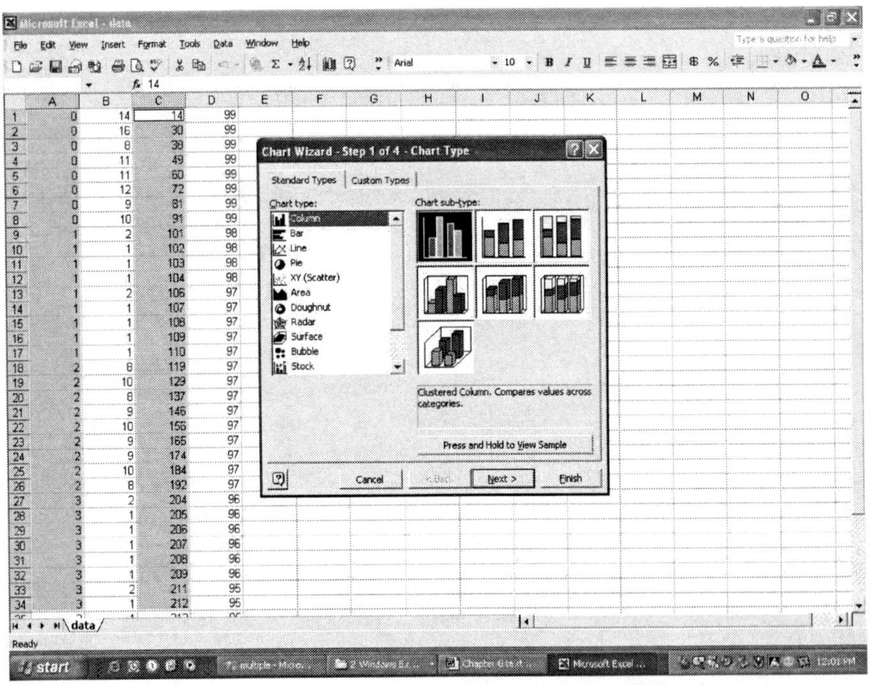

Figure 8.19 displays the first screen of the Chart Wizard.

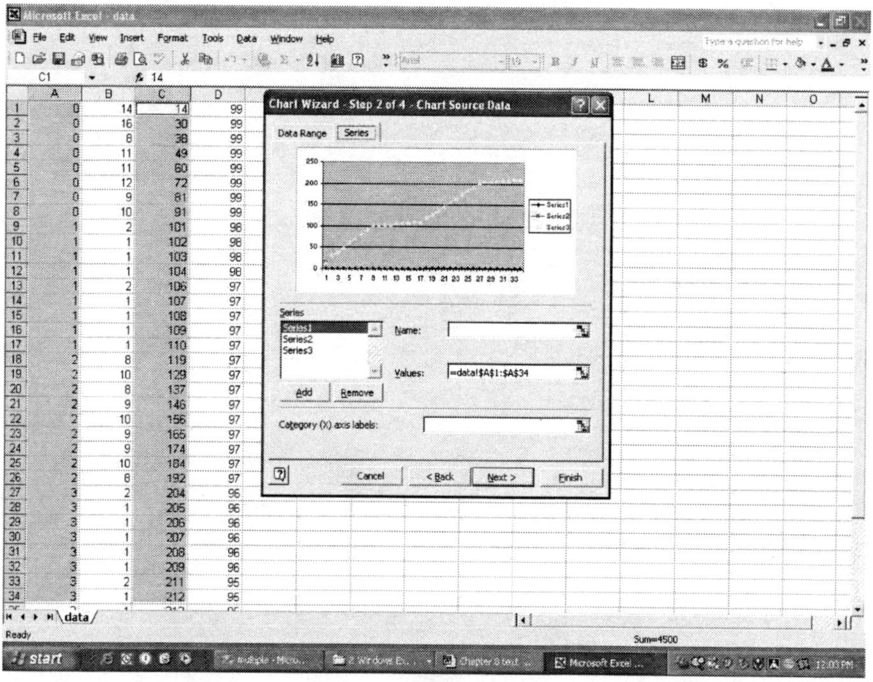

Figure 8.20 displays the second screen of the Chart Wizard.

The third screen of the Chart Wizard allows you to add a title, y-axis label, and x-axis label to your chart. Enter the text "Sample Data" for your title, "Cumulative Responses" for the y-axis label, and "3 second Intervals" for your x-axis label. Note the changes to the little graph in the Wizard as shown in Figure 8.21.

At this time, you should click on the *Next* button to advance to the final screen of the Chart Wizard, which is shown in Figure 8.22. This final screen asks if you wish to place the newly created chart in an existing worksheet in your spreadsheet "As object in", or on its own worksheet "As new sheet". Select the "As new sheet" option and click *Finish*. The resulting chart should look like that found in Figure 8.23.

Initial modifications to this graph would be to delete the legend found on the right side, eliminating the irrelevant data series, and removing the grey background color. To make all three of these changes you will follow the same sequence of steps. First, click on the item (series, legend, background) once to highlight it, then press the *delete* key. The resulting graph appears in Figure 8.24.

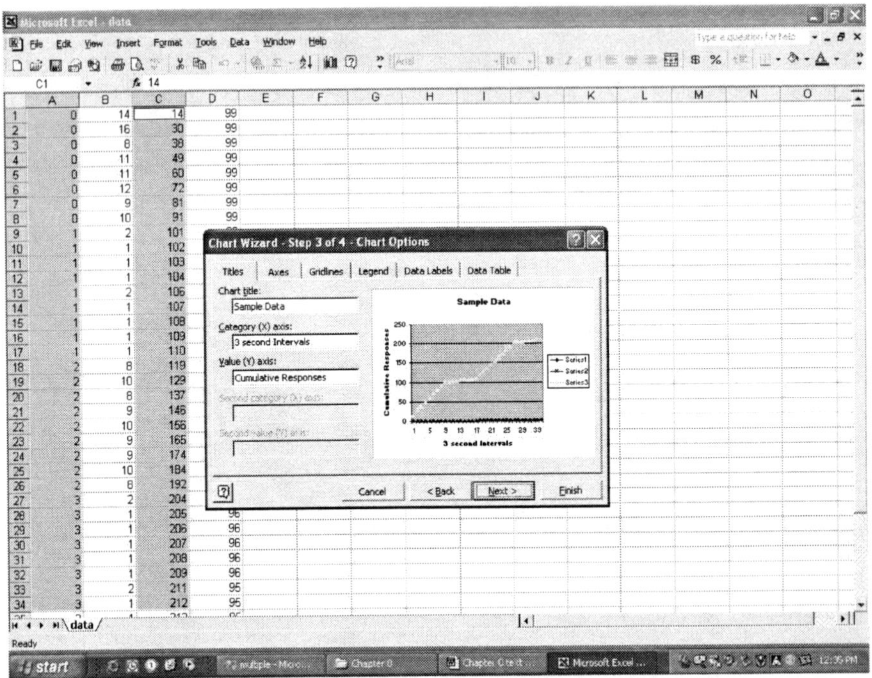

Figure 8.21 displays the modifications to the graph found within the Chart Wizard after entering text into the titles section.

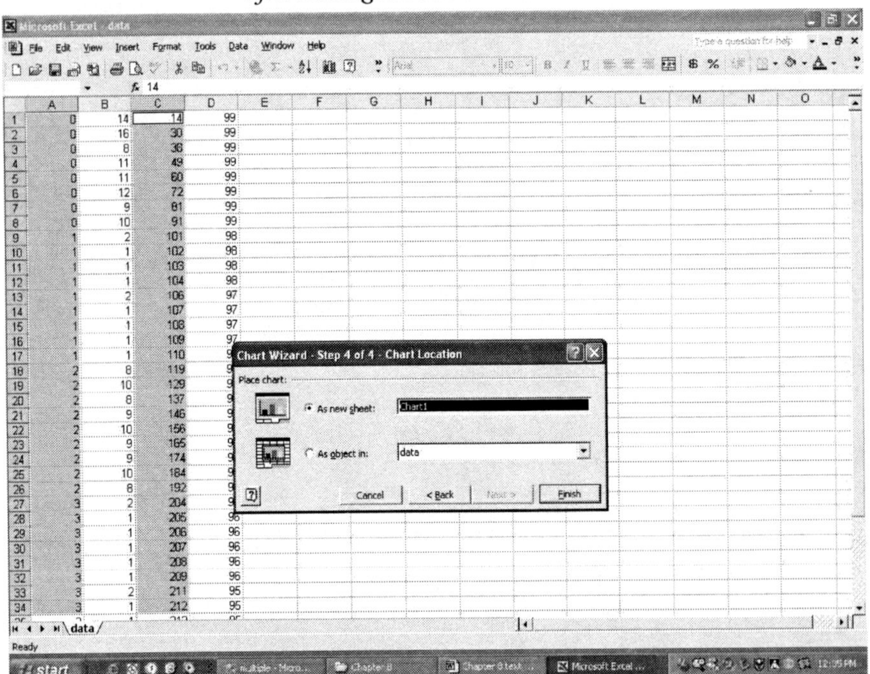

Figure 8.22 displays the final screen of the Chart Wizard.

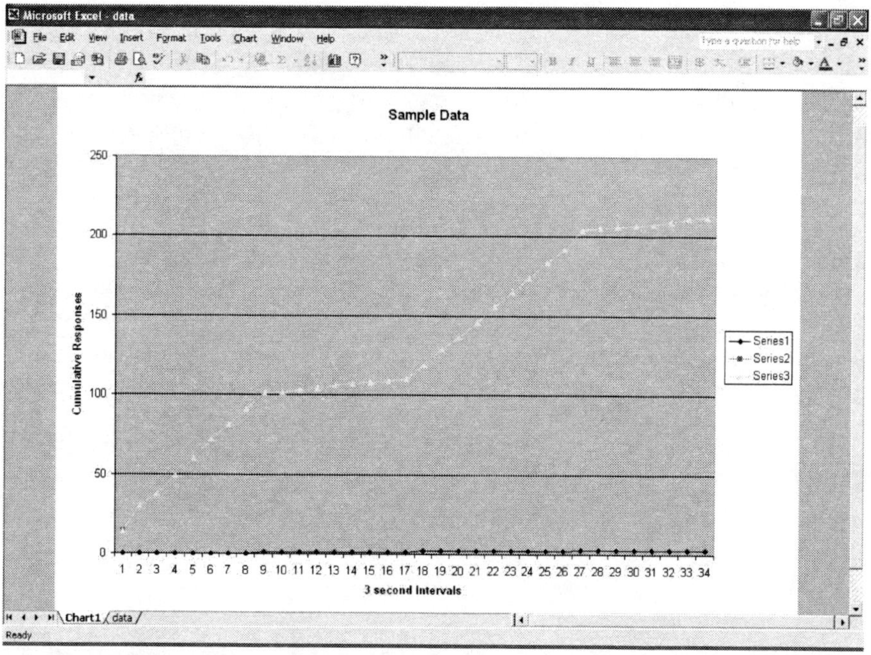

Figure 8.23 displays the chart created using values of vSwitch and vCumm

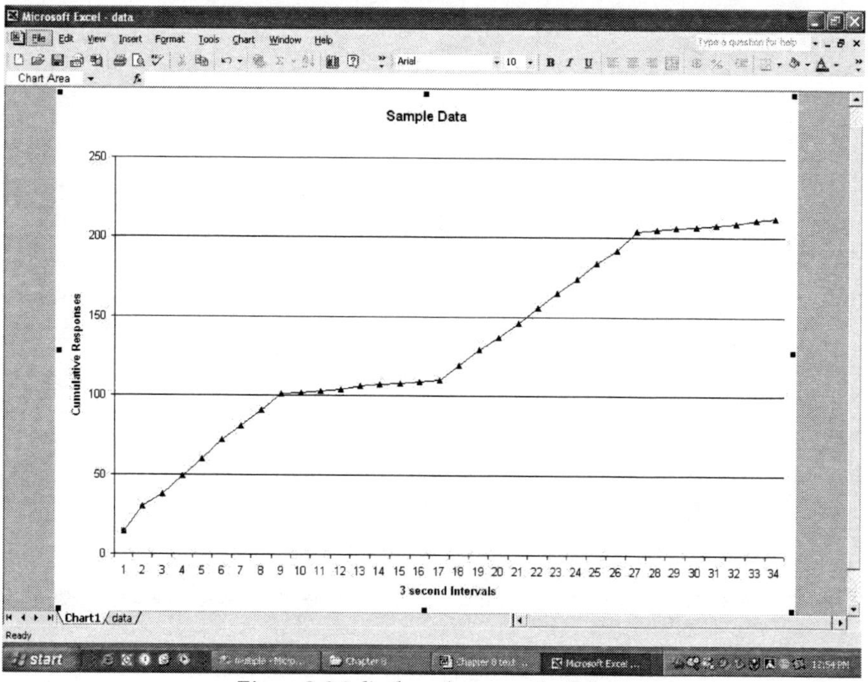

Figure 8.24 displays the customized chart with legend, background, and unneeded data series removed.

The last modification you may wish to make to your graph is the labeling of schedule component presentations. This can be done by drawing vertical lines between the data points that end one component and begin the next. For example, after nine 3 second intervals of the FR component, the DRL component goes into effect. As a result we would want to draw a line between the 9th and 10th data point and label the components accordingly. To do this, click on *View* from the main menu and then on *Toolbars*. Select the *Drawing* toolbar if it is not already selected. Upon locating the drawing toolbar, select the diagonal line next to the word *AutoShapes*. This is called the "line drawing tool." Position the mouse cursor on your chart between data points 9 and 10 and draw the line between them. Repeat this process for the other component changes displayed on your chart. The existing gridlines on the chart are now complicating the visual display you wish to get across using the new vertical lines. Delete these gridlines by selecting them and pressing the *delete* key. The final step is to add labels above the components to identify FR (DRH) or DRL contingencies. Four tools to the right of the line tool is the *Text tool*. Select this drawing option and place it on your chart in the desired location. Type the desired text. Repeat this process for the other components. The resulting chart should look similar to Figure 8.25.

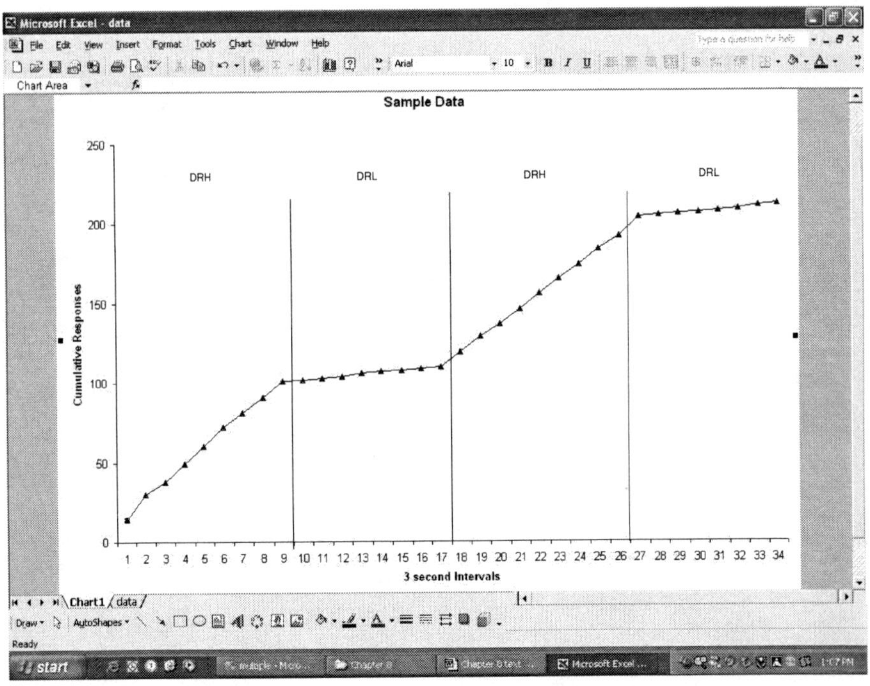

Figure 8.25 displays the final chart layout for the cumulative record of responses.

Building a Mixed Schedule of Reinforcement

A Simple Modification

If you wish to conduct research using a mixed schedule of reinforcement instead of a multiple schedule, only one simple modification is needed to the existing program. A mixed schedule is identical to a multiple schedule except that the mixed does not have a discriminative stimulus associated with each schedule component. In our working example, that discriminative stimulus is *BackColor*. Alter the BackColor properties of both forms so they are the same color. Now, you should have a working version of a mixed schedule.

Building a Concurrent Schedule of Reinforcement

Creating the Interface

Altering the multiple schedule to a mixed schedule was very simple. It is also quite easy to alter the multiple schedule to a concurrent schedule of reinforcement. In a concurrent schedule, both schedule components are presented simultaneously, and the participant selects which of the two components he/she wishes to respond to. Sometimes participants may have "forced choices" when only one component is available for selection, and other times when they may have "free choices" when both components are available. The forced or single choice trials are presented to ensure the participant has made contact with the programmed contingencies associated with each component, and therefore can make an "informed" choice when presented with a free or two choice trial.

We will need to add another form to our existing project to serve as the "choice" interface for our two schedule components. To do this, add a Windows form by clicking on the Project option in the main toolbar, and on the sub-option "Add Windows form". Name the form frmChoice and click *Open*. Change the Text property of this form to *Choice*, the WindowState to *Maximized*, and the MaximizeBox and MinimizeBox properties to *False*. Next add two Buttons to the form, to which we will link the components of the schedule. Change the names of these Buttons to butLeft and butRight and the Text property to *blank*. If we are going to use discriminative stimuli for each schedule component, as we did in the multiple schedule, place those stimuli on frmControl as well. In our example, we used screen BackColor. Our frmFR had a green BackColor and our frmDRL had a red BackColor. Change the BackColor of your butLeft to resemble the green BackColor of frmFR and the BackColor of butRight to resemble the red BackColor of frmDRL. We will not describe how to randomize the positions of these Buttons on frmChoice, but you may wish to have them randomized at each choice point control for a position bias. Randomization code examples are found throughout this book and can be incorporated into this situation as well if desired.

To link the butLeft and butRight Buttons to their respective forms, you need to place some code under each of them. Start with butLeft by double-clicking on it to enter the edit mode. Under Private Sub butLeft_Click type the following:

```
Dim x As New frmFR()
x.Show()
me.Hide()
```

Now place the following code under butRight:

```
Dim x As New frmDRL
x.Show ( )
me.Hide( )
```

A few other alterations need to be made to our individual component forms as well. First, go to frmFR and change the line of code under tmrSwitch from:

```
Dim x As New frmDRL()
to
Dim x As New frmChoice()
```

Second, repeat the same steps on frmDRL by changing the code under tmrSwitch from:

```
Dim x As New frmFR()
to
Dim x As New frmChoice()
```

Third, change the location of the code that opens the data file and checks to see if vSwitch is greater than 10 from frmFR's Private Sub frmFR_Load to frmChoice's Private Sub frmChoice_Load. Specificially cut and paste the following code:

```
If vSwitch = 0 Then vPoints = 100 'TO SET THE INITIAL POINT
   VALUE
If vSwitch = 0 Then FileOpen(1, "C:\data.txt",
   OpenMode.Append)
If vSwitch > 10 Then
FileClose(1)
End
End If
```

Forth, move the following line of code to the beginning of the tmrSwitch_Tick subroutines on both frmFR and frmDRL:

```
vSwitch = vSwitch + 1
```

The resulting subroutine should look like this for frmFR:

```
vSwitch = vSwitch + 1
Dim x As New frmChoice()
x.Show()
me.Hide()
tmrCheck.Enabled = False
tmrSwitch.Enabled = False
vClicks = 0
```

and look like this for frmDRL:

```
vSwitch = vSwitch + 1
Dim x As New frmChoice()
x.Show()
Me.Hide()
tmrCheck.Enabled = False
tmrSwitch.Enabled = False
vClicks = 0
```

The movement of this line of code is critical. If you fail to do it an error will occur the second time you return to frmChoice because you load frmChoice prior to adding one to vSwitch. As a result, frmChoice attempts to re-open data.txt, a file that is already open, and VB.NET shoots you an error.

Finally, change the startup object from frmFR to frmChoice. Run the program and check your progress. If all goes well you should have a working concurrent schedule of reinforcement. Enjoy.

Summary

In summary, this chapter has provided you with a series of new tools to create more complex schedules of reinforcement you can use for research purposes. In addition, this chapter has shown you the steps necessary to import your data files into spreadsheets such as Microsoft Excel and how to make simple charts from the data. Any researcher that takes the information found in this chapter along with the control panel from Chapter 4 and the multimedia from Chapter 5 will be able to develop an endless array of research projects incorporating schedules of reinforcement.

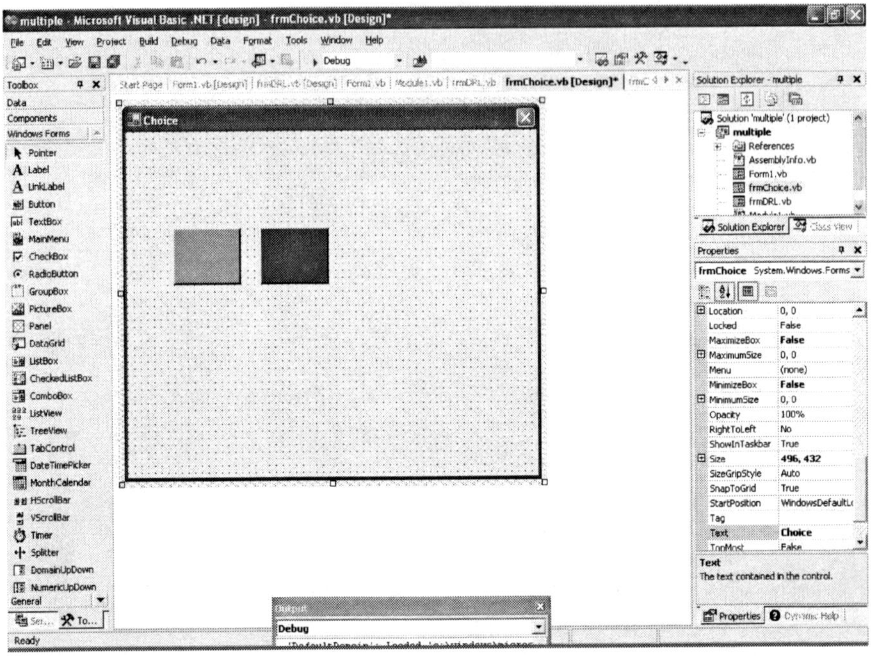

Figure 8.26 displays the graphical layout of frmChoice.

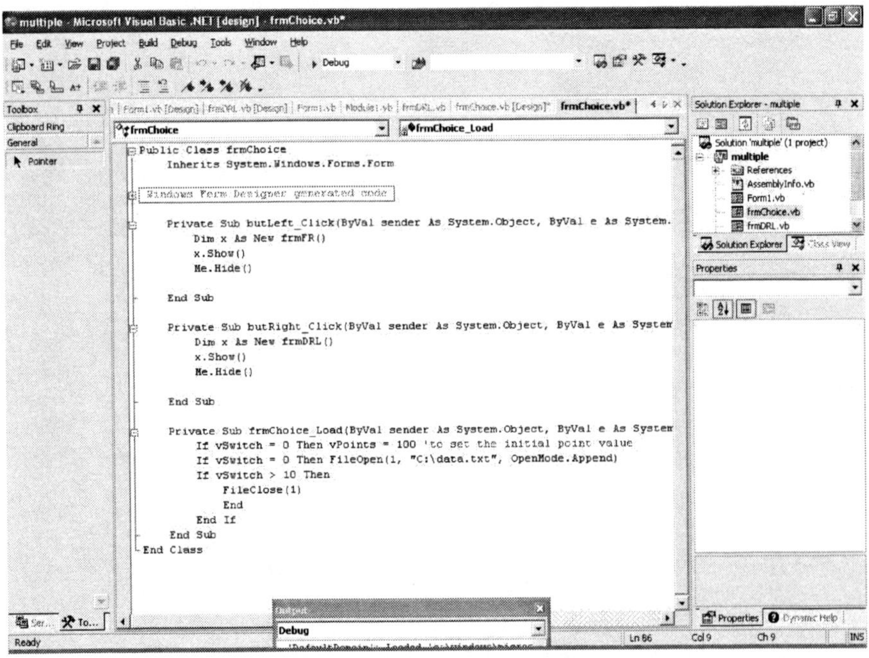

Figure 8.27 displays the correct code of frmChoice.

Chapter 9: Relational Responding and Contextual Control

Overview

Beyond Matching to Sample

To date, most of the published literature which has examined derived relational responding has utilized matching to sample procedures such as those described in Chapter 7. Many successful advances have come from the use of this methodology, and many more will surely occur in the future. Yet, in an effort to ensure that our descriptions of behavior are not merely descriptions of a procedural artifact, an increasing number of behavior analysts are moving beyond the sole use of matching to sample procedures in their research programs. For example, Leader, Barnes, and Smeets (1996) developed a respondent training procedure whereby subjects simply observed pairs of stimuli on the computer screen and were later able to make derived relations in matching to sample test trials. Fields, Reeve, Varelas, Rosen, and Delanich (1997) also developed an alternative procedure whereby subjects viewed stimulus pairs on the computer screen and were required to respond on one of two keys (a yes or a no key) following the presentation. Many of Fields et al., (1997) subjects were subsequently able to derive relations following this type of training-type procedure. Most recently, Cullinan, Barnes-Holmes, and Smeets (2001) developed a procedure they termed *pREP* or a precursor to the relational evaluation procedure. In pREP a single stimulus was presented on the computer screen, followed by a presentation of either a positive or negative comparison stimulus, then followed by two response options representing *same* or *different*. Together these alternatives to simple matching to sample procedures provide behavior analysts with different means of assessing relational responding.

pREP as an Illustrative Example of Database Control

In this chapter we outline how you can construct alternative training and testing procedures to evaluate relational responding and contextual control. Although we have chosen the pREP procedure described by Cullinan et al., (2001) as our illustrative example, the techniques we will present can be modified very simply to craft variations of the respondent type or the go / no-go training procedures. Furthermore, even if your immediate research plans are far from examining relational responding, this chapter will show you something new and extremely powerful in Visual Basic.NET – incorporating the use of external databases into your VB.NET program. In this chapter we will use an Excel spreadsheet as a data file to receive and pass data parameters into our program. We will show you how to link objects in the program to the Excel spreadsheet. This will allow you to create a data input file, similar to that done in Chapter 7, yet with even more flexibility in Excel.

It will also allow you to have your data output file write directly into the same file you are using for data input, just in different spreadsheet cells.

Program Requirements

Creating the Interface

Open a new Visual Basic.NET project, from the start page, click on the New Project button. Click on the icon for a Windows Application, change the name to *pREP*, and chenge the directory to C:\. Change the following properties of the form: Name to frmPrep, text to *Blank*, KeyPreview to True, and WindowState to Maximized. We will require several objects for the pRep program. The pRep program we will create will require 4 PictureBoxes on the form. The first two will display the initial and comparison stimuli; while the second two will display the response options the subject is presented with. Add 4 PictureBoxes of the same size. Change the name of your PictureBoxes to *picPrep0-3*. Position the images in the center of the form as shown in Figure 9.1 with picPrep0 in the top position, picPrep1 just below and picPrep2 and picPrep3 to the left and right of the form respectively. For all PictureBoxes change the visible property to equal *False* and the SizeMode property to *StretchImage*. This will ensure that the images we use for samples and comparisons will not be visible when the form loads (i.e. Visible = False), but when they are, the images we load ill stretch to fit into the PictureBoxes (i.e., SizeMode=StretchImage). We can even add another image to function as a context cue for further relational explorations whereby context changes may signal differing response – reinforcer relationships. To do so, add another PictureBox and locate it to the left of the form. Name this image picContext, change the *Visible* and *SizeMode* properties as above.

Adding a Timer to Control Stimuli Presentations

Add a timer object from the toolbar, and change the following parameters: Name to tmrPrep, Enabled to False, and Interval to 1000. These alterations will disable the timer when the form loads and set the length of the timer interval to 1 sec or 1000 milliseconds. Next add a Label to the pREP form that can be used for instructions you wish to provide to your subjects. Change the name of the Label to *lblPrep0* and change the text property to " " or blank. Enlarge the Label and position it in the center of the form over the top of picPrep0 and picPrep1 like displayed in Figure 9.2.

Adding Windows Media Player

The pRep program we will design will give subjects auditory feedback along with points following correct responses as well as take away points following incorrect responses on training trials. Both these consequences can easily be withheld during test trials if we decide to do so. To set up pREP to accept code necessary to play auditory stimuli, you must add the Windows Media Player. If the Windows Media Player object is not located in your toolbox, right click your mouse over the toolbox and select the *Customize Toolbox* option. Scroll down the list of options to near the end of the list. Select *Windows Media Player*. The MediaPlayer

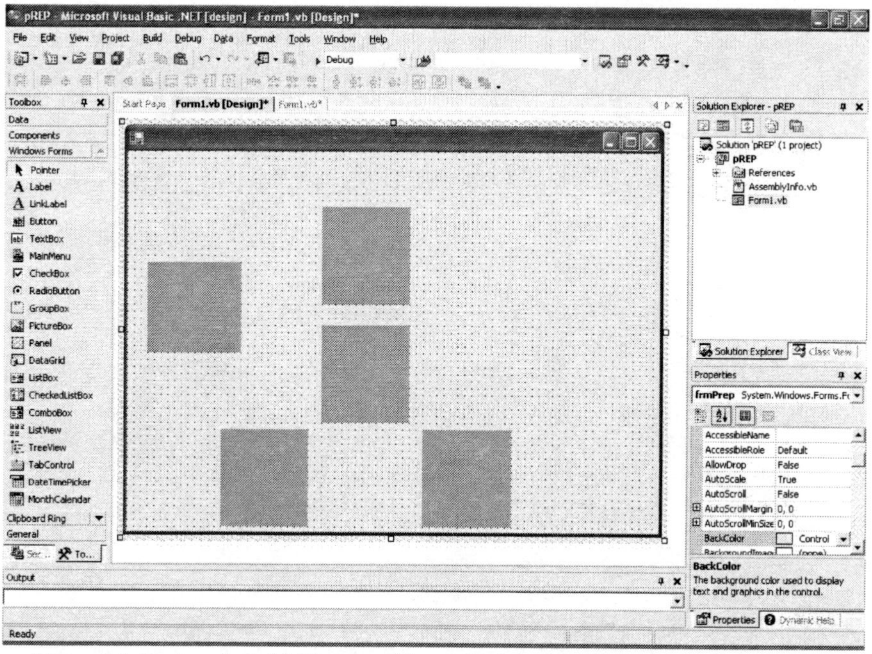

Figure 9.1 displays the initial layout of the pREP form with PictureBoxes arranged for stimuli, context, and response image presentations.

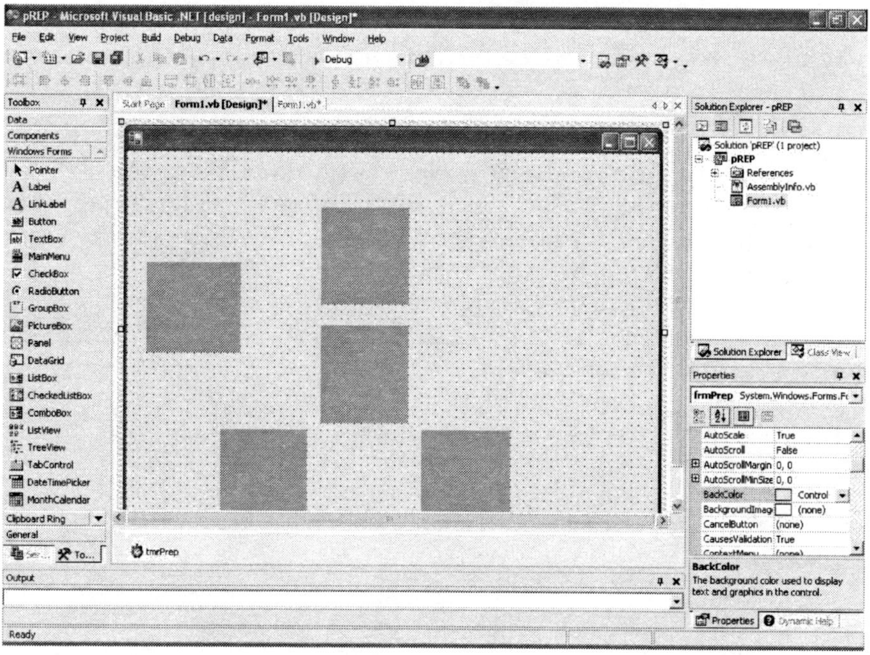

Figure 9.2 displays the pREP form with the addition of the Timer object and Label used for instructions.

object should new be available to add to frmPrep. Place it anywhere you like as it will not be displayed once the program is running. Once the MediaPlayer is added change the name to *ampFeedBack* and the visible property to *False*.

Adding Point Counters

To display a point counter which will serve as feedback to subjects following correct and incorrect training responses, add a GroupBox to frmPrep and change the name to gbPoints. Position the gbPoints GroupBox at the top center of the form. Next, add a Label to gbPoints and rename it lblPoints. Add a TextBox to gbPoints called txtPoints. You can keep the text of these objects as they are, or change them to blank. When the program actually starts, these pre-existing text will be replaced with information we provide in our data input spreadsheet. Note: make sure that lblPoints and txtPoints are actually located in the GroupBox by dragging it to another location. If the other objects are in the GroupBox they will move as well. If not, delete these incorrect objects and begin again.

Creating Communication Between Excel and Visual Basic.NET

The last sequence of steps we need to do to complete the program's graphic interface is link communication between Excel, our data input spreadsheet, and Visual Basic.NET. To do this we have to add a series of TextBoxes to use as *portals* to the Excel sheet. For ease of reference we will also add a series of Labels so we know which TextBox contains which information from the spreadsheet. While these Labels do nothing to make the program actually work correctly, they aid in the construction process by identifying which data are transferring from Excel into which TextBoxes, thus highlighting possible errors one might make when programming.

Making the Excel Spreadsheet

Before adding the data linkage to frmPrep, we will have to create the spreadsheet for it to hook up to. Begin by opening a new Excel spreadsheet and save it as *pRep.xls* in the same directory you are creating your Visual Basic.NET project for this chapter in. For illustrative purposes of this chapter place all of your files into the C:\ directory. Now, return to the spreadsheet and in the first row type the following column headers. Where C1= column 1, C2 = column 2, and so on, type the following column headers in row 1:

C1 = Record
C2 = Command
C3 = Sample
C4 = Comparison
C5 = Option1
C6 = Option2
C7 = Correctresp
C8 = PosFB

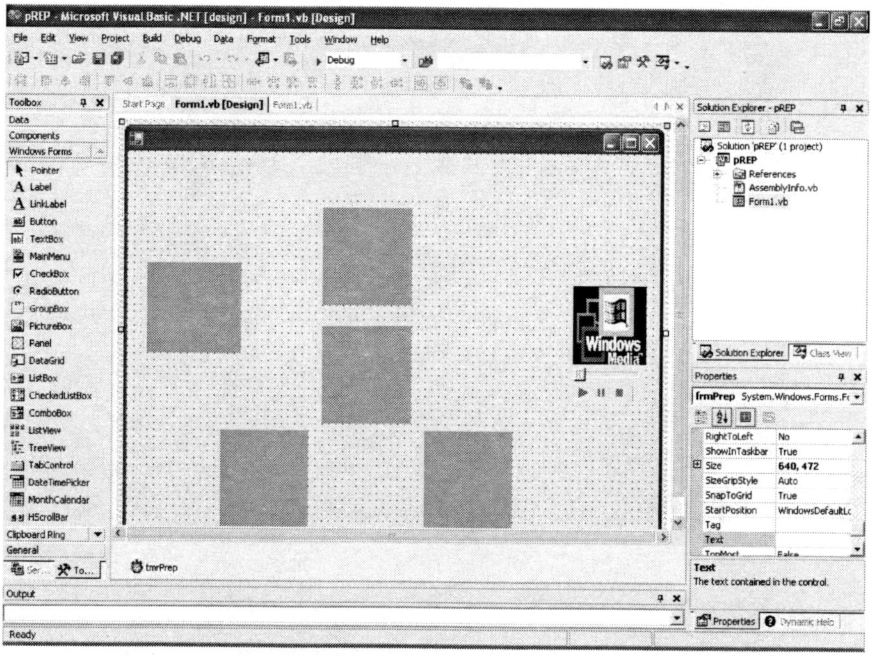

Figure 9.3 displays frmPrep along with the newly added ampFeedBack object.

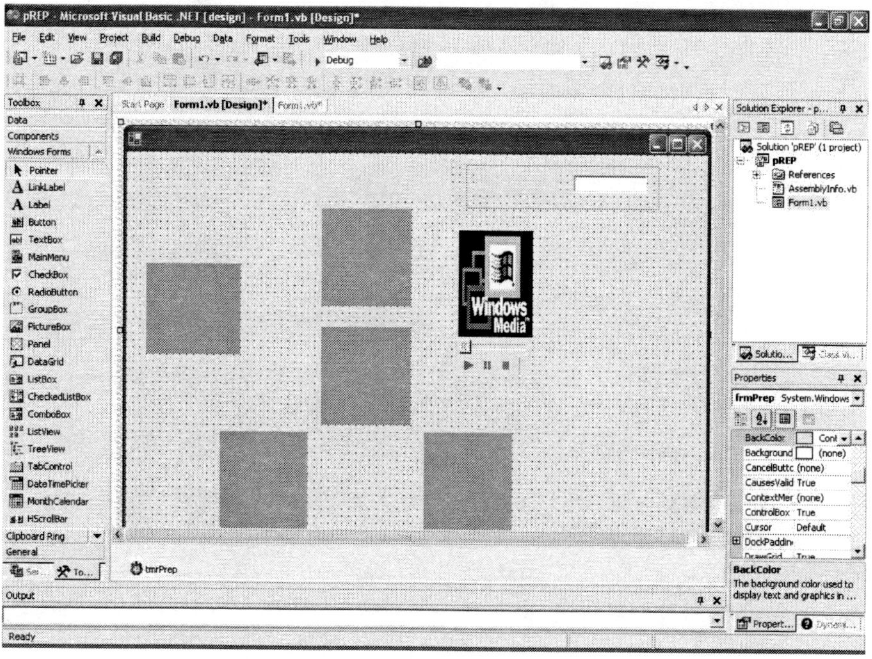

Figure 9.4 shows the new GroupBox and associated objects added to frmPrep.

C9 = NegFB
C10 = PosPoints
C11 = NegPoints
C12 = TotalPoints
C13 = Resp
C14 = Instructions
C15 = Criteria
C16 = Context

The spreadsheet should now look like the one in Figure 9.5. Delete the additional worksheets on your spreadsheet ("Sheet 2" and "Sheet 3") and save your file asMicrosoft Excel Workbook. Again, make sure that you save the spreadsheet in the same folder as where the pRep program will be saved to and run from. In this example we are using the C:\ directory.

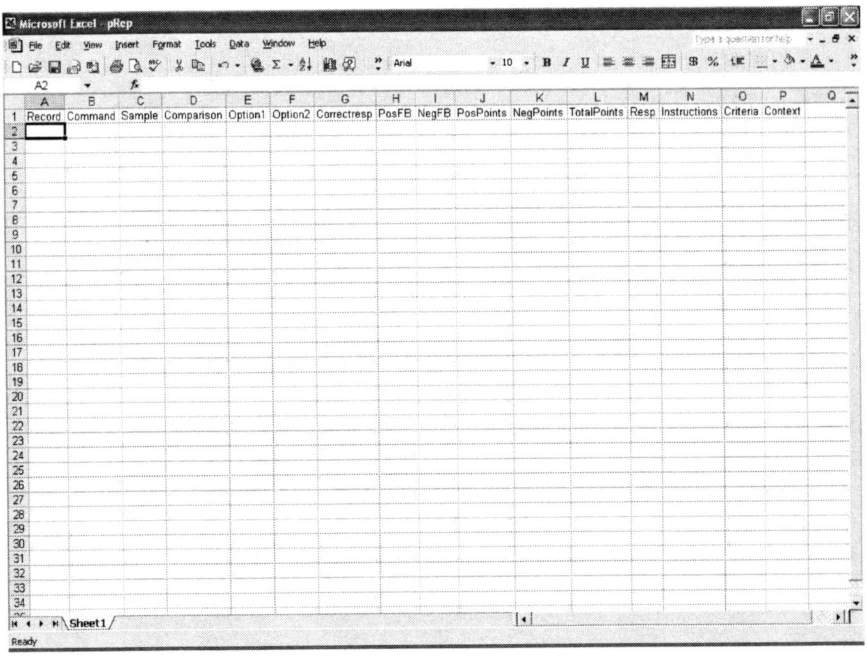

Figure 9.5 shows the Excel spreadsheet created for the pRep program.

Adding the Data.OleDB

We now need to link the pREP project with Excel. To do so we will use a COM-based database linking tool of VB.NET called *OleDB*. VB.NET has many means by which it can be linked to other programs. OleDB is probably the easiest to use. Programmers interested in other means should explore the use of ADO.NET and

ASP.NET tools. To add the Data.OleDB, type the following code at the very first line in the text editor (above *Public Class*):

```
Imports System.Data.OleDb
```

Next we have to provide some specifics. Under the Public Class frmPrep and Inherits System.Windows lines, add the following three lines of code (make sure that you take care to type the following code exactly; upper and lowercase need to remain as such):

```
Private vConnString as String =
   "Provider=Microsoft.Jet.OLEDB.4.0;" &  "Data
   Source=C:\pRep.xls;" & "Extended Properties = ""Excel
   8.0;HDR=YES"""
Private vConn as New System.Data.OleDb.OleDbConnection
   (vConnString)
Private cmd1 as New System.Data.OleDb.OleDbCommand
   ("Select * From [pRep$]", vConn)
```

Note: the section of the above code which refers to "C:\" and Excel 8.0" will need to be altered when you redesign your program to run in a different directory or with a different version of Excel.

Using this rather intimidating code VB.NET will communicate back and forth with Excel and concurrently read and write data to the spreadsheet. When reading in the data, VB.NET will need to "store" it somewhere in order to use it. A great place to "store" the data is in a series of TextBoxes which remain invisible to the subject, but constantly store and pass information through them. What we need at this point is a series of textboxes that correspond to the cells we created in Excel. Plus we probably should have corresponding labels wihch aid in our programming process.

For the labels, add 16 identically sized labels and rename them lblPrep1-16. The new lblPrep should start with lblPrep1 and end with lblPrep16. Change the text property of each box to the names of the column headers we created in our Excel worksheet as shown in figure 9.6.

Next, add the TextBox series that will be used to store data during program runtime. Name the first textbox *txtPrep0,* change the text property to *blank*, add 15 more TextBoxes and name them txtPrep1-15. The visible property should be true for the lblPrep1 to 16 and the txtPrep0 to 15 so you can see how the information is passed during run time. Before you run participants in an actual experiment, you will want to change the visible property of these objects back to false.

Finally, we need to add a Button to the bottom of the form called cmdPrep. Change the text to Start. Don't forget that you can change the size and font of the text for this Button in the properties window.

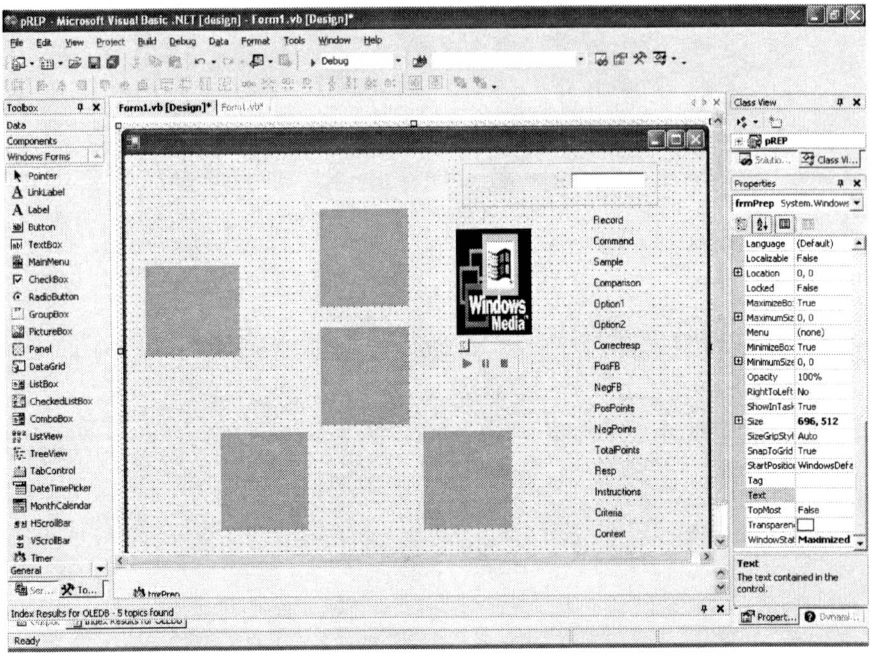

Figure 9.6 shows the series of Labels.

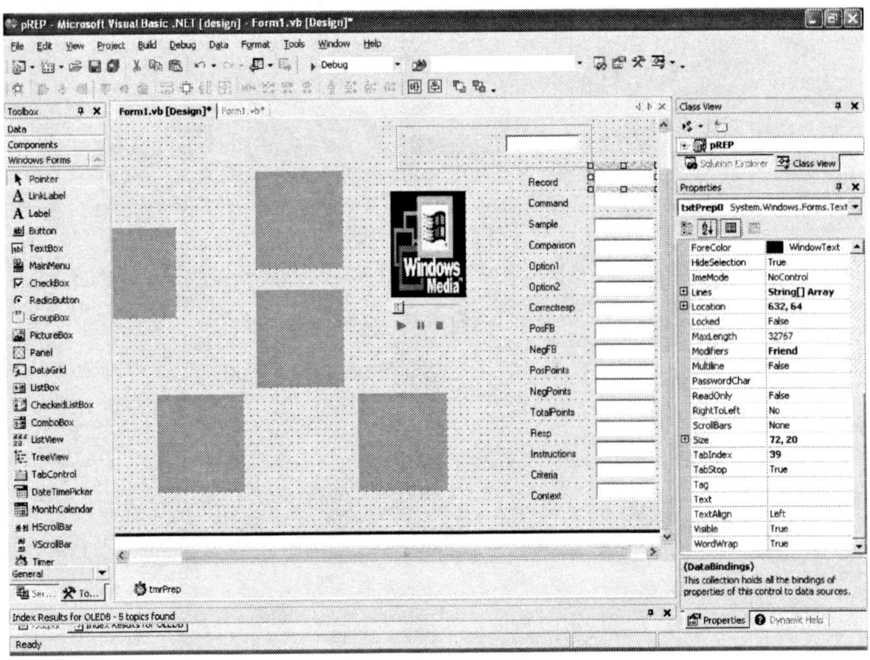

Figure 9.7 shows the newly added TextBox array.

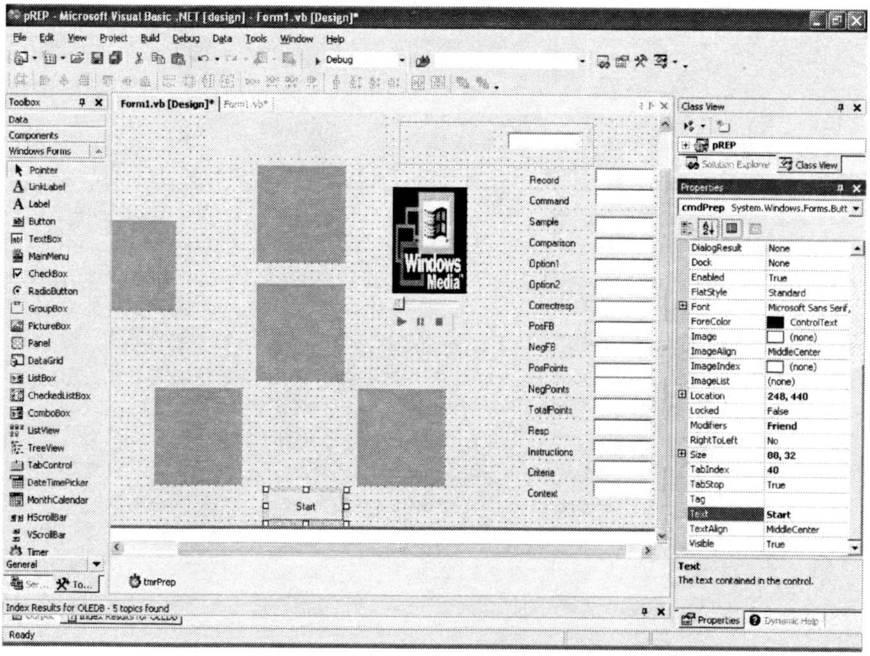

Figure 9.8 shows the location of the new Button on frmPrep.

Customizing your Excel Spreadsheet

Using an Excel spreadsheet gives you the freedom to create any sequence of stimuli trials imaginable. Best of all this method allows you to predetermine an actual sequence of trial presentations and hold that sequence constant across participants because VB.NET will pull the information in row by row from Excel. Randomized presentations can be accomplished in two ways. First, the experimenter can pre-randomize the trial information that he/she wishes to add to the Excel data file. Second, the method described for Matching to Sample procedures in Chapter 7 could be used. In this chapter we will create a very brief example of series of training and testing trials. Actual experimental investigations can be adapted to this program by simply adding more trials. If you suspect that participants might take many blocks of trials to meet a given criteria, make sure that you place enough possible trial blocks in your Excel file. In this case, reaching the end of the file (i.e. never mastering criterion) could be considered part of your participant exclusion criterion.

Open the Excel program, and access *pRep.xls* for editing. In the column *Record*, create the number sequence from 1 to 100. The program requires numbers in an ascending sequence, so make sure you add them. As written, this file will allow for up to 100 trial types. If you wish to make more trials in a given experiment, add numbers beyond 100. In the *Command* column we will use one of the following codes to signal to VB.NET what type of trial is being presented. Specifically, we will use the codes: INS (instructions), TRAIN (program provides feedback), TEST (no feedback is provided), CRITERIA (will check to see if criteria is met), and END (will terminate the program). Column "Sample" contains the image names used as sample stimuli. *CONTEXT* is used for the image to be presented as the contextual stimulus. *INS* is for instructions, and will be displayed in lblPrep0. The program will look for images in the C:\ or the directory in which the application program is located. In this chapter example we are using C:\, so make sure all your files are contained in the same directory. The *Comparison* column is for the image names used as comparison stimuli. Option1 and Option2 are for the image names used for the response option stimuli located to the left and right of the form at the bottom (left to right respectively). *Correctresp* tells the program which response Option is correct where 1 = Option1 and 2 = Option2. *PosFB* identifies the name of the wav file to be played for positive feedback and *NegFB* is for the name of the wav file to be played for negative auditory feedback. Again, these files must be located in the C:\directory. *PosPoints* determines how many points are given for a correct response and *NegPoints* are the points subtracted for an incorrect response. Keep in mind that to have the program run correctly you will need to create these stimuli (i.e. images and sound files) and make sure the names you saved them by match identically to those names typed into the prep.xls file.

Up to this point all of the columns are used to pass information into the pRep program. Yet, information can also be passed back from pRep into the spreadsheet. The column *Total Points* will actually display the total points earned by the participant up to that point in the experiment. Obviously this column will be empty when you create the input file, yet will actually contain values after you run the program. The *Resp* column will be used for the pRep program to write the participant's response back to the Excel sheet. Keep in mind that the pRep program will overwrite these values (Total Points and Resp) every time you run the program. As a result, these values need to be saved after each run if you want to keep the data. A good practice to get in the habit of doing is to save the pRep Excel file under a different name after each running where you wish to keep the participant data. During your exploratory programming in this chapter, make sure you delete these data in between each use of the program so that the Total Points and Resp data do not interfere with your running of the program.

Criteria is the number of correct responses that need to be made by the participant to terminate the program. If the criterion is not met the program will continue through to the next series of trials until it sees the *CRITERIA* command again and the criterion is met, or the command END is encountered. As you may have noticed already in this text, criteria are usually set up in code like the following: If vTotalPoints < Criteria then repeat the phase. This will make more sense after you start writing the code, but since a simple < sign is used, you need to make the criteria entered into the Excel spreadsheet one less than what your criteria actually is for the program to work how you want it to.

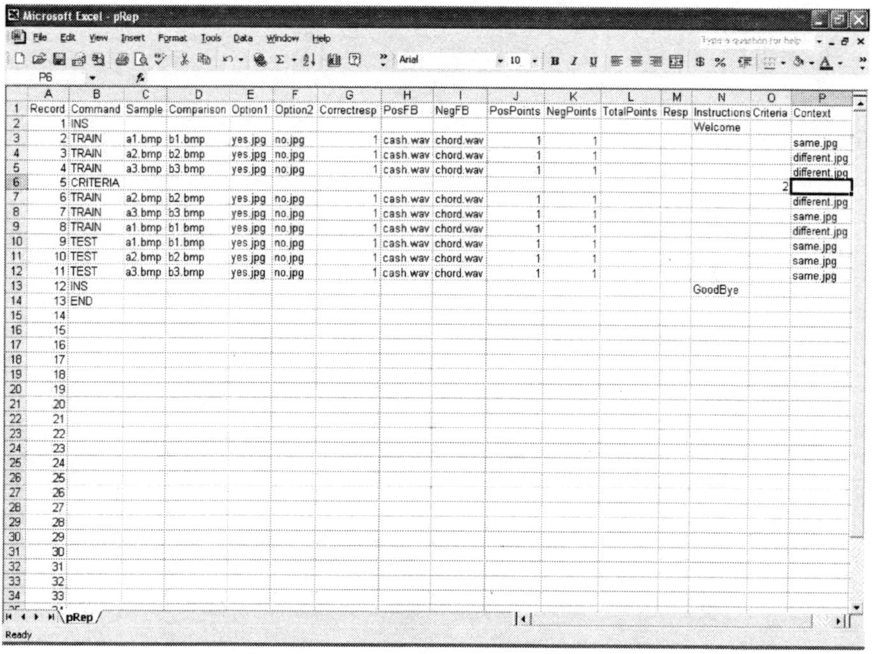

	A	B	C	D	E	F	G	H	I	J	K	L	M	N	O	P
1	Record	Command	Sample	Comparison	Option1	Option2	Correctresp	PosFB	NegFB	PosPoints	NegPoints	TotalPoints	Resp	Instructions	Criteria	Context
2	1	INS												Welcome		
3	2	TRAIN	a1.bmp	b1.bmp	yes.jpg	no.jpg	1	cash.wav	chord.wav	1	1					same.jpg
4	3	TRAIN	a2.bmp	b2.bmp	yes.jpg	no.jpg	1	cash.wav	chord.wav	1	1					different.jpg
5	4	TRAIN	a3.bmp	b3.bmp	yes.jpg	no.jpg	1	cash.wav	chord.wav	1	1					different.jpg
6	5	CRITERIA													2	
7	6	TRAIN	a2.bmp	b2.bmp	yes.jpg	no.jpg	1	cash.wav	chord.wav	1	1					different.jpg
8	7	TRAIN	a3.bmp	b3.bmp	yes.jpg	no.jpg	1	cash.wav	chord.wav	1	1					same.jpg
9	8	TRAIN	a1.bmp	b1.bmp	yes.jpg	no.jpg	1	cash.wav	chord.wav	1	1					different.jpg
10	9	TEST	a1.bmp	b1.bmp	yes.jpg	no.jpg	1	cash.wav	chord.wav	1	1					same.jpg
11	10	TEST	a2.bmp	b2.bmp	yes.jpg	no.jpg	1	cash.wav	chord.wav	1	1					same.jpg
12	11	TEST	a3.bmp	b3.bmp	yes.jpg	no.jpg	1	cash.wav	chord.wav	1	1					same.jpg
13	12	INS												GoodBye		
14	13	END														
15	14															
16	15															
17	16															
18	17															
19	18															
20	19															
21	20															
22	21															
23	22															
24	23															
25	24															
26	25															
27	26															
28	27															
29	28															
30	29															
31	30															
32	31															
33	32															
34	33															

Figure 9.9 shows the Excel spreadsheet (pRep.xls) with sample trial information.

Figure 9.9 presents a small sample of trials that illustrate the functioning capabilities of the pREP program. Notice that rows have different data depending on the command in the *Command* column. Save the Excel file and return to Visual Basic.

Generating the Necessary Code

Linking Visual Basic.NET to Excel

Save the form and program as pRep if you have not already done so in a while. Go to the edit level and declare the following variables under the Public Class section:

```
Private vTimeCount as Integer
Private vTotalPoints as Integer
```

vTimeCount will be used to determine the timing for the appearance of the stimuli and feedback (if any), while vTotalPoints will be used to keep track of the total points earned.

Next we have to do some additional linking of VB.NET to the Excel spreadsheet. First we will want a subroutine to clear out existing values of the

TextBoxes and do so repeatedly after each trial. Therefore, create the following subroutine by typing the following code immediately above the *End Class* text:

```
Private Sub clear_inputs()
txtPrep1.Text = ""
txtPrep2.Text = ""
txtPrep3.Text = ""
txtPrep4.Text = ""
txtPrep5.Text = ""
txtPrep6.Text = ""
txtPrep7.Text = ""
txtPrep8.Text = ""
txtPrep9.Text = ""
txtPrep10.Text = ""
txtPrep11.Text = ""
txtPrep12.Text = ""
txtPrep13.Text = ""
txtPrep14.Text = ""
txtPrep15.Text = ""
End Sub
```

Next we want to read the next line of data from Excel into the textboxes. Add the following subroutine by typing the following code immediately above the *End Class* text:

```
Private Sub move_next_input()
Dim cmd1 as New System.Data.OleDb.OleDbCommand ("Select *
   From [pRep$]", vConn)
Dim rdr as OleDbDataReader = cmd1.ExecuteReader
Dim x as Integer
Dim array(15)
clear_inputs() 'REMOVES VALUES FROM INPUT BOXES
x = txtPrep0.Text + 1
Dim i

For i = 1 to x
rdr.Read()
Next i
For i = 0 to 15
x = i - 1
If rdr.IsDBNull (i) Then array (i) = 1
Next
```

```
If array(0) <> 1 Then txtPrep0.Text = rdr.GetValue (0)
If array(1) <> 1 Then txtPrep1.Text = rdr.GetValue (1)
If array(2) <> 1 Then txtPrep2.Text = rdr.GetValue (2)
If array(3) <> 1 Then txtPrep3.Text = rdr.GetValue (3)
If array(4) <> 1 Then txtPrep4.Text = rdr.GetValue (4)
If array(5) <> 1 Then txtPrep5.Text = rdr.GetValue (5)
If array(6) <> 1 Then txtPrep6.Text = rdr.GetValue (6)
If array(7) <> 1 Then txtPrep7.Text = rdr.GetValue (7)
If array(8) <> 1 Then txtPrep8.Text = rdr.GetValue (8)
If array(9) <> 1 Then txtPrep9.Text = rdr.GetValue (9)
If array(10) <> 1 Then txtPrep10.Text = rdr.GetValue (10)
If array(11) <> 1 Then txtPrep11.Text = rdr.GetValue (11)
If array(12) <> 1 Then txtPrep12.Text = rdr.GetValue (12)
If array(13) <> 1 Then txtPrep13.Text = rdr.GetValue (13)
If array(14) <> 1 Then txtPrep14.Text = rdr.GetValue (14)
If array(15) <> 1 Then txtPrep15.Text = rdr.GetValue (15)

rdr.Close ()
End Sub
```

This subroutine may initially appear intimidating, but is is really rather simple. First it states to created a new instance of the OleDb and identify the worksheet pRep as the one we are interacting with. We have already told the program that vConn is pRep.xls. Next we need to create a new instance of the OleDbDataReader. The data reader doesn't like blank spaces in the Excel sheet so we have to create a data array, array(15), to help us check the value of each cell we are reading from. We call on the clear_inputs subroutine to clear out old values that may have been entered into the TextBoxes.

This may sound like a bit of work, but each time we want to read in the next record we have to start at record one and move to the record of interest. Regardless of this rather cumbersome mess, Visual Basic.NET makes this happen very fast, so fast you can't even notice it. The following code is used to tell pREP which is the next line:

```
x = txtPrep0.text + 1
```

The FOR/NEXT statement then advances the reader (rdr) to the next record. The following FOR/NEXT statement checks for the empty or *NULL* cells in Excel. If the cell is empty, then the corresponding array value is flagged and the value "1" is entered. Next, the series of IF/THEN statements tell VB.NET to read the value from Excel into the corresponding txtPrep if it is not NULL. The reader (rdr) is then closed.

When the program begins the Start Button should be visible, yet it needs to become invisible when it is clicked, so multiple clicks are not possible which could disrupt stimuli presentations. Restricting the Start Button to one click has an additional advantage. It can be used to generate stimuli and advance the program to the next trial. To make this happen, double-click on cmdPrep and enter the edit mode. Add the following code under cmdPrep_Click:

```
cmdPrep.Visible = False
lblPrep0.Text = ""
Move_next_input()
load_images ()
```

To load the images create a new subroutine called *load_images*, as described above, and enter the following code:

```
Private Sub load_images()
Select Case txtPrep1.Text
Case "INS"
gbPoints.Visible = True
lblPrep0.Visible = True
lblPrep0.Text = txtPrep13.Text
cmdPrep.Visible = True
Case "TEST", "TRAIN"
tmrPrep.Enabled = True
picPrep0.Image = Image.FromFile ("C:\" & txtPrep2.Text)
picPrep1.Image = Image.FromFile ("C:\" & txtPrep3.Text)
picPrep2.Image = Image.FromFile ("C:\" & txtPrep4.Text)
picPrep3.Image = Image.FromFile ("C:\" & txtPrep5.Text)
If txtPrep15.Text <> "" Then picContext.Image = Image.FromFile
   ("C:\" & txtPrep15.Text)
Case "CRITERIA"
gbPoints.Visible = False
If Int (vTotalPoints) < Int(txtPrep14.Text) Then
cmdPrep.Text = "Continue"
cmdPrep.Visible = True
Else
End
End If
Case "END"
Close ()
End
End Select
End Sub
```

The next section of code is a *Select Case.* What this code does is read in the new value of txtPrep1 which corresponds with the *Command* column. Depending on the value, or keyword that is placed in the command line of our Excel file, Select Case, txtPrep1 reads in the program, it will look for that instance in the Select Case code and follow those series of commands. Notice that the cases are in caps "INS." Quotes are required since these values are literals or strings. This means that the commands in your spreadsheet should be all caps. If you wanted to write the program to accept other combinations you would have to modify the line such as: Case *INS* to *Ins* or *ins*. If the Command is *INS* then lblPrep0 becomes visible and the text under the Instructions column is displayed. The next case in this Select Case is: Case *TEST, TRAIN* either one is accepted as the training and the testing are essentially the same in the way they present the stimuli, except one has feedback.

The next lines load the stimuli listed in the Excel sheet and place them into the proper PictureBoxes:

```
picPrep0.Image = Image.FromFile ("C:\" & txtPrep2.Text)
picPrep1.Image = Image.FromFile ("C:\" & txtPrep3.Text)
picPrep2.Image = Image.FromFile ("C:\" & txtPrep4.Text)
picPrep3.Image = Image.FromFile ("C:\" & txtPrep5.Text)
```

Additionally, if during the training or testing a contextual cue is required the following line of code will load the image. Notice that it checks to see if the textbox is blank first. In some cases the experimenter may not want a contextual cue and can just leave the space blank:

```
If txtPrep15.Text <> "" Then picContent.Image = Image.FromFile
("C:\" & txtPrep15.Text)
```

The next case in the Select Case is:

```
Case "CRITERIA"
gbPoints.Visible = False
If vTotalPoints < Int(txtPrep14.Text) Then
cmdPrep.Text = "Continue"
cmdPrep.Visible = True
Else
End
End If
```

This last section under CRITERIA evaluates the criteria to either continue accessing subsequent information from the spreadsheet (repeat the training or testing) or to end the program (criteria met). There is text in the *Instructions* column for the criterion command so this is displayed to the participant. If vTotalPoints is less than the criteria then the Button cmdPrep appears with the text *Continue* and the Label with the message to the participant disappears. If a criterion is met, the program closes. Finally, if the command is *END* the program will close the spreadsheet session and end the program:

```
Case "END"
Close
End
End Select
```

As we mentioned above, under certain conditions, the program will wait for the experimenter to terminate the program. Because we set the keyPreview property of frmPrep to equal *True*, we can press any key on the keyboard and execute a line of code. In this case we chose the *F1* key that is associated with KeyCode number 112 to activate the following subroutine that is created under the Form (Note: remember to change the subroutine from *Click* to *KeyUp* by first selecting *(Base Class Events)* from the left drop down menu of the editor, and *Key Up* from the right drop down menu of the editor. Once done, the new subroutine `Private Sub frmPrep_KeyUp (ByVal sender as Object, ByVal e as System.Windows.Forms.KeyEventArgs) Handles MyBase.KeyUp` should appear. Type the following code in this subroutine:

```
If e.KeyCode = Keys.F1 Then
Close ()
End
```

Customization for Actual Experimentation

This chapter has been constructed so that it reads from one Excel file from top to bottom, terminating either when a criterion has been met by the participant, or after all trials have elapsed and an *End* command is encountered in the file. Assuming you do not want your participant to end after he or she meets a criterion, you can add a new phase or condition to this project by just adding a new form to your existing project, and making that form Visible when the criterion is met. For example, you may wish to establish relations of *same* and *different* using pREP and then test the transfer of these relations to novel stimuli using a matching to sample preparation. All you need to do is make your current form (*Me*) Hide and your other form (*frmM2S*) Show when the If vTotalPoints < Int(txtPrep14) statement in the above code has been satisfied. You can use this same technique to load other pRep type forms for training or testing other types of relations like same / opposite, same / different, greater than / less than, and so on.

Stimulus Presentation

To display the images on each trial we will use the timer object we named tmrPrep. Specifically, we want picPrep0 to display, then a brief period of no stimuli present, then picPrep1 to display followed by a brief period of no stimuli present, and finally the two *option* or *response* stimuli to appear and wait for the participant's response. This is accomplished with the following code, which should be easy to understand if you have been following along with earlier chapters in this text. We have added comments to highlight specifics that might be useful when modifying this program for your own research purposes. Under Sub tmrPrep_tick, type:

```
Select Case vTimeCount
Case 0
gbPoints.Visible = False
If txtPrep15.Text <> "" Then picContext.Visible = True
vTimeCount = 1
tmrPrep.Interval = 1000 'THIS RESETS THE STIMULI
   PRESENTATION
Case 1
picPrep0.Visible = True 'INTERSTIM INTERVAL
vTimeCount = 2
Case 2
picPrep0.Visible = False 'SHOWS NEXT STIMULUS
vTimeCount = 3
Case 3
picPrep1.Visible = True 'INTERSTIM INTERVAL
vTimeCount = 4
Case 4
picPrep1.Visible = False
vTimeCount = 5
Case 5
picPrep2.Visible = True
picPrep3.Visible = True
vTimeCount = 0
tmrPrep.Enabled = False
tmrPrep.Interval = 3000 ' TIME OF GBPOINTS DISPLAY FOR NEXT
   TRIAL
End Select
```

Tracking Participant Responses Using a Control Array

The next task is to add a subroutine to capture the participant's response. This can be accomplished by double clicking on one of the picPrep response objects (i.e., picPrep2 or picPrep3) and creating a control array similar to that done in Chapter 2.

First add the text:

```
,picPrep3.Click
```

at the end of the Private Sub picPrep2_Click text.

This code will create a control array between the two objects allowing for similar code to be placed under just one object, yet it will be accessed when either object is clicked upon. While accessing the same code is very useful, sometimes you might want a certain event to occur when picPrep2 is clicked and another event to occur when picPrep3 is clicked. At this point in our program we want both to occur. We want a different value to be written into txtPrep12.Text depending on which picPrep response option was clicked, but after that, point delivery, .wav file playing, and initiating the subsequent trial is identical for both response options. Start by creating the array section of code which is different for each picPrep. Add the following code under picPrep2_Click:

```
Dim buttonClicked as PictureBox
buttonClicked = CType (sender, PictureBox)
If buttonClicked.Name = picPrep2.Name() Then txtPrep12.Text
   = 1
If buttonClicked.Name = picPrep3.Name() Then txtPrep12.Text
   = 2
```

Next add the code which is identical for each picPrep under the lines you just typed:

```
picContext.Visible = False
If txtPrep1.Text <> "TEST" Then 'MAKE SURE THIS IS NOT A
   TRAINING SESSION
If txtPrep6.Text = txtPrep12.Text Then 'PLAY POSITIVE
   FEEDBACK AND ADD POINTS
ampFeedBack.FileName = ("C:\" & txtPrep7.Text)
ampFeedBack.Play()
lblPoints.Text = "GOOD: POINTS ="
vTotalPoints = vTotalPoints + 1
txtPoints.Text = vTotalPoints
gbPoints.Visible = True
Else 'PLAY NEGATIVE FEEDBACK AND SUBTRACT POINTS
ampFeedback.FileName = ("C:\" & txtPrep8.Text)
ampFeedBack.Play()
lblPoints.Text = "BAD: POINTS ="
vTotalPoints = vTotalPoints - 1
txtPoints.Text = vTotalPoints
gbPoints.Visible = True
```

```
End If
End If
picPrep2.Visible = False
picPrep3.Visible = False
txtPrep11.Text = vTotalPoints
write_response()
move_next_input()
load_images
End Sub
```

Recording Responses

When the participant clicks on one of the images we want to write the value of either 1 (left) or a 2 (right) to the Excel sheet by entering the value into the TextBox linked to the spreadsheet for the Response column txtPrep12.

Writing to Excel

Once the response is entered into the txtPrep12, we need to enter it into the Excel sheet. This can be done by creating a new subroutine called write_response. Created this subroutine and enter the following three lines of code within it (make sure you type this exactly as presented, with spacing and capitalization):

```
Dim cmd1 as New System.Data.OleDb.OleDbCommand ("Select *
   From [pRep$]", vConn)
cmd1.CommmandText = "UPDATE [pRep$] " & "SET Resp = " &
   txtPrep12.Text & ", TotalPoints = " & txtPrep11.Text &
   " WHERE Record = " & txtPrep0.Text
cmd1.ExecuteNonQuery()
End Sub
```

Wrapping Up

The last code to add to the program is under the Form_Load subroutine. This code will initialize the program and variables used in the program. Type the following lines under Private Sub frmPrep_Load:

```
Dim vRecord as Integer
vConn.Open()
txtPrep0.Text = 0
vTotalPoints = 0
move_next_input()
lblPrep0.Text = txtPrep13.Text
```

A Little Bug

The program is now capable of running, and you should attempt do to so now to check your progress. There is one small "bug" in this program if you programmed it correctly to this point, and probably many more if you did not. Assuming you did indeed program all the steps correctly, the bug that exists concerns the criteria. If a subject arrives at the criteria "Command" and does not make the criteria, they will advance onward in the experiment. The next time the criteria "Command" is encountered, however, the formula that exists for checking criteria is not correct. Take a look again at the line of code that was put into our Select Case statement:

```
If Int(vTotalPoints) < Int(txtPrep14.Text) then
```

Imagine the following scenario...You set the mastery criteria on your pREP spreadsheet to be checked at Record 20. So, after 20 trials, VB.NET pulls in Record 20, and displays the criteria in txtPrep14.Text. Let's say the criteria is 18, and the subject has made 15 correct responses. Going back to our above equation this would result in the following values being placed in the variables:

```
If 15 < 18 then
```

So far everything should work fine. The subject did not meet criteria, and the program continues onward, moving down the pREP spreadsheet. When the next record, lets assume Record 40, comes up with a criteria of 18 the problem arises. The subject has now made 16 correct since the last criterion check, and therefore should still fail this second criterion check (16 is still less than 18). Yet this will not happen. Here is why. vTotalPoints was not reset to 0 when the previous criterion check occurred. We could easily do this, but vTotalPoints is also being displayed in txtPoints.txt for our subject as an accumulating point counter. This is where the problem lies. Using our equation above, the following values are placed in the variables:

```
If 31 < 18 then
```

Instead of moving forward in the pREP spreadsheet, at this point the program ends.

There are a variety of ways we could solve this problem by resetting vTotalPoints after we place the value into txtPoints and shifting that value into another variable, or we could solve it by creating another temporary variable to momentarily hold vTotalPoints values upon reset. A third easy way to solve the problem is to create another variable just for storing correct responses up to the criterion point and resetting it after checking the criterion. This way vTotalPoints could be left alone, and still be used for point counter information that is displayed in txtPoints.

Proceeding with this last option, we need to create and declare a new variable under the existing `Inherits System.Windows.Forms.Form` section. Type the following code under `Private vTotalPoints as Integer`:

```
Private vPointcounter
```

A slight modification is needed in the Select Case code. Add the following line of code which will clear out vTotalPoints' value after a criterion is checked:

```
vTotalPoints = 0
```

The new section of the Select Case should look like:

```
Case "CRITERIA"
gbPoints.Visible = False
If Int(vTotalPoints) < Int(txtPrep14.Text) Then
cmdPrep.Text = "Continue"
cmdPrep.Visible = True
vTotalPoints = 0
Else
Close()
End
End If
```

A few changes also need to be made to the control array we designed using picPrep2 and picPrep3. Specifically, we need to add code which will advance the value of vPointcounter each time the subject makes a correct response and subtract the value of vPointcounter each time the subject makes an incorrect response. Also, the display of txtPoints needs to be altered so that it displays the value of vPointcounter and not vTotalPoints. Begin by adding the following code after the line `vTotalPoints = vTotalPoints + 1 (which is found in the Private Sub picPrep2_Click:`

```
vPointcounter = vPointcounter + 1
txtPoints.Text = vPointcounter
```

This resulting section of code should now look like:

```
If txtPrep1.Text <> "TEST" Then
If txtPrep6.Text = txtPrep12.Text Then
ampFeedBack.FileName = ("C:\" & txtPrep7.Text)
ampFeedBack.Play()
lblPoints.Text = "GOOD: POINTS ="
vTotalPoints = vTotalPoints + 1
vPointcounter = vPointcounter + 1
txtPoints.Text = vPointcounter
```

```
gbPoints.Visible = True
```

Also modify the next section of this subroutine after the line `vTotalPoints = vTotalPoints - 1` (which is also found in the `Private Sub picPrep2_Click`)

```
vPointcounter = vPointcounter - 1
txtPoints.Text = vPointcounter
```

Finally remark out, or put a ' mark in front of the code: vTotalPoints=vTotalPoints – 1 because this code is no longer being used to keep track of points. Instead it keeps track of correct responses made since the last criterion had been assessed. We do not want correct responses to be subtracted. The resulting section of code should be:

```
Else
ampFeedBack.FileName = ("C:\" & txtPrep8.Text)
ampFeedBack.Play()
lblPoints.Text = "BAD: POINTS ="
'vTotalPoints = vTotalPoints - 1
vPointcounter = vPointcounter - 1
txtPoints.Text = vPointcounter
gbPoints.Visible = True
End If
```

Once again we have taken you on a windy road to completion of the final program. For sake of clarity here is a listing of all the code necessary to program the pRep project.

```
Imports System.Data.OleDb
Public Class frmPrep
Inherits System.Windows.Forms.Form
Private vConnString As String =
   "Provider=Microsoft.Jet.OLEDB.4.0;" & "Data Source =
   C:\pRep.xls;" & "Extended Properties = ""Excel 8.0;
   HDR=Yes"""
Private vConn As New
   System.Data.OleDb.OleDbConnection(vConnString)
Private cmd1 As New System.Data.OleDb.OleDbCommand("Select
   * From [pRep$]", vConn)
Private vTimeCount As Integer
Private vTotalPoints As Integer
Private vPointcounter
```

```
Private Sub frmPrep_Load(ByVal sender As System.Object,
   ByVal e As System.EventArgs) Handles MyBase.Load
Dim vRecord As Integer
vConn.Open()
txtPrep0.Text = 0
vTotalPoints = 0
move_next_input()
lblPrep0.Text = txtPrep13.Text
End Sub

Private Sub lblPrep_Click(ByVal sender As System.Object,
   ByVal e As System.EventArgs) Handles lblPrep7.Click
End Sub
Private Sub clear_inputs()
txtPrep1.Text = ""
txtPrep2.Text = ""
txtPrep3.Text = ""
txtPrep4.Text = ""
txtPrep5.Text = ""
txtPrep6.Text = ""
txtPrep7.Text = ""
txtPrep8.Text = ""
txtPrep9.Text = ""
txtPrep10.Text = ""
txtPrep11.Text = ""
txtPrep12.Text = ""
txtPrep13.Text = ""
txtPrep14.Text = ""
txtPrep15.Text = ""
End Sub
Private Sub move_next_input()
Dim cmd1 As New System.Data.OleDb.OleDbCommand("Select *
   From [pRep$]", vConn)
Dim rdr As OleDbDataReader = cmd1.ExecuteReader
Dim x As Integer
Dim array(15)
clear_inputs() 'REMOVES VALUES FROM INPUT BOXES
x = txtPrep0.Text + 1
Dim i

For i = 1 To x
rdr.Read()
Next i
```

```
For i = 0 To 15
x = i - 1
If rdr.IsDBNull(i) Then array(i) = 1
Next
If array(0) <> 1 Then txtPrep0.Text = rdr.GetValue(0)
If array(1) <> 1 Then txtPrep1.Text = rdr.GetValue(1)
If array(2) <> 1 Then txtPrep2.Text = rdr.GetValue(2)
If array(3) <> 1 Then txtPrep3.Text = rdr.GetValue(3)
If array(4) <> 1 Then txtPrep4.Text = rdr.GetValue(4)
If array(5) <> 1 Then txtPrep5.Text = rdr.GetValue(5)
If array(6) <> 1 Then txtPrep6.Text = rdr.GetValue(6)
If array(7) <> 1 Then txtPrep7.Text = rdr.GetValue(7)
If array(8) <> 1 Then txtPrep8.Text = rdr.GetValue(8)
If array(9) <> 1 Then txtPrep9.Text = rdr.GetValue(9)
If array(10) <> 1 Then txtPrep10.Text = rdr.GetValue(10)
If array(11) <> 1 Then txtPrep11.Text = rdr.GetValue(11)
If array(12) <> 1 Then txtPrep12.Text = rdr.GetValue(12)
If array(13) <> 1 Then txtPrep13.Text = rdr.GetValue(13)
If array(14) <> 1 Then txtPrep14.Text = rdr.GetValue(14)
If array(15) <> 1 Then txtPrep15.Text = rdr.GetValue(15)

rdr.Close()
End Sub

Private Sub cmdPrep_Click(ByVal sender As System.Object,
   ByVal e As System.EventArgs) Handles cmdPrep.Click
cmdPrep.Visible = False
lblPrep0.Text = ""
move_next_input()
load_images()
End Sub
Private Sub load_images()
Select Case txtPrep1.Text
Case "INS"
gbPoints.Visible = False
lblPrep0.Visible = True
lblPrep0.Text = txtPrep13.Text
cmdPrep.Visible = True
Case "TEST", "TRAIN"
tmrPrep.Enabled = True
picPrep0.Image = Image.FromFile("c:\" & txtPrep2.Text)
picPrep1.Image = Image.FromFile("c:\" & txtPrep3.Text)
picPrep2.Image = Image.FromFile("c:\" & txtPrep4.Text)
```

```
picPrep3.Image = Image.FromFile("c:\" & txtPrep5.Text)
If txtPrep15.Text <> "" Then picContext.Image =
   Image.FromFile("c:\" & txtPrep15.Text)
Case "CRITERIA"
gbPoints.Visible = False
If Int(vTotalPoints) < Int(txtPrep14.Text) Then
cmdPrep.Text = "Continue"
cmdPrep.Visible = True
vTotalPoints = 0
Else
Close()
End
End If
Case "END"
Close()
End
End Select
End Sub

Private Sub frmPrep_KeyUp(ByVal sender As Object, ByVal e
   As System.Windows.Forms.KeyEventArgs) Handles
   MyBase.KeyUp
If e.KeyCode = Keys.F1 Then
Close()
End
End If
End Sub

Private Sub picPrep2_Click(ByVal sender As System.Object,
   ByVal e As System.EventArgs) Handles picPrep2.Click,
   picPrep3.Click
Dim buttonClicked As PictureBox
buttonClicked = CType(sender, PictureBox)
If buttonClicked.Name = picPrep2.Name() Then txtPrep12.Text
   = 1
If buttonClicked.Name = picPrep3.Name() Then txtPrep12.Text
   = 2

picContext.Visible = False
If txtPrep1.Text <> "TEST" Then
If txtPrep6.Text = txtPrep12.Text Then
ampFeedBack.FileName = ("c:\" & txtPrep7.Text)
ampFeedBack.Play()
```

```
lblPoints.Text = "GOOD: POINTS ="
vTotalPoints = vTotalPoints + 1
vPointcounter = vPointcounter + 1
txtPoints.Text = vPointcounter
gbPoints.Visible = True
Else
ampFeedBack.FileName = ("c:\" & txtPrep8.Text)
ampFeedBack.Play()
lblPoints.Text = "BAD: POINTS ="
'vTotalPoints = vTotalPoints - 1
vPointcounter = vPointcounter - 1
txtPoints.Text = vPointcounter
gbPoints.Visible = True
End If
End If
picPrep2.Visible = False
picPrep3.Visible = False
txtPrep11.Text = vTotalPoints
write_response()
move_next_input()
load_images()
End Sub

Private Sub picPrep3_Click(ByVal sender As System.Object,
   ByVal e As System.EventArgs) Handles picPrep3.Click,
   picPrep2.Click
End Sub

Private Sub tmrPrep_Tick(ByVal sender As System.Object,
   ByVal e As System.EventArgs) Handles tmrPrep.Tick
Select Case vTimeCount
Case 0
gbPoints.Visible = False
If txtPrep15.Text <> "" Then picContext.Visible = True
vTimeCount = 1
tmrPrep.Interval = 1000 'THIS RESETS THE STIMULI PRESEN
   TATION
Case 1
picPrep0.Visible = True
vTimeCount = 2
Case 2
picPrep0.Visible = False
vTimeCount = 3
```

```
Case 3
picPrep1.Visible = True 'INTERSTIM INTERVAL WHEN NO STIM
   IS DISPLAYED
vTimeCount = 4
Case 4
picPrep1.Visible = False
vTimeCount = 5
Case 5
picPrep2.Visible = True
picPrep3.Visible = True
vTimeCount = 0
tmrPrep.Enabled = False
tmrPrep.Interval = 3000 'THIS KEEPS GBPOINTS DISPLAYED FOR
   3 SECONDS
End Select
End Sub
Private Sub write_response()
Dim cmd1 As New System.Data.OleDb.OleDbCommand("Select *
   From [pRep$]", vConn)
cmd1.CommandText = "UPDATE [pRep$] " & "SET Resp = " &
   txtPrep12.Text & ", TotalPoints = " & txtPrep11.Text &
   " WHERE Record = " & txtPrep0.Text
cmd1.ExecuteNonQuery()
End Sub
```

Think about ways you could change your spreadsheet file name during run time instead of here in the code. The solutions are in Chapter 4 where we created a menu form that asked for file name inputs by the user. The next line of code ensures that vTimeCount will be set to 0 when the form loads. You may recall that variables are usually given a default value of 1 when the form loads. This code overrides that default.

Final customizations for your pRep program might include a cumulative point counter that transfers values across forms. You might also want to eliminate the subtraction of points for incorrect responses. To do this, simply delete the vTotalPoints = vTotalPoints – 1 lines of code. Other customizations might entail shorter or longer stimulus presentations, concurrent presentations of both stimuli, placing limited holds on participant responses to be considered a correct response, or changing the actual stimuli images partially through completion of the spreadsheet to test for transfers of relational control. The possibilities are endless. Hopefully your programming skills have come along far enough by now to conquer many the programming challenges that lay ahead.

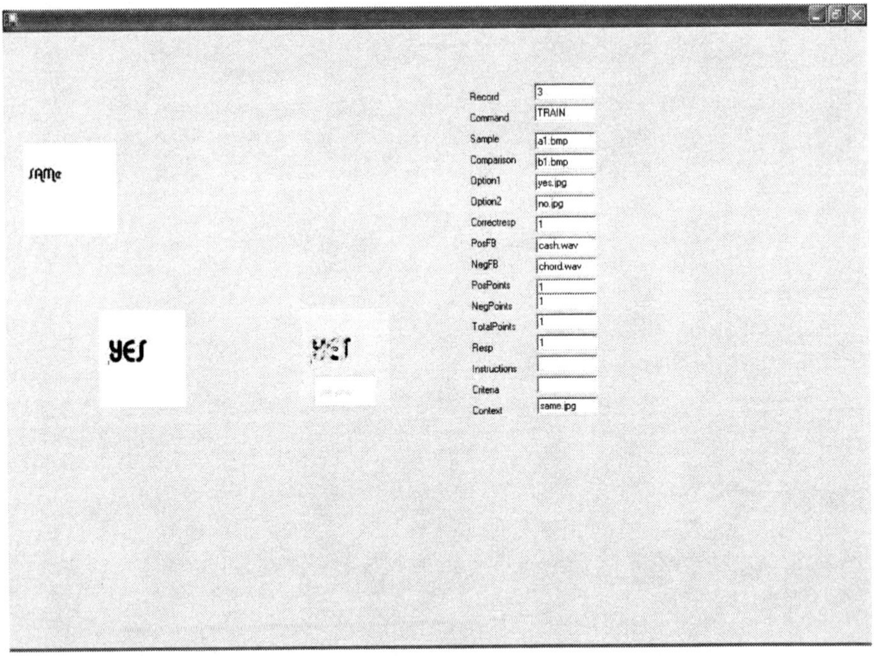

Figure 9.10 displays a run time image of the pRep program with stimuli and response options loaded.

References

Cullinan, V. A., Barnes-Holmes, D., & Smeets, P. M. (2001). A precursor to the relational evaluation procedure: Searching for the contextual cues that control equivalence responding. Journal of the Experimental Analysis of Behavior, 76, 339-349.

Fields, L., Reeve, K. F., Varelas, A., Rosen, D., & Belanich, L. (1997). Equivalence class formation using stimulus-pairing and yes-no responding. The Psychological Record, 47, 661-686.

Leader, G., Barnes, D., & Smeets, P. M. (1996). Establishing equivalence relations using a respondent-type training procedure. The Psychological Record, 46, 685-706.

Chapter 10: Software Packaging and Deployment

Overview

This last chapter will provide you with the skills necessary to take any completed program you developed in Visual Basic.NET and package it for actual experiment running, installation on another computer, or distribution to other users.

Until now, you have created Visual Basic.NET applications that are saved as *Windows Applications* consisting of a project, forms, and perhaps a module or two. This collection of files is considered your application. As a result, if you were to attempt to transfer these files over from your development computer to a laboratory computer or share the program with a colleague, you would have to copy and save all of these files independently. Furthermore, you might need to copy a variety of system files that are needed to ensure that the program will run correctly. The problem is compounded when the location you wish to transfer your application to does not have a copy of Visual Basic.NET already installed on it. Luckily there is an easier way. It is called Packaging and Deployment using something called a *Setup Project*.

Adding the Output to Your Setup Project

The eventual goal of the Setup Project is to have a single file package that can be copied and shared across computers and users. VB.NET refers to this file as the *Output*. It is at this point we need to create the VB.NET project that we wish to convert into an *Output*. Rather than use an existing project you created during the course of this book, make a very simple new application at this time called *Test*. To do this you will need to click on *File* from the main menu, select the *Visual Basic Projects* folder, select *Windows Application*, and rename the project *Test*. Once you have changed the directory, click *OK* and begin the construction of this simple project. Rename the form *frmTest* and change the BackColor to Light Blue. Next add a Button and name it *butHello*, and change the text to *Hello*. Add a second Button named *butGoodbye* and change the text to *Goodbye*. Now add a PictureBox, change the name to *picHello*, the SizeMode to *StretchImage*, and place an image within this PictureBox.

Double-click on the *butHello* Button and enter the edit mode. Add the following code under the butHello_Click subroutine:

```
picHello.Visible = True
```

Under the butGoodbye_Click subroutine type:

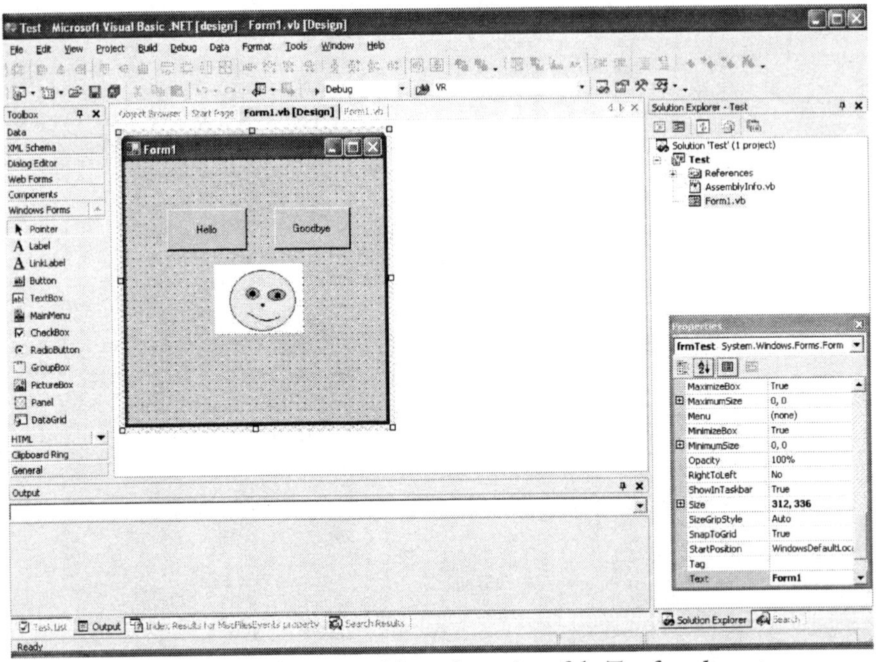

Figure 10.1 displays a possible configuration of the Test form layout.

```
picHello.Visible = False
```

Finally change the Startup object to frmTest, and run the program to make sure it works. The program should now result in *imgHello* appearing when you click on *butHello* and disappearing when you click on *butGoodbye*. Click on the buttons a few times, and stop the program. Save this new, yet rather not too exciting, Test project by clicking on *File* and then *Save All* from the main menu and exit Visual Basic. Now you are ready to return to creating your Setup Project.

Initial Setup Using the Setup Wizard

Creating the Setup Project

Right-click your mouse on the *Solution Test* option in the *Solution Explorer* Window. Select *Add* from your available options, and then select *New Project* as shown in Figure 10.2. Now instead of clicking on *Windows Application* as you have done previously throughout this book, select the folder *Setup and Deployment Projects* and note the project option changes as shown in Figure 10.3. Now select from these new options *Setup Wizard.*

Rename the project *Installprogram* and also change the Location for your project to a new folder you should place on your desktop entitled *VB.NET*. Now click *OK*. The reason we want you to create an entirely new folder for this exercise is so that you are not attempting to place files for this Setup Project into the same folder they

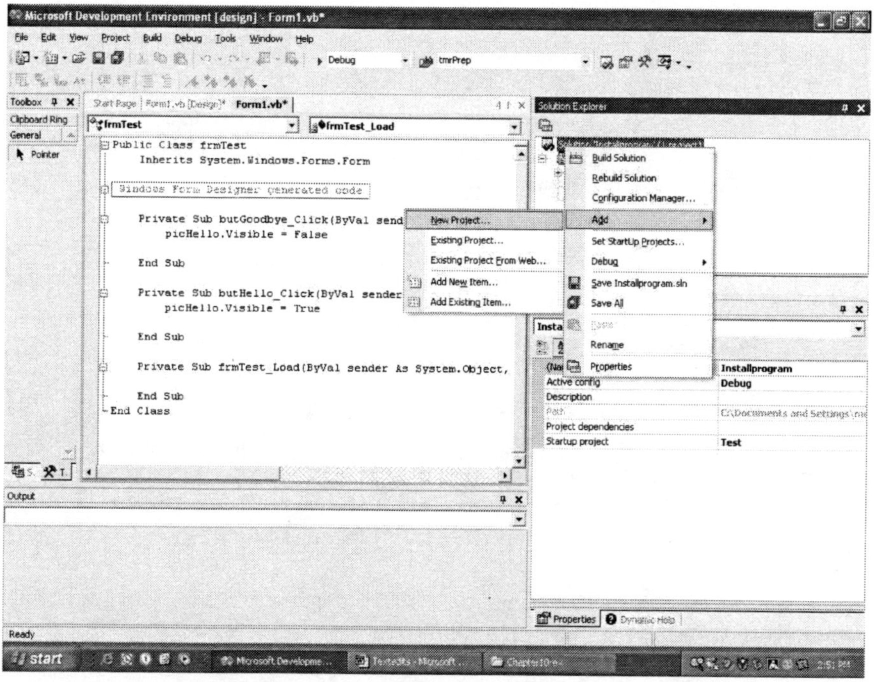

Figure 10.2 displays the interface for creating the Setup program.

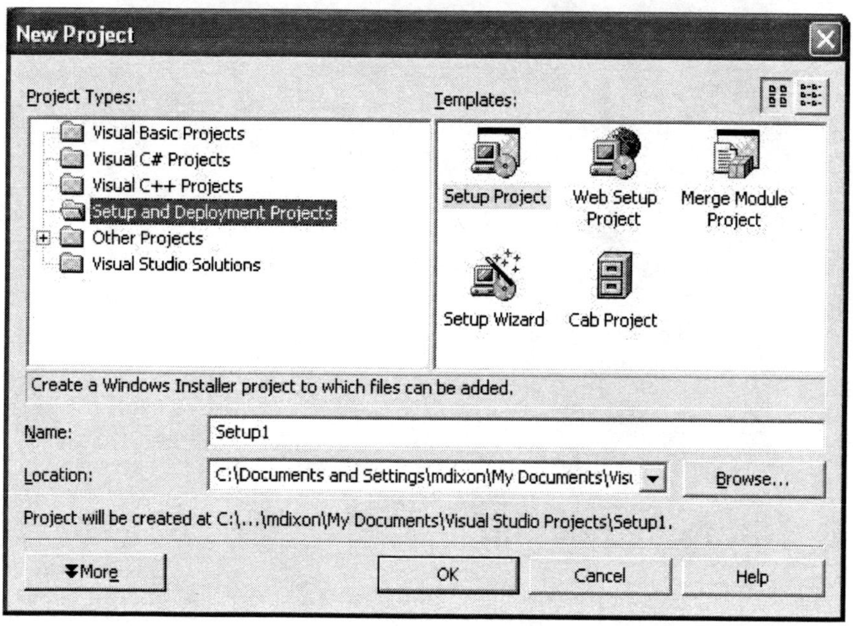

Figure 10.3 displays the appropriate "New Project" options found in the "Setup and Deployment Projects" folder.

may have already been located in. Plus, having this project on your desktop allows you easy access to it for emailing or transferring to floppy disc or CD-ROM.

At this point a new window will appear in VB.NET that states "Welcome to the Windows Setup Project Wizard" as shown in Figure 10.4. This excellent new tool found in Visual Basic.NET will provide you with a step-by-step guide to creating your own professional looking installation program. At this point, click on the *Next* button to continue the development process. The second window of the Setup Wizard asks you what of project you wish to develop. You can choose between a Windows or Web application. For the types of programs you have been developing in this book, you should select a *Windows Application*. Yet, a *Web Application* is just as easy to create and deploy when created in a similar fashion to what we have taught you. The second set of available options on this window asks if you wish to create a redistributable package. The CAB file is a type of compressed file that can easily be passed over the web or via email to other users, while the Merge Module is a distributable package that can be customized in a variety of ways by the person whose computer will eventually hold your software. In most cases, neither of these options is needed, so leave them both unchecked and click on the *Next* button as shown on Figure 10.5.

The third window of the wizard asks which project output files that you wish to add to the Setup Project. The first option *Primary Output from Test* will be often enough for other users to run your program. By only including this option, the user will not be able to see what your code is, as the actual form, will not be included in

Figure 10.4 displays the first window of the Setup Wizard.

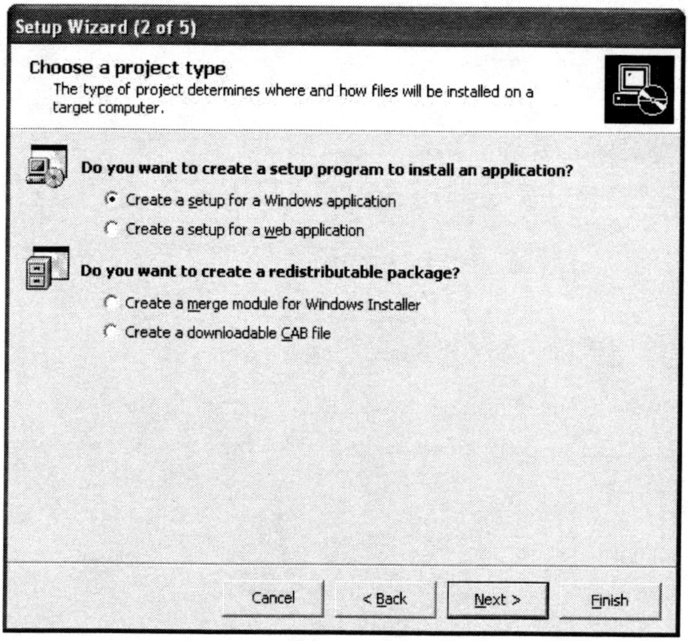

Figure 10.5 displays the second window of the Setup Wizard.

the Setup Project. Selecting only this option might be a really good idea if you do not want to "give away" your code to other users. However, if you wish to have your intended user(s) modify the code or alter your program (as might be the case when two people are working at a program from remote locations) then check the remaining four options. At this point, let's just select *Primary Output from Test* and click on Next as shown in Figure 10.6.

The fourth window of the wizard asks which additional files you wish to package with your Setup Project. It is here where you would add all your individual stimuli image files, .wav files, media files, etc. that should be included in the final computer program, but do not reside within Visual Basic.NET when the program is run. Leave this option blank and click *Next* as shown in Figure 10.7, because right now our Setup Project is completely blank. Luckily if you forget a file or two at this point, there is another way to add files to the Setup Project. We will show you how to add files that way too.

The last window of the wizard displays your previously selected choices and asks that you review them now, alter them if needed via clicking on *Back* or accept them by clicking on *Finish*. Click on *Finish* as depicted in Figure 10.8. Visual Basic.NET will now reopen and look much different than it has in the past. There is a new main window on the screen containing two smaller panes as shown in Figure 10.9.

The pane on the left side depicts *File System on Target Machine* and the pane on the right depicts a variety of folders including *Application Folder*, *Global Assembly*

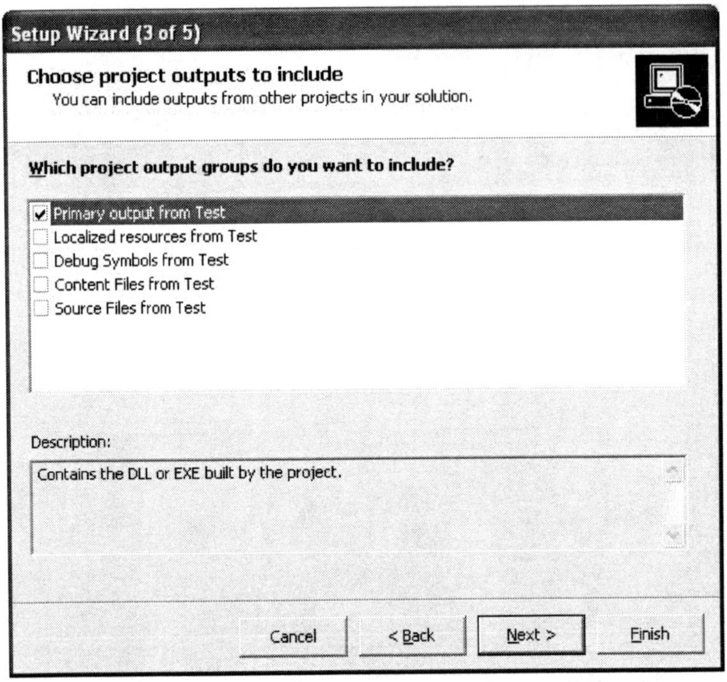

Figure 10.6 displays the third window of the Setup Wizard.

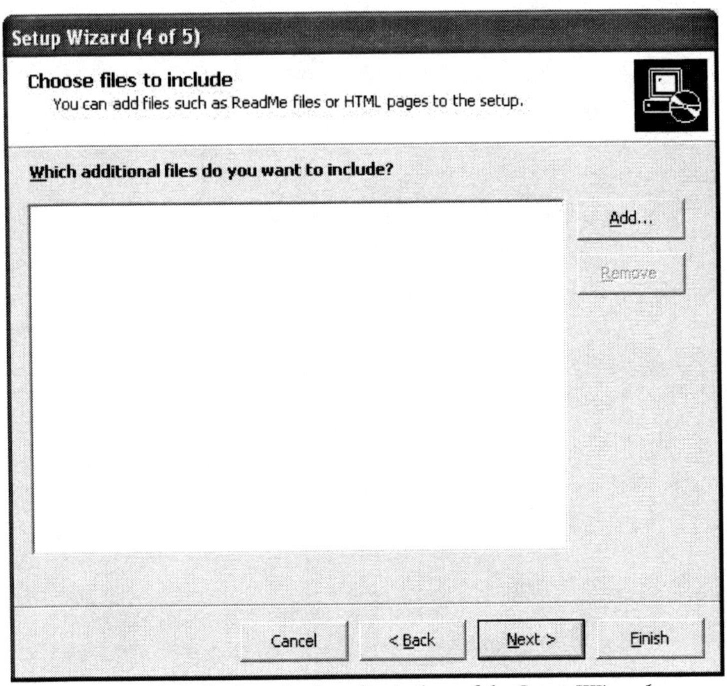

Figure 10.7 displays the fourth window of the Setup Wizard.

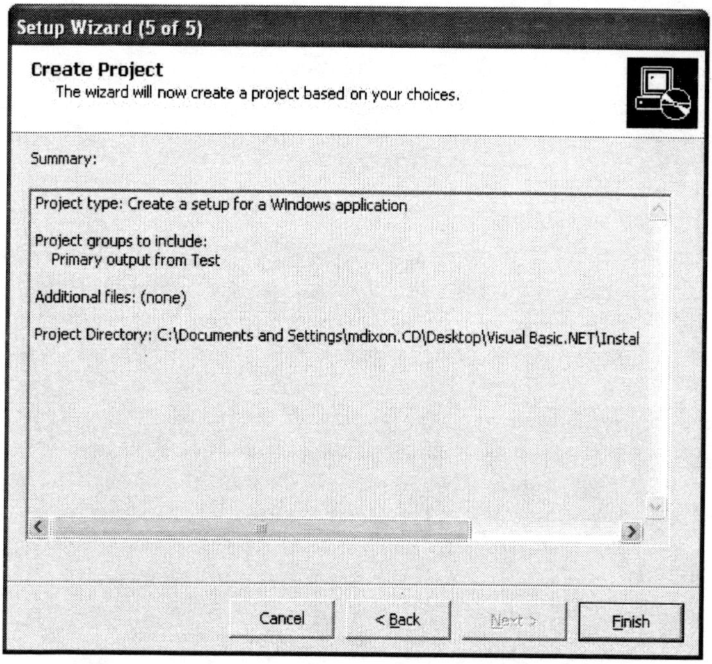

Figure 10.8 displays the fifth window of the Setup Wizard

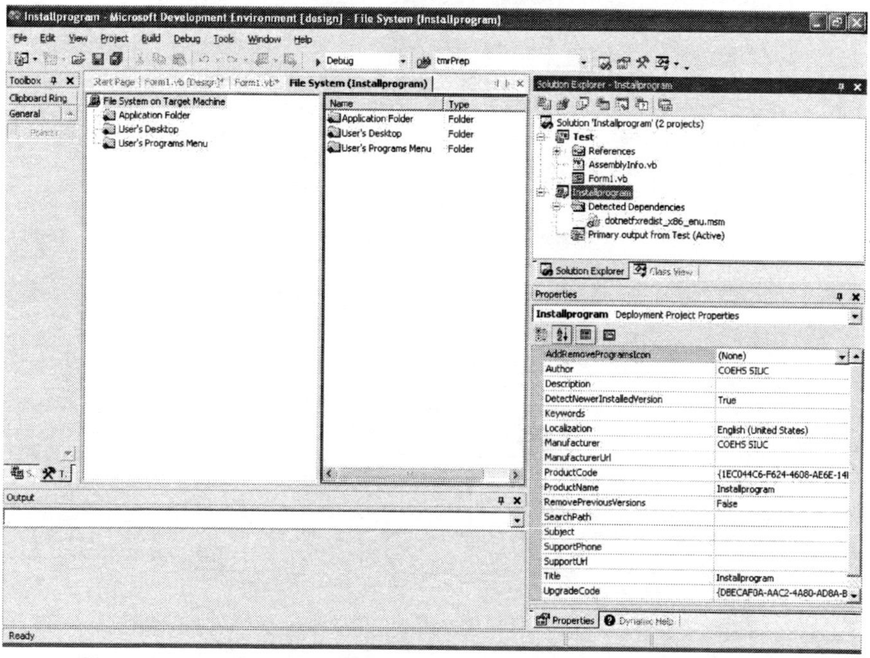

Figure 10.9 displays the layout window for customizing your Setup Project.

Cache Folder, *User's Desktop*, and *User's Programs Menu*. Plus the Solution Explorer now contains an entire second project titled *InstallProgram*. We now have two projects sitting in one solution. One project is our test project and the other is our Setup Project.

Customizing the Setup Project

File Output Properties

A new and useful feature found in Visual Basic.NET is the ability to specify the actual location you wish to install the Output program. In other words, once you create the Output, you can tell VB.NET where it should install it when it is loaded on another computer. Users can change this if they want to, but your specification might be helpful to ensure proper installation of more complex programs that require additional supporting materials like images or video clips.

Click your mouse once on the *Applications Folder* that is located in the left pane of the main project window to highlight it. Now press the F4 key. Your properties window will appear and present the specific properties that exist for your Output application as shown in Figure 10.10. Notice the *Default Location* property currently is set to:

[ProgramFilesFolder][Manufacturer]\[ProductName]

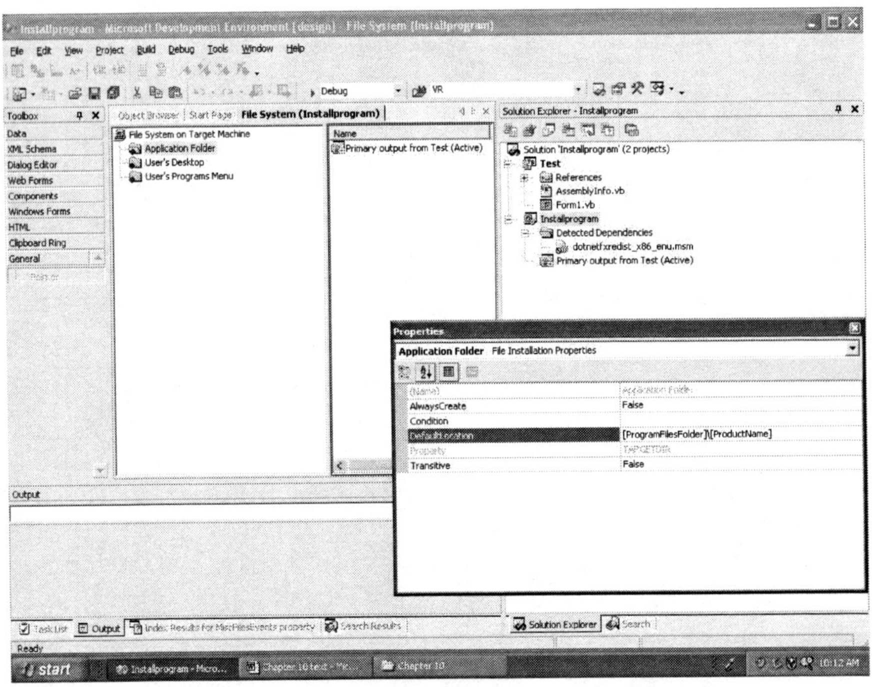

Figure 10.10 displays the suggested Default Location property.

What this means is that the Output file will be installed in the Program Files folder, in a subfolder with the name of the company you entered when you first installed Visual Basic.NET, and in a subdirectory with the name of the actual Output project. You can change this to better suit your needs. Perhaps, eliminate the middle folders so that your *Default Location* property now reads:

[ProgramFilesFolder]\[ProductName]

Changing Additional Output Properties

In addition to specifying the file folder for the project Output, you can also specify the image icon that will be placed on the desktop of the user, add additional support files, and create a shortcut on the Start Menu. These options may seem like overkill for a simple transfer from your office computer to your lab computer, but they may come in handy once you start selling your VB.NET masterpieces.

To change the icon, right-click your mouse on the Test project title that is displayed in the Solution Explorer window. From the pop-up menu, select the option entitled *Properties*. Yes, this is the exact same way that you have changed the Startup object of your many programs you have written throughout this book. Yet, now look to the left pane of this dialog box and click your mouse once on the text *Build*.

Right now there is a pretty boring looking icon selected for your program. Click on the three "..." located to the right of the icon and search your computer for a more exciting one. Keep in mind this file needs to be an icon file type and not a .jpg or .gif file type. Leave *Option Compare* as is, on *Binary*. Click *OK* and notice that your icon has actually been added to your Solution Explorer window.

Many commercially available software programs contain a text file called a *Readme document* with them. The *Readme* file often explains installation instructions, tips for troubleshooting, and copyright information. Your *Installprogram* program probably does not need any of these but just for fun, make a one line text file using NotePad called *Sample Information* that contains the text "This is my Installprogram information" and save it in an easy to find directory.

You can also add a new custom folder to the user's computer when the installation process occurs. To do this, return to VB.NET and right-click your mouse on the text *File System on Target Machine* which is found in the left pane of the main split pane project window, select the option *Add Special Folder* and then *Custom Folder*. Once selected, a new folder will appear in the left pane and it will allow you to change its name. Change the name of this new folder to *Chapter10* and press *Return*.

It is here where you have a second chance to place any sort of files that might be useful for the user when running the program that were forgotten during the running of the Setup Project Wizard. These might include images, video or audio

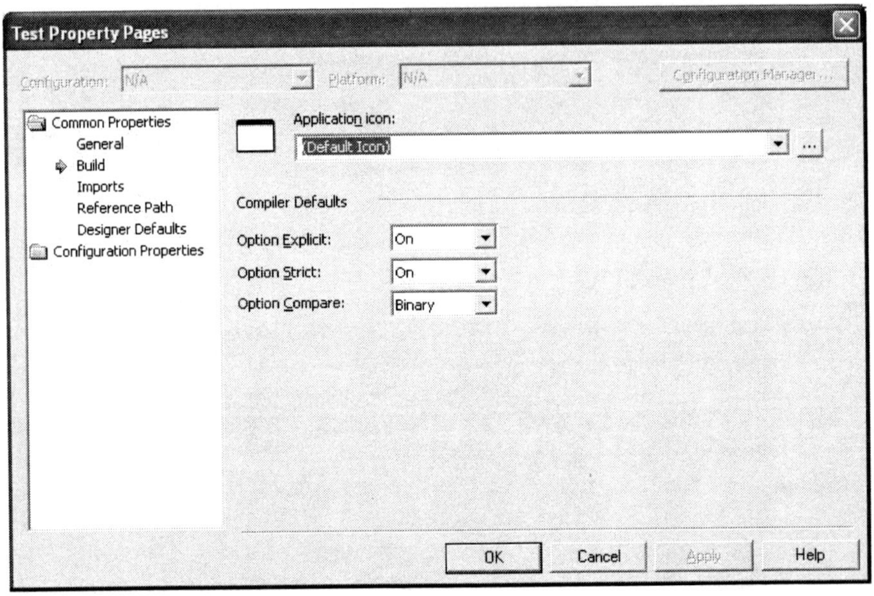

Figure 10.11 displays the Build option required to alter the Output program icon.

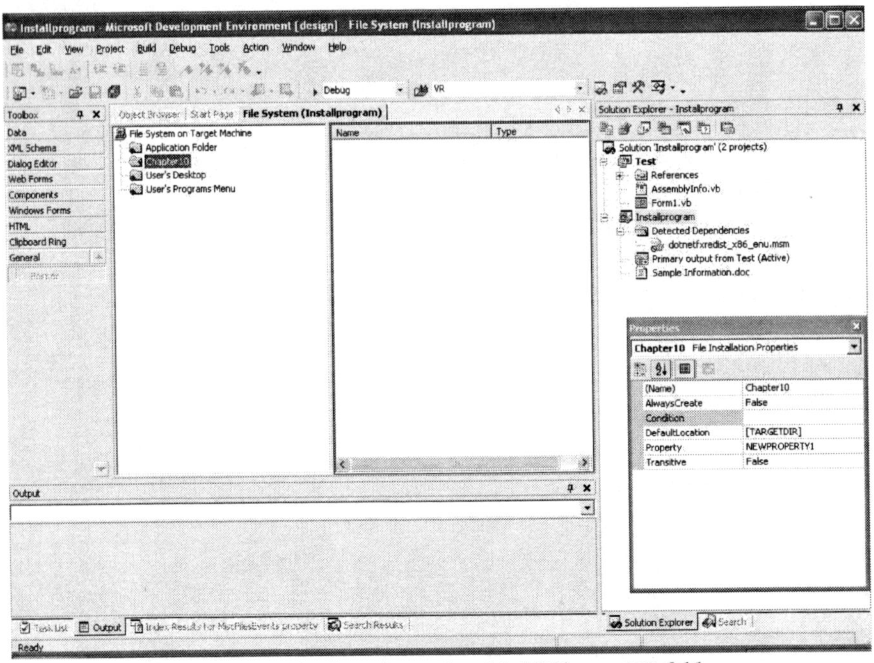

Figure 10.12 displays the newly added "Chapter10" folder.

files, or Readme files. Because we recently created the informative *Sample Information* text file, let's put it into this new folder. To do so, right-click on the *Chapter 10* folder in the left pane of this main window, select *Add* from the Popup Menu, and then select *File* . Locate your *Sample Information* file and press *Open*. Now when the program is installed, your Readme file will be located in this new customized folder.

To create a shortcut on the Start Menu of your user's computer, click once on *Application Folder* in the left window pane to highlight it. You should see the text *Primary Output from Test* in the right window pane. Highlight this text and right-click your mouse. Select the first option *Create Shortcut to Primary Output for Test (Active)* and notice you will have added a shortcut to Test in this right window pane. Now, drag this shortcut over to the folder entitled *User's Programs Menu* in the left window pane. This will result in a shortcut being placed on the user's computer from the Start Menu.

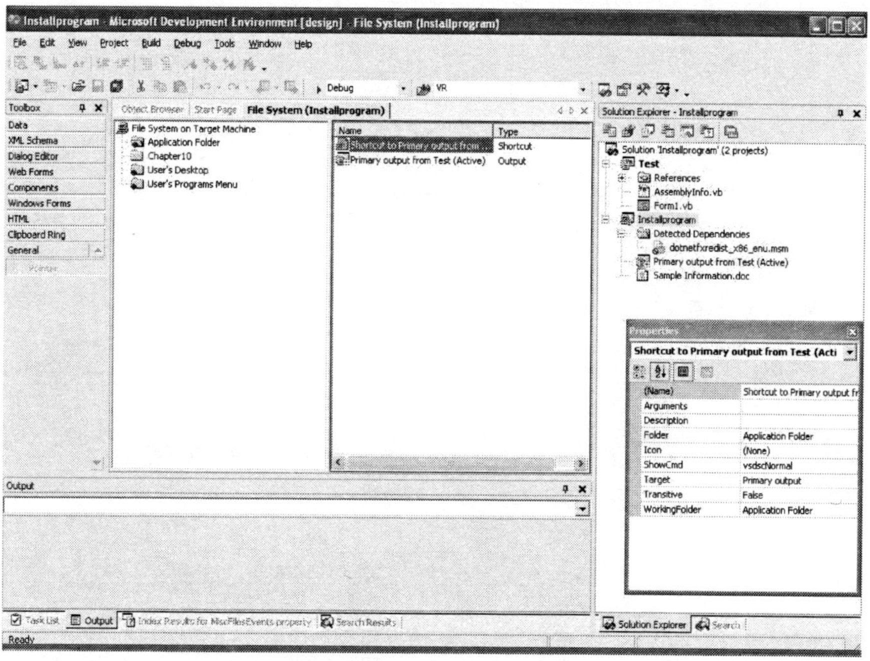

Figure 10.13 displays the newly added shortcut prior to transferring it into the "User's Programs Menu" folder.

By the time you are ready to package your program up and transfer it over to your users, you will have hopefully corrected any programming errors that your program contained. Unless your user wishes to have the large and cumbersome Debugging features of Visual Basic.NET installed on his/her computer for further error correction, you will need to change one last option from the *Build* option on the main toolbar. Click on *Build*, and select the last option, *Configuration Manager.* A new dialog box will appear that shows a grid containing your Test project and your Output project Installprogram. Under the *Configuration* row, change both from *Debug* to *Release*. This change will result in your user's computer being spared from the unneeded and cumbersome Debugging files of VB.NET. Finally, make sure that both Projects are checked in the *Build* row.

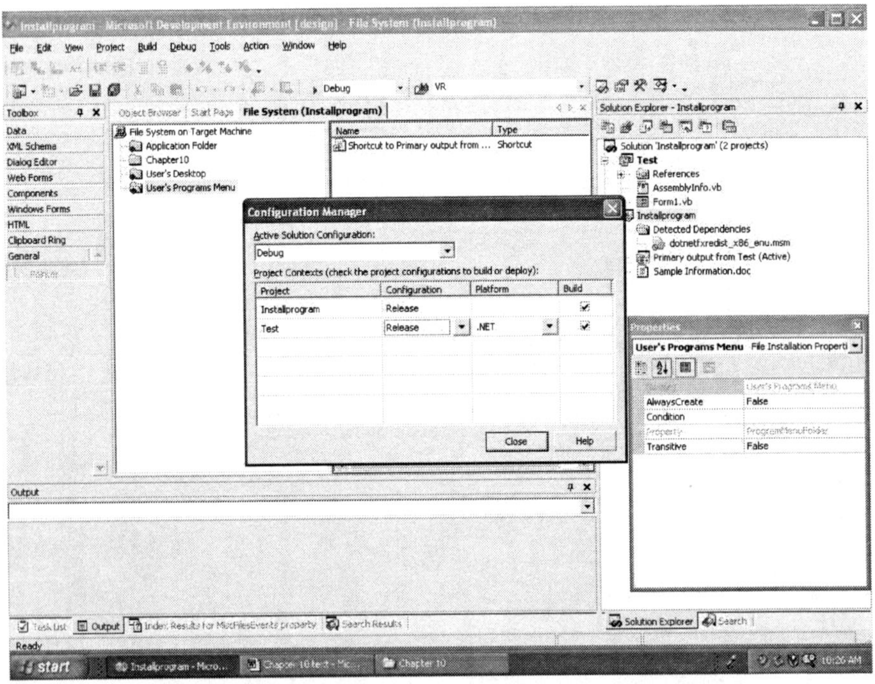

Figure 10.14 displays the Configuration Manager dialog box.

Running Your Program on a Computer without Visual Basic.NET

Common Runtime Language

By default, your Installprogram Output will not contain a very large set of files called *Common Language Runtime.* This set of files allows for your Visual Basic.NET program to be installed on any computer, even those without the Visual Basic.NET program installed on it. The *Common Language Runtime* is a lifesaving new feature on VB.NET that programmers of earlier versions of Visual Basic will surely appreciate. The lack of these files was responsible for many, many errors that users would get when attempting to run a program Output on a computer other than the one it was originally created on. If you know for sure your user already has VB.NET

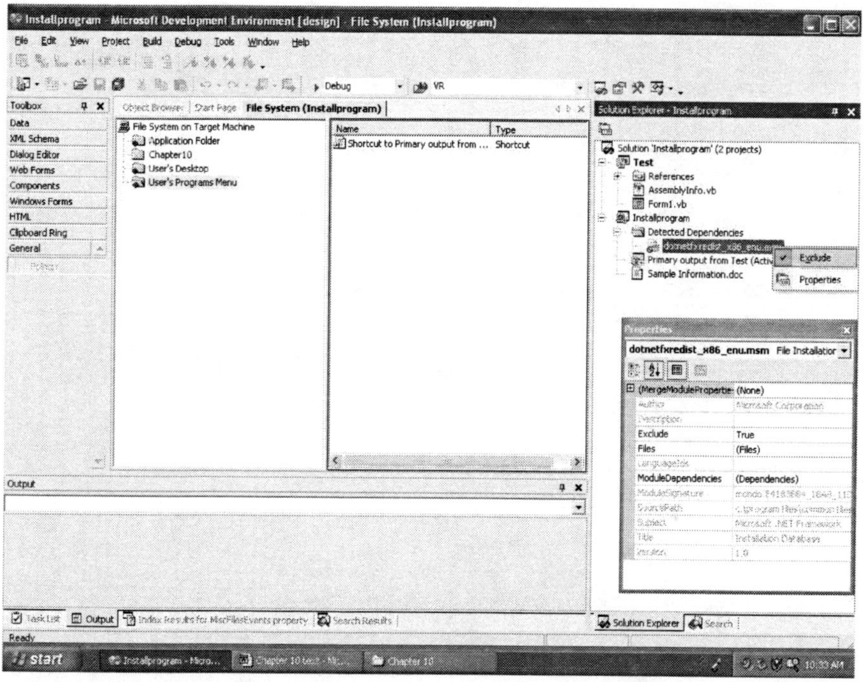

Figure 10.15 displays the steps necessary to include the Common Runtime Language.

installed on their computer, you can remove this large set of files. Yet, if you do not know if they do or not, it is safer to include them when you create your Output. Since these files are excluded by default, let's just add them to demonstrate how it is done. To include the Common Language Runtime file right-click your mouse on the file *dotnetfxredist_x86_enu.msm* that should be displayed in the Solution Explorer window under the *Detected Dependencies* folder. Select the option *Exclude* from the pop-up menu.

The final step in this rather user-unfriendly process is to generate the Output file. To do so, click on *Build* from the main toolbar, and select the option *Build Solution.* Visual Basic.NET will now begin the compiling process of packaging all your individual files into a single installation file to share on your user's machine. Once VB.NET has accomplished this task, it will return a message stating "Build Succeeded."

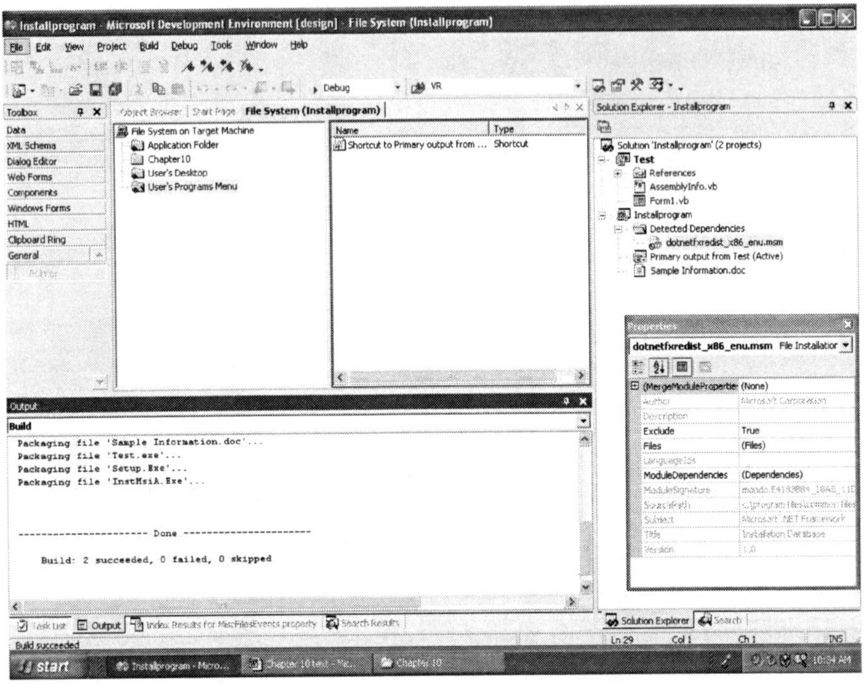

Figure 10.16 displays a successful building of the Installprogram Output.

To locate your newly created Output, browse your file directories and find your desktop directory and the "VB.NET" folder you created at the start of this chapter. Double-click on this folder to open it. Now double-click on the *Installprogram* directory, and then on the *Release* directory. Your Installation file will reside here. It is named *Installprogram* and will have the file type of *Windows Installer Package*. Figure 10.17 displays the contents of your "VB.NET" folder's *Release* directory.

Deploying Your Setup Program

Running the Setup

Let us begin by attempting to install your newly created Installprogram right on the same computer you just created it on. We can copy the files in the VB.NET directory and transfer them to another computer later. This step will ensure your packaging of all the necessary files was done correctly, prior to your transferring attempts. Locate your VB.NET directory on your desktop, open it, and go to the *Release* folder, and double-click on *InstallProgram*. After you do so, a dialog box similar to that found in Figure 10.18 will be displayed on your computer screen.

At this point, click on the *Next* option located in the bottom right hand corner of the screen, and view the subsequent dialog box requesting you to choose the directory you wish to place this program in (remember we created this option when we packaged our files earlier in this chapter!), and to determine if you wish to install

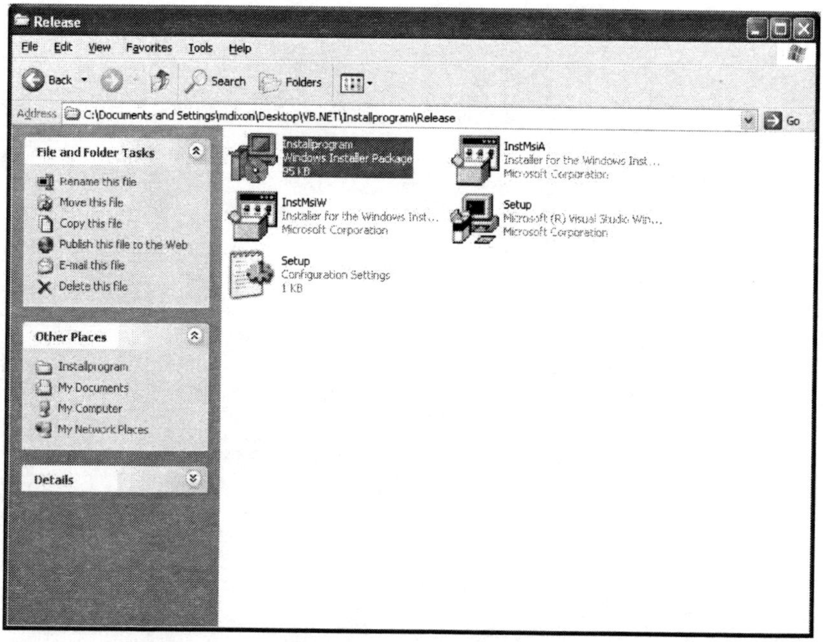

Figure 10.17 displays the contents of the Release directory.

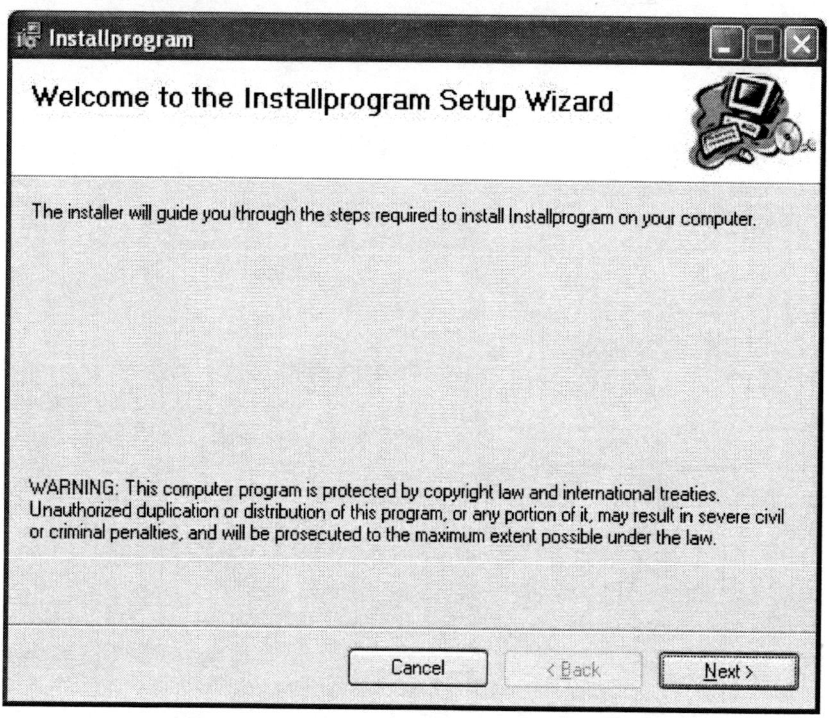

Figure 10.18 displays the welcome dialog box for the Installprogram.

this program for everyone who uses the computer or just yourself. Make your appropriate selections. Now notice the option entitled *Disk Cost.* Clicking here will display the system resources you have available and the "cost" or amount of space needed to install the program.

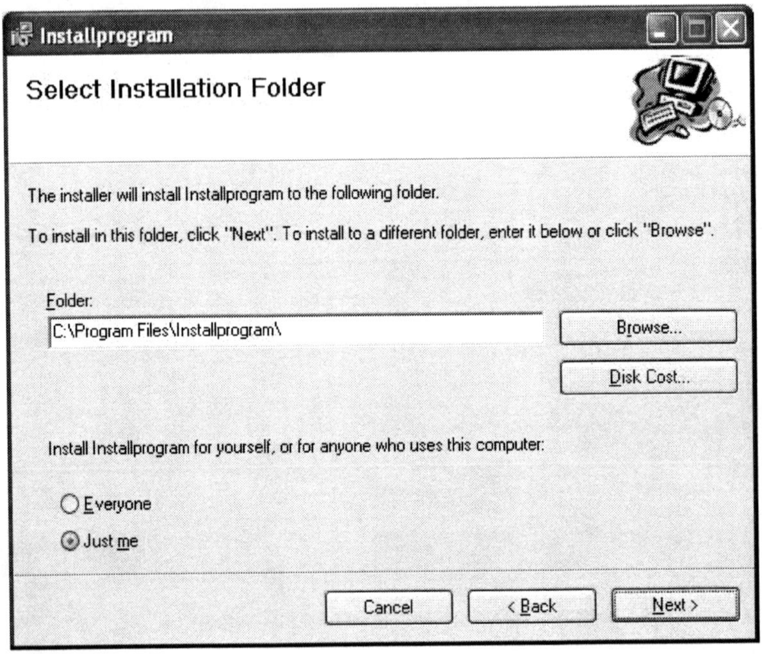

Figure 10.19 displays the Select Installation Folder dialog box for the Installprogram.

Once satisfied with your selections, click on the *Next* option. You will be prompted one last time to confirm that you wish to have the *Intsallprogram* program installed on your computer. If you are sure you wish to do so, click on the *Next* option. Once done, your computer will begin to install the program as depicted in Figure 10.20.

Running the Program

All that is left to do is check to see if your program runs. Remember, the program that we want to run is the exciting *Test* program that has a *Hello* and a *Goodbye* Button on it. The reason we did not call our installation program *Test* is that Visual Basic.NET will not allow you to have the installation program and the Output named the same. You may wish to name all your installation programs after your own name followed by a suffix, like *Dixoninstall1*. Just make it something useful and easy to remember. Locate your *Test* program by clicking on the *Start* image located on the bottom left corner of your computer screen. Next select *Programs*. Browse through your existing programs and you will see a new shortcut listed named *Shortcut*

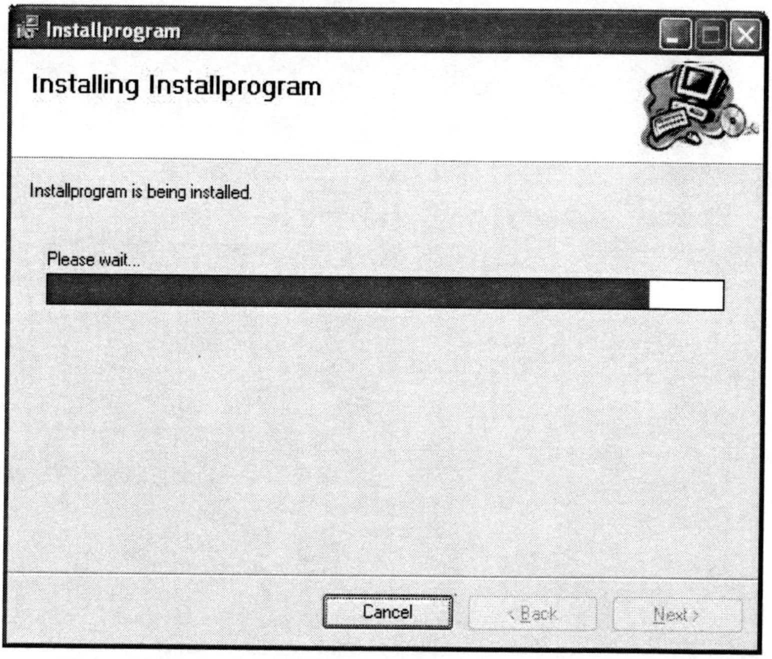

Figure 10.20 displays the Installing dialog box with progress indicator.

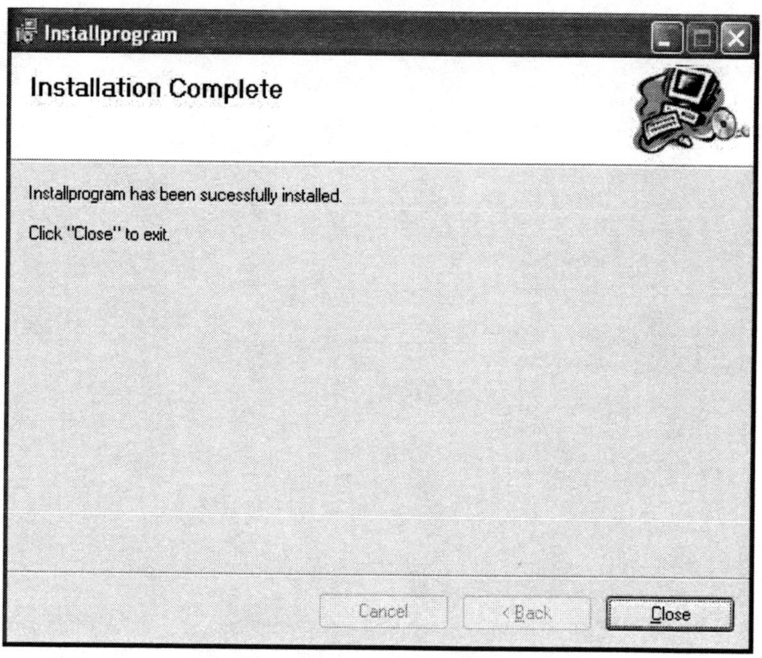

Figure 10.21 displays the Install Complete dialog box that appears following a successful installation.

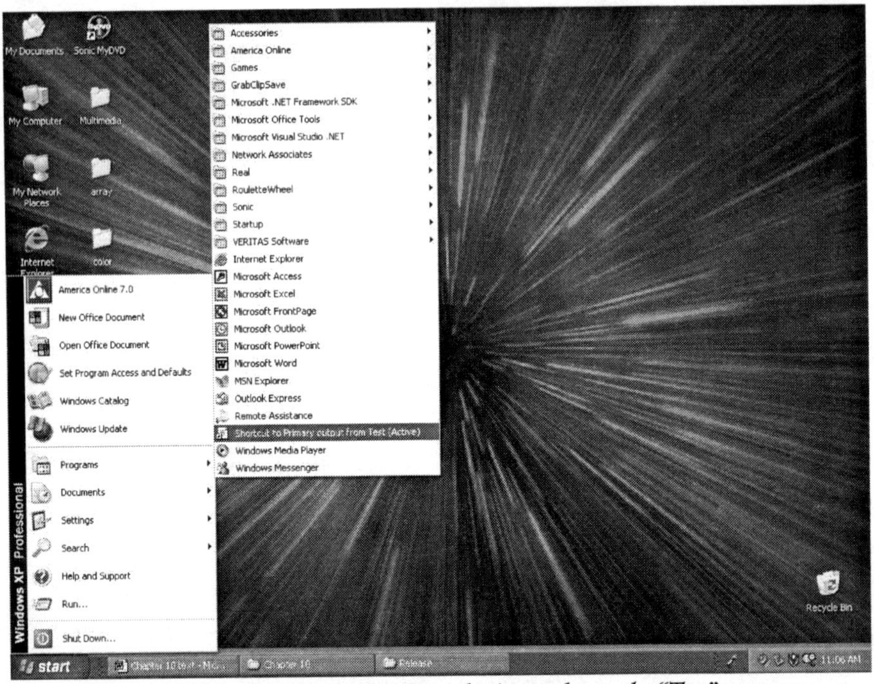

Figure 10.22 displays the appropriate selections to locate the "Test" program from the "Start" button.

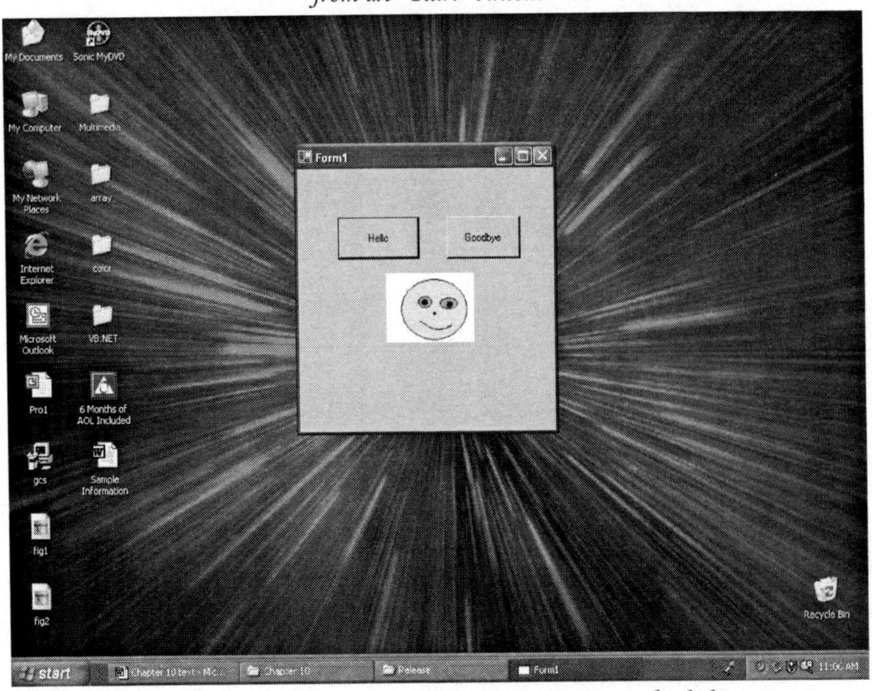

Figure 10.23 displays the "Test" program in action on the desktop.

to Primary Output from Test (Active). This is it. Not too fancy of a name, but it works. You can change this later to something more attractive if you wish. Select this option and your *Test* program will magically begin to run on your computer. It does so, without ever opening Visual Basic.NET. It even has a little bit of a professional look to it. The reason why your goofy little *Test* program looks professional is because you have become a computer programmer. Congratulations.

Removing the Application You Have Installed

There are two ways in which you can remove the newly installed application from your computer. Both are relatively simple. One way to do so is to simply double-click on the *Installprogram* file in your *Release* directory that you previously did to install the program. The resulting dialog box has different features this time though. The dialog box now asks you if you wish to either repair the program or remove it from your computer. Select *Remove* and click on the *Finish* option. That is it. The program will be removed.

Although the above removal process was about as simple as it gets, it may not work in every circumstance. For example, you may have copied your VB.NET folder from your desktop to a CD-ROM so a different user could install this program on a different computer. If you did, and the user no longer has the CD-ROM this removal feature would not be available because the files were installed from a CD

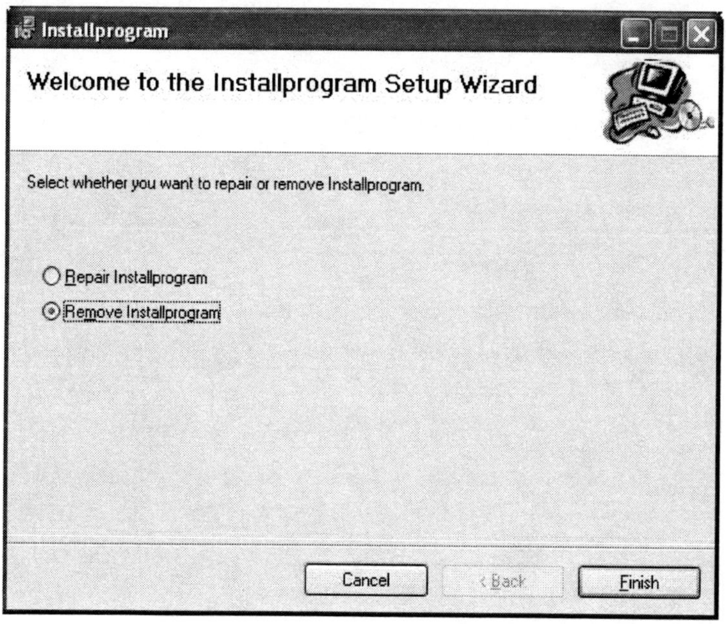

Figure 10.24 displays the dialog box allowing you to remove the Testprogram from your computer.

that is no longer available. Luckily, Microsoft Windows has a general program removal feature that you can use to accomplish the same task.

To take advantage of this process, you simply need to click on the *Start* button on the bottom left corner of your computer screen, and select *Settings* and then *Control Panel.* Locate the option within the Control Panel named *Add/Remove Programs* and double-click your mouse on it. Scroll down the various program selections and locate the *Installprogram* program. Uninstall the program by selecting it, and then clicking the mouse on the *Remove* option. Return to your programs from the Start button and examine your options. The *Shortcut to Primary Output from Test (Active)* has been removed.

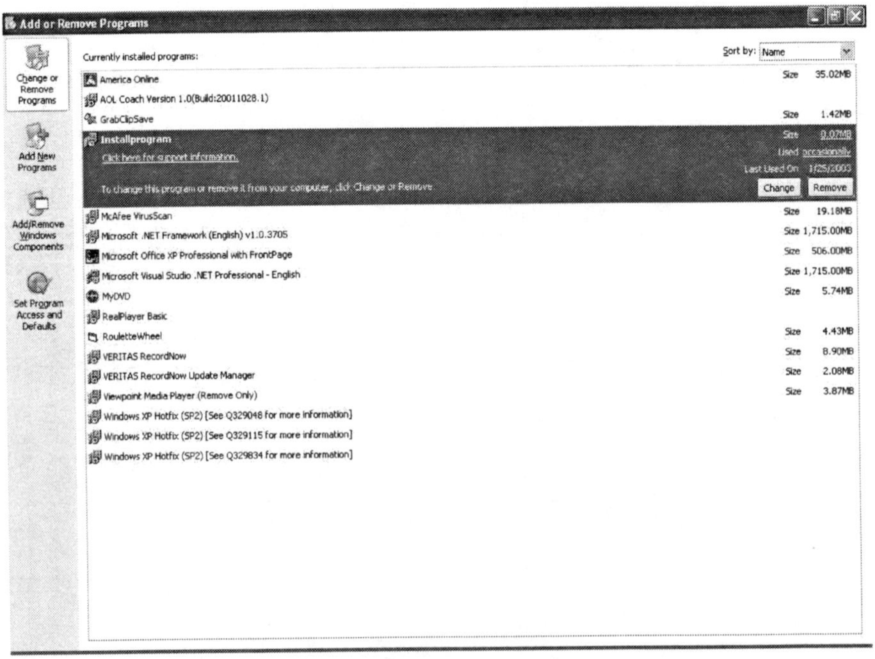

Figure 10.25 displays the Add/Remove Programs dialog box.

Final Thoughts

Throughout this book we have highlighted the most commonly used features of Visual Basic.NET that behavioral psychologists might utilize when designing their own computer programs. All together, the features we have illustrated are less than 10% of what Visual Basic.NET is capable of. Most of the additional 90% is designed for database programmers or commercial business software development. Yet buried in the myriad of seemingly useless information are a few treasures. Finding additional information out about Visual Basic.NET that is useful to you will be a labor intensive process. For example, we spent over three weeks attempting to figure out how to display a second form when a user clicked on a Button. That comes to about one line of code per week! The process of acquiring new and useful information can also be very rewarding. Our advice is to search everywhere – as we have done. Buy books, join chat rooms, trade information at conventions or via emails with colleagues. The problem you may have been struggling with for weeks could be nothing more than two lines of code a colleague uses on a regular basis.

Visual Basic.NET has new features included within it that were not available in any previous editions. In .NET, applications can now be developed for distribution over the Internet. Imagine the endless supply of experimental participants! The steps to distribute your programs over the web are similar to those we have highlighted in this text, but you will need to seek out additional resources for the specifics. VB.NET also now lets you work seamlessly with data contained within spreadsheets and databases much more extensively than we illustrated in Chapter 9. In fact, there is a whole programming language found within the Visual Studio.NET family called ADO.NET that works hand in hand with Visual Basic.NET to acquire, manipulate, and transform data stored in external files and/or programs.

As this book goes to print, Microsoft is releasing a new version of .NET that will incorporate additional features to allow for the programming of many handheld devices such as the Pocket PC, cell phones, and pagers. Over the course of the next few years there will be an increasing shift from the desktop computer to such mobile computing solutions. Learn how to program these devices soon; you will eventually need to do so.

In closing, hopefully reading this book has provided you with many tools you can use to enhance or completely recreate your research agenda. We wish you the best of luck with all your programming adventures that lie ahead. Along the way, remember to pause every now and then to teach the skills to others.

Index

This index provides a quick reference to many frequently used features of Visual Basic.NET. Indexed pages are not exhaustive but rather indicate the initial presentation of the feature as well as highlight selective examples of application.

About the Authors

Dr. Mark R. Dixon is a faculty member in the Behavior Analysis and Therapy program in the Rehabilitation Institute at Southern Illinois University. Mark has been writing computer programs for over 15 years, the last 10 exclusively in Visual Basic versions 3.0-6.0 and .NET. Mark's programs have been incorporated into a variety of areas of research including choice and self-control, verbal behavior, gambling, relational frame theory, and stimulus equivalence.

Dr. Otto H MacLin is a faculty member in the Psychology Department at the University of Northern Iowa. Otto has been writing computer programs for over 25 years, the last 10 have included Visual Basic versions 3.0-6.0 and .NET, Visual C++, JAVA, and XML. Otto's programs have been incorporated into a variety of areas of research including gambling, stimulus equivalence, eyewitness lineup administration, examination of the cross-race effect, and face recognition.